Civil Wars in the Democratic Republic of Congo, 1960–2010

Civil Wars in the Democratic Republic of Congo, 1960–2010

Emizet François Kisangani

LYNNE RIENNER PUBLISHERS

BOULDER
LONDON

Published in the United States of America in 2012 by
Lynne Rienner Publishers, Inc.
1800 30th Street, Boulder, Colorado 80301
www.rienner.com

and in the United Kingdom by
Lynne Rienner Publishers, Inc.
3 Henrietta Street, Covent Garden, London WC2E 8LU

Library of Congress Cataloging-in-Publication Data
Kisangani, Emizet F.
   Civil wars in the Democratic Republic of Congo, 1960–2010 / Emizet
François Kisangani.
   Includes bibliographical references and index.
   ISBN 978-1-58826-827-3 (alk. paper)
   1. Civil war—Congo (Democratic Republic)—History. 2. Civil war—
Social aspects—Congo (Democratic Republic). 3. Congo (Democratic
Republic)—Politics and government—1960–1997. 4. Congo (Democratic
Republic)—Politics and government—1997– I. Title.
   DT658.K475 2012
   303.6'409675109045—dc23   2011040665

British Cataloguing in Publication Data
A Cataloguing in Publication record for this book
is available from the British Library.

Printed and bound in the United States of America

∞   The paper used in this publication meets the requirements
    of the American National Standard for Permanence of
    Paper for Printed Library Materials Z39.48-1992.

5 4 3 2 1

To my family, love always

Contents

Illustrations

Tables

Figures

Maps

Acknowledgments

I am grateful to my friend and colleague Jeffrey Pickering for his insightful comments. His careful reading and constructive recommendations helped improve the original draft. I would also like to thank the anonymous reviewers for their critical comments and much-needed recommendations that greatly improved the manuscript. My thanks also go to Jeremy Aber, PhD student in the Geography Department at Kansas State University, for making the maps included in this book.

1

The Context of
Congo's Internal Wars

The Democratic Republic of Congo (DRC or Congo)[1] is a leading laboratory of civil wars. Since it became independent on 30 June 1960, secessions, insurrections, rebellions, mutinies, invasions (by Congolese with sanctuary in Angola), revolts, and ethnic wars have been part of the political landscape of the DRC. As used in this book, a civil war, or internal war, is any domestic armed conflict between at least two groups or "political organizations" (Levy and Thompson 2010, p. 5), one of which is perceived to be linked to the state, and during which the violence kills more than 1,000 people and internally displaces more than 2,000 persons in the first three months of the conflict.[2] This definition includes internally displaced persons who, unlike refugees, represent another major human dimension of civil war. The duration of civil war captures the length of intense violence from its initiation until one party is defeated or agrees to a peace settlement that lasts at least three months. As Table 1.1 records, and given these definitions, Congo has had seventeen civil wars from July 1960 to December 2010, ranging in duration from twenty-three days (Shaba war II) to 2,204 days (Hema-Lendu war). The average of Congo's internal wars is 538 days, or almost eighteen months. More than four million people have been killed in Congo wars.

Why have so many civil wars erupted in the DRC? What theoretical approach best captures both the micro- and the macro-processes of Congo's wars and their duration? Was there any effort to manage these conflicts? These are the questions that I attempt to answer in this book.

Scholars and practitioners have long been preoccupied with the question of why civil wars occur. Zartman (2005, p. 256) summarizes the literature in terms of greed or resources, grievance or basic needs, and creed or identity. However, I depart from the extant literature in several ways by contending that the politics of exclusion is a major trigger of most civil wars in Congo rather than tensions over resources, basic needs, or identity.[3] The common greed, grievance, and creed approaches have highlighted a number of problems, which are also apparent in the history of Congo. As Lemarchand (2006, p. 29) has pointed out,

Table 1.1 Internal Wars in the Democratic Republic of Congo

Conflict	Beginning	Ending	Number of Deaths (IDPs)[a]	Days Duration
Katanga secession (South Katanga)	11 July 1960	14 Jan. 1963	65,000–92,000 (15,000–30,000)	917
South Kasai secession	8 Aug. 1960	2 Feb. 1962	2,500–6,500 (350,000)	543
North Katanga insurrection	5 Sept. 1960	19 Dec. 1961	65,000–80,000 (6,000–10,000)	470
Northwestern South Kasai insurrection	1 Oct. 1962	15 Apr. 1964	2,500–4,800 (6,000–12,000)	561
Kwilu rebellion	6 Jan. 1964	31 Dec. 1965	3,000–6,500 (7,000–15,000)	725
Eastern rebellion	15 Apr. 1964	1 July 1966	45,000–75,000 (150,000–200,000)	807
Mutiny of Baka Regiment	24 July 1966	25 Sept. 1966	1,100–4,200 (5,000–10,000)	63
Mercenaries' mutiny	5 July 1967	5 Nov. 1967	2,000–6,000 (7,000–18,000)	123
Shaba war I	8 Mar. 1977	27 May 1977	1,000–1,500 (5,000–9,000)	80
Shaba war II	11 May 1978	3 June 1978	1,600–3,500 (8,000–12,000)	23
Kivu ethnic war I	20 Mar. 1993	31 Aug. 1993	7,000–16,000 (200,000)	164
Kivu ethnic war II	17 July 1995	21 Dec. 1995	1,500–3,000 (150,000)	156
Kivu ethnic war III	17 Apr. 1996	12 Oct. 1996	25,000–30,000 (220,000)	178
Anti-Mobutu revolt	17 Oct. 1996	17 May 1997	236,000–237,000[b] (100,000)	211
Mai Mai insurrection	5 Sept. 1997	26 July 1998	4,500–8,800 (15,000–25,000)	324
Anti-Kabila revolt	2 Aug. 1998	17 Dec. 2002	3,200,000–4,200,000 (1,457,000)	1,598
Hema-Lendu war	19 June 1999	1 July 2005	65,000–75,000 (42,000)	2,204

Notes: a. IDPs: internally displaced persons. b. This number also includes some 233,000 Hutu refugees who were killed by the Rwandan troops between October 1996 and May 1997 (see Kisangani 2000a, p. 179; United Nations High Commissioner for Refugees cited in Human Rights Watch 1999).

frequent reference to confrontations among warring factions as "resource wars" points to a misconception. Although resources may sustain an internal war, rebel leaders are rarely political outcasts. Rather, they are often former members of the government or other elites excluded from power who are trying to (re)insert themselves into the state apparatus.

With regard to the grievance approach, it is also incorrect to characterize excluded elites as an impoverished or an uneducated grieved group. On the contrary, these elites not only tend to be among the best-educated members of society but almost by definition they have enough resources to challenge the incumbent regime. Once in power, they are likely to continue the same system of predation as their predecessors, setting an unending cycle of predation and conflict. Furthermore, excluded elites in many multiethnic societies may not care about their identities. More often than not, they will create coalitions of individuals from a variety of different cultural backgrounds in their quest to oust the government. Political violence provides these coalitions with a rationale for fighting, but their ambitions may not be to sustain societal welfare, to improve governance, or to foster national identity.

Of course, stating that the politics of exclusion triggered Congo's internal wars still leaves a number of questions unanswered and a number of details to be explained. One of the most important details in this book is understanding why the masses or ethno-political constituencies follow excluded elites marching in or initiating civil war in Congo's multiethnic society. Three broad perspectives on ethnicity have attempted to answer this question. First is the primordialist perspective that takes ethnic identity as given (Smith 1986). As a consequence, conflict that emerges from ethnic differences does not necessarily need an explanation. The main criticism of this approach is its failure to account for the emergence of new identities or the transformation of existing identities as well as variations in the level of conflict over time and space (Lake and Rothchild 1998, p. 4).

The second is the instrumentalist approach that views ethnicity as a tool or a political instrument used by the elites for material goals (Brass 1985). Critics of this approach contend that ethnicity is not like any other social or political affiliation, which can be decided by individuals at will but can only be understood within a "relational framework" (Easman 1994, p. 13). As proponents of the third perspective, or constructivists, argue, ethnicity is not an individual attribute but a social phenomenon and the product of human actions and choices (Anderson 1983; Young 1993). Conflict emerges from pathological social systems that individuals cannot control. By itself, ethnicity is not a cause of violent conflict because most ethnic groups, most of the time, pursue their interests peacefully through established political channels (Lake and Rothchild 1998, p. 7). However, opponents of this approach contend that constructivists cannot elucidate how particular ethnic groups endure and why people are usually willing to die for their nations (Smith 1993). Furthermore, constructivists failed to account for the masses' motivations to follow the elites and for mechanisms that account for such following (Fearon and Laitin 2000).

This book takes a different perspective and argues that the masses are likely to follow excluded elites not because of primordial ethnic bonds or because of the social context in which such elites operate. Rather, they will follow such elites only if they believe the conflict is legitimate. As the remaining chapters will show, however, one tragedy in Congo's history lies in the fact that the mobilized masses often organize to support what they believe are wars of legitimacy only to discover later that their leaders are seeking nothing more than state spoils and are thus waging wars of replacement or convenience.

Because civil wars are not a cohesive class of events, the book refers to "a civil war of legitimacy" (Sobek and Payne 2010) as an attempt by political entrepreneurs to fundamentally alter the relationship between the state and society. A civil war of legitimacy is thus different from a war of replacement and a war of convenience. In a war of replacement, rebel leaders seek to remove the incumbent regime but intend to keep the state relatively unchanged. A war of convenience aims to suffocate or weaken the incumbent regime without replacing or altering it. The advantage of this categorization is that critical historical factors that help excluded elites to mobilize the masses for collective action may differ across civil wars even though the politics of exclusion remains the common trigger. Therefore, the duration of civil wars should also differ, and the expectation is that a civil war of legitimacy should be shorter than the other two because of its popular support to fundamentally transform the relationship between the state and society. Empirically, this book refers to any war that lasts more than the mean of 538 days as a long war, while a short war lasts less than the average. The advantage of this operational definition is to take the context into account rather than to rely on quantitative large N analysis that either considers a seven-year mean (Collier, Hoeffler, and Söderbom 2004) or a twelve-year mean (Fearon 2004).

Legitimacy alone is not sufficient to mobilize the masses, however. An opportunity must provide players with the expectation to gain from violence. This opportunity emerges only in a weak state as citizens interact strategically while competing for scarce resources. A weak state refers to a polity that lacks the capacity to penetrate society, to provide order, to protect groups, to arbitrate groups' issues, and to produce social goods. It thus supplies ample opportunities for civil war because it creates a fear of the future that excluded elites can bank on to mobilize the masses through violence in order to re(insert) themselves into the political system. In a sense, the nationalist discourse by political elites only provides the ideological legitimation of their strategy (Englebert and Hummel 2005). They often have no true desire to transform the state apparatus. Rather, political elites view government institutions as means to access or control the country's resources and tools that can be used to thwart political rivals. Political competition is perceived here as competition for power to control access to scarce resources by excluding potential contenders.

The book uses a process-tracing strategy to illustrate the utility of an approach focusing on the politics of exclusion for understanding Congo's many civil wars. This comparative historical method highlights the uniqueness and the commonality among Congo's internal wars. Because the process-tracing technique used in this book is relatively intricate, it must be outlined in detail. Goldstone (1991) refers to process-tracing as a critical mechanism that can illuminate the issue of confounding variables because many causes can have their own causes. Such "causes of causes" are what methodologists have in mind when they warn about infinite regress (every cause has a cause in its own right). To identify the process by which some causes are critical in explaining the outcome, or civil war, "researchers must perform the difficult cognitive feat of figuring out which aspects of the initial conditions observed in conjunction with *which simple principles* of the many that may be at work, would have *combined* to generate the observed sequence of events" (Goldstone 1991, p. 57, emphasis in the original). A detailed narrative or a story presented in the form of a chronicle provides the best way to understand the outcome of interest because it throws light on how an event came about. In essence, too little attention to history can hinder causal explanation of a social phenomenon.

The process-tracing approach used here links critical junctures to critical antecedents to explain the outcome of interest—civil wars. Critical juncture refers to a period "in history when the presence or absence of a specified causal force pushes multiple cases onto divergent long-term pathways, or pushes a single case onto a new political trajectory that diverges significantly from the old" (Slater and Simmons 2010, p. 888). As this book demonstrates, most critical junctures in Congolese history were episodes when the politics of exclusion came into particularly sharp focus.

Critical antecedents, on the other hand, are factors or conditions preceding a critical juncture that combine with causal forces during a critical juncture to produce a long-term divergence in outcomes.[4] Critical antecedents thus combine with causal forces operative at a critical juncture in at least two ways (Slater and Simmons 2010, pp. 890–891). In one scenario, critical antecedents are successive causes and exhibit a direct effect on the causal force that emerges during the critical juncture. According to John Stuart Mill, a useful rule of thumb is to truncate historical analysis at the point when causes can be understood without being expressed (cited in Rigby 1995, p. 236). The issue is to limit oneself to nontrivial causes to avoid infinite regress. Moreover, the kind of successive causes that lead to infinite regress are usually background similarities, not critical antecedents. In another scenario, critical antecedents are conditioning causes that vary before a critical juncture and predispose (but do not predestine) cases to diverge as they ultimately do (Slater and Simmons 2010, p. 891). They usually help to determine the differential causal effect of the independent variable across cases when the critical juncture exogenously comes about (Slater and Simmons 2010). In sum, critical antecedents condition a critical juncture to explain the outcome of interest.

Having indentified the politics of exclusion as a critical juncture that explains Congo's internal wars begs the question of what constitutes critical antecedents in the context of Congo. The book refers to critical antecedents as elements of continuity, or the colonial legacy, and elements of change, or the postcolonial setting. As developed in more detail later in this chapter, elements of continuity include the state itself with its artificial colonial boundaries, the integration of Congo into the world economy as a supplier of raw materials, urbanization as a modernization process, and the coexistence of unwritten communal land tenure and colonial private land system. Elements of change are a weak army or a deinstitutionalized military and the institutionalization of a patronage system.

Figure 1.1 illustrates the theoretical model of the argument. The book thus focuses on specific aspects of social life in the DRC since colonial times to capture both continuity and change, including events, actions, symbols, rituals, and words that dramatize sociocultural and economic phenomena. It also examines the motives, reasons, and justifications for citizens' behavior in civil wars by concentrating on actions and sequences as well as by looking at time and process as essentials because people construct social reality through actions that occur over time. This procedure requires a sensitive analysis of the ever-present tension between agency and structure. The former describes the changing social reality, while the latter describes the fixed regularities and patterns that shape social actions or perceptions. Not only do people create and change social reality, but social reality also imposes restrictions on human choices.

The book's process-tracing approach is important and significant for a number of reasons:

- It helps disaggregate a civil war and allows for more detailed analyses of actors' conflict characteristics.
- It provides a way of evaluating how these characteristics influence prospects for settlement, the duration of the conflict, and the likelihood of specific outcomes.
- By using a process-tracing strategy that traces the behavior and interactions of subnational actors in individual conflicts, this microlevel analysis features a broader variety of within-country information sources.
- With a larger set of conflicts, such as in the DRC, the book makes multiple comparisons, and this helps identify the idiosyncrasies of individual conflicts and evaluate whether modal patterns exist across conflicts.
- Process-tracing allows a detailed analysis of aggregate data in historical perspective as well. Thus, a combination of both microlevel and macrolevel analyses provides a way of avoiding what Kalivas calls "reckless extrapolation from the micro to the macro level" (2008, p. 398).
- By highlighting why the politics of exclusion can lead to civil war in some settings (DRC and most of its neighbors) and not in others (Tanzania and Zambia, two other neighbors), process-tracing provides a handy framework that can help analysts develop a better understanding of civil wars in most polities. More than this advantage, process-tracing can also be a useful approach to explain within-country variations.

Figure 1.1   Process-Tracing Model of Civil Wars

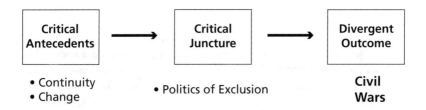

The remainder of this chapter sets the stage for the book's analysis of the politics of exclusion and Congo's civil wars. The next section is a brief literature review and a quantitative analysis of Congo's civil wars in terms of broad trends and limitations of this approach to studying civil wars. The statistical analysis is followed by a brief historical background that highlights both elements of continuity and elements of change in Congo's history. The last section of this chapter provides the goals and a brief outline of the book.

A Brief Literature Review and Statistical Exercise

Three approaches dominate the literature on the causes of internal wars. As outlined earlier, they include greed, grievance, and creed analyses. However, most statistical studies have modeled civil wars in terms of structural, economic, and political approaches rather than in terms of creed, greed, and grievance because they tend to use creed or identity as an explanatory variable.

First, the structural approach considers the nature of the country and society. Correlates of civil wars are geographical features such as a country's size, population characteristics, renewable resources, and degree of cultural affinities (Homer-Dixon 1999). Large and populous countries with young and urbanized populations have an increased probability of experiencing internal wars and even potential separatism. Neo-Malthusians also contend that population pressure on natural renewable resources makes societies prone to conflict (Urdal 2005). Ethnic heterogeneity, as a measure of identity, is also important. The more heterogeneous a state is, the more likely it will experience conflict. Operational definitions of country size and its characteristics include the natural logarithm of population, logarithm of population per square kilometer, percentage of urban population, and the age dependency ratio (the percentage of working-age population). Arable land per capita measures pressures on renewable resources. Data used in the statistical analysis are from the World Bank (2010). The last variable is social fractionalization that measures societal heterogeneity (see following greed model).

Second, economic analyses of civil wars rely mostly on the idea of greed. Rebels resemble organized criminal groups rather than freedom fighters struggling against injustice. Because a civil war is a rational decision, it is determined by the financial viability of the organization and the opportunities that arise for high expected returns. Collier and Hoeffler (1998, 2002) have popularized this greed approach in a series of quantitative analyses. Their model focuses on opportunities rather than motivations as the driving factor of civil war.

The first factor to influence opportunities is the availability of finances. Finances come from extortion of natural resources, donations from diasporas (data unavailable for Congo), and subventions from hostile governments. Collier and Hoeffler used primary commodity exports as a share of gross domestic product (GDP) and a post–Cold War dummy to operationalize the first and third variables. The relationship between primary commodities and civil wars is not linear, however. The second factor to explain opportunity is the cost of rebellion because recruits must be paid, and their cost may be related to the income foregone by enlisting as rebels. The opportunity cost of a civil war tends to be low in states that have low economic growth rates, low income, and a high number of unemployed youth (male secondary school enrollment). Third, opportunity for civil war is likely where supply of military hardware, or conflict capital, is cheap (defined by peace years and previous wars) and in states where governments have difficulties expanding their reach throughout society (defined by population dispersion and forests or mountains as a share of the country's area). Finally, weak social cohesion is an antidote to civil wars, and its operational definition is social fractionalization (see Collier and Hoeffler 2002). Because the sample is small and given the issue of multicollinearity, the variable "peace years" is removed from the analysis. Another variable, mountains as a percentage of total area, is not included because it is constant for the case of Congo. Most data are from the World Bank (2010) and the variable "forests" is from the Food and Agriculture Organization (1965–2008, annual issues).

The third approach deals with the dynamics of the political system and process. It relies on the idea of grievance or motivations. First, intergroup hatreds tend to be stronger in fractionalized societies than in homogeneous societies. Thus, civil war is carried on by political entrepreneurs willing to redress past wrongdoing. The grievance approach uses social fractionalization, political repression (autocracy, from Marshall and Jaggers 2010), ethnic dominance, and economic inequality (Gini coefficient of inequality and land inequality). Grievance may also increase with population size (logged population) to capture conflict-induced grievances. The measure of ethnic dominance is zero in Congo (there is no dominant group), and measures of economic inequality are nonexistent.

Still other scholars in the political science tradition argue that it is the instability of the political system or a political transition that weakens the state and drives states to separatism as ethnic identities are intensified (Laitin 2001). A variant of this argument is Posen's (1993) idea of internal security dilemmas.

From this perspective, the end of the Cold War (post–Cold War dummy) caused superpowers to gradually disengage from costly commitments in faraway places that did not immediately affect their national interest. This withdrawal allowed old ethnic animosities to resurface and old scores to be settled once and for all. Horowitz (1985, pp. 12–13) has also identified riots as forerunners of civil wars, especially secessionist wars. Data on riots are from Banks (2010). The dynamics affecting internal security dilemmas are upheld by living in a "bad neighborhood" (a region prone to conflicts), and external military intervention also affects the dilemma (Weiner 1996). Bad neighborhood is a constant because civil war has been endemic in Central Africa since the early 1960s. Data on military intervention are from Kisangani and Pickering (2008).

The statistical analysis uses data from 1959 to 2009. Most statistical studies on civil war operationalize it as a dummy variable, one coded as presence of civil war and zero otherwise. Because "intrastate war" is a dummy variable, the statistical model used is logit. The last methodological issue relates to the dependent variable and autocorrelated errors. Most studies that employ binary discrete dependent variables tend to assume that residuals are white noise. To deal with autocorrelated residuals, lagged civil war is used, which corrects for the inefficiency caused by autocorrelation. Table 1.2 provides the statistical results in a nonmathematical format to ease interpretation of the findings. *Positive* or *negative* expressions in parentheses below the variables suggest that this variable is likely to increase or lower the chance of civil war onset, holding other variables constant. Statistically significant (SS) means that this variable explains the onset of civil war, while SNS (statistically not significant) implies that the variable has no impact on the onset of civil war. In other words, significance relates to the probability that the given variable actually has no effect on civil wars.

The three models seem to fit the data well as illustrated by statistically significant chi-square statistics. Lagged civil war remained statistically insignificant in all models, and its removal did not affect the results. The structural model shows that only the age dependency ratio is likely to increase the chance of civil war, while population growth is negatively related to civil wars. The second model also highlights two statistically significant variables. The variable "previous wars" has the wrong sign, but geographic dispersion is positively related to civil wars as hypothesized. However, the most critical variable in the greed model—exports of primary commodities as a percentage of GDP—is not related to civil wars. Despite Congo's mineral wealth, the statistical results suggest that the greed model does not help to explain its many civil wars. This finding reinforces a number of studies that have challenged the Collier-Hoeffler model (Fearon 2005; Lujala, Gleditsch, and Gilmore 2005).

The statistical analysis of the political model highlights the fact that the democratic transition and external military intervention were critical in initiating civil wars in the DRC. Civil wars may not have been carried out by political entrepreneurs willing to redress past wrongdoing. Although these findings

Table 1.2 Three Models of Civil Wars in Congo, 1959–2009

Structural Approach	Economic Approach	Political Approach
Lagged civil war (negative & SNS)	Lagged civil war (positive & SNS)	Lagged civil war (negative & SNS)
Population (positive & SNS)	Exports/GDP (negative & SNS)	Social fractionalization (positive & SNS)
Population density (negative & SNS)	Exports/GDP^2 (negative & SNS)	Autocracy (positive & SNS)
Age dependency ratio** (positive & SS)	Post–Cold War dummy (positive & SNS)	Democratic transition* (positive & SS)
Arable land per capita (positive & SNS)	Secondary enrollment (positive & SNS)	Post–Cold War (positive & SNS)
Population growth** (negative & SS)	Economic growth (positive & SNS)	Forest (negative & SNS)
Urban population (positive and SNS)	GDP per capita (negative and SNS)	Riots (negative & SNS)
Social fractionalization (negative & SNS)	Economic growth (negative & SNS)	External military intervention** (positive & SS)
	Previous wars* (negative & SS)	
	Forests (negative & SNS)	
	Geographic dispersion* (positive & SS)	
	Social fractionalization (negative & SNS)	
Chi-square = 22.30*** Pseudo-R^2 = 0.39	Chi-square = 25.19*** Pseudo-R^2 = 0.44	Chi-square = 20.19*** Pseudo-R^2 = 0.36

Notes: Constants are omitted.
* = less than 10 percent level of significance (two-tailed test)
** = less than 5 percent level of significance (two-tailed test)
*** = less than 1 percent level of significance (two-tailed test)

counter the role of ethnicity in spurring rebellion, they do not capture how ethnic entrepreneurs exacerbate ethnic tensions to mobilize their kin. These entrepreneurs can only ply their trade in an ethnically polarized society. The critical factor is whether the counterelites can overcome obstacles to recruit partisans, control them, and maintain discipline to achieve the group's goals.

Moreover, the statistical analysis highlights some useful insights to understand civil wars, although it also has limitations. As pointed out later in this chapter, each Congolese civil war reveals a different level of intensity, duration, casualties, internal group unity, and intergroup animosity that defies any generalization conforming to existing quantitative literature on the onset and duration of civil wars. For example, most studies on Congo's wars usually refer to the first secession in 1960 as the Katanga secession and overlook the fact that two-thirds of the Katanga Province was not under the control of the seceded government because northern Katanga citizens refused to recognize it. People of North Katanga challenged both the secession and its legitimacy. What extant literature hardly considers is that wars fought within ethnic groups may have different antecedents than wars fought across ethnic lines. The quantitative literature disregards this possibility because it treats civil war as an aggregate category, implicitly assuming that a typology that distinguishes, for example, a war of legitimacy from a war of convenience or a war of replacement would not be meaningful. Any analysis that treats civil wars as if they were homogenous is likely to lead to faulty inferences about the causal links among variables. Of course, such concern about proper methods is not merely an academic issue. The substantive impact resonates widely. If decisionmakers refer to the growing body of quantitative studies when crafting policy to deal with civil wars, the results could be disastrous. Thus, the next section provides a brief historical background of Congo's internal wars to set the stage for qualitative analysis.

Political and Socioeconomic Context of Congo's Internal Wars

The political history of the DRC started on 1 July 1885, or four months after the signatories of the Berlin Conference recognized King Leopold II of Belgium as the sovereign of the Congo Free State (CFS). The CFS became a Belgian colony on 15 November 1908 and the Republic of Congo on 30 June 1960. After the promulgation of the Luluabourg constitution, it became the DRC on 1 August 1964 and remained so until 27 October 1971 when President Mobutu Sese Seko named it Zaire. On 29 May 1997, President Laurent Kabila changed the name back to the DRC. Although these names indicate that the DRC has undergone many changes in terms of players and goals, change and continuity have coexisted, and both forces have simultaneously exerted their influence on the political landscape of Congo. This section briefly outlines the political history of Congo to provide the context necessary to understand the case chapters that follow.

From Formation to Consolidation of the Colonial State

Before the European scramble for Africa in the 1860s, both acephalous societies and hierarchical polities dominated the Congo basin or present-day DRC (Ndaywel 1997). Although the precolonial Congo basin operated within essentially a subsistence economy, it was also an area of intense long-distance trade (Vansina 1962). By the mid-1870s, when agents of King Leopold II of Belgium entered the Congo basin to conquer it, four groups of alien forces dominated long-distance trade and had significantly altered the political landscape of the region: the Ovumbundu and the Cokwe (Tshokwe) from Angola, Tippo Tip and his Afro-Arabs from Zanzibar, and Ngelekwa Mwenda, or Msiri, and his Yeke from the eastern shore of Lake Tanganyika (Miller 1970; Page 1976). In the mid-1880s, most empires and chieftaincies in the Congo basin were thus weakened or ruled by foreign traders except for a few principalities and kingdoms (Vansina 1966; Ntahokaja 1981). By the time the Berlin Conference ended on 26 February 1885, most major powers had recognized King Leopold as the sovereign of the International Association of Congo (IAC), which he created on 9 October 1882, not only because his agents, among them Henry Morton Stanley, had signed a number of treaties with local rulers, but also because Leopold II had guaranteed freedom from slavery in the IAC, freedom of navigation in the Congo basin, and freedom of trade in the area.

To rule his domain, the king set up an administrative apparatus that remained in Brussels. The administrator general, and later governor general, served as the king's chief agent in the CFS and resided in Leopoldville (now Kinshasa). The decree of 1 August 1888 was the first to divide the CFS into eleven districts headed by district commissioners to make the CFS manageable. In 1895, the number of districts was increased to fifteen and remained at that number until 1910. King Leopold also established an army, called the Public Force (Force Publique), and its task was to occupy the Congo basin and to maintain law and order. Despite three mutinies in the early years of colonial state formation, the army remained an instrument to enforce authority (Flamant et al. 1952). Moreover, the king promulgated a decree on 1 July 1885 that allowed his administration to establish the state's right to dispose of all lands that were not effectively occupied by Africans by declaring them as vacant land. This expropriation of land meant that Africans were not allowed to undertake any activity outside subsistence production.

The final set of Leopold's policies was to secure resources. First, he used a mixed economic system and traditional authorities to exploit his domain.[5] Second, he passed laws on taxation as a means to force natives to collect resources such as wild rubber and ivory. In 1904, export earnings from rubber stood at 43.48 million francs gold, or $205 million in 2010 prices (2010 = 100),[6] which represented about 83 percent of exports (Gann and Duignan 1984, p. 122). This mono-exporting economy would continue to dominate the economic history of Congo. As a personal domain of King Leopold, the CFS also had to sustain or pay for itself. This managerial style is similar to pillage or exploitation and is known in Marxist language as "primitive accumulation." The king's domain had to generate profits and pay for different types of costs to bring natural resources to the nearest seaports. Thus, to collect rubber and other products,

Africans were overworked, coerced, and underfed. Resistance to the CFS emerged almost everywhere. Millions of Africans were either killed by Leopold's agents or died from starvation, disease, forced labor, mutilations, and inhumane conditions while gathering wild rubber (Hochschild 1998; James 1943; Morel 1906).

Both external and internal pressures forced Leopold II to officially cede the CFS to Belgium on 15 November 1908. Article 1 of the Colonial Charter stated that the colony had a separate and distinct legal personality from Belgium and must be self-financing. The Belgian Congo was henceforth under the Ministry of Colonies, which had to carry out a number of reforms to make the Belgian rule more humane. Although some excesses of the Leopoldian state disappeared, most reforms were cosmetic because they only reproduced the same Leopoldian apparatus under a different label. In other words, Leopoldian legacies remained the pillars of the colonial rule "though certainly there was refinement of that component" (Anstey 1966, p. 262).

In fact, the first administrative reform after the annexation followed practices dating back to the CFS. The royal decree of 28 July 1914 reorganized the colony by incorporating the districts into four provinces: Congo-Kasai, Equateur, Orientale, and Katanga. The last reform occurred in 1933 when the administration established six provinces: Leopoldville, Equateur, Costermansville (later Kivu), Elisabethville (Katanga), Orientale, and Lusambo (later Kasai).

The second Leopoldian legacy relates to traditional authority and land tenure. After 1908, a halfhearted attempt was made to restore traditional authority by creating chieftaincies and subchieftaincies. Although Belgian administrators theoretically recognized the authority of traditional chiefs, in practice every effort was made to replace them with trustworthy elements whose only claim to chieftaincy was their personal loyalty to the colonial state. The colonial administration thus enacted a series of decrees in 1910 and 1933 that completely transformed the chiefs into subaltern functionaries of the colonial administration (Nzongola-Ntalaja 2002, p. 35). Moreover, the system of land expropriation continued after the annexation.

A related legacy after 1908 was the nexus between the state and private enterprises to exploit the colony. In the late 1910s, Minister of Colonies Louis Franck realigned the Congolese franc to the Belgian franc to encourage foreign investment that increased from 3.85 million francs in 1909 to 101.02 billion francs in 1956 (Belgium 1958). This is an equivalent increase from $544,169 to almost $14.28 billion (2010 = 100). The share of mining averaged 25 percent of foreign investment and was second only to the banking and insurance sectors, which averaged 36 percent a year. Provincial division favored Katanga's copper. Just like rubber, copper came to represent more than 55 percent of total exports by 1928 (Peemans 1997a, p. 30).

Another Leopoldian legacy was a coercive state apparatus epitomized by political repression, compulsory or forced labor, and extorted individual tax. For example, legislation requiring sixty days per year (forty-five after 1955) of forced labor (or other public works) was applied until 1957. Like its Leopoldian counterpart, the harsh colonial system provoked rebellions in many parts of the colony in the form of peasant revolts, messianic and syncretic movements, and strikes (Young 1965, pp. 281–290). Moreover, Belgians ruled their colony in a climate of authoritarianism coupled with a massive dose of racism under the "paternalistic" assumption that "Negroes have the souls of children, souls that mould themselves to the methods of the educator" (Moutoulle 1946, p. 54). Unlike the Leopoldian state, however, paternalism encouraged strong state intervention in the social realm, especially in health care. A survey by the European Common Market indicated that, by 1958, the medical infrastructure in the Belgian Congo was "the best in Tropical Africa" (cited in Brausch 1961, p. 8).

The result of paternalism was also apparent in the economy. For example, Belgians isolated their colony from the world and isolated Congolese from one another. This policy was based upon the theory that the Belgian Congo could develop and eventually be transformed "from a backward and underdeveloped colony dependent upon Belgium to a fully industrialized modern state capable of running its own affairs" (Hoskyns 1962, p. 8). To some extent, this policy succeeded because the industrialization of the colony started as early as 1921. After World War II, the colony had an exceptional economic growth averaging 8 percent per year from 1946 to 1955 (Huybrechts 1970, p. 373). By the 1950s, the manufacturing industry grew at an exceptionally fast rate, averaging 14.5 percent a year; as a result, local industrial production of consumer goods covered by national production increased from virtually zero in the early 1920s to 36.5 percent of equivalent imports of similar goods by the mid-1950s (Lacroix 1967, p. 163). This percentage jumped to 44 percent in 1958 (Lacroix 1967, p. 309). As a number of scholars contended, the Belgian Congo was the most industrialized territory on the continent apart from South Africa (Lacroix 1967; Prunier 2009). For example, by 1958, more than 35 percent of all adults were in salaried employment, a proportion unknown elsewhere in Africa (Merlier 1962, p. 166).

This number may be deceptive given the fact that most of these salaried workers never finished middle school and were mostly unqualified workers, farm laborers, and petty clerks. In any case, the postwar boom ran out of steam in the late 1950s, and migrants to cities soon exceeded employment opportunities. Foreign enterprises, which represented the wealthiest sector of the economy, received a tax break and were even allowed to transfer their profits abroad rather than reinvesting them in the colony. This transfer averaged almost 9.1 billion francs per year between 1950 and 1959; the transportation and insurance sectors had the largest transfer, averaging 5 billion francs per year (Peemans 1975, p. 198). In brief, some 90.9 billion francs, or $12.73 billion (in 2010 prices), were transferred to Belgium from 1950 to 1959, depriving Congo of needed investments to create jobs. As the demand for labor fell in the private sector and urban wages started declining, the colonial state had to step up, becoming the largest employer in urban areas. Salaries paid by the state jumped from 10 percent of total salaries in 1950 to 25 percent in 1958 (Peemans 1975, pp. 198–199). At independence in June 1960, the state became a battleground because it was not only one of the main sources of employment but also remained the main access point for scarce resources.

The final effect of paternalism was in education. Until the University of Lovanium was created in 1954, the colonial system never allowed Congolese to continue schooling beyond high school. The sole avenue for secondary schooling and higher education was through the seminaries because the colonial state used the Catholic Church to create its colony (Young 1965, pp. 198–199). For example, the first African priest was ordained in 1917. At the time of independence, there were nearly 500 Congolese priests and four bishops (Young 1965, p. 199). However, the Belgian Catholic hierarchy forbade these priests or "university graduates" to accept any administrative role in the colony. Thus, from the time that Belgium took over the CFS in 1908 to the eve of independence in 1959, the vast area of the Belgian Congo was under effective and firm control exercised by the Belgian administration and supported by European investments and the Catholic Church.

Nonetheless, those few African university graduates who decided to take a different route than the priesthood and Africans who were granted education up to the middle school were the first to challenge the colonial system. This group was called *évolués*, or civilized Africans, and occupied mostly clerical jobs in the colonial system. Because the Belgian system prohibited organizations with political overtones, these évolués created cultural groups with strong ethnic connections. For example, the Alliance of Bakongo (Alliance des Bakongo or ABAKO) in Leopoldville was established in the early 1950s by Edmond Nzenza Nlandu as a social and cultural group to protect the interests and the language of the Kongo people. It later became a political party led by Joseph Kasavubu. Hundreds of other associations followed. The increasing number of African townships and the related rise of évolués made it imperative for the colonial state to think about political reforms.

One of these reforms occurred with the decree of 26 March 1957, allowing major urban centers to freely elect a council. In turn, elected council members had to nominate burgomasters from their members. The electoral system was based on single-member constituencies. In late 1957, the process took place in Leopoldville and Elisabethville and was extended in 1958 to other provincial capital cities. As expected, electoral results fell mostly along ethnic lines.

Politically, the reforms stimulated the growth of political parties because they invited competition among various contestants. After urban reforms, the formation of parties accelerated. Several political figures and parties emerged, among them Patrice Lumumba and his Congolese National Movement (Mouvement National Congolais, or MNC). Later the MNC split over leadership style into MNC/Lumumba (MNC/L) and MNC/Albert Kalonji (MNC/K). On 11 October 1958, a group of southern Katanga évolués created the Confederation of Tribal Associations of Katanga (Confédération des Associations Tribales du

Katanga, or CONAKAT). To counter the influence of CONAKAT in Katanga, the northern Luba created the Baluba of Katanga, or BALUBAKAT, in November 1959. Among many other political parties that emerged before 1960, only the MNC/L and the conservative National Party of Progress (Parti National du Progrès, or PNP) made a serious effort to organize nationally.

As the movement toward independence accelerated, political parties started seeking supporters from ethno-political constituencies. Urban areas were the first arena for competition, but urban mobilization became so tense that it produced a wave of riots among unemployed youths. The most important riot, in Leopoldville on 4 January 1959, shook the foundation of the model colony and presaged the inability of colonial structures to capture, direct, and channel youth dissatisfaction. The Belgian government responded to increasing political unrest in urban areas by convening a political roundtable conference on 20 January 1960, which most politicians attended, and a less-publicized economic roundtable that included most university graduates and a few politicians from the mining belt. On 20 February 1960, the participants in the former roundtable adopted sixteen resolutions, which represented a compromise between two fundamental issues: the timing of independence and the form of state organization afterward. The first issue positioned supporters of immediate independence against proponents of gradual independence, and the second issue pitted supporters of unitarism against proponents of federalism. From these two opposing issues emerged four political views: radical nationalism (immediate independence in a centralized structure), radical federalism (immediate independence in a federal structure), moderate nationalism (gradual independence in a unitarist structure), and moderate federalism (gradual independence in a federal structure). The essence of most political parties before independence can be reduced to these issues. For example, the MNC/L was radical and nationalist, while the ABAKO was radical and federalist; the PNP was moderate and nationalist, while the CONAKAT was moderate and federalist.

The Belgian legislature also adopted an electoral law, based on proportional representation, and a constitution, or the Fundamental Law, which created a parliamentary system. In the legislative elections, which took place in May 1960, some 250 political parties competed for seats in the lower house and provincial legislatures. Because no political party received an absolute majority in the lower house, political coalitions were necessary to form the first government. Legislators reached a compromise whereby Patrice Lumumba became prime minister and Joseph Kasavubu, the ABAKO leader, president. The new government also included Vice Premier Minister Antoine Gizenga. On 30 June 1960, the Belgian Congo became independent.

From Secessions to the Mercenaries' Mutiny

Four days after the new government took office on 4 July 1960, it confronted an army mutiny. African noncommissioned officers felt they were being left out of the distribution of the fruits of independence. While civilians were taking political power, the last European military commander, General Emile Janssens, refused to promote Africans to senior positions, stating on 5 July 1960 that "before independence = after independence" (Gérard-Libois and Verhaegen 1961, p. 350). The result of the mutiny was to deprive the new state of its effective monopoly of force and to set in motion an environment favorable to perpetuating violence. In addition, most Belgian civil servants left behind, in panic, empty administrative chairs that would be filled by unknowledgeable and inexperienced Congolese clerks.

President Kasavubu, as commander in chief, and Prime Minister Lumumba, as minister of national defense, promoted a former master sergeant, Victor Lundula, to the rank of major general and placed him in command of the new Congolese National Army (Armée Nationale Congolaise, or ANC). Joseph Mobutu, a former sergeant in the colonial army, became a colonel and chief of staff and was ordered by Lumumba to promote noncommissioned officers to officer ranks in the ANC. Despite a quick Africanization, disorder in the army continued, and soldiers at Camp Massart in Elisabethville also mutinied on 9 July 1960. Moïse Tshombe, as the governor of Katanga, appealed to Brussels for troops to restore order. The next day, two Belgian companies from Kamina military base under Major Guy Weber occupied Camp Massart. Other Belgian troops were also dispatched to a number of major cities to protect Europeans. While the United Nations (UN) Security Council was debating the Congolese crisis, the Katanga Province seceded on 11 July 1960 with Tshombe as president. He immediately hired white mercenaries, and a few weeks later he created an army, the Katanga Gendarmerie, to defend the new state. Three days after the proclamation of the Katanga secession, the UN Security Council adopted Resolution S/4387 calling for the withdrawal of Belgian troops from Congo and providing for UN assistance. The first UN military contingent, from Ghana, arrived in Kinshasa on 14 July 1960. Within four days there were some 4,000 UN troops in Congo.

While Lumumba was trying to assert his authority over Katanga, South Kasai (or Sud-Kasai), a region rich in diamonds, seceded on 8 August 1960. Its president was Albert Kalonji, the leader of MNC/Kalonji. Three days later, an insurrection in North Katanga (Nord-Katanga) broke out to oppose the Katanga secession. In early September 1960, tensions mounted between Lumumba and Kasavubu on the issue of defeating the Katanga secession. After UN Secretary-General Dag Hammarskjöld refused Lumumba's request to end the Katanga secession, Lumumba requested and received military aid from the Soviet Union. Lumumba's act alienated the United States, which pressured Kasavubu to dismiss Lumumba and nominate Joseph Ileo as the new prime minister, on 5 September 1960. A legitimacy crisis ensued, resulting in a coup d'état by Colonel Mobutu on 14 September 1960 to neutralize Lumumba, who was perceived by the West as a communist sympathizer (Kalb 1982). Mobutu installed a Council of General Commissioners on 20 September 1960, mostly composed of college graduates, to serve as a caretaker government. Mobutu's actions automatically excluded most pro-Lumumba followers or "nationalists" from power.

By early October, it became clear that Lumumba and his coalition were losing power, and the possibility of a negotiated reconciliation with President Kasavubu was more remote than ever. Lumumba's strategy was to form a countergovernment in Stanleyville (now Kisangani) where he had a majority constituency. In mid-November 1960, his supporters started heading for the town, and in late November 1960, Gizenga, the former deputy prime minister, reached Stanleyville, where he immediately received the support of the provincial government. He quickly removed pro-Mobutu officers from army battalions and replaced them with trusted officers. Within a week a pro-Lumumba government controlled the whole Orientale Province. On 12 December 1960, Gizenga announced that Stanleyville had become the capital city of Congo. The new central government had 5,500 troops under General Lundula. On Christmas day, a handful of gendarmes from Stanleyville overturned the pro-Leopoldville government of Jean Miruho in Bukavu, Kivu. Gizenga's troops penetrated as far as Manono in North Katanga in support of the northern Katanga uprising against the Katanga secession.

While these events were unfolding, Lumumba was caught by Mobutu's soldiers in early December at Lodi on the left bank of the Sankuru River after escaping from Leopoldville and trying to reach Stanleyville. He was handed over to the deputy director of security services, Gilbert Pongo, at Port Francqui (now Ilebo). On 17 January 1961, Lumumba was transferred with Senate Vice President Joseph Okito and former Youth Minister Maurice Mpolo to Elisabethville (now Lubumbashi), where the three men were assassinated a few hours after landing. The account of Lumumba's death has been developed elsewhere but suffice it to say that it was the result of a conspiracy that involved the United States, Great Britain, and Belgium (De Witte 2001; Hochschild 1998).

In early 1961, Mobutu handed power back to Kasavubu, who appointed the government of Joseph Ileo to replace the Council of Commissioners on 8 February 1961. Thirteen days later, the UN Security Council passed Resolution S/4741 that authorized its troops to use force if necessary to prevent a long civil war in Congo and called for the withdrawal from Congo of mercenaries, foreign troops, paramilitary personnel, and all political advisers not under the UN command.

The Ileo government remained in power until Cyrille Adoula took office on 2 August 1961. The Adoula administration included two prominent Lumumba followers as deputy prime ministers: Gizenga and Jason Sendwe. Their inclusion was a compromise of a parliamentary convention convened under UN pressures at Lovanium University. Six months later, on 2 February 1962, the Kasai secession was defeated by the UN and the army. With partial control of Congo secured, Adoula initiated constitutional reform with the promulgation of the law of 27 April 1962, which amended Article 7 of the Fundamental Law related to the number of provinces. By late 1963, the Congolese government had created twenty-one provinces in response to local demands for autonomy (see Map 1.1).

The creation of new provinces hardly solved the issue of political legitimacy. For example, the inauguration of a new provincial government in South Kasai ignited an insurrection in the northwestern part of the province on 1 October 1962 when a group of youths attacked unarmed civilians from the Bena Mutu wa Mukuna (people from highlands) region who were living in the Bena Tshibanda (people from lowlands) region. By mid-January 1963, nearly 4,800 people were killed, and 6,000 to 12,000 people were internally displaced (*Africa Diary* 1963, p. 973; Ilunga 1973). This insurrection coincided with the defeat of the Katanga secession by the UN on 14 January 1963. The mercenaries and most soldiers of the Katanga Gendarmerie disappeared with their arms, and many gendarmes became refugees in Angola.

Thus, the first phase of violence in Congo ended with the restoration of central authority in many parts of the country. A new political equilibrium

Map 1.1 Provinces of Congo, 1960 and 1963

emerged, and violence diminished to small-scale intraprovincial skirmishes. After a four-year mission, UN troops withdrew from Congo on 30 June 1964. Its strength of 19,828 troops from thirty-five countries cost $400.1 million (Lefever and Joshua 1966, p. 431), or $2.64 billion (2010 = 100).

As the UN was withdrawing from Congo, a new kind of warfare emerged in western and eastern Congo. A rebellion led by Pierre Mulele, the minister of education in the Lumumba government, broke out on 6 January 1964 in the Kwilu Province. Another rebellion in eastern Congo followed the Kwilu rebellion on 15 April 1964. By late 1964, the civil war in eastern Congo succeeded in eliminating government authority from Uélé (northeastern Congo) to North Katanga.

On 9 August 1964, President Kasavubu removed Prime Minister Adoula, who had been in office since August 1961. He then appointed the former president of the seceded Katanga state, Tshombe, as prime minister to quell the two rebellions. Tshombe called his former Katanga soldiers back from Angola and recruited white mercenaries to reinforce the flagging national army. Meanwhile, on 5 September 1964, the insurgents in eastern Congo declared the Popular Republic of Congo, with Stanleyville as its capital and Christopher Gbenye, former minister of interior in the Lumumba government, as its president.

In addition to quelling the two rebellions, Prime Minister Tshombe had to organize legislative elections according to Article 185 of the Luluabourg constitution promulgated on 1 August 1964. In early 1965, he renewed the Leopoldville branch of his political party, the CONAKAT, in anticipation of the upcoming elections. Some forty-nine tribal organizations also joined the party to form the Congolese National Convention (Convention Nationale Congolaise, or CONACO) on 20 February 1965 in Luluabourg. The second legislative elections, from 18 March to 30 April 1965, occurred without violence and without foreign observers. The CONACO received 122 legislative seats, or 73 percent, of the votes from most electoral districts (Gérard-Libois and Van Lierde 1966, pp. 222–223). Instead of letting Tshombe compose the government, President Kasavubu nominated Evariste Kimba from the minority coalition, the Congolese Democratic Front (Front Démocratique Congolais), on 13 October 1965 as the prime minister. This minority coalition was created by a group of politicians behind Victor Nendaka, security police chief, to oppose the CONACO. Nendaka was a member of the Binza Group, which worked closely with US, Belgian, and UN officials and imposed its will on President Kasavubu.[7] Unfortunately, the CONACO's ascendancy led to tensions between Kasavubu and Tshombe. On 24 November 1965, Mobutu, now general, took power under this uncertainty. By this time, the Kwilu rebellion was winding down and ended in late December. The eastern rebellion continued afterward but was quite weak by July 1966 and posed no major threat to the central government. The two rebellions did, however, cost more than 60,000 lives and internally displaced more than 100,000 people (Verhaegen 1969).

In his quest to consolidate power, Mobutu decided in early 1966 to integrate both the mercenaries and former Katanga soldiers who had fought the eastern rebellion in the national army. As he was reforming the army, a mutiny broke out in Kisangani on 24 July 1966 that involved the Baka Regiment, a unit of the national army consisting of 2,000 Katangan soldiers under Colonel Ferdinand Tshipola (Gérard-Libois 1967, p. 346). The mutiny ended on 25 September 1966 after more than 3,000 deaths and the displacement of most people in the town (Gérard-Libois 1967, p. 356). Nine months later, on 5 July 1967, a mutiny instigated by eleven white mercenaries began in Kisangani. Within a week, the mutineers were joined by some 150 additional mercenaries, 600 Katangan soldiers, and 400 renegades from the former rebel army. When the mutiny ended on 5 November 1967, the death toll was 2,000 to 6,000 people (Gérard-Libois and Verhaegen 1969, pp. 349–407).

The Second Republic: From Consolidation to Collapse

For almost thirty-two years Mobutu remained the uncontested president of Congo. This political longevity was the result of many factors, among them the unintended consequence of the anti-Communist policies of the United States. In addition to US support, Mobutu used a number of key domestic strategies to remain in office. First was his quest for legitimacy after his second coup d'état in November 1965. Legitimacy is a belief by the ruled that the ruler has a right to exercise authority (Kisangani 2000b, p. 209). Habermas (1979) describes the distance between shared belief of the governors and the governed as a legitimacy gap. To bridge the gap, most leaders resort to "legitimation devices" that establish "how and why existing or recommended institutions are fit to employ power" (Habermas 1979, p. 183). Mobutu initiated five such devices to secure early legitimacy of his power and to create not only a sense of nationhood but also a strong state. First, he dealt with the collapse of the early political consensus by coopting some twenty-two civilians from different ethno-political constituencies and major political parties in his first government to give it a sense of national unity (Kisangani 2000b).

Second, he proclaimed Patrice Lumumba, the symbol of the 1964 rebellions, as a national hero and appropriated Lumumba's nationalist principles. More specifically, he promulgated the Bakajika Law in June 1966, which stipulated that "all public land was the domain of the Congolese nation-state, and formally extinguishing all grants and concessionary powers delegated by the colonial state" (Young and Turner 1985, p. 288). The Bakajika Law cleared the way for new mineral concessions by abolishing colonial arrangements and undeveloped colonial claims. The law also paved the way for the nationalization of the Union Minière du Haut Katanga (UMHK) in January 1967 that became the Générale des Carrières et des Mines (Gécamines). The Belgian government reacted quickly by imposing an embargo on copper exports to cripple the Congolese economy.

Third, five years later, Mobutu banned all Christian names. Colonial names of cities, such as Leopoldville and Stanleyville, were changed to Congolese names, Kinshasa and Kisangani. This policy was known as "authenticity" and was also extended to lifestyle (Kisangani and Bobb 2010, pp. 35–36). These decisions were the first devices to create a sense of "belonging" to the state and the nation. Authenticity sought to create a truly national identity by developing indigenous institutions and national forms of expression in the nation's political, economic, and cultural life.

Fourth, Mobutu sent a strong signal early on that opposition would not be tolerated. In early June 1966, he publicly hanged four former cabinet members before 50,000 spectators in what was called the "Pentecost Plot" to overthrow Mobutu (Kisangani 2000c, p. 261). Fifth, Mobutu began modernizing the army with new equipment to provide prestige to the military. He also accelerated the level of education and training of the officer corps by sending hundreds of military officers and high school graduates to the best military schools in the West (Kisangani 2000b). His efforts were intended to create a professional army that not only reflected the Congolese ethno-political constituencies but that was also capable of defending the nation.

Although Mobutu's populist actions were a real start in the legitimacy process, they were not enough to help him develop strong state institutions. As a result, he created the Popular Movement of the Revolution party (Mouvement Populaire de la Révolution, or MPR) to broaden his political support. Then, in December 1970, he amended the 1967 constitution to institutionalize the one-party state. All citizens, including the unborn, were all declared Mobutists or members of the single party. The MPR's slogans projected a novel promise for a better and just society for the future. Meanwhile, Mobutu's speeches also became force of law. He was thus able to develop a sense of Congolese (then Zairian) nationhood and strong institutions that helped maintain peace and order, supply public goods, penetrate society, and sustain economic growth for almost ten years. This quasi-strong state minimized most opportunities for civil wars.

In sum, the goal of Mobutu's legitimation devices was to strengthen the state as an instrument of authority and to enhance its capabilities. However, by placing Mobutu above the law, state-building efforts to legitimize Mobutu's rule were also the first mechanisms to weaken the state-building process. Institutionalized violence became common as state secret services and the military were used as instruments of terror against opponents of the Mobutu regime (Kisangani 2000c). His early nationalist rhetoric also turned out to be a way of accumulating resources to finance his patronage system. Mobutu was able to monopolize all sources of revenue and distribute them to his clients as he pleased. This strategy was, however, based on a weak economic foundation that precipitated the collapse of his regime. Thus, an analysis of the economy since the 1960s will help explain the emergence of a new round of civil wars.

Foundations of the Second Republic, Shaba wars, and beyond. Six major periods characterize the postcolonial economy up to 2010: 1960–1965, 1966–

Figure 1.2 Economic Growth, 1960–2009

Source: Data from World Bank 2010.

1973, 1974–1979, the 1980s, the 1990s, and the post-1990s. Figure 1.2 illustrates these periods. In the first era, the rate of economic growth oscillated between positive and negative, but the growth rate remained, on average, positive as the result of the growth impetus of the 1950s. Because prices and the trade deficit were on the rise, the government devalued the Congolese franc in 1961 and 1963. These policies failed because the central government had lost its major sources of revenue from Katanga, Kasai, Kivu, and Orientale provinces as the result of secessions and Gizenga's control of the last two provinces. Despite a few shocks from the demand side, economic growth averaged 3.68 percent per year in 1960–1965.

Economic growth also remained positive in the second period, 1966–1973, averaging 3.78 percent per year as inflationary pressures remained low. The economic model pursued by Congo seemed to work relatively well as the result of the economic reform of 24 June 1967 by the International Monetary Fund (IMF), which narrowed the gap between aggregate demand and aggregate supply. The centerpiece of the reform was a sharp devaluation of 300 percent that realigned the new currency, the zaire, to its parallel market value at the fixed exchange rate of 1.00 zaire per $2.00. The net result of the 1967 monetary reform was positive because the economy benefited from favorable prices of copper in the world markets. Thus, from 1967 to 1970, the financial contribution of the state mining company, Gécamines, as a share of government revenue, represented 49 percent of the national budget (Bézy, Peemans, and Wautelet 1981, p. 84). The mineral sector, especially copper, provided some 65 percent of export earnings.

The third period, from 1974 to 1979, began with supply side shocks. The economy weakened and averaged a negative growth rate of –1.88 percent a year. Recession also set in as inflationary pressures accelerated, averaging 67 percent a year. The economy deteriorated after 1973 for many reasons. First, the government nationalized foreign businesses on 30 November 1973, and the takeover by new owners (*acquéreurs*) occurred within a month of the announcement. Foreign businesses and plantations were handed over to the political ruling group, which ran them into the ground a few months later. The result was a breakdown of production as well as a decline in agricultural and manufacturing production. Not only did the nationalization deindustrialize Congo, but it also destroyed tradable agriculture. For example, official export earnings from agriculture declined drastically to 12 percent of total export earnings in 1974 from 40 percent in 1958–1959 (Bézy, Peemans, and Wautelet 1981, p. 84). This was the lowest percentage since the end of World War II. Despite some efforts in 1976 to revitalize agriculture, less than 4 percent of official export earnings originated from agriculture, which paradoxically employed more than 60 percent of the Congolese population.

Second, the economic crisis also reflected the collapse of copper prices in the world markets and the concomitant decline in foreign exchange. These prices plummeted from 98 cents a pound in 1973 to 59 cents in 1974 and remained on average below 70 cents a pound from 1974 to 1978. The result was a decline in export earnings despite the production of copper averaging more than 450,000 metric tons a year in 1974–1978. Meanwhile, the price of oil skyrocketed in the same period. As a result, foreign debt also increased, averaging some 30 percent of GDP from 1976 to 1979 (World Bank 2010). As a consequence of these macroeconomic imbalances, Mobutu was forced by the IMF to stabilize the economy in the second half of the 1970s, but all stabilization measures were unsuccessful. The result was a spiral of devaluation and inflation that reduced the value of the national currency from $1.00 = 0.86 zaire in 1976 to $1.00 = 2.04 zaires in 1979 (Kisangani 1987).

Despite this weak economy, Mobutu appeared firmly in control in the mid-1970s, although this control was more apparent than real. Economically, Mobutu's state ceased to penetrate the countryside from the mid-1970s on, as smuggling activities across borders largely escaped government control (Kisangani 1998; MacGaffey 1991). Politically, the state had no control in eastern Congo. For example, Congolese opponents of Mobutu's regime from the Front for the National Liberation of Congo (Front pour la Libération Nationale du Congo, or FLNC), based in Angola, invaded Katanga on 8 March 1977, initiating a civil war called Shaba I. When the invasion ended on 27 May 1977, the death toll was between 1,000 and 1,500, with more than 5,000 people internally displaced. Another invasion, or Shaba II, occurred between 11 May 1978 and 3 June 1978. Although Shaba II was shorter than Shaba I, the number of casualties was much higher, ranging between 1,600 and 3,500 deaths, with an average of 10,000 internally displaced persons. The Congolese rebels were driven back to their sanctuary in Angola by French and Belgian paratroopers. The United States also played a role, providing air transport and materials during the drop of paratroopers.

Economic troubles and the Shaba conflicts were only the most visible signs of the weakness of Mobutu's regime. A number of less conspicuous phenomena also wore away the foundations of the Mobutu state. One example is the growth of the public sector. As a consequence of uncontrolled government spending, inflation soared in the late 1970s as Mobutu was spending more than 32 percent of government outlays on himself (Kisangani 1997, p. 41). Meanwhile, state revenue plummeted as the result of copper price fluctuations, which forced the government to borrow massively from abroad. Foreign debt increased from less than 50 percent of GDP in the 1970s to more than 100 percent of GDP in the late 1980s. It averaged more than 200 percent of GDP a year in the first half of the 1990s (World Bank 2010).

Another symptom of state weakness was patronage, with the major source being a position in the executive branch. Mobutu's key strategy was frequent reshuffling of the government—more than forty times from 1966 to 1989 (Kisangani 2000c, p. 269). The result was frequent embezzlement and mismanagement in the public domain. Corruption became the "system" (Gould 1980, p. xvii) because, out of greed and fear for their survival, the elites institutionalized corruption and locked their subordinates into corrupt practices in a systematic way. By the early 1980s, kleptocracy emerged as the mode of governance.

Despite this, the 1980s, categorized here as the fourth period, were unique because they averaged a positive economic growth rate of 1.81 percent a year. This period also remained politically stable despite the presence of ample opportunities for civil war. Even one of Mobutu's opponents in exile titled his book *Le Pouvoir à la Portée du Peuple* or "The Power within People's Reach" (Kamitatu 1977). Congo thus remained relatively calm until the early 1990s, except in November 1984 when a group of dissidents labeled the Party of Popular Revolution (Parti de la Révolution Populaire, PRP) under Laurent Kabila confronted the regular army in Moba, North Katanga. The PRP held the town for two days before the army regained control. Because the conflict ended with less than seventy-eight casualties, it does not qualify as a civil war. The PRP attacked again in June 1985 without much success.

From Kivu ethnic wars to anti-Mobutu revolt. The end of the 1980s also marked the end of the Cold War and the beginning of the fifth economic period. Mobutu was compelled by the West and domestic political forces to announce the liberalization of his political system on 24 April 1990. Soon after, the euphoria of having a free press and multiparty political system developed into social agitation on campuses. The unrest rattled Mobutu and led to an overreaction when soldiers killed 297 students on the campus of the University of Lubumbashi on 11–12 May 1990 (Kisangani 1997, p. 44). This act resulted in the suspension of foreign aid, except humanitarian aid, from his major aid donors—Belgium, France, and the United States. Overall levels of foreign aid consequently dropped from 7 percent of GDP in 1990 to 2 percent of GDP in 1992 (World Bank 2010). Meanwhile, economic growth also declined by 4.1 percent in 1991, with a major drop of 14 percent in 1993. This negative trend continued until 2001, except for a slight positive growth of 0.1 percent in 1996. The consumer price level, which had dropped by 81 percent from 1989 to 1990, jumped by 2,154 percent from 1990 to 1991, and then by 4,129 percent a year later, despite government efforts to control it (World Bank 2010). Although the increase in consumer prices from 1992 to 1993 was lower than the preceding year, or 1,986 percent, prices jumped again by almost 23,773 percent from 1993 to 1994, then dropped to almost 542 percent in 1995 and slightly in 1996. This inflationary period also coincided with political instability as the process of democratization was proceeding.

Despite Mobutu's efforts to stall the process, hundreds of political parties emerged in the early 1990s as the result of Law no. 90/009 of 18 December 1990. More specifically, pro-Mobutists, or "dinosaurs," a term used by Braeckman (1992),[8] created a plethora of parties to undermine the opposition. The number of political parties swelled from 43 in July 1990 to 382 in November 1993. A small group of these parties created a coalition called the Sacred Union (Union Sacrée) and insisted on the organization of a national conference to create new institutions. One major party in the coalition was Union for Democracy and Social Progress (Union pour la Démocratie et le Progrès Social, or UDPS), which was created in 1982 by a group of thirteen dissident legislators during the single-party regime.

The national conference opened on 7 August 1991, but Mobutu flooded it with his supporters, resulting in a walkout by the opposition. For several weeks, tensions mounted, and, on 23 September 1991, dissatisfied soldiers in Kinshasa mutinied, going on a looting spree that spread throughout the country, initiating a culture of "pillage" that would epitomize the economic history of Congo for the next two decades.

Under pressure from the West, Mobutu appointed Etienne Tshisekedi from the Sacred Union as the prime minister to deal with the crisis. A week later, Mobutu dismissed him because Tshisekedi refused to swear allegiance to the president. Then, in mid-January 1992, Prime Minister Nguza Karl-i-Bond called off the national conference indefinitely on the grounds that the dominance of the conference by the opposition was contributing to violence and the conference was costing the national treasury thousands of dollars a day. Pressures from the Catholic clergy, which organized the Christian March of Hope on 16 February 1992, and from the West forced Mobutu to reopen the proceedings on 6 April 1992. The conference, now called the sovereign national conference, declared its own status and its decisions binding on all citizens. The conference, which was chaired by Archbishop Laurent Monsengwo of Kisangani, also elected Tshisekedi, a Luba from Kasai, as the prime minister of the transitional government, voting overwhelmingly for the resignation of Karl-i-Bond, a Lunda from Katanga. The nomination of Tshisekedi and the expulsion of Karl-i-Bond sparked ethnic conflict in early September in Katanga, where the Lunda targeted the Luba clans of Kasai for harassment. By the time the conflict ended, around 215 Luba and other non-Katanga people were killed by the Lunda (Kisangani 1997). Because this conflict does not meet the 1,000-death threshold, and does not thus qualify as a civil war, it will not be discussed here. Suffice it to say that the causes of this conflict are rooted in the colonial period discussed in Chapter 2.

Mobutu was able to stall the democratization process even after the conference ended and officially elected Tshisekedi as the prime minister of the transition under a new legislature, the High Council of the Republic (Haut Conseil de la République, or HCR). On the economic front, Mobutu asked the governor of the central bank in January 1993 to introduce a five-million zaire banknote worth less than $2 to cope with the country's hyperinflation. However, merchants and traders obeyed Tshisekedi's call to refuse the banknotes. Despite this popularly supported move, Mobutu decided to pay the military with the new banknotes, and when the merchants refused to honor them, the soldiers went on another rampage on 28 January 1993 with casualties of about a hundred people killed, including Philippe Bernard, the French ambassador to Congo.

Tshisekedi's popularity resulted in his dismissal in March 1993 by Mobutu, who also discharged the HCR and called on his supporters from the defunct national assembly for a "conclave of the last chance" (Kisangani 1997, p. 49). After two weeks, he appointed Faustin Birindwa, a former UDPS member, as the new prime minister. However, Birindwa was not recognized by the West and the opposition, resulting in a dual executive system. As Mobutu tried to reassert his authority, an ethnic conflict broke out in Nord-Kivu Province on 20 March 1993 in Walikale. A week later, the conflict spread to Masisi territory. By the end of August 1993, between 7,000 and 16,000 people were dead and 200,000 were internally displaced (U.S. Committee for Refugees 1994, p. 73).

While this ethnic conflict was unfolding, the national economy continued its nosedive in 1993 as inflation accelerated. To deal with hyperinflation, a presidential decree promulgated a new currency called the "new zaire" on 19 October 1993, equivalent to three million old zaires and worth only $0.33. Four weeks after the reform, the new zaire dropped from 3.00 to 4.09 per dollar as the result of intense speculation. The government was also far behind in its debt payments with arrears estimated in 1994 at $4.46 billion (Kisangani 1997). On 1 February 1994, the World Bank closed its offices in Congo, declared Congo insolvent, and canceled all credits allocated to Congolese projects. To say that the Birindwa administration failed to stabilize the economy is thus an understatement. As an example, the exchange rate plummeted from $1.00 = 3.00 new zaire in mid-1993 to $1.00 = 1,194.49 in October.

Meanwhile, the opposition and Mobutu's supporters signed political accords to create a unicameral legislature that merged the defunct national assembly and the HCR into HCR/Parliament of Transition, or HCR/PT. This parliament appointed Mobutu's protégé Léon Kengo wa Dondo as the new prime minister. His nomination also ended the dual executive system because the West approved it, given Kengo's previous cordial relations with Bretton Woods institutions in the 1980s as prime minister. Kengo promised to take appropriate measures to end the economic catastrophe that had plagued Congo since the early 1990s.

A few days after being nominated prime minister, Kengo wa Dondo was faced with the problem of nearly 1.2 million Hutu refugees from Rwanda who had abruptly entered eastern Congo on 18 June 1994 (Kisangani 2000a). The refugees were fleeing a Tutsi group called the Rwandan Patriotic Front (RPF), the political wing of the Rwandan Patriotic Army (RPA), which had seized power in Rwanda. These refugees were eventually relocated to Goma (850,000), Bukavu (200,000–300,000), and Uvira (62,000) (see Kisangani 2000a, p. 173). Among the refugees were some 20,000 to 25,000 former Rwandan soldiers and 30,000 to 40,000 Hutu militiamen who had committed genocide in Rwanda. These armed groups even attempted to create a Hutuland in Congo to serve as a sanctuary from which to launch massive attacks on Rwanda.

The fear of a Hutuland in Kivu prompted the transitional parliament on 28 April 1995 to adopt a resolution that stripped Congolese of Rwandan origin, known as Banyamulenge and Banyarwanda, of their citizenship. The Banyamulenge are Congolese of Tutsi origin who migrated to Sud-Kivu in the late eighteenth century (Kabamba and Lanotte 1999, p. 126). The Banyarwanda include natives of Nord-Kivu (Banyabwisha), Rwandan subjects cut off from Rwanda in 1910 when the boundaries in the Great Lakes region were redrawn by the colonial powers, and Rwandan immigrants during the colonial period (see Chapter 6). The result of the parliamentary decision of April 1995 was a new wave of ethnic clashes in Nord-Kivu from 17 July 1995 to 21 December 1995 as local Congolese politicians used Hutu refugees to exploit the rivalry between the Tutsi and other groups in Nord-Kivu. The death toll reached 1,500 to 3,000 people, and some 150,000 people were internally displaced. After almost four months of relative calm, another ethnic conflict erupted in Nord-Kivu Province on 17 April 1996, and sporadic clashes continued until 12 October, with 25,000 to 30,000 deaths and more than 220,000 internally displaced people (U.S. Committee for Refugees 1997, p. 105).

While this new round of ethnic conflict was unfolding, the deputy governor of Sud-Kivu asked the Banyamulenge on 6 October 1996 to leave, in accordance with the April 1995 parliamentary resolution. However, they refused and turned to the Rwandan Tutsi government for help. On 17 October 1996, a full-scale war erupted in Sud-Kivu as the Banyamulenge confronted the regular national army. By the end of the year, some 3,000 people were dead, and more than 6,000 people were internally displaced (U.S. Committee for Refugees 1997, p. 105). Kabila emerged as the spokesperson of the rebel group known as the Alliance of Democratic Forces for the Liberation of Congo (Alliance des Forces Démocratiques pour la Libération du Congo, or AFDL) and he announced the group's intention to oust President Mobutu. The rebel forces, spearheaded by Mai Mai (or Mayi Mayi) militias as well as troops from Angola, Rwanda, and Uganda, entered the capital city on 17 May 1997. On 29 May 1997, Kabila became president (Braeckman 1997).

From Civil Wars Against Kabila to Hema-Lendu Ethnic War

The rise of Kabila marked a new period for Congo. As Kabila was consolidating his power, the Mai Mai groups that helped him during the anti-Mobutu war confronted the Banyamulenge battalion of the Congolese army and Rwandan troops on 5 September 1997. The Mai Mai accused Kabila of betraying them or "selling" the Kivus (Nord-Kivu and Sud-Kivu) to Rwanda. The conflict resulted in the death of 4,500 to 8,800 people, and more than 15,000 to 25,000 people were internally displaced in Kivu by the time the insurrection ended in late July 1998.

Despite political instability in eastern Congo, the Kabila government was able to restore the confidence of the international community in the Congolese economy by paying, in June 1998, some $1.5 million of debt arrears to the IMF. This gesture marked the de facto resumption of relations between Congo and the IMF. Kabila also embarked on a major economic reform on 30 June 1998 when his government replaced the new zaire with the franc. The buying rate was fixed at 1.43 franc to a dollar and the selling rate at 1.38 franc to a dollar. Less than a month after this monetary reform, Kabila decided to free himself from the kingmakers, Rwanda and Uganda, by ordering all foreign troops to leave, thus ending the military cooperation that overthrew President Mobutu. Backed by Rwanda, an anti-Kabila revolt began on 2 August 1998. Angola, Namibia, and Zimbabwe sent troops to the DRC and rescued the Kabila government. By the end of 1998, the war had cost the lives of more than 12,500 people and had displaced more than 250,000 (U.S. Committee for Refugees 1999, pp. 58–60).

The anti-Kabila revolt was mostly dominated by the Congolese Rally for Democracy (Rassemblement Congolais pour la Démocratie, or RCD) and its backer, the Rwandan government. Uganda also joined later as Rwanda's ally (Clark 2001), and other groups emerged, such as the Movement for the Liberation of Congo (Mouvement pour la Libération du Congo, or MLC) of Jean-Pierre Bemba. The rebels and the government met in Lusaka, Zambia, to conclude a cease-fire agreement in July 1999 called the Lusaka Peace Accord. Despite the agreement, the war against Kabila and other ethnic conflicts continued unabated. One example is the Hema-Lendu conflict in the Ituri region. It began on 19 June 1999 and continued until 31 December 1999 with 6,000 to 8,000 deaths and more than 25,000 internally displaced persons. The fighting resumed again in early 2000. A year later, on 16 January 2001, President Kabila was assassinated by his bodyguard, Rashidi Kasereka (Prunier 2009, pp. 249–255).

Kabila left the DRC in total economic chaos, half-occupied by foreign troops and rebel groups. On 26 January 2001, Joseph Kabila succeeded his father. The only document that offered any hope for peace since the outbreak of the war was the Lusaka Peace Accord. It called for a UN peacekeeping operation and an Inter-Congolese Dialogue (ICD) of all Congolese belligerents and representatives of civil society, which effectively started in Sun City, South Africa, in February 2002. The dialogue ended with the signing on 17 December 2002, in Pretoria, of the Global and Inclusive Act of the Transition. Another peace agreement followed, on 2 April 2003 in Sun City, which sought to restore democracy in Congo after the deaths of 3.2 million to 4.2 million people and the internal displacement of some 1.5 million persons as the result of the war against Kabila (computation from diverse sources). The peace accord also resulted in a national transitional government in June 2003, which included Joseph Kabila as president, four vice presidents, and thirty-five ministers with their deputies. Two years later, the Hema-Lendu war officially ended.

After postponing elections once in 2005, the government sent a draft constitution to voters in late 2005. Some 84 percent of the registered electors voted for the new constitution, which was promulgated in February 2006. Free and fair legislative elections took place on 30 July 2006, the third since the country became independent. The first presidential elections through universal suffrage also occurred on the same day. After the second round of presidential elections, Kabila was sworn in as the fourth president of the DRC on 6 December 2006, ending the democratic transition to the Third Republic that started in April 1990.

However, by late 2010, political instability remained a major issue in eastern Congo as the result of a number of factors, including a government incapable of restoring peace, an undisciplined army terrorizing people throughout the country, and the existence of a number of peace spoilers,[9] foreign rebels from Rwanda and Uganda with sanctuary in Congo, and autocrats in neighboring countries refusing to open up their own political processes, causing their own rebels to cross the borders. More specifically, the peace blueprint of the international community failed to bring peace in Congo because it required the hasty creation of a transitional government and the holding of "free elections" before all the warring parties were disarmed and demobilized. Political instability in eastern Congo also prompted the UN Security Council to unanimously adopt Resolution 1925 on 8 October 2010, calling for the establishment of the UN Stabilization Mission in the DRC (Mission de l'Organisation des Nations Unies pour la Stabilisation du Congo, or MONUSCO) under Chapter VII. The goal was to protect civilians, humanitarian personnel, and human rights defenders under imminent threat of physical violence and to protect UN personnel, facilities, installations, and equipment. Thus, continuing conflicts in eastern Congo by late 2010 and issues of governance prevented Joseph Kabila from delivering any form of peace dividend to the people.

Interplay of Continuity and Change in Congo's Civil Wars

As Figure 1.1 illustrates, this brief historical review highlights two sets of factors that help contextualize Congo's internal wars, including elements of continuity and change. The first element of continuity remains the state itself with its artificial and juridical boundaries. As a consequence, these boundaries have sustained ethno-political constituencies across borders with multiple national allegiances. Moreover, the colonial state was an idea in the mind of the colonized. This is line with Geertz's (1980, p. 13) contention that the state should be seen as "a legitimating idea and a teleological construct ingrained in the minds of people without which no legitimate existence of power relations would exist in society." Viewing the state as an idea helps explain the repressive and paternalist colonial state. In the mind of the colonized, it was a brutal and oppressive entity. They called it *Bula Matari* (*Bula Matadi*) or "he who breaks rocks" (Young 1965, p. 98). This metaphor came to describe an entity capable of crushing all resistance. Little changed with independence because the notion of an all-oppressive state was perpetuated by the Congolese leadership. Although the personnel at the top changed, the same repressive and exploitative structure remained.

The second element of continuity is the integration of Congo into the world economy. Initially, the colonial system drew Africans into production for the global economy. The six provinces or colonial administrative divisions reflected an economic structure characterized by a few dominant mineral commodities in total exports. This dominance has been perpetuated in the postcolonial period. Like the colonial apparatus, the postcolonial provinces represent clusters of economic markets that also include various ethnic groups under one roof. In other words, provincial markets have become battlegrounds to access state power and scarce resources rather than to administer the land and citizens.

Third is urbanization. Instead of being an agent of modernization, increased urbanization has only reinforced ethnic affinities. The politicization of ethnicity became salient in the early 1960s largely because the colonial state socialized Africans to grant ethnic identity more importance than any other type of affiliation. However, the elimination of overt electoral competition under Mobutu's rule did not diminish the role of ethnicity. On the contrary, ethnic affinities increased because he relied on a core group from his own province to rule. Post-Mobutu state managers have also reinforced ethnic affinities.

Traditional land tenure and traditional authority represent two other elements of continuity. Although the colonial state appropriated all native lands, it never destroyed customary land tenure and even upheld traditional authority as long as it did not interfere with colonial order and its economic exploitation of the Belgian Congo. Thus, traditional authorities were not only colonial representatives but also remained guardians of African traditions. This ambiguity has continued in the postcolonial period.

Congo became independent on 30 June 1960 and gained a new set of institutional arrangements. With these new rules of the game also emerged a new set of players. One major change in government functions was the deinstitutionalization of the army. The military collapsed briefly after independence in a mutiny that destroyed a number of old institutional arrangements and produced new tensions that prevented new institutions from developing. Since then, the army has remained not an instrument to keep law and order or to protect national borders but rather a self-perpetuating undisciplined corps that is incapable of defending national boundaries and an efficient instrument of terror preying on unarmed civilians.

A second change after independence was the institutionalization of patronage. Those in power developed clientelist networks to gain support from the elites, not the masses. In the mid-1960s, a new group of players appeared, mostly college and university graduates, who revolved around Mobutu. As early as 1974, kleptocracy was born and has perpetuated itself since. Although government pillage of Congolese resources seems to be an element of continuity dating back to the CFS in the nineteenth century, the postcolonial pillage differs from the colonial system in that reinvestment of a small portion of this pillage in basic social and physical infrastructure as well as in mines and agriculture completely vanished by the mid-1970s. Moreover, unlike the colonial leviathan with a strong superstructure able to penetrate society and extract both labor and taxes, the postcolonial state has remained extremely weak, except perhaps from 1967 to 1975. One consequence is that a politicized judicial system has developed a culture of impunity and allowed incessant grave human rights abuses by the government and its military.

The interaction between continuity and change provides a way of understanding the historical roots of Congo's civil wars and how the masses or ethnopolitical constituencies respond to elites' call to arms, although a major trigger of Congo's civil wars remains the politics of exclusion. So far, no study has tried to analyze these wars in the context of the interaction between continuity and change. Most qualitative studies in the context of grievance are, for example, limited to either one civil war (Katanga secession, anti-Mobutu civil war, or anti-Kabila conflict) or a few civil wars (rebellions, Shaba wars, or anti-Mobutu and anti-Kabila wars).

Goals and Structure of the Book

Several issues emerge from the statistical exercise and the brief historical context of Congo's wars, which provide the two major goals of this book. The first goal is empirical. By following a qualitative method, I subject extant theoretical research on civil wars to detailed historical investigation in one of the most war-torn countries of the postcolonial period. Although the book focuses on one country, an attempt is made to discover similarities and differences diachronically in the discussion of Congo's civil wars. I thus aim to explain the process by which Congo's wars occurred and why some lasted longer than others. I use data on individual actions and also macrolevel data to describe conditions under which individual decisionmaking takes place, helping to disentangle complicated multicausal relationships at the micro- and macrolevels. By doing so, the qualitative approach reconstructs the chronology of Congo's internal wars to identify interactions among explanatory variables that have been undertheorized in quantitative studies. By providing "richness," "thickness," and "depth," qualitative methods help to contextualize the material that is developed in quantitative studies (King, Keohane, and Verba 1994). Although the qualitative approach can also identify the causes that influence a particular outcome, as in the quantitative approach, its major hurdle is to specify a causal sequence that connects multiple causes and interactions with the outcome of interest. To deal with this hurdle, the book follows the process-tracing strategy (Figure 1.1), which hypothesized that the politics of exclusion is a critical juncture of most Congolese civil wars.

The historical context also highlighted a number of factors of continuity and change as critical antecedents to explain Congo's internal wars (Figure 1.1). The interaction between elements of continuity and change creates opportunities where ethno-political constituencies compete for state power because the state controls scarce resources and provides access to these resources and the income streams that flow from them. Individuals and groups that possess political power can often gain access to these resources and increase their own welfare (Hardin 1995, pp. 34–37). As subsequent chapters show, the politics of exclusion emerges as a promising option to access state power and scarce resources this access commands because its goal is to prevent political contenders from gaining power.

The second goal of the book relates to policies. Any statistical exercise is sometimes too abstract or complicated for policymakers. The statistical output, in particular, is largely incomprehensible to most policymakers and even to many academics. Sometimes statistical analyses provide unfeasible policies that deepen the skepticism of policymakers. For example, the greed approach contends that reducing economic dependence on primary commodities, improving development policies by reducing negative economic growth, and increasing income should make civil wars less likely. Other variables include secondary school enrollment and population control. Although a number of variables are not statistically significant, they constitute parts of policy proposals related to these models. However, using these variables as policy instruments to prevent civil wars is questionable. Most variables are structural and not easily manageable over the short term, and those that can be changed require long lead times. For example, the role of primary commodities requires a policy to diversify the economy. Usually, economic diversification takes time and resources. These resources may be beyond the means of most war-torn societies. Extant quantitative models also underline the importance of providing employment to young males of military age, but they remain silent on how to achieve this noble goal. Reducing the population growth rate requires planned education in societies that culturally espouse large families. Also, leveling mountains or clearing forests to destroy rebels' hideouts remains impractical as a policy choice.

The grievance and structural approaches also have their problems. For example, the former highlights minimizing the source of need but overlooks the means to achieve it. The satisfaction of needs requires resources. In many societies, such resources are scarce and may not even exist. As history has repeatedly shown, transforming a society characterized by increasing resource scarcity and Malthusian pressures into a resource-abundant society is far easier said than done.

One final problem with the quantitative approach is that it cannot provide a fully satisfactory answer for why civil wars end. While some civil wars end with decisive outcomes on the battlefield, others end through a long process of political or diplomatic bargaining (Zartman 1995). Despite many studies on civil wars, little is yet known on how and under what conditions diplomatic efforts succeed in ending them (Licklinder 1993; Stedman, Rothchild, and Cousens 2002).

In the next chapter I analyze the first four cases of civil wars: the two secessions, Katanga and South Kasai, and the two early concomitant insurrections, North Katanga and northwestern South Kasai. Although the Kasai secession was shorter than the Katanga secession, both appear to have their roots in colonial history. Chapter 2 also explains how the two secessions endured and how key players attempted to manage them. Chapter 3 extends the analysis to the Kwilu and the eastern rebellions of 1964. There I attempt to identify similarities and differences with previous civil wars. The fourth chapter deals with the specter of Tshombe or the mutinies of the Baka Regiment and mercenaries in the second half of the 1960s as well as the Shaba wars of the 1970s. The Shaba wars were the first major challenges to the Mobutu regime. These four cases illustrate how inadequate disarmament processes can influence the recurrence of civil wars. In fact, for more than ten years, the specter of the Katanga secession haunted Congo. In both Shaba wars, Mobutu was rescued by the international community.

Chapter 5 starts with the anti-Mobutu war by first explaining the absence of civil wars for at least thirteen years, from 1979 to 1992. Then it analyzes the wars against President Kabila. The first war against Kabila was the Mai Mai insurrection in September 1997. The second war against Kabila, which started in August 1998, was the only war in the history of Congo to end through negotiations. Chapter 6 focuses on ethnic wars in Nord-Kivu and the Hema-Lendu conflict in Ituri in the 1990s. The book concludes with a summary of major findings as well as with suggested adjustments to existing paradigms and a set of policy proposals.

Notes

1. The DRC became independent on 30 June 1960 as the Republic of Congo. The DRC and Congo are used here interchangeably. The former French colony, today Republic of Congo, is herein referred to as Congo-Brazzaville.

2. This definition implies that at least 5 percent of this number are caused by the weakest side and at least 100 people die each year until the war ends. See Small and Singer (1982), pp. 214–215. For a discussion of operational definitions of civil wars, refer to Sambanis (2004).

3. See also Buhaug, Cederman, and Rød (2008).

4. Slater and Simmons (2010) distinguish critical antecedents from noncritical antecedents and argue that only critical antecedents help cause the outcome of interest.

5. One of the earliest companies to penetrate the Congo basin was the Compagnie du Congo pour le Commerce et l'Industrie, established in 1887. Later Leopold II created mixed companies to collect rubber, called concessionary companies.

6. The book uses US 2010 dollar equivalent because the time frame is 1960 to 2010. For conversion factors, refer to Sahr (2008).

7. Other members of the group included Joseph Mobutu (army commander), Justin Bomboko (perennial foreign minister), Albert Ndele (national bank president), and Damien Kandolo (interior minister). See Young (1965), pp. 379–380.

8. She used the term to describe Mobutu's power and wealth. Congolese now use the term to describe all pro-Mobutists who siphoned millions of dollars of taxpayers' money to Swiss bank accounts.

9. Spoilers include people and groups that have an interest in keeping the war going because it provides them with material advantages. See Stedman (1997).

2

Wars of Secession

On 11 July 1960, Moïse Tshombe of the Lunda ethnic group became the president of the seceded state of Katanga. A month later, the Luba elite of North Katanga, who had opposed the secession, began an insurrection against the secession. On 8 August 1960, a group of elites from the Luba of Kasai declared the independence of South Kasai, with Albert Kalonji as president. The South Kasai secession ended on 2 February 1962, but an insurrection followed in northwestern South Kasai on 1 October 1962, which pitted two groups of Luba against one another: the Bena Tshibanda (people from the lowlands) and the Bena Mutu wa Mukuna (people from the highlands). The North Katanga insurrection ended on 19 December 1961, and the UN defeated the Katanga secession on 14 January 1963. The insurrection in South Kasai ended on 15 April 1964. This chapter analyzes the two secessions and the two concomitant insurrections. Secession is a subcategory of nationalism that has territorial reorganization as its primary goal and is thus an organized attempt to establish a separate sovereign state (Emizet and Hesli 1995, p. 494). An insurrection is an internal war between former allies in a previous conflict. Map 1.1 locates the areas of these early civil wars.

Katanga Secession

Katanga was the most industrialized province in the Belgian Congo. Its share of wage earners was 36.2 percent in the 1950s, the highest in Congo (Bézy, Peemans, and Wautelet 1981, p. 84). This industrialization was, however, the work of a single employer, the UMHK. Because Katanga was economically more advanced than other provinces, it also attracted many Europeans. In 1958–1959, it had 32,143 Europeans, who comprised 29 percent of the population in the colony; only 52 percent of these Europeans claimed Belgian nationality (Young 1965, p. 199). According to a number of observers, this high percentage of Europeans and their business interests provide perhaps the best explanation of the Katanga secession (Gérard-Libois 1963; O'Brien 1962).

This argument rejects the idea of creed (identity), greed (resources), or grievance (basic needs) and suggests that the Katanga secession was independent of Africans' action. Thus, Tshombe's CONAKAT party was "an African party that the Europeans had intelligently sponsored at baptism, and whose strings they clearly pulled in the wings" (O'Brien 1962, pp. 84–85). However, this view ignores the fact that Katanga was also home to 1.65 million Congolese as of June 1960—roughly 12.5 percent of the country's African population (Gérard-Libois and Verhaegen 1961, p. 222). This population was also diverse: southern Katanga included the Lunda, Bemba, Yeke, and Tabwa, while the Luba dominated northern Katanga. The interplay of these groups provides a starting point for understanding the Katanga secession.

Background to Conflict:
Critical Juncture and Critical Antecedents

The discovery of copper in the late nineteenth century gave Katanga a privileged status when, in June 1900, the CFS and the Katanga Company set up the Comité Special du Katanga (CSK) to occupy and exploit mineral resources in the area. From 1906 to 1910, the CSK controlled Katanga. Then the royal decree of 22 March 1910 made the Katanga District a vice-government headed by a vice governor-general; other administrative units remained districts under district commissioners. Because Katanga was integrated late into the Belgian Congo, and given its special status as vice-government, this probably helped to stimulate separatist sentiments among white settlers. In 1920, a group of prominent European settlers submitted a reorganization plan to the minister of colonies and requested provincial autonomy, the transfer of the governor general office to Brussels, the integration of colonial services, and "the adaptation of the administrative services to the real needs of the colony" (Lemarchand 1964, p. 60).

However, Belgian authorities never considered these suggestions, except the last one. In 1933, the minister of colonies promulgated a decree that divided the Congo-Kasai and Orientale Provinces into four units, bringing the total number of provinces to six. One portion of Lomami District in the Katanga Province became part of the Sankuru District attached to Lusambo Province. The 1933 reform caused vehement protests among Europeans in Katanga who called it "a demolition enterprise" (Lemarchand 1964, p. 61) because it reduced the size of Katanga for the first time since 1910. Between 1910 and 1933, Katanga remained the only area with no major transformations. This apparent administrative stability gave it some semblance of continuity. Though colonial efforts to adapt district boundaries to ethnic divisions encouraged Africans to identify themselves along ethnic lines elsewhere, natives of Katanga became accustomed to identifying themselves as "Katangans," not Bemba, Luba, Lunda, Tabwa, or Yeke.

Another element of separatism among Europeans was hostility toward the central government because the proportion of public spending devoted to

Katanga appeared minute compared with its contribution to colonial revenue. By 1957, the GDP of Katanga as a share of Congo's GDP was 31.5 percent compared with 27.3 percent for the Leopoldville Province, while its share of tariffs was even more impressive, accounting for 42.2 percent of the total from all six provinces (Bézy, Peemans, and Wautelet 1981, pp. 150–151).

White settlers showed the first sign of secession in May 1944 when they created the Union for Colonization (Union pour la Colonisation), or UCOL-Katanga, as an affiliate of the Federation of Associations of Colonists in Belgian Congo and Ruanda-Urundi. After 1952, the UCOL began a campaign to settle whites in Katanga and Kivu, targeting "one hundred thousand Belgian settlers within ten years to make Congo truly Belgian" (Gérard-Libois 1963, pp. 18–19). In May 1958, the UCOL established a political party called the Katangan Union (Union Katangaise) to make its demands politically feasible and credible. The new party stressed the division of the Belgian Congo into several federal or autonomous regions and encouraged European immigration to Congo. However, the colonial government refused to promote any federal system or any extensive autonomy for the provinces. This was a real setback for Katanga white settlers, who then changed their strategy by turning to educated Africans (Katanga évolués) hoping to promote the idea of federation and provincial autonomy. However, autonomy was not the main issue among Katanga évolués, who were concerned about the overwhelming visibility of "strangers," mostly the Luba from Kasai Province, working in the UMHK and living in the southern mining towns of Katanga, especially Elisabethville, now Lubumbashi.

In the early twentieth century, the UMHK began recruiting labor from Kasai and settling the Luba from Kasai in Katanga. As the population of Elisabethville increased, so did the proportion of Luba from Kasai. By 1958, the town's population was about 171,477: 26 percent were Luba from Kasai, and 18.1 percent were Luba of North Katanga. Those who called themselves locals, such as the Lunda and Bemba, represented 6.3 percent and 4.3 percent of the population, respectively (Ilunga 1973, p. 120). The Luba's demographic visibility was further enhanced by their socioeconomic and political status. Although the Luba of Kasai were only 26 percent of the population of Elisabethville in 1958, they represented 56 percent of African workers of the UMHK. In the African Katuba quarter, where the Luba represented 40 percent of the population, they owned 42 percent of the houses; only 12.3 percent of Luba of Katanga and 6.5 percent of the Songe owned houses (Ilunga 1973, p. 123). The various ethnic groups from southern Katanga owned the remaining 20 percent of the houses. In other words, 80 percent of the houses in the African quarters of Elisabethville belonged to "strangers."

Politically, the Luba from Kasai became more visible after the consultative reforms of 1957 in Elisabethville. As pointed out in Chapter 1, the reforms established urban institutions based on popular elections. Major urban centers were divided into communes roughly equal in population, and each commune had to elect a council, which chose a burgomaster from its members. In Elisabethville, the electoral process took place in late December 1957 and resulted in the nomination of four non-Katanga burgomasters: two Luba from Kasai, one Songe from Kasai, and a Kusu from Kivu (Rubbens 1958). Among Katangans, this defeat caused a sense of exclusion or separatism. As a reaction to the growing power of the Luba from Kasai in the mining towns of southern Katanga, the évolués from southern Katanga decided to create the CONAKAT on 11 October 1958. According to Tshombe, the goal of the movement "was from the beginning a reaction against the existing situation: it is the work of 'authentic Katangans' . . . it saw the light after the 1957 elections" (Gérard-Libois 1963, p. 12). "Authentic Katangans" meant those who belonged to the indigenous groups, such as the Lunda, Luba of north Katanga, Yeke, Sanga, Tshokwe, Tabwa, and Bemba, while "strangers" were those people the UMHK recruited to work the mines, especially the Luba from Kasai. Thus, the union of "authentic Katangans" was mainly a self-defense mechanism in urban areas stemming from political exclusion in the late 1950s.

The relationship between the CONAKAT leaders and the white settlers' party, the Katangan Union, strengthened as independence approached. The alliance, however, created a fissure between the CONAKAT and the Luba of Katanga, or the BALUBAKAT. As independence approached, the BALUBAKAT was created in 1959 to counterbalance the CONAKAT and oppose the latter's tenet of "authentic Katangans," which targeted the Luba of Kasai, with whom the Luba of Katanga had strong ethnic affinities dating back to the Luba Empire in the seventeenth century. Attempts at reconciliation failed when the CONAKAT refused to denounce publicly the accord it had reached with the Katanga Union and to revise its attitude toward the Luba from Kasai, a condition imposed by the BALUBAKAT. Instead, in mid-June 1959, the CONAKAT leadership welcomed the European Katangan Union as an "authentic Katangan party." Tshombe outlined his party's vision by contending that "a sovereign Katanga accepts the idea of a federal unity under certain minimal conditions" and "whether a federal Congo with a Katangan state is possible or not, Katanga will, in any case, seek a community with Belgium" (Lemarchand 1964, pp. 32–33).

A number of events seemed to have triggered the Katanga secession. However, one critical juncture was the result of the national elections of May 1960 and the concomitant politics of exclusion. The CONAKAT received eight seats in the lower house, while the BALUBAKAT cartel won seven seats. At the provincial level, the CONAKAT received twenty-five out of sixty seats and also acquired fifteen additional seats from individual tickets and traditional representatives, while the cartel gained twenty-two seats (Gérard-Libois and Verhaegen 1961, p. 262). The cartel complained about serious electoral irregularities and contested the results of the balloting by introducing twenty-one appeals in Elisabethville and Jadotville (now Likasi). Despite overwhelming evidence of irregularities, Belgium rejected these appeals.[1]

To show its disapproval, the BALUBAKAT cartel boycotted the first meeting of the provincial legislature on 1 June 1960. This action paralyzed the proceedings because the law required two-thirds of all members of the provincial legislature to deliberate and vote. One solution was to amend the law on quorums. During the impasse, the CONAKAT members addressed a petition to the minister of colonies and requested that he amend the Fundamental Law. Three days later, however, the cartel members attended the second session. In the meeting, the CONAKAT used its majority to appropriate the presidency and the two vice presidencies of the provincial parliament. In the next session, the assembly elected ten senators from traditional authorities, but the cartel received only three and withdrew from the proceedings before the provincial legislature could elect members of the provincial government. The cartel's decision created indignation among the CONAKAT members, and rumors began to circulate in Elisabethville that the CONAKAT's leadership was planning to secede on 13 June 1960 (Gérard-Libois and Verhaegen 1961, p. 246). In response to these rumors, members of the cartel also threatened to establish a separate government in North Katanga if the CONAKAT seceded from Congo. On 14 June 1960, the government declared a state of emergency for the entire province of Katanga to prevent any action that might split the province along the two major party lines (Gérard-Libois and Verhaegen 1961, p. 249).

On the same day, the Belgian Parliament amended Articles 110 and 114 of the Fundamental Law. According to the amendment, "if after two consecutive meetings of the assembly, the presence of at least two-thirds of its members has not been obtained, the Assembly may duly proceed, provided a majority of its members are present" (Gérard-Libois 1963, p. 81). This amendment permitted the CONAKAT-dominated provincial assembly to proceed and even to vote without the cartel. Since the amendment emphasized "two meetings" and remained silent on whether these meetings should be scheduled consecutively on the same day or over a certain period, the CONAKAT decided to meet on 16 June 1960 at 10:00 am, 3:00 pm, and 8:00 pm. The underlying intention was that if the cartel members refused to attend the first two meetings, then the CONAKAT could proceed at the 8:00 pm session without them.

As expected, the first two meetings took place without the cartel. At 8:00 pm, the CONAKAT elected members of the provincial government, with Tshombe as the president. When the cartel received no positions in the provincial government, it announced its own government on 21 June 1960 and lobbied in Leopoldville for a major position in the Lumumba government. Two days later, Lumumba announced his government and nominated Jason Sendwe, the leader of BALUBAKAT, as the state commissioner for Katanga, a position established by the Fundamental Law (Articles 190 and passim). A three-year office, the state commissioner represented the central government in the province, with full veto powers over the provincial government. While the CONAKAT considered this nomination as a provocation, the BALUBAKAT viewed it as a victory. Thus, the amendment of the Fundamental Law, which allowed the CONAKAT to exclude the BALUBAKAT from provincial government, was a critical juncture of the Katanga secession.

The last two subsequent events of the Katanga secession were the mutiny of the national army and the response by the Belgian military. Five days after the mutiny in Leopoldville on 4 July 1960, soldiers at the military Camp Massart in Elisabethville also mutinied. Immediately, Tshombe appealed to Belgium for troops to restore order. A day later, Belgium unilaterally decided to send two Belgian companies under Commander Guy Weber to restore order in Katanga. On the evening of 11 July 1960, Tshombe proclaimed the independence of Katanga. Several reports indicated that Belgium even attempted to foment secessions in Equateur and Kivu provinces in order to destabilize its former colony (Gérard-Libois and Verhaegen 1961, pp. 979–982).

Conflict Management and Duration of the Katanga Secession

The Katanga secession lasted thirty months and involved two major external players: Belgium and the UN, plus a number of domestic players. Belgium supported the seceded state, and the UN backed the central government. According to extant literature, such rival intervention is likely to prolong civil wars (see Regan 1996). Nine days after the proclamation of Katanga independence, Belgian prime minister Gaston Eyskens dispatched his deputy chief of staff, Harold d'Aspremont Lynden, to Elisabethville on a special mission to assess the possibility of extending aid to Katanga. Thus, the Belgian intervention helped the Tshombe government to gain momentum and organize a military strategy.

The second factor was financing from the UMHK. Until 1962, the UMHK continued to support the seceded state by providing it with more than 80 percent of revenue because Katanga became de facto and de jure collector of all taxes, mining royalties, and obligations due to the state. The parastatal CSK also paid some 431 million Belgian francs ($60.91 million in 2010 prices) between 30 June 1960 and 31 March 1962 to Katangan authorities because the seceded state replaced the Congolese state (Gérard-Libois 1963). Katanga was thus assured of important sources of revenue that helped it survive both economically and militarily. Economically, the money paid to the Katanga treasury helped the Tshombe government pay its colossal government payrolls. Militarily, the funding provided the Katanga government a means to recruit mercenaries to protect itself against Leopoldville and Stanleyville forces. These mercenaries, called *Affreux* (the frightful ones), were recruited in Europe, Northern Rhodesia (now Zambia), and South Africa. In August 1961, the UN estimated there were 250 mercenaries in Katanga and some 19,000 troops of the Katanga Gendarmerie (Verhaegen 1962).

Several attempts were made to negotiate an end to the secession. First, the UN Security Council adopted Resolution S/4741 on 21 February 1961 to deal with the weakness of the Leopoldville government and the increasing military strength of southern Katanga. It thus authorized its troops to use force if necessary to prevent a long civil war. The resolution also called for the withdrawal of mercenaries, foreign troops, paramilitary personnel, and all political advisers not under the UN command. In addition, it urged the government to reorganize the national army. The key elements of the resolution were to disarm all factions and to have all parties organize conferences for national reconciliation.

The French government sponsored the first conference, held from 8 to 12 March 1961 in Tananarive, Malagasy Republic. Tshombe had three objectives at the conference: (1) to denounce the UN February resolution, (2) to adopt a confederal system with decisions made unanimously, and (3) to call for the pacification of the whole country and normalization of the situation. The central government accepted most of Tshombe's demands. However, his arrogance and refusal to compromise helped precipitate an agreement between President Kasavubu and the UN in April 1961 in which Kasavubu accepted the February UN resolution and rejected Tshombe's demands.

A second conference, in Coquilhatville (now Mbandaka in Equateur Province) from 24 to 28 May 1961, was far more fruitful than the Tananarive meeting. In Tananarive, the delegates tried to create sixteen sovereign states by adopting a confederal formula. One weakness of this formula was that each of the sixteen confederal states had veto power, an even more destabilizing system than the one created by the Fundamental Law. One state could paralyze the entire political machinery. The Coquilhatville conference, on the other hand, rejected the confederal formula and supported a real central power by giving secondary powers to member states. The conference also emphasized the reintegration of Katanga according to the UN resolution. Moreover, all participants agreed to have a parliamentary meeting before September 1961 in order to end the constitutional crisis, which started in September 1960 after the fall of Lumumba. This meeting occurred at Lovanium University, Leopoldville, before the September deadline.

Under UN pressures, the Stanleyville and Leopoldville governments convened a meeting of the upper and lower houses on 22 and 23 July 1961. Tshombe's CONAKAT refused to attend. Despite ideological differences, members of the parliament accepted Cyrille Adoula as the new prime minister on 2 August 1961. His government represented a careful balance of political groups. The task of the new government was to end the Katanga secession, to restore socioeconomic circuits damaged by the long political crisis, and to replace the Fundamental Law with a new constitution. To achieve these goals, the Kennedy administration provided planes and heavy military equipment to the UN in late 1961, after the British declined to engage in the Congo crisis (Young 1965). The US intention was to have the UN apply force if necessary to end the Katanga secession, which forced Tshombe to agree to a new round of negotiations with Prime Minister Adoula, sponsored by the United States at the UN base of Kitona. The result of the meeting was an accord on the unity of Congo and the authority of the central government, but the Katangan assembly had to ratify the Kitona agreements. Without actually denouncing the accords, Katanga authorities never implemented them.

The last series of talks between Adoula and Tshombe occurred from 18 March to 26 June 1962 in Leopoldville under the auspices of the officer-in-charge of UN operations, Robert Gardiner from Ghana. However, these talks also faltered. After the death of Dag Hammarskjöld, the second UN policy was the "U Thant plan" (named for UN Secretary-General U Thant) for Katanga's reintegration in Congo and national reconciliation, which was made public on 20 August 1962 (Lefever and Joshua 1966). The plan called for a federal and representative government and was nonnegotiable and binding on all parties in its entirety. All the players accepted the plan within two weeks. Although Tshombe was given every opportunity to embrace it, the UN believed that he preferred the status quo, which was a strategy intended to wear down the UN.

The final round of force began in December 1962 when UN forces relocated to southern Katanga with 13,500 men at the height of the operation. On the eve of Christmas, the Katanga Gendarmerie opened fire on a UN post and continued to harass UN installations. Late in the afternoon of 28 December, the UN Secretary-General ordered the UN troops to move against the Katangan forces. This order began the final attack against the seceded state. By early 1963, the UN captured most strategic locations in southern Katanga. In the final analysis, U Thant ended up doing exactly what the late Prime Minister Lumumba insisted upon—using force to end the Katanga secession.

The Katanga secession had little negative impact on capital assets. First, the installations of the UMHK, productive capital, and other installations were spared during the conflict, and even economic infrastructure (transport and communication) was not disrupted. The main loss from the war was the frayed social capital between the north and the south as the result of the northern Katanga insurrection (see later in this chapter). In sum, the role of the UN Security Council, especially the United States, to end the Katanga secession using force was necessary, as trust in the central government grew within the international community. On 14 January 1963, Tshombe announced the end of the Katanga secession.

South Kasai Secession

The autonomous state of South Kasai (Sud-Kasai) or the Mining Republic (République Minière) was officially established on 8 August 1960. Albert Kalonji and other Luba leaders were in Elisabethville, where they justified their decision to create a separate state based on the UN Charter, especially its section on "the right to self-determination" and their unanimous rejection of the Lumumba "communist regime" (Gérard-Libois and Verhaegen 1961, pp. 800–801). The latter reason, they thought, would strongly appeal to Western powers. However, the new Mining Republic had no legal basis because the leadership was in exile and the state had neither a constitution nor an army. It was not until 20 August 1960 that the Luba leaders were able to recruit 250 police officers and 200 soldiers from the Luba ethnic group living in southern Katanga (Gérard-Libois and Verhaegen 1961, p. 802). Most members of the "exiled" government reached Bakwanga, the capital city of South Kasai, in October 1960. Kalonji, the leader of MNC/K, became the president and Joseph Ngalula the prime minister of the seceded state.

Unlike Katanga, South Kasai is a recent administrative creation. During the scramble for Africa in the second half of the 1800s, the Kasai region was engulfed in political and social turmoil arising from the slave trade by Afro-Arabs from Zanzibar and their Tetela and Songe allies. After the annexation of the CFS by Belgium, the southern end of the Luba homeland was part of the Katanga Province until 1933. However, the northern section was divided among different territories and districts. After World War II, Lusambo Province was renamed Kasai Province, and, in 1954, the Luba were grouped together in the Bakwanga and Kanda Kanda territories. In 1956, the territories of Bakwanga, Ngandajika, and Mwene-Ditu became part of the Luba land. However, the Luba and Bena Kanyoka, who made up a distinct group of the Luba cluster, share the territory of Mwene Ditu, where the latter make up the majority. The three territories and most areas inhabited by the Songe ethnic group were lumped into the multiethnic district of Kabinda. Thus, Kasai Province in 1960 was the traditional homeland of some twenty ethnic groups, with Lulua, Luba, and Songe being the three most important clusters.[2]

Sociologically, the Luba of Kasai are internally divided in two major lineages called Mutu wa Mukuna (Mutu) and Bena Tshibanda (Tshibanda). This division is rooted partly in geography and partly in culture. Geographically, the Luba are subdivided from the central position of Bakwanga, the provincial capital, into those who live upstream and downstream of the Lubilanji River. Mutu wa Mukuna refers to the Luba who live in the hills in the south, or people from the highlands, and Bena Tshibanda refers to the Luba who inhabit the valley in the north, or people from lowlands (Kanyinda-Lusanga 1970, pp. 9–10). The main lineages of the two groups are listed in Table 2.1 (Ilunga 1973, p. 389).

Culturally, the two Luba groups differ as the result of the modernization brought about by colonization (Ilunga 1973). First, the colonial administration created a no-man's land in Bakwanga where the diamond mining company, Société Internationale Forestière et Minière du Congo (Forminière and later Minière de Bakwanga), was located. Because this area was clearly divided into two parts, this colonial decision slowed social intercourse between the two lineages. The Forminière had prospection rights over 110 million hectares and ownership of 2,150 hectares (Ilunga 1973). Encompassing about fifty diamond mining sites in Tshikapa and Bakwanga, it produced about 60 percent of the world's industrial diamonds and most gem diamonds in Congo (Bézy 1957). The Forminière contributed significantly to Congo's budget. In 1959, it paid 391.3 million francs, or $55.3 million (2010 = 100), to the

Table 2.1 Lineages of Bena Tshibanda and Bena Mutu wa Mukuna

Bena Tshibanda Lineages	Bena Mutu wa Mukuna Lineages
Bena Mulenge	Bakwanga
Bena Mpuka	Bakwa Nsumpi
Bakwa Disho	Bakwa Ndoba
Bakwa Tembwe	Bena Tshitolo
Bakwa Nsumba	Bakwa Kanda
Bashilange	Bena Kaniki
	Bena Kalambayi
	Bena Nshimba
	Bakwa Lonji
	Bena Kapuya
	Bakwa Kalonji
	All the lineages referred to as "Bena Tshiyamba"

state in taxes and 201.8 million francs, or $28.5 million, in export duties (Tshilombo 1964, p. 125). Its workers were totally isolated and lived in a compound in the midst of this no-man's land, which was off limits to other Africans. In the Belgian paternalistic tradition, the life of the workers was carefully regulated.

Second, because of the way communication networks were established in Kasai, the Mutu had relatively easy access to Katanga, while the Tshibanda were attracted to nearby Luluabourg, the capital city of Kasai Province. Thus, the Mutu were more in touch with the Bena Kanyoka and the Luba of North Katanga than with the Tshibanda, who interacted more with the Lulua. Third, the colonial administration built better schools near the Tshibanda than near the Mutu. As a consequence, the Tshibanda received better education than the Mutu (Ilunga 1973). Taken together, all these factors resulted in a stereotyped distinction between the two Luba groups well before independence. The Tshibanda were reputed to be more "educated" and "intelligent" but more prone to "immorality" than the Mutu (Ilunga 1973, p. 392).

Economically, Kasai was less developed during the colonial era than Katanga. Kasai thus served as a labor reservoir for southern Katanga mining industries (Ilunga 1973). In 1958, with a population representing 16 percent of the country's total population, Kasai Province had only 10.5 percent of the nonagricultural labor force (Tshilombo 1964, p. 118). It ranked third in available labor but scored last in the number of people engaged in the wage economy.[3] The tremendous increase in the diamond mining production by the Forminière over decades was realized with no more than 6,000 workers (Tshilombo 1964, p. 120). Despite its financial contribution to the national economy, the Forminière never developed its social environment to the same degree as the UMHK did in Katanga. The Luba homeland was therefore socioeconomically an underdeveloped entity without major cities (Ilunga 1973; Tshilombo 1964). The absence of urban centers resulted in little to no political consciousness. However, the colonial state built one of the first Catholic schools in the area, which would play a major role in the spread of the Luba to other parts of the Belgian Congo.

Critical Antecedents and Juncture of the South Kasai Secession

The South Kasai secession has its historical causes in the Luba-Lulua conflict (Ilunga 1973; Lemarchand 1964). The conflict started in the early 1950s and reached its climax in late 1959 in Luluabourg where arson, murder, and terrorism between the two groups were common. The saddest part of this conflict is that the two groups, the Luba and the Lulua, are culturally identical and close to one another; they even speak the same language, Tshiluba. The main differences between the two groups stem from their differing precolonial migrations and subsequent responses to modernization.

The Lulua were part of the first migratory wave from the Luba Empire, and after a war of conquest throughout the seventeenth century against the Kete and Bashilele, they settled in the valley of the Lulua River (Ilunga 1973). The Lulua were subdivided into many autonomous lineages ruled by chiefs. Until 1870, the Lulua continued to refer to themselves as "Luba coming from the South," but they were called Bashilange by the neighboring Tshokwe group (Mabika 1959, p. 69). The term "Lulua" was first used by the German Hermann von Wissmann around 1885 to designate a group of Luba located on the western bank of the Lulua River (Lemarchand 1964, p. 206). The Lulua kept this appellation to distinguish themselves from the Luba immigrants, who followed Europeans in the late 1890s, and helped these newcomers build several stations in northern Kasai, included the town of Luluabourg. In a sense, the term "Lulua" as used today is a foreign creation. Shortly before the conquest of the area by agents of King Leopold II, the Lulua entered into profitable slave-ivory trading relationship with Angola-based traders. This relationship allowed a Lulua chief, Mukenge Kalamba, to acquire firearms and establish authority over some Lulua groups. He later exploited his good relations with Europeans and tried to establish hegemony over his peers but did not succeed, even though Europeans referred to him as king of Lulua (Ilunga 1973).

The Luba of Kasai, on the other hand, were among the last groups to migrate into the Kasai area between 1800 and 1850. During the 1860s–1870s, the Luba were victims of the slave networks. African auxiliaries of Tippo Tip and other Afro-Arabs from Zanzibar carried out a number of destructive raids in the Luba-Kasai area, leaving in their wake a dislocated and demoralized populace unable to defend itself (Ilunga 1973, pp. 219–221). Thousands of Luba fleeing slave raids and internal conflicts within their respective lineages found refuge among the Lulua who welcomed them as kinfolk and even gave the newcomers plots of land. These newcomers kept their own lineage identity and organized themselves accordingly, but the Luba were considered as second-class citizens in the Lulua land (Ilunga 1973).

The Lulua's refusal to be associated with the Belgian colonial enterprise later exacerbated the conflict between Luba and Lulua. Because they did not fully understand the potential advantages of the new colonial system, the Lulua let Luba children attend European enterprises (schools, missions, and firms), but the Lulua kept their own children away from attending schools. Beginning in 1891, Luba children dominated schools under the jurisdiction of the Catholic Scheut priests. The Luba quickly and massively capitalized on their relationship with Europeans. As Belgians used them as catechists, teachers, clerks, and manual workers, they became dynamic agents of colonization. Their language, Tshiluba, was even imposed upon the entire Belgian Congo.

As the Luba became associated with the colonial enterprise, they also started spreading into Lulua land. The colonial administration encouraged this migration by allocating land in the Lulua area to the Luba. The construction of a rail line from Ilebo (former Port Francqui) to Katanga opened up important opportunities, which the Luba group was first to exploit, including an extremely lucrative market for maize and other staples produced by the Luba along the rail line (Lemarchand 1964). At first, the policy to allocate land to Luba in Lulua land caused little dissension among the Lulua, but the steady influx of the Luba into the Lulua area made land scarcity quite acute. The Luba responded to the scarcity of cultivable land by squatting in urban areas of Luluabourg in the early 1920s, where they managed to secure land at the expense of the Lulua. They also dominated most colonial clerical jobs, especially in 1950, when Luluabourg became the capital city of Kasai Province.

By the time the Lulua had the opportunity to move into the modern sector in large numbers after World War II, land was already scarce, and many Luba were already in powerful clerical positions in the colonial administration. Because the administration was never willing to reinstate land that had already been occupied by European enterprises, the intrusion of the Luba farmers into Lulua land resulted in Lulua opposition, which became manifest in the 1950s. Thus, a sense of loss among the Lulua and awareness of their status compared with that of the Luba resulted in the creation of the Association of Lulua Brothers (Association des Lulua Frères) in 1952 to raise the status of their ethnic group. According to Chomé (1959), the colonial administration and Catholic missionaries were also instrumental in setting up this organization to counterbalance the increasing social power of the Luba.

Given this background, two events precipitated the secession of South Kasai. The first was the the organization of popular elections in Luluabourg in December 1958, which left the Luba feeling excluded from the political process. In the two African quarters of Luluabourg, Nganza and Ndesha, eighty-three Luba, twenty-nine Lulua, and other candidates competed for thirty-six council seats (Ilunga 1973, p. 289). The Lulua cast their votes along ethnic lines and received sixteen seats, although they represented only 26 percent of the Luluabourg population, while the Luba group, with 56 percent of the population, gained only seventeen seats.

Following this victory, the Lulua became more aggressive in their demand for land and social status. On 6 May 1959, Sylvestre Kalamba[4] requested that the Belgian government recognize him as the "King of all Bena Lulua" (Ilunga 1973). After Assistant District Commissioner A. Dequenne investigated the demand, he advised the provincial governor, in his report, to grant Kalamba's request. The government acknowledged Kalamba's claim that all the Luba settlers be declared aliens and be subject to the authority of the "king." Dequenne's report went even further by stating that those Luba who had settled on Lulua land since the beginning of the twentieth century should be required to pay an annual tribute to Lulua chiefs. In a sense, the decision to recognize Kalamba as chief of Lulua automatically made the Luba "strangers" in the Lulua land and excluded them from owning land. Dequenne's report radicalized the Luba against the colonial administration. Led by Luba leaders in Luluabourg in August 1959, a wave of protests resulted in the arrest and temporary banishment from Luluabourg of three prominent Luba leaders—Albert Kalonji, Evariste Kalonji, and Albert Nyembwe—accused by the colonial administration of racial hatred (Ilunga 1973). This anti-Luba move escalated tensions between the Lulua and the Luba.

The first major bloody confrontation between the two groups took place in Luluabourg on 11 October 1959.[5] Three months later, the colonial administration set up a conciliation commission headed by Judge Rae to settle the "land dispute" between the Lulua and the Luba (Lemarchand 1964, p. 208). After only two days of discussion at Lake Munkamba, the commission decided that 100,000 Luba must return to their homeland in South Kasai within two months, as violence against them spread in Lulua-dominated areas (Lemarchand 1964, pp. 208–209). The governor-general vetoed this decision, but it was too late to stop the violence against the Luba, resulting in massive waves of Luba returning to South Kasai.

The manipulation of ethnic identity seems to indicate how modernity can divide a group into antagonistic factions. In 1959, when the conflict reached its apex, neither group could remember that no ethnic distinction between the Luba and the Lulua existed prior to 1885. More specifically, not only was the term "Lulua" nonexistent in the Luba lexicon prior to 1885, but it was a foreign creation. Yet, by late 1959, the Lulua saw themselves as disadvantaged compared to the Luba group, which provided a reference point to judge Lulua livelihood and social place in the Lulua land.

The movement of the Luba back to South Kasai created a tense climate as they crowded their homeland. It was in this confused atmosphere that the May 1960 general elections took place in Kasai Province. The critical juncture was the electoral outcome and the ensuing exclusion of a number of Luba from the government. With 2,158,633 inhabitants, Kasai had to fill seventy seats in the lower house and provincial institutions. Major ethnic groups cast votes along their own political parties. The net winners were the MNC/Kalonji with twenty-one seats, the MNC/L with seventeen, the Lulua's Union Nationale Congolaise with ten, and the Songe Unity with six (Gérard-Libois and Verhaegen 1961, pp. 214–215).

On 1 June 1960, Patrice Lumumba flew to Luluabourg and met with provincial legislators of the MNC/L, Lulua party, and Songe Unity and asked them to present a common front in their votes. This political maneuver was intended to exclude his rival's party the MNC/K from the provincial government. As a result, the coalition behind the MNC/L was able to secure seven positions out of ten in the provincial government, while the MNC/K received only three seats despite having won more seats than each individual political party (Gérard-Libois and Verhaegen 1961, pp. 216–218). The MNC/K also failed to secure two important positions in the provincial government, namely, interior and finance ministries, which could have ensured them some safety in the Lulua-dominated capital of Luluabourg.

Having failed to get satisfaction at the provincial level, the MNC/K leadership decided to set up its own government in South Kasai. A cabinet of ten members, led by Joseph Ngalula, was elected on 14 June 1960 by twenty-one Luba assembly members. On 30 June 1960, Kasai Province, just like Katanga Province, had two parallel provincial governments, one legally recognized under the leadership of Governor Barthélémy Mukenge and an illegal Luba government presided over by Joseph Ngalula. Ngalula justified the decision of Luba leaders to set up their own province as a direct reaction to Lumumba's success in setting up an anti-Luba majority coalition in the Kasai provincial government. Luba leaders also demanded that the Belgian legislature modify Article 7 of the Fundamental Law to make room for a seventh province. Receiving no positive reply to their demands, they later informed the UN Secretary-General of their decision to "secede" while "keeping close ties" with their "brothers" within the framework of a "confederation" (Gérard-Libois and Verhaegen 1961, p. 800).[6] They claimed that their move was motivated by the lack of any prospect of continued peaceful coexistence between the Luba and Lulua within the framework of Kasai Province.

Another incident that precipitated the proclamation of an autonomous state of Kasai was Kalonji's personal ambition. In June 1960, he was elected a member of the lower house and expected to become prime minister of Congo. However, he failed to gather sufficient parliamentary support in the lower house to legally unseat his political opponent, Lumumba. His personal ambition drove him to fly to Elisabethville where he joined other Luba leaders to proclaim the independence of South Kasai.

Duration of the South Kasai Secession

Two key factors seem to have shortened the South Kasai secession, which lasted only 543 days, or eighteen months. First was the politics of exclusion within the

Luba group, starting with the division within the elite of the two Luba clans—Mutu and Tshibanda. President Kalonji was from the Tshibanda, and his prime minister, Ngalula, was from the Mutu. Increasingly, Kalonji relied on the elites from the Tshibanda at the expense of those from the Mutu (Ilunga 1973).

Evidence of these politics was the ratio of ministers from the two groups in Kalonji's successive cabinets. Although the Mutu represented two-thirds of the Luba group (Ilunga 1973), their number in the South Kasai government declined as Kalonji consolidated his power by relying on the elites from the Tshibanda. For example, the ratio of Tshibanda to Mutu ministers was four to nine in the "exile" cabinet of August 1960; this ratio was eight to seven in early 1961, nine to six in May 1961, and twelve to four in September 1961 (Ilunga 1973). By then, the key portfolios of finance, army, and interior were in the hands of Tshibanda. The removal of Thomas Kabangu, a Mutu, as the head of the army and his replacement by Floribert Dinanga, a Tshibanda, in late September 1961 only confirmed the already general feeling of exclusion among the Mutu with respect to Kalonji's cabinet. The Mutu elite felt excluded from state spoils and discriminated against in most administrative nominations. By October 1961, sixteen Mutu out of the twenty-one Luba assembly members joined Ngalula in Leopoldville to create a new political party, the Congolese Democrats (Démocrates Congolais). The objective of the party was to reestablish the peaceful reintegration of South Kasai into Congo. Thus, the defection of the Mutu from the ruling coalition hastened the end of the South Kasai secession.

Politics of exclusion also manifested itself between the Luba and other groups living in South Kasai. In June 1960, the Luba considered their homeland as including the territories of Bakwanga, Ngandajika, and Mwene-Ditu, which comprised the Kabinda District of the former Kasai Province. However, the Bena Kanyoka were against the secession. Not only did they consider themselves a different ethnic group, but they were mostly Lumumba's followers who overwhelmingly voted for the MNC/L and strongly opposed the secession. Armed clashes even occurred between Bena Kanyoka and South Kasai soldiers, with 870 Kanyoka and some 145 soldiers killed in less than a week in early 1961. The Kanyoka did not want permanent and total domination by the Luba in their own territory of Mwene-Ditu. Their claim to be a separate political entity ended only after the first administrative reform in 1966. Even the Luntu, another ethnic group in South Kasai, opposed the seceded state and confronted South Kasai soldiers. After they had killed some 120 Luba soldiers in early 1961, the soldiers killed 600 Luntu (Epstein 1965, pp. 100–101).

Another factor that shortened the South Kasai secession was recruitment challenges due to the illegal trade of diamonds. One important issue in South Kasai was the number of Luba, estimated at about 350,000, who were forced to return to South Kasai in 1959 (Tshilombo 1964). Local authorities launched a resettlement program to encourage people to engage in farming. However, most Luba migrants were used to urban life and not enthusiastic about returning to villages they had left many decades earlier (Tshilombo 1964). The result was a tremendous increase in the informal sector, primarily in illicit diamond exploitation. Small bands quickly developed, working closely with West Africans who organized parallel market export networks to move diamonds.

Many internally displaced Luba, especially young men fifteen to twenty-five years old, quickly gathered large amounts of money from trading illegal diamonds and were reluctant to serve in the South Kasai army, about which they understood little. Even soldiers of the seceded state were involved in providing services to private entrepreneurs. Lack of discipline was widespread in both the officer corps and the rank and file that weakened the seceded state.

Early Insurrections in Congo

Two insurrections occurred in the early 1960s: North Katanga and northwestern South Kasai. North Katanga's opposition to the Katanga secession appears to support the idea that ethnic fragmentation may be an antidote to civil war. The insurrection in South Kasai, where opposing sides were from the same ethnic group divided along clan lines, contradicts this argument, however. The analysis that follows is an attempt to explain this inconsistency.

Insurrection in North Katanga

The insurrection in North Katanga started on 5 September 1960 when a mercenary patrol and several gendarmes of the seceded Katanga state ran into an ambush. Eight gendarmes, one Belgian captain, and a Belgian adjutant were killed, while the survivors were quickly disarmed and arrested by the UN to assure their protection (Gérard-Libois 1963, p. 124). Repeated attacks of North Katanga by Tshombe's soldiers only hardened the position of North Katanga's leadership to oppose the Katanga secession. On 20 October 1960, the BALUBAKAT leaders proclaimed the autonomous province of Lualaba, or North Katanga. Prosper Mwamba-Ilunga became president and Jason Sendwe was high commissioner of state. The capital city of the province was Manono. After a temporary victory of the Stanleyville army over the seceded Katanga Gendarmerie, the provincial government was installed on 11 January 1961. Because North Katanga represented two-thirds of Katanga Province, two-thirds of the state was not under the control of Tshombe and the secessionist Katanga. One month later, Tshombe's soldiers and mercenaries counterattacked with some 3,000 soldiers and mercenaries. For almost two years, the rural Luba youth of North Katanga attacked military forces from South Katanga for what the youths perceived as an attempt to conquer their lands. The rural youths dominated the insurrection, and they used both magic and drugs to fight the establishment. Magic potions were used to supposedly make insurgents invulnerable to bullets. With no leadership to control the youth, the insurrection became a source of terror and disorder.

From the declaration of the insurrection in early August to October 1960, more than 10,000 people were killed. The full-scale insurrection against the established authority of the Tshombe regime spared nobody, and even traditional chiefs were killed along with their notables. One high-profile case was the grand chief of the Luba, Kabongo Kaluwa Dibwe, who was killed in Kongolo by a band of Luba young men because he was associated with the Tshombe government (Gérard-Libois and Verhaegen 1961, p. 778). Normally, a Luba chief must die without blood, but Kabongo was chopped to pieces to undermine both the chief as a symbol of the state and the chieftaincy as a symbol of tradition.

Causes and duration of the insurrection. North Katanga is inhabited mostly by the Luba and other minority groups such as Tshokwe, Bembe, Hemba, Songe, Zela, Lubasania, Holoholo, and Lumotwa (Gérard-Libois and Verhaegen 1961, p.780). Mostly agricultural, North Katanga was part of the seventeenth century Luba Empire, which began to disintegrate with the coming of Afro-Arabs from Zanzibar in the mid-1800s. When Belgium eliminated the Afro-Arabs in 1895, certain Luba chiefs became interested in strengthening their collapsing power by collaborating with Belgian administrators. This collaboration made North Katanga a reservoir of labor for the UMHK. As the colonial system became more oppressive, natives' reactions took many forms, and the most important was the Kitawala (to reign) movement, a Congolese version of Watch Tower (Deschamps 1965, p. 118). It was at the root of social demands from mining workers in Manono to railways workers in southern Katanga. Other than the Kitawala movement, North Katanga remained relatively calm until 1960.

As pointed out earlier, the critical juncture of the North Katanga insurrection was the amendment of the Fundamental Law by the Belgian legislature on 14 June 1960 after the BALUBAKAT contested the national electoral results of May 1960. This amendment allowed the CONAKAT to elect a provincial government two days later and thus to exclude all members of the BALUBAKAT. On 21 June 1960, the BALUBAKAT elites formed their own autonomous government. The Luba and other minority groups felt unrepresented in the Tshombe government and feared a regime where they would be subject to the unrestrained domination of southern ethnic groups such as the Lunda, Tabwa, and Yeke. The proclamation of the Katanga secession in July 1960 made reconciliation between the two parties impossible. Thus, one critical juncture of the insurrection was the exclusion of North Katanga leaders from the provincial government (O'Brien 1962, pp. 140–166). The Katanga secession thus produced the insurrection.

A few weeks after the beginning of the North Katanga insurrection, Tshombe's army began periodically raiding the area to subdue the BALUBAKAT. The result was the death of some 80,000 people by the time the insurrection ended on 19 December 1961. Without UN intervention in North Katanga, counterinsurrection and youth attacks could have continued, with a devastating toll in human lives. The principal UN effort against the Katanga troops was to recapture areas under BALUBAKAT control (Hoskyns 1962, pp. 391–394).

Insurrection in Northwestern South Kasai

On 14 August 1962, President Kasavubu promulgated the law establishing South Kasai Province in accordance with the law of 27 April 1962. Provincial electoral results gave an overwhelming majority (fifteen of the twenty cast votes) to Ngalula, prime minister of the seceded state of South Kasai. On 1 October 1962, several weeks after he was sworn in as provincial president, a group of Tshibanda youths attacked unarmed civilians from the Bena Mutu wa Mukuna region who were living in Bena Tshibanda. These Mutu eventually managed to run away and took refuge in the village of Chief Badibanga, a Tshibanda senator, but Badibanga handed them back to the youths, who killed them (Ilunga 1973, pp. 433–440). When this incident was reported to the provincial government, army troops were sent to punish the youths, who then retaliated. Within three weeks, the death toll on both sides rose to about 800. Ngalula quickly preempted the opposition's initiative by proclaiming a state of emergency in the troubled area and appointing an extraordinary general commissioner (*commissaire général extraordinaire*) from Tshibanda directly accountable to Ngalula. Under these circumstances, the central government was denied a pretext to intervene directly in the conflict. The fact that the provincial extraordinary commissioner was a Tshibanda also had the effect of undermining an insurrection fomented by the Bena Tshibanda.

As the conflict escalated, a tragic incident occurred in April 1963. Some seventeen traditional chiefs from the area, on their way to Mbujimayi where they had been summoned by Ngalula, were killed by the Tshibanda youths (Ilunga 1973). This massacre further undermined support for the insurrection, and Ngalula used it as an excuse to escalate repression in the area. More troops were sent in, and more villages were burned. Villagers reacted by using spears and other arms to defend themselves. When the insurrection ended in August 1964, some 4,800 people were dead, and more than 5,000 were internally displaced in the area.

Causes and duration of the conflict. The insurrection of northwestern Kasai was mostly an issue of exclusion and control of state spoils. In early October 1962, the election of Ngalula as the provincial president formalized the division of South Kasai into two groups of rival lineages. The Mutu perceived the electoral outcome as a victory over the Tshibanda. This victory, which occurred after Kalonji's downfall, consolidated this primary subdivision. Ngalula was quickly besieged by the Mutu, who sought jobs, rewards, and even revenge against the beneficiaries of the previous regime dominated by the Tshibanda under Kalonji's seceded state (Ilunga 1973).

Ngalula behaved like Kalonji before him. Like Kalonji, who excluded the rival Mutu lineage from the government, Ngalula also excluded most Tshibanda from major offices when he became provincial president. Of the ten ministers in the provincial government before the insurrection, seven were from the Mutu, and only three minor portfolios went to the Tshibanda (Ilunga 1973). A group of legislators from the Tshibanda addressed a petition to the central government about their exclusion from the provincial government. This resulted in the Tshibanda's insurrection in South Kasai, which Kalonji seemed to have financed in part from exile in Spain, or at least gave it his moral support (Ilunga 1973). The Tshibanda opposition even requested the central government create a province that would include all the Tshibanda territories.

Discussion of Early Civil Wars and Extant Research

Since the early twentieth century, Katanga had been the mineral hub of Congo. Not only did its mineral wealth attract more Europeans than did any other region, it also became more industrialized and more developed than other provinces. Unlike Katanga, South Kasai remained an underdeveloped region and a reservoir of labor for Katanga's mining towns. The two provinces provided some 80 percent of mineral output in the 1950s, certainly justifying an economic analysis of civil wars. Political explanations of civil wars, on the other hand, tend to rely on grievance. However, the analysis of the four early civil wars shows that politics of exclusion remains perhaps the best critical juncture explaining these wars, although their critical antecedents are different.

Causes of Early Civil Wars

Critical juncture. The process leading to independence of the Belgian Congo began with the electoral law of March 1960 that institutionalized proportional representation. A fundamental hypothesis in legislative studies is that the electoral system largely determines the party system and, through it, the structure of the government (Duverger 1955; Lijphart 1977). Proportional representation favors minority groups because candidate slates are chosen by party leaders. It also creates multiparty system and coalition governments, while plurality elections favor a two-party system and single-party government. However, the advantage of having multiple parties in a proportional representation system is counterbalanced by government instability because coalitions are postelectoral strategies that aim to gain a majority in the upper house or provincial legislatures in order to exclude noncoalition members from the government.

The proportional representation system thus exacerbated conflict in Congo by polarizing groups because most political parties were "ethnic" political parties. Political entrepreneurs excluded from state spoils activated ethnic affinities to seek power (Kisangani 1999). As Englebert and Hummel (2005, p. 400) have pointed out, the politics in Africa "often amounts to zero-sum games, as states are captured by one ethnic group or coalition, which frequently exerts its domination over others, largely excluding them from state benefits if not persecuting them." For example, the Katanga secession as a conflict between the north and south made some ethnic groups, such as the Yeke, more "authentic Katangans" than the Luba of North Katanga. In early June 1960, the Luba of Katanga were suddenly no longer authentic Katangans, while the Yeke remained authentic Katangans. According to historical records, the Yeke migrated to South Katanga in the mid-nineteenth century from the eastern shore of Lake Tanganyika, while the Luba have been in the area since before the establishment of the Luba Empire in the sixteenth century. In a sense, the Yeke qualify as "strangers," while the Luba are autochthons. The same politics of exclusion seems to have motivated the South Kasai secession.

The two insurrections show some temporal institutional dependence resulting from the two secessions. The Katanga secession created the North Katanga insurrection, and the South Kasai secession indirectly caused the northwestern insurrection in South Kasai. The BALUBAKAT's call to arms resulted from its exclusion from state spoils. In South Kasai, the Tshibanda reacted because they felt excluded from state spoils controlled by the Mutu. Ultimately, because colonial provinces were economic entities rather than administrative units, the two secessions were urban affairs attempting to control state spoils, while the two insurrections were rural protests against increasing control over provincial spoils by an urban elite.

As these early internal wars indicate, neither greed nor grievance provides any critical juncture to explain them. Most rebel leaders were not political outcasts but former members of the government who tried to reposition themselves in the state apparatus. These excluded elites had the opportunity to rebel because the state that emerged in the early 1960s was weak, having lost its instrument of coercion after the army's mutiny. Thus, law and order disappeared overnight. Moreover, the state was unable to arbitrate, which provided a favorable setting for civil wars. Also, the rebel leaders were not among the grieved ones but had the best education, given the standards of that period, and appropriated all the houses and material benefits enjoyed by Europeans. In the words of one observer, these leaders were "new whites" in the post-Lumumba Congo (Nzongola-Ntalaja 2002, p. 124).

More specifically, a few operational definitions of the greed model illustrate the point that extant research on civil wars provides no explanation of the four early cases of internal wars in Congo. For example, the economic approach operationally defines "greed" in terms of primary commodity exports as a percentage of GDP. It thus contends that the risk of civil war rises by about 22 percent when exports of primary commodities as a percentage of GDP constitute about 32 percent of GDP (Collier, Hoeffler, and Sambanis 2005, p.16), but this risk declines thereafter. Katanga's share of primary commodities and mineral exports in GDP hardly supports these numbers. Nationally, mineral exports represented an average of 12 percent of GDP between 1959 and 1963, and an average of almost 11 percent in the 1960s. These numbers are on the ascending inverse U-shaped curve of the greed model. At the regional level, the share of mineral exports to provincial GDP in Katanga was 97 percent and in South Kasai 86 percent—numbers not captured by the greed model. Therefore, critical antecedents of the two secessions and the two insurrections lie elsewhere because there is little indication that the mineral sector played much role in their causes.

Furthermore, the greed approach argues that the use of looted resource wealth in the prewar period should provide rebel leaders enough financial resources to fund start-up costs of hiring soldiers and initiating civil war. One should then expect to observe an increasing military buildup in the prewar phase of a civil war. If this is correct, then the two secessions and the two insurrections should clearly show leaders amassing money before the onset of conflict by extracting and selling natural resources or by extorting resources from the two mining companies—the UMHK and Forminière. However, this is not apparent. According to historical evidence, only after their defeat in the 1957 elections did the excluded elites begin to mobilize their rank and seek an autonomous institutional formula for Congo. The same argument can be extended to South Kasai. First, the Belgian mining company Forminière stood against the Luba in the late 1950s. Moreover, the colonial administration supported the Lulua (see Dequenne's report), resulting in the deterioration of the relationship between the Luba and the colonial administration.

Politics of exclusion also provides a better explanation to civil wars in North Katanga and northwestern South Kasai than both the greed and grievance approaches. For example, the leaders of North Katanga insurrection had no access to mineral wealth, because the mineral wealth of Katanga was mostly found in the south. In sum, natural resource abundance did not provide an opportunity for insurrection by serving as a source of funding in these four civil wars.

The second major factor in the economic approach to civil wars relates to declining economic opportunities; its proxies are low GDP per capita, negative or low economic growth, and low level of secondary school enrollment (Collier and Hoeffler 2002). In 1960, the GDP per capita in Congo was still rising, following the economic impetus that began in the late 1940s. Moreover, economic growth was positive from 1958 to 1959. These results show that little opportunity for civil war existed in the entire Congo in 1960. Regional differences are contradictory, however. Katanga had the highest GDP per capita, and economic growth was increasing in the region.

Turning to education, statistical analysis shows no relationship between secondary school enrollment and civil wars. Compared to the national average, Katanga and Kasai provinces had many undereducated young males. This represents a factor that, in the context of abundant natural resources, contributes to the risk of greed-driven conflict. In the 1950s, the colonial administration carried out a ten-year plan that increased the level of primary education without providing a concurrent expansion of secondary education. By 1959–1960, some 1.64 million primary school pupils nationwide competed for fewer than 30,000 seats in secondary schools (Mabusa 1966, p. 26). Thus, secondary school bottlenecks in the late 1950s increased youth mobilization and helped to explain civil wars. However, the absence of secession in other mineral-rich provinces, such as Kivu and Orientale provinces, undermines this argument because these provinces suffered the same bottlenecks.

Critical antecedents. Extant research in political science tradition argues that grievance and ensuing ethnic polarization are critical factors in explaining civil wars. Thus, resource extraction can create a sense of economic loss among the local population. If resource exploitation leads to civil wars through grievance, then one should observe the rebels criticizing resource firms, the resource sector, or the group benefiting from the system before the onset of civil wars. Rebel leaders believe these issues are salient concerns in the population they wish to mobilize and that raising these issues will help them gain popular support. However, the rebels never criticized the firms.

Furthermore, Horowitz (1985) provides a theoretical argument that links colonial legacy to civil wars. He contends that fortuitous location in or near a center of investment gives local ethnic groups opportunities for education and employment denied to those less well situated, but advanced migrants from backward regions to the area may take advantage of these opportunities to the exclusion of local ethnic groups. Thus, the indigenous population or a backward group becomes disadvantaged in an advanced region, resulting in secessionist tendencies.

This argument is partly substantiated because the UMHK, facing a major labor shortage in the 1920s, relocated a number of Luba (advanced groups) from Kasai (a backward region) to work the mines in southern Katanga (an advanced region). These newcomers became better adapted than the autochthons (backward group) to the new colonial roles and soon dominated key administrative and business positions at the expense of the local population.

South Kasai provides an example of a developed group, the Luba, from a backward area. According to Horowitz's framework, such a group tends to favor a unitary system rather than secessionist tendencies because it constitutes a population exporter. The group is likely to secede only if it feels discriminated against outside its province. As strangers, the Luba suffered discrimination in Katanga and in Lulua land, creating a massive wave of migrants back to Kasai and propelling them to declare in desperation the independence of South Kasai. The primary cause of the South Kasai secession was land scarcity and expulsion of Luba from Lulua land.

Several factors of continuity were important in the early civil wars. First, provinces as economic entities were ripe for secession. The colonial state erected a centralized administrative system by dividing some 336 ethnic groups into six provinces that were mostly economic entities. Because the provinces were economic entities rather than administrative institutions, they provided political leaders with a more attractive political market than the national arena. The two secessions were thus attempts to control provincial economic activities and the spoils that went with them. For example, rather than attacking the UMHK or white settlers in Katanga, a convergence of economic interests emerged among southern Katangans. The most important economic factor was the need to keep the fruits of industrialization that Katangans had gained during the colonial period. In fact, Katanga was the first to secede. In this case, economic development is probably the most important reason to secede earlier than later. This is in line with the modernization literature that early seceders tend to be within economically advanced regions. The CONAKAT leaders and white settlers wanted to secede because they lived in an advanced region and had "interest in protecting and safeguarding achievements already made" (Emizet and Hesli 1995, p. 524).

In sum, economic well-being, not greed or grievance, was more important to secession in Katanga. Its leaders reasoned that their privileged status arising out of the colonial period could be best maintained and amplified through secession or autonomy. However, the other three civil wars—the South Kasai secession and the two insurrections—hardly fit the modernization framework because those three areas were not as economically advanced as South Katanga.

Urbanization is another colonial legacy. In the postcolonial setting, the competitive response to modernization opportunities engendered serious tensions in urban centers. The two secessions were urban based, with the ruling group attempting to eliminate rival contenders to control centers of power and enjoy state spoils, while totally neglecting the countryside. The politics of exclusion thus helped the urban elite mobilize rural masses to oppose the provincial government. However, the politics of exclusion is possible only when the state becomes the sole employer.

In 1960, several new elements emerged and interacted with these colonial legacies to shape early civil wars. Independence meant the transfer of power to Africans. This was a new element in the constellation of continuity epitomized by ethnicity. Although ethnicity was a familiar part of the history of Congo, it was not inherently an issue until the eve of independence. Increasing urbanization in the 1950s made towns prone to conflict as an educated group of Africans, or évolués, began to use the newly crystallized ethnic categories in a more self-conscious way. The politicization of ethnicity became salient in the 1957–1958 urban reforms and continued to shape the electoral process after independence. The Katanga secession made ethnicity a "divisible value" among the people of Katanga, thus showing its malleability.

Independence also meant new institutional arrangements, including the Fundamental Law and the electoral law. This institutional framework or an element of change seemed to pave the way toward politics of exclusion that triggered early civil wars. Institutions usually constrain individual choices so that individuals' expectations take into account what other citizens' choices will be. The Fundamental Law froze the six economic provinces, the keys for accumulation and power. Rather than providing the Luba a province of their own, the Belgian government rallied the unitarist call for centralization. The prevailing assumption was that providing the Luba of Kasai a homeland of their own in 1960 would stir up demands for autonomy everywhere. The amendment of the Fundamental Law in April 1962, which increased the number of provinces from six to twenty-one, only indicated the obvious.

Evaluation of Civil War Duration

The four early civil wars were wars of convenience rather than wars of legitimacy and lasted longer than the average of Congo's civil wars, except the the insurrection in North Katanga. Geographers and students of international relations have long claimed topography and location to be important determinants of state behavior. Thus, civil wars that occur far from the capital, near international borders, and in mountainous areas are likely to last longer than any other conflict (see Buhaug, Gates, and Lujala 2009). Economic approaches to explain the duration of civil wars view rebellion as investment, business, or mistake (Collier, Hoeffler, and Söderbom 2004).[7] Political approaches tend to rely mostly on the bargaining model of war. Military means constitute part of the bargaining process to advance political ends either through absolute war or limited war (von Clausewitz 1976). How do these approaches help explain the duration of the four early cases of civil war in Congo?

First, all these early civil wars occurred far from the capital, and two were near international borders. However, the fact that the state lost its instrument of coercion after the army mutiny perhaps explains the duration of civil wars rather than does distance or location. Second, economic literature of civil wars provides several mechanisms by which natural resources explain the duration of civil wars. The first mechanism is looting, which can prolong civil wars if it provides rebels enough funds to keep fighting or maintain the status quo. In Katanga, however, mines were fenced by the UMHK and thus the resource was not lootable and could not be easily appropriated by the belligerents. However, the Katanga secession benefited from the mineral sector because the UMHK financed the seceded state and helped Tshombe sustain his military operations and pay for his administration. This financing strengthened the South Katanga position in dictating a confederal formula in most negotiations with the central government. Thus, financial resources from the UMHK enabled CONAKAT leaders to recruit mercenaries and harden their positions at the negotiating table.

In contrast, South Kasai had diamonds both as a nonlootable resource (industrial diamonds) and a lootable one (gems). Although Forminière fenced part of the resource, a large portion of alluvial diamonds was never under the control of either the seceded state or the mining company. Moreover, the lootable resource was labor intensive and thus benefited a wider segment of the population and limited the viability of the South Kasai secession. The illicit exploitation of diamonds and the control of trade networks by noncombatants prolonged the secession because it encouraged locals to loot instead of fight.

The presence of a lootable resource also exacerbated the principal-agent issue (Fearon 2004) in South Kasai. Soldiers could accumulate personal wealth because they had better information on the location of alluvial diamonds than their superior ranking officers. Undisciplined soldiers personally benefited from resource looting, which made it harder for the South Kasai secession to survive long enough to consolidate power. Not only did looting encourage a lack of discipline and undermine the command structure of the secession, but it also lowered the chance of recruiting young men into the army of the seceded state. The Luba youths preferred digging diamonds to volunteering in a secession they probably did not fully understand. In further contrast, the two insurrections had almost no organizational structure. They were characterized by carjacking, extortion, kidnapping, and small theft, such as looting houses and businesses.

The duration of the South Kasai secession was also affected by several events. Unlike the ruling group in South Katanga, which remained unified, the elite in South Kasai fragmented, thus precipitating the end of the secession. The Tshibanda and the Mutu both perceived the distribution of state spoils as unequal or a zero-sum game. As Mutu representation in the government declined, they felt excluded from state spoils and migrated to Leopoldville where they rallied to the central government against the seceded state of South Kasai. The exclusion of the Mutu destroyed internal cohesiveness and helped to end the civil war. The same can also be said of the Katanga secession. The excluded BALUBAKAT refused to be part of the secession and allied to the central government to oppose the secession.

Another critical factor affecting the duration of civil wars is the role of third parties. The UN's late involvement, in fact, affected the early civil wars. Howard (2008) argues that one of the key factors determining peacekeeping success or failure is the degree to which the UN Security Council is interested in a given case. In Congo, the UN hesitated for more than a year before committing resources to end the two secessions. More specifically, the United States was instrumental in ending the Katanga secession by providing the UN resources to compensate for government's weakness.

In sum, the involvement of the UN was instrumental in shaping the duration of early civil wars because the UN saw them as infringing on the territorial sovereignty of the new state. Despite the argument from southern Katangan elites that Katanga Province was incorporated in the Belgian Congo at a later date than the rest of the colony and thus deserved to be a separate and autonomous state, the international community sent a strong signal to secessionist movements everywhere that it considered decolonization an acceptable form of self-determination. With its efforts to defeat the Katanga secession, the UN thus enshrined the explicit stipulation that colonies have a right to sovereign independence only within their colonial boundaries, which were considered sacrosanct.

Consequences and Postconflict Rebuilding

The first set of consequences of early internal wars includes socioeconomic issues. Usually, civil wars tend to destroy infrastructure and leave the postconflict administration with the hard work of rebuilding. Of all the regions mobilized, Katanga, especially South Katanga, suffered the most because both sides used aircraft and heavy artillery. Although some bridges were lost, they were quickly rebuilt in 1963 by the UMHK so it could export its minerals. In South Kasai, the secession almost wiped out subsistence agriculture because most rural dwellers became involved in illegal diamond mining.

The first three years of independence thus saw an increase in prices of goods not seen since the end of World War II. From 1960 to 1963, inflation rose by more than 20 percent as the result of political instability and disarticulation of the state. At the national level, the real GDP per capita started showing signs of decline under inflationary pressures. Smuggling flourished along borders in eastern Congo, especially in the Kivu area where the central government lost more than $50 million in revenue in less than three years (Masson 1970). In the absence of an adequate administrative infrastructure to collect taxes, the central government resorted to printing money under the newly created banking system, Conseil Monétaire. Because the government made ample use of its discretionary power to print money to fill the shortage of revenue, the budget deficit more than doubled from 1960 to 1963, reaching a record high of four billion francs ($180 million in 2010 prices). During these civil war years, increased imports and declining exports created balance-of-payments disequilibria.

To correct these macroeconomic imbalances, the government responded with economic policies. First, it destroyed the Katanga currency to regain monetary sovereignty. Second, the central government devalued the franc from 85 francs per US dollar in 1961 to 150 francs per dollar, or 100 francs for 33.33 Belgian francs on export transactions. On the import side, the exchange rate was 180 francs per dollar, or 100 francs for 27.78 Belgian francs. The goal of the devaluation was to eradicate internal and external macroeconomic disequilibria in order to increase revenue through this dual exchange rate, to control inflation, and to stimulate exports of agricultural products through legal channels. However, by early 1964, exports plummeted again, and the price level further increased by more than 20 percent as the result of monetary expansion to cover government deficits. In brief, the monetary reform was a total failure.

At the political level, the two secessions had the ironic consequence of removing any stigma from demands for provincial autonomy. They also brought to light the need for a new institutional framework. Federalism emerged as the right formula for the new republic. A trend toward corporate provincial solidarity against the central government also surfaced in the first three years of independence. By mid-1963, twenty-one new provinces had been created (see Map 1.1). However, the central administration never succeeded in developing a genuine popular base and thus failed to control the provinces.

Finally, because of its victory over the early civil wars, the government never envisioned the need to build an army and demobilize combatants. The central government did not feel obliged to inflate its army by more than 25 percent with the Katanga elements. More specifically, the UN began its withdrawal from Congo in mid-1963 without any plan to demobilize Tshombe's military forces or to build the Congolese army. Only 2,500 former Katanga gendarmes were actually absorbed into the national army (Beys, Gendebien, and Verhaegen 1964). More than 16,000 men simply disappeared with their weapons, and a number of these troops regrouped in Angola. By early August 1963, UN forces had dropped to 7,700 troops. The diminishing capabilities of the UN were matched by diminishing law and order in Congo. Thus, in mid-1963, Congo was more chaotic and vulnerable to another major civil war than ever before because the UN's goal of ending the Katanga secession never envisioned building either the Congolese army or any decent police force to keep law and order.

Summary and Policy Implications

The purpose of this chapter was to analyze the first four civil wars in Congo. These civil wars ended with government victories—outcomes that appear to contradict the view that African wars are more likely to end with rebel victories than are wars on other continents (DeRouen and Sobeck 2004). Taken together, the four cases of civil war offer several lessons and generalizations for those concerned with policies related to conflict and conflict resolution. Most notably, the politics of exclusion seems to have triggered all these early civil wars.

Several factors of continuity were also critical in explaining this politics of exclusion. First was the insertion of Congo in the world economy because its administrative provincial divisions were organized as economic entities in order to respond to the demand for raw materials in the global markets. Second was urbanization. As urban elites monopolized the political discourse, the competitive response to modernization engendered tensions as these elites competed to control provincial scarce resources. The two secessions were thus urban based. Because the politics of exclusion is possible only when the state becomes the sole employer, an alternative long-term strategy is to make the private sector more attractive than the public sector.

A few elements of change emerged after independence, which meant the transfer of power to Africans. Despite calls for institutional changes, the new Fundamental Law froze colonial provinces. Rather than providing the Luba with a province of their own, the Belgian government rallied the unitarist call for centralization. Thus, an early and well-planned autonomy in 1958–1959 would likely have diffused conflict.

Electoral maturity is critical to making proportional representation work and avoiding conflict. The plurality system may prove to be an antidote to conflict for any emerging and new polity because plurality-based elections force political parties to coalesce before balloting. However, such political compromise is nonexistent in proportional representation, which places the responsibility of choosing both the personnel and the policy of the new state on party leaders, who deliberate out of public view and after the votes have been cast. In Congo's early history, this process reinforced the politics of exclusion.

Notes

1. First, electoral rolls were irregular and incomplete to the extent that many Rhodesians of Bemba origin were included in the ballots, while votes of the Luba from Kasai were missing. Second, ballot boxes that contained favorable votes for the cartel disappeared before the counting of votes. Third, violence against partisans of the cartel was widespread in many places. For example, on 22 May 1960, pro-cartel Luba from Kasai were attacked in Kamina where Chief Kasongo Nyembo rallied to the CONAKAT. See Gérard-Libois (1963, pp. 67–68).

2. The Luba of Kasai are surrounded in the west by the Bena Lulua, Tshoko, Pende, and Bashilele; in the north by the Bakwa Luntu, Kuba, Bindji, Dengese, Songo Meno, Kela, Kuntshu, Hamba, and Tetela; in the east, by the Songe and Luba Shankadi; and in the south by the Bindji, Kete, Sala Mpasu, and Bena Kanyoka.

3. Scores of other provinces have the following percentages of people engaged in the wage economy in each province: Leopoldville (59.9), Katanga (50.9), Kivu (47.2), Orientale (31.3), and Equateur (27.8). Refer to Merlier (1962), p. 146.

4. Kalamba was the grandson of Mukenge Kalamba, paramount chief of the Lulua in the nineteenth century, who welcomed Europeans in the Lulua land.

5. Some Luba youngsters returning from a soccer game jeered at a number of Lulua leaders who were coming out of a meeting of the Lulua-dominated political party, Congolese Union (Union Congolaise). A group of Lulua women nearby took offense and danced naked in the streets of Luluabourg. Such dance amounts to a declaration of war. On the same night, there was a generalized attack on the Luba by the Bena Lulua in Luluabourg. See Ilunga (1973).

6. The new state was to include the Kabinda District in which the Luba were a majority, as well as Luisa, Dimbelenge, and Lusambo territories inhabited by Kete and Kuba.

7. The idea of investment is that rebel leaders carry out a civil war today to provide citizens a better tomorrow. However, rebel leaders are businessmen if they intend to gain personally from civil war. A mistake implies that the society is well-off without rebel leaders because the economy is working well for all.

3

A Tale of Two Rebellions

On 14 September 1960, Colonel Joseph Mobutu removed the leader of the nationalist bloc, Prime Minister Patrice Lumumba, from power. His removal was linked to Cold War rivalry after the prime minister turned to the Soviet Union to help end the Katanga secession because his army was leaderless, but the UN, as the surrogate of the army, had a different priority than that of Lumumba. In fact, the UN's goal was to prevent the Congo conflict from becoming a major international crisis, while the prime minister intended to consolidate the authority of the government. A major consequence of Mobutu's coup d'état was to isolate the nationalist bloc and to maintain the pro-Western group in power.

As developed in Chapter 2, the nationalist bloc was slowly being removed from power as the UN was attempting to defeat the Katanga secession. Demands for provincial autonomy by the pro-Western bloc, which resulted in the amendment of the Fundamental Law in April 1962 and the creation of twenty-one provinces in 1963, automatically isolated the nationalist bloc from provincial politics. By mid-1963, the nationalist group had lost political positions at all levels acquired in the 1960 elections. It then decided to overthrow the government, beginning with the rebellion in Kwilu on 6 January 1964 and in eastern Congo on 15 April 1964.[1] The former ended in late December 1965, while the latter lasted until mid-1966. Although the Kwilu rebellion was confined to the Mbunda and Pende regions, the eastern rebellion spread like the tentacles of an octopus as its Popular Liberation Army (Armée Populaire de Libération), called the *simba* (lions) and using *dawa* (magic, for invulnerability), almost toppled the government.[2] A "rebellion" refers to a violent rural uprising that aims to change state structures and has the usual threshold of fatalities and displaced persons. The fact that massive rural masses followed the rebel leaders' message indicated that the rebellions were viewed as legitimate struggles.

Historical Context of the Two Rebellions

The two rebellions occurred hundreds of kilometers apart and had no connections because they never had a common organizational structure. The areas involved were geographically distant and culturally different (see Map 3.1). Moreover, the essential difference between the two rebellions was the more radical aims of the Kwilu rebellion under Pierre Mulele, who had a comprehensive program of social transformation in contrast to the eastern rebellion, which was based on narrow class interests (Nzongola-Ntalaja 2002, p. 128). In a political sense, however, there was one rebellion because the leaders of both civil wars wanted to destroy existing institutions by mobilizing rural masses in their quest for what they called "second independence" (Fox, de Craemer, and Ribeaucourt 1965). As Amilcar Cabral stated, the concept of "second independence" consists of two phases in the liberation struggle: (1) the national phase in which all classes of colonial society unite to fight the colonial system and (2) the social phase of reconstruction and transformation, in which the essential aspect of the problem is the struggle against neocolonialism and its internal allies (cited in Nzongola-Ntalaja 2002, p. 124).

Unlike the two early internal wars of secession, leaders of the two rebellions intended to have legitimate access to the state apparatus within a unitary state. Unitarist rather than federalist, they were not interested in establishing their own states. While competing for state access for the benefit of the particularistic interests of their own group, rebel political elites used nationalist discourse as a platform to build a minimum winning coalition and to define others as nonpatriotic or nonnationalist. By the time the two rebellions ended, 48,000 to 81,500 people were dead, and some 157,000 to 215,000 persons were internally displaced (Kisangani and Bobb 2010, pp. 81–82). A brief historical background of the two areas is warranted to understand the causes of the 1964 rebellions.

Kwilu Rebellion

Kwilu was a district of the Leopoldville Province before it became a province on 14 August 1962 (see Map 1.1 for Kwilu's location). In 1963, Kwilu had 1,448,128 inhabitants and was home to several ethnic groups, although dominated by six groups. First, the Mbunda occupy Idiofa territory. The leader of the Kwilu rebellion, Mulele, was a Mbunda. The Pende in the Gungu territory adjacent to Idiofa form the second group. They also occupy a portion of Kikwit, Kasai Province (sector Kitanpwa), and a small portion of Kwango (sector Mukoso). Antoine Gizenga is a Pende. The third group, the Mbala, resides in the Bulungu territory. An early important political leader from this group was Cleophas Kamitatu, from the Ngongo clan. The fourth group is the Yanzi in Bandundu territory. The two other groups are the Suku in the Masi-Manimba and Feshi territories; and the Dinga along the Kasai River and Kamtsha area.

Map 3.1 Rebellions in Congo

Note: Shaded areas are from Young (1970), p. 908.

Kwilu relies economically on agriculture and specifically on the production of palm oil, which first involves cutting palm fruits. In the early 1960s, one out of five men in Kwilu received income from cutting palm fruits (Fox, de Craemer, and Ribeaucourt 1965). Historically, any activity that affected palm oil production tended to have profound sociopolitical repercussions in Kwilu. In May 1931, the Pende revolted as the result of depressed prices of palm fruits and the colonial decision to increase taxes (Gize 1973). In 1931, a cutter of palm fruits had to spend six hard weeks to gather 1,500 kilograms of fruits to pay the required taxes. Using war charms that they believed made them invulnerable to army bullets, the Pende attacked the installations of the Huilleries du Congo Belge palm oil company and killed most of its agents. When the revolt ended, 550 Pende had been killed by the colonial army.

Kwilu remained calm until 1959 when a politico-religious sect, called Mpeve (spirit), appeared among the Dinga and Mbunda groups. The movement considered all Europeans as hostile forces and foresaw independence as a cataclysmic political event when all colonial vestiges would disappear and African ancestors would bring economic prosperity. On 30 June 1960, however, their ancestors did not respond to the millennial dream and the Mbunda livelihood deteriorated still further. Some observers trace the root of the Kwilu rebellion to the Mpeve deception and the appearance three years after independence of Mulele, who attempted to make the millennial dream real (Gize 1973).

Mulele started his political career in the African Solidarity Party (Parti Solidaire Africain, or PSA) founded by Sylvester Kama in February 1959 (Weiss 1967). The PSA was a regional political party embracing federalism. In early 1960, Gizenga became its general president and Mulele its first general secretary. The PSA acquired a solid regional base by collaborating with a group of intellectuals from Kikwit headed by Kamitatu, called the Association of Former Pupils of Jesuit Fathers (Association des Anciens Elèves des Pères Jesuites). In the 1960 elections, the PSA received thirteen out of 137 seats in the lower house (Gérard-Libois and Verhaegen 1961, p. 262). The failure of the party to compete with the MNC/L at the national level forced it back to its provincial roots. This move increased political tension within the province because national leaders of the PSA, such as Gizenga, had to compete with the provincial PSA leaders like Kamitatu. To this tension should be added ethnic and regional cleavages. As Maps 1.1 and 3.1 indicate, the Mbunda and Pende are located in eastern Kwilu. Unlike the Mbala and Ngongo groups, they rarely trusted people of Kikwit, the provincial capital, and their isolation from the town prevented them from effectively participating in provincial politics. Moreover, because they were a minority in the city of Kikwit, the Pende and Mbunda became a political minority in provincial institutions, which helped push them into the opposition. Thus, conflict within the PSA emerged when provincial and national governments formed in spring 1960.

The unity of the PSA was saved when its leaders adopted the unitary stand of the MNC/L before independence, and the PSA became de facto part of the nationalist coalition under Lumumba. Three leaders of the PSA were members of the government of Lumumba: Gizenga as vice prime minister, Mulele as minister of education, and Kama as state commissioner for Leopoldville Province. These nominations diffused the conflict within the PSA by leaving provincial politics to Kamitatu and his supporters. When Gizenga was reappointed vice prime minister in August 1961, Kamitatu was eclipsed in PSA politics. A few months later, in January 1962, Gizenga was accused of treason and sentenced to life in prison after his unsuccessful attempt to secede in late 1961.[3] Meanwhile, Kamitatu was named minister of interior. The result was the division of the party into PSA/Gizenga and PSA/Kamitatu. While the Mbunda and Pende were affiliated with the former, the Mbala, Ngongo, Yanzi, and other groups were affiliated with the latter. Moreover, the Mbunda and Pende felt excluded from provincial politics and accused the provincial government of being unrepresentative. When Mulele returned to Kwilu in July 1963, the province was already polarized along two factions (PSA/Kamitatu against PSA/Gizenga), two regions (eastern Kwilu against the other areas), two ethnic groups (Pende/Mbunda against all others), and two ideologies (radical in eastern Kwilu against moderate in western Kwilu).

Political polarization in Kwilu started after Mobutu's first coup d'état in September 1960 to neutralize Lumumba. As a result, in late 1960, members of the nationalist bloc, including Mulele, installed a parallel government in Stanleyville with Gizenga as their leader. Although part of the Stanleyville government, in early 1961, Mulele was appointed ambassador to Egypt. In 1962, he traveled via Prague and Moscow to Peking, where he underwent a training course in guerrilla warfare (Verhaegen 1969). Upon his return to Kwilu in mid-1963, he began organizing ideological camps in the Mbunda areas where young men were indoctrinated and taught the elements of guerrilla warfare to overthrow the government, which he described as oppressive, corrupt, and "sold out" to the West, notably to the United States. By late December 1963, Mulele had perhaps 10,000 followers age fifteen to twenty (Verhaegen 1969, p. 258). He emphasized patriotism, social justice, and the vision of a "second independence," in which disappointed hopes of prosperity would finally be fulfilled. About six months after the first camps were set up in the Mbunda and Pende regions, the Kwilu rebellion broke out when rebels attacked and burned the administrative center of Mungindu, in Kwilu, on 6 January 1964. By the end of January, large parts of the Idiofa and Gungu were under siege. Although the rebel bands possessed only spears, machetes, and bows and arrows, they overwhelmed the police and army detachments. By mid-1964, the Kwilu rebellion was contained, but not defeated, but its capacity to generate massive participation, and to pit spears against firearms, demonstrated the state of the national army. Ironically, the Kwilu rebellion, which intended to destroy the foundation of the Congolese society, never expanded beyond the Pende and Mbunda in Idiofa, Kenge, and Ngungu territories where it initially originated.

The Eastern Rebellion

The eastern rebellion started on 15 April 1964 at 6:00 am when rebel columns attacked the town of Bukavu and several areas in the Uvira territory, the sectors of Luvungi, Luberizi, Mulenge, and the posts of Kaliba and Lemera (Verhaegen 1969). Two days later, the Fulero rebels seized the town of Uvira. On 27 May, some 5,000 to 7,000 Bembe rebels took Fizi. Fulero and Bembe live in Kivu Central (see Maps 1.1 and 3.1). Equipped with spears, bows and arrows, and a handful of firearms, the rural insurgents routed two army battalions. The rebels, or simba, under the leadership of General Nicolas Olenga advanced along the old Zanzibari trade route from Fizi to Kabambare and Kasongo. On 5 August 1964, Stanleyville came under rebel control. Thereafter, rebel columns fanned out in all directions. The zenith of rebel self-confidence was marked by the proclamation on 5 September 1964 of a revolutionary government in Stanleyville under the leadership of Christophe Gbenye, former minister of interior in the Lumumba government. By the end of 1964, Gbenye's rebel forces occupied almost half the area that coincided with the quasi-empire of Tippo Tip in the late nineteenth century, which covered the Swahili zone except South Katanga. The collapse of the Leopoldville government appeared a real possibility, but, in early 1965, the rebellion suddenly showed signs of disintegration. By July 1966, the eastern rebellion was defeated. Although several pockets of resistance remained, the rebels no longer posed any threat to the central government because most of its leaders had fled into exile.

The eastern rebellion is known as the Uvira-Fizi rebellion because these areas were the centers of rebel activity before it expanded into other regions (Verhaegen 1969, p. 258). Thus, the rebellion could not have started without the involvement of the Bembe of Fizi and the Fulero of Uvira, who migrated to their present areas in the late eighteenth century and imposed their rule on the Rega, Kumu, and Vira. During the colonial period, the Fulero were easily subdued. From 1960 to 1963, they were subject to arbitrary decisions by special administrators or provincial authorities because of their isolation. For people of Fizi and Uvira territories, any political renewal was acceptable as long it aimed to overthrow the incumbent regime and destroy all of its institutions of coercion.

At the national level, federalism had almost isolated the nationalist-unitarist bloc by mid-1963, thus keeping its leaders from mobilizing the masses. The result was rivalry within the MNC/L leadership as its moderate members were co-opted by a central government controlled by the pro-Western bloc. Then, on 29 September 1963, President Joseph Kasavubu adjourned the parliament indefinitely. This decision brought together a disoriented nationalist bloc and increased its cohesiveness. From 29 September to 3 October 1963, the group met in Leopoldville and created the Union of Nationalist Parties, with the MNC/L and the PSA/Gizenga among them.

In early October 1963, this group crossed the Congo River and set up its headquarters in Brazzaville, where a socialist government had been established under the labor leader Alphonse Massaba-Debat. The group established the National Council of Liberation (Conseil National de Libération, or CNL) to overthrow the Adoula government and realize "the total decolonization" of Congo. Among its leaders was Gbenye, who sent his two lieutenants, Gaston Soumialot from Maniema and Laurent Kabila from North Katanga, to eastern Congo in February 1964 to direct military action against the government in these regions.[4] He gambled that he could count on the eastern population that had, since 1960, supported the MNC/L.

In February 1964, Soumialot and a few members of the CNL arrived in Bujumbura, where they applied for asylum. Soumialot enrolled young Congolese refugees living in Bujumbura into the CNL and organized small groups of these refugees into armed bands that slipped into Kivu. A report of the Embassy of Congo in Bujumbura provided details of Soumialot's activities in Bujumbura as follows:

Daily conventicles in Paquidas Hotel, with representatives of the opposition in Bujumbura, expedition of tracts in Bukavu and Uvira to incite people to civil disobedience. . . . It seemed that the intention of rebel leaders is to force the youth of their party residing in Burundi after a brief military education to attack authorities in order to carry on revolution that would bring the central government down. (Gérard-Libois and Van Lierde 1965, p. 56)

On 18 February 1964, the first antigovernment tracts from the CNL began circulating in Bukavu, inviting the populace and soldiers to rebel against the state. Less than two months later, on 15 April 1964, the rebels attacked Bukavu and several areas in the Uvira-Fizi territories.

Causes of Rebellions

The following analysis provides both economic and political causes of the two rebellions by distinguishing critical junctures from critical antecedents. The most important critical juncture in both rebellions was the exclusion of the nationalist bloc from power. The top leadership of the two rebellions came from hard-line opposition politicians and from those who had not found a place in the Leopoldville government or provincial capitals after the removal of Lumumba from power. These politicians were pro-Lumumba, all of whom, after September 1960, were slowly being pushed aside or excluded from state spoils while losing the provincial and national political bases they acquired at independence. The institutionalization of federalism in 1962, which created twenty-one autonomous provinces, completely isolated the nationalist-unitarist bloc by mid-1963, thus keeping its leaders from mobilizing the masses. The dismissal of the parliament by President Kasavubu on 29 September 1963 completely excluded the nationalist bloc from voicing its opinion and gave the pro-Western bloc freedom to "exercise power unfettered by legislative oversight and the probing eye of the Lumumbist coalition" (Nzongola-Ntalaja 2002, p. 125).

Although the politics of exclusion was a critical juncture of the two rebellions, the challenge of rebel leaders was to motivate the masses and recruit followers. The following subsections explore how they were able to mobilize the masses and make the two rebellions legitimate struggles against a "corrupt and exploitative regime" (Young 1970, p. 970).

Critical Antecedents

The literature on the causes of civil war shows a significant divide between opportunities and motivations. The first relies on greed and the second on grievance. In the greed model, lootable commodities remain central in financing civil wars. An analysis of Kwilu, however, reveals an agricultural region that relies exclusively on palm fruits, a nonlootable commodity. Although eastern Congo is rich in mineral resources, the mineral sector apparently provided no financing for the rebellion (Ndikumana and Kisangani 2005). More specifically, Fizi and Uvira, where the eastern rebellion started, are predominantly agricultural, with an economy based on cotton and sugarcane. Therefore, it is difficult to argue that lootable goods played any substantial role in the onset of either rebellion.

The second factor in the greed model is the cost of rebellion defined in terms of positive economic growth, increasing GDP per capita, and secondary school enrollment. First, the two rebellions occurred when economic growth was still positive, from 1962 to 1963, and GDP per capita was higher than in subsequent decades. Not the least of the paradoxes was the fact that the first violence appeared in Kwilu, the province that in 1963 was widely advertised as a "pilot province" and a local incarnation of the recovery process, because Kwilu Province operated with impressive effectiveness (Willame 1964). The eastern provinces were not so administratively effective, however.

Although the administrative machinery seemed to operate effectively in Kwilu, national socioeconomic indicators revealed a different story. Nearly 50 percent of the Congolese population in the early 1960s was younger than twenty years of age. By 1962–1963, almost 1.9 million primary school pupils competed for 36,951 available places in secondary school (Table 3.1). Thus, more than 1.8 million primary school pupils had no hope of a secondary education. In other words, the mobilization of young men was important at the beginning of both rebellions. The youths often migrated to urban centers only to find no jobs. Although they had received a rudimentary education in mission schools, where they were often encouraged to abandon their traditional beliefs, they were not given enough education, or contact with the modern world, to obtain economically useful skills or to develop a new and coherent system of values (Young 1970). Unemployment was massive, averaging no less than 68 percent per province, except in South Katanga and Lower Congo, which represented two zones of prosperity. Large numbers of young men probably frustrated by unemployment expressed a great degree of aggression. While they had no op-

Table 3.1 Evolution of Primary and Secondary School Enrollments

Number of	1959–1960	1960–1961	1961–1962	1962–1963	1963–1964
Primary schools	1,644,000	1,732,000	1,830,000	1,894,000	1,995,000
Teachers	1,500	38,000	43,000	48,000	53,000
Secondary schools	37,386	—	—	36,951	92,273

Sources: Data from DRC (1964) and Mabusa (1966), p. 26.

portunities for themselves, the elites associated with the government enjoyed relative prosperity.

Economic literature on civil wars also views a weak government as another factor of conflict. A proxy for weak government in the economic literature of civil wars is forest and mountains as a percentage of land. The argument is that Congo's forests and mountains provide rebels a safe haven to hide from government forces. Moreover, geographic dispersion of the population should inhibit government capability as well. Accordingly, Congo seems prone to civil wars because its population lives around the edges of the country (Herbst 2000).

This argument, although sound, has no empirical foundation for explaining the two rebellions. Forests and mountains were not crucial because the government had no military of its own. Rebellions could have broken out in any sort of terrain because the Congolese government did not meet the Weberian test for statehood: it did not have a monopoly on the use of force within its borders. From 1960 to 1963, the UN forces served as a surrogate for the normal governmental monopoly of coercion to provide order during the Katanga secession. After defeating the secession, the UN withdrew without rebuilding the army. Primarily because of budgetary constraints, the UN refused to train and organize the national army, despite repeated requests from Prime Minister Adoula that the UN coordinate the modernization of the army. In his report to the Security Council, the Secretary-General pointed out in February 1963 that he had a dilemma: on the one hand, the state of the army required a rapid reorganization, and, on the other hand, the grave financial situation of the UN made it impossible to engage in new spending, no matter how dire the need (Beys, Gendebien, and Verhaegen 1964, p. 110). The presence of the UN forces as a surrogate only delayed the inevitable period when power deflation became an open invitation for rebellion.

The situation in 1963 was deplorable for many, justifying an explanation for the rebellion based on grievance. In 1958–1959, most Congolese visualized a vast improvement in their standard of living after independence, giving them the dignity and material advantages that Belgians held under colonial rule; rather, the anticipated standard sharply declined in rural areas. However, a simple or even sharp decline in living standards is not enough to explain a rebellion. Some reference point is needed to make people aware of their deteriorating standard of living. This point emerged after independence when the rural constituencies were largely abandoned by their elected leaders. No political structures existed that could engender a minimum of loyalty from the rural masses and help them identify with the state and its political leadership (Young 1970). No political parties maintained the extraordinarily successful grassroots organizations they established in the few months before independence. Instead, leaders migrated to the national and provincial capitals, where they participated in endless and sterile games of parliamentary politics (Young 1970). Because elected officials were not forced to seek the support of their followers and keep their pre-independence promises, local governments in the rural areas became crippled and economically bankrupt, completely forgotten by provincial capitals.

A sense of deprivation in 1963 was not only widespread but was also perceived by the masses in terms of temporal space, vertical social space between strata, and horizontal communal space among groups (Young 1970). This tridimensional nature of relative deprivation helps explain the masses' responses to the nationalist call to arms in late 1963.

Mass level perceptions of deprivation. The time dimension of deprivation has two aspects: (1) the immediate recollection of a more ordered and materially prosperous life and (2) a utopian vision of future well-being. Table 3.2 provides an overview of the palm oil economy in Kwilu. A seesaw pattern started in 1959, and this instability of production also meant income instability. Although independent producers increased their production in Congo from 153,396 tons in 1962 to 159,363 tons a year later, Kwilu's production registered a sharp decline of 5,848 tons from 1962 to 1963. Even palm oil in barrels registered a net overall decline. These declines meant a serious loss of income for farmers who depended on palm fruits. Meanwhile, the state imposed exorbitant taxes on peasants.

The economic situation of eastern Congo was no different, even though most of Congo's mineral wealth was located there. Before independence, the two dominant crops in Fizi and Uvira were cotton and sugarcane. Cotton output per acre was one of the highest in the Belgian Congo. From 1945 to 1959, national production remained almost stable, averaging 147,000 tons per year. Compared with the national average of 204 kilograms per farmer in 1959, the Fizi-Uvira average output was 667 kilograms per farmer (Verhaegen 1969, p. 273). However, after 1960, cotton producers were badly hit by deteriorating economic conditions. In the Fizi Territory, where the output per acre was favorable, by December 1963 cotton production plummeted, and the income of the average farmer was less than half of its 1959 level. In 1959, the revenue from cotton per farmer was 5,500 francs ($777 in 2010 prices), but a few years later, 1962–1963, it was around 3,000 francs ($135). In 1963, total revenue from

Table 3.2 Production of Palm Oil (in metric tons)

	1958	1959	1960	1961	1962	1963	1964
Palm oil in bulk							
Kwilu	30,362	29,602	33,751	28,730	33,031	27,183	23,633
Total	143,765	158,613	158,576	142,064	153,396	159,363	126,321
Palm oil in barrels							
Kwilu	12,082	10,868	11,271	9,881	12,961	6,821	4,750
Total	35,585	34,638	27,271	22,559	22,419	14,913	9,825

Source: Data from Pierre Dupriez (1968), p. 655.

cotton was 50 million francs ($2.1 million in 2010 prices) compared with 123.84 million ($16.7 million in 2010 prices) in 1960.

Another cash crop was sugarcane. In 1958, the refinery of Kiliba in Sud-Kivu Province, Sucreries d'Afrique, produced 3,099 tons of sugar (Verhaegen 1969, p. 273), representing almost 18 percent of sugar produced by the Moerbeke Company in Lower Congo. In 1960, production in Fizi-Uvira rose to 13,800 tons but then dropped to 11,000 tons in 1962–1963, compared with 30,000 tons for the same period in Lower Congo. Finally, the minimum salary in Fizi-Uvira in 1962–1963 was among the lowest in Congo: 47 francs ($0.28) per day in Uvira and 49 francs ($0.31) in Fizi, compared with the national average of $1 in 1960 and $0.81 (133 francs) in 1963.

To these nominal losses must be added the declining buying power of Congolese currency, which was devalued in 1961 and 1963. Thus, the Congolese franc dropped from $1 = 50 francs in June 1960 to $1 = 160 francs by December 1963. By the end of 1963, prices of imported manufactured goods soared in the local markets. Most small farmers could not afford to buy agricultural inputs because inflation kept their average income far below what it had been a year earlier. In sum, living in the countryside left citizens without hope.

Another reference point was the performance of political leaders compared with the former colonial ruler. The adage that "those were salad days" is quite common in all cultures. For the masses, salad days did not mean a resurrection of the colonial period. The masses had paid the colonial taxes, supplied the forced labor to build the roads, worked the mines, and sold the crops they were forced to grow at well below market prices. Their land was expropriated to make room for new towns, roads, plantations, and mines. Although the colonial system was harsh and oppressive, it started getting better in the early 1950s when jobs were plentiful, roads were kept in good repair, bureaucracies were reliable, local hospitals possessed both adequate personnel and medical supplies, and schools had desks and chalk (Fox, de Craemer, and Ribeaucourt 1965). As noted in Chapter 1, the Belgian Congo had the best medical infrastructure in Africa and relatively fast economic growth after World War II. Independence was not an ideal abstract for the masses, who specifically wanted a free society, freedom from injustice, improved standards of living, better housing, and decent prices for crops. However, after independence, life got worse, and the vision of a brighter future quickly evaporated.

The empty promises politicians made in early 1960 compounded the masses' disappointments. The following illustrates the PSA political campaign promises in June 1960 in Kwilu (Weiss 1967, p. 9):

- Complete elimination of unemployment and work for all
- Expansion of school facilities, especially in rural areas, and elimination of all school fees for primary and secondary schools
- Salary increases for everybody

• Improved housing in rural areas
• Free medical care for all nonwage earners
• Mechanization of peasant agriculture and indexed prices for peasant crops
• A lifestyle modeled on that of the Belgian rulers

These aims were said to be within reach on 30 June 1960, when the country became independent, but independence brought only misery. Even the embryonic welfare apparatus of the terminal colonial state atrophied. This diminished well-being opened an enormous abyss between promise and performance, past and present.

The second dimension of deprivation is social stratification, or vertical inequality. This dimension refers to the rapid development of huge differences in economic rewards between those who are able to move into powerful positions and those who lack those opportunities. If citizens view the gap as widening, not narrowing, this inequality is likely to be a source of resentment and an agent of mobilization.

Table 3.3 Evolution of Salaries of Political Elites (in Congolese francs [CF])

	Salaries		Representation Premium	
	1960	1964	1960	1964
National Government				
President	1,200,000	—	200,000	—
Prime minister	700,000	650,000	300,000	360,000
Vice PM	650,000	600,000	200,000	300,000
Other ministers	600,000	550,000	100,000	300,000
(Foreign affairs)			300,000	
State secretaries	550,000	500,000	70,000	240,000
& state ministers				
Presidents (Houses)	650,000	540,000	200,000	
Other MPs	300,000	360,000		
Chief of staff	350,000			
(government)				
Provincial Government				
President		550,000		300,000
Vice president		500,000		220,000
Members		475,000		210,000
President assembly		450,000		
VP assembly		375,000		
Assembly secretary		335,000		
MPs assembly		300,000		

Sources: For 1960, see Gérard-Libois and Verhaegen (1963), p. 647; for 1964, refer to Gérard-Libois and Van Lierde (1965), p. 430.
Note: For 1960, $1 = 50 CF; for 1964, $1 = 160 CF.

Until the eve of independence, the colonial civil service maintained two different reward systems. Salaries of Europeans were ten times Africans' salaries. However, the salaries of Congolese petty functionaries were at a modest level not far removed from the wage levels of the average urban worker (Young 1965). Prior to 1960, African society was thus stratified by prestige and education, not by large disparities in wealth or power. The highest prestige occupations, in both the public and private sectors, were clerical positions, drawing an average annual salary of $900 in 1959, or $6,359 in 2010 prices (Sklar 1967, pp. 1–11).

The flight of Belgian functionaries and army officers in 1960 suddenly opened up 5,900 upper-level positions in the administration, 3,681 in the middle level, and 1,000 officer positions in the army.[5] Moreover, some 1,500 highly paid "political" positions were created in 1960 at the central and provincial levels. Former clerks, teachers, and noncommissioned officers were well positioned for sharp increases in pay. They enjoyed a swift vertical ascent up the scale, from a clerical position in 1959, drawing an average annual salary of 45,000 francs ($6,359 in 2010 prices), to a rank earning perhaps twenty times that salary in 1960. Table 3.3 offers a general picture of the pattern of salary increases from independence to the period of the rebellions. By 1963, this salary gap was clear to all. Roughly some 45,000 citizens, representing less than 1 percent of the economically active population, or less than 18 percent of salaried workers, benefited materially from independence. Table 3.4 highlights the evolution of the real wages of those who were not able to move into political positions. By December 1963, the minimum real wage had lost 90 percent of its 1960 value.

Added to the decline in real minimum wage was increased unemployment, which rose from 29 percent in early 1960 to 68 percent in early 1962 (Raymaekers 1964, pp. 35–47). Unemployment was also affected by a trend toward mechanizing industry. Moreover, government-imposed minimum nominal wage rates had risen to a point where industries could not afford to employ a superabundance of unskilled hands. Pay arrears became a general pattern in the provinces, especially in the lower ranks of the administration. By the time of the two rebellions, salary arrears of up to two years were quite common in the countryside. For example, some 20,000 primary school teachers received no salary in 1962 and 1963 for periods ranging from nine to twenty-one months, while the politico-administrative elite were paid regularly and consumed more than 30 percent of the budget (Mabusa 1966, p. 24).

Conspicuous consumption among the newly wealthy also added to the rapid polarization between socioeconomic strata. The opulent lifestyle of the colonial establishment served as a reference point for the administrative bourgeoisie. Politicians and civil servants inherited the housing attached to ranking positions in the state hierarchy and became removed from the humbler strata by those devices that had once served to preserve the segregated character of colonial society (Young 1970). The postcolonial society became segregated, not by

Table 3.4 Evolution of Nominal and Real Minimum Wage

	1959	1960	May 1963	Dec. 1963	1964	1965
Minimum						
nominal wage (CF)	41.37	50.80	50.80	133.00	133.00	133.00
Real wage (CF)	41.37	50.80	25.37	64.55	37.31	31.28
Real wage ($)	1.00	1.00	0.15	0.10	0.01	0.005

Source: Data from Gerard Dupriez (1968), pp. 392–395.

race, but along income lines between former clerks, now the new "whites," and the rest of society.

The third dimension of grievance or social inequality is horizontal and runs across diverse cultural groups (see Stewart 2010). In Kwilu, the Pende and Mbunda perceived provincial politics as providing the Mbala and Ngongo groups with privileged access. Most intriguing was that the Pende and Mbala groups were not historical enemies whose endemic strife had only been temporarily halted by the enforced truce of colonial rule. No chronicler who visited the area in the nineteenth century ever mentioned any conflict between the two groups (Ndaywel 1997). The same goes for the Mbala and Mbunda. Ambitious young men of these groups sought clerical jobs in Kikwit or Leopoldville before independence and competed for places in the district secondary schools without animosity. However, one group, the Mbala, had more évolués than the other two groups, Pende and Mbunda. After Belgium disappeared from political prominence in June 1960, the Pende/Mbunda became aware that they had fewer educated sons to fill the administrative positions vacated by Belgians than did the Mbala. They also perceived the provincial government as dominated by the Mbala. Although rural Mbala and Ngongo shared the same material grievances with the Pende/Mbunda, they did not follow Mulele's banner because they viewed the political system as their own. In such a context, ethnic identity becomes associated with social class. Ethnicity and class overlap, creating a volatile political setting. Thus, political power was with the Mbala, while exclusion from power characterized the Pende-Mbunda group.

The eastern rebellion also reflects this perception of horizontal inequality across ethnic groups, which helps explain the onset of the rebellion. Despite the complexity of the eastern rebellion, which included many ethnic groups and affected a wide area, its historical background reveals the importance of the ethnic thread in the rebellion texture. Two clusters of ethnic affinities stand out in the eastern rebellion. First, the Fulero-Bembe and the Kusu-Tetela clusters supported the rebellion because they felt excluded from provincial politics dominated by the Shi and Rega. The Shi-Rega groups resisted the rebellion because they thought its symbols represented the Kusu-Tetela group. Real grievances could not break these ethnic ties.

In general, among the masses was a sense of relative deprivation with a concomitant disappointment in how political promises failed to generate solutions to economic problems. Moreover, those who were most deprived economically saw the gap between rich and poor widening dramatically. Initially, those who were most deprived saw ethnicity as the basis for this economic disparity, and, in both rebellions, common interests gave way to kinship ties.

However, a sense of deprivation is not a sufficient factor to unleash violence. Political entrepreneurs have to provide incentives to the masses to mobilize them. A number of incentives, such as ideology, political parties, and the power of dawa, indicates that the masses were convinced that the two rebellions were legitimate struggles.

Overcoming collective action I: Ideology and party. Mulele's ideology was based on the fact that, in Congo, the two main classes were the capitalists and the impoverished masses (Verhaegen 1969, pp. 129–130). Reduced to its simplest terms, "Mulelism" argued that the central government incarnated the national bourgeoisie, definitively corrupt by its alliance with imperialist forces represented by Belgium and the United States. His conception of a new society was a "gigantic village, composed of smaller villages where people will recover their own authentic identity, the satisfaction of all their material needs, justice, creative activity, and joy in working the soil in common" (Fox, de Craemer, and Ribeaucourt 1965, p. 19). Mulele set up a process to evaluate the level of commitment of potential recruits, using Marxist-Leninist-Maoist thought. He opened ideological camps to indoctrinate new recruits to the rebel movement and to teach them Marxism. By replacing the working class as a revolutionary force with a view extolling the pristine virtues of the village, Mulele made his Marxism intelligible to the rural youth.

The Marxist-Leninist contribution to the rhetoric of the eastern rebellion was much more fragmentary. The eastern rebellion relied on the MNC/L to mobilize a heterogeneous following. The MNC/L had to approve any new recruits to the rebel cause. The radical political thought—a vague nationalism epitomized by Lumumbism in 1960—was enough to attract followers in late 1963. An antibourgeois or antigovernment rhetoric was the leitmotif; the ruling political and administrative class was accused of being part of the old conservative party (the PNP) and an enemy of the people. The MNC/L recruited most members of the rebel army, and it was the sole avenue to belong to the simba (Verhaegen 1969, pp. 483–484).

Overcoming collective action II: Dawa. Grievance alone is not sufficient to incite rebellion. Potential recruits must believe that they will gain something from victory and will not be open targets marching to their death. The most important incentive that made potential recruits believe in victory and in an almost "cost free" rebellion was the role of dawa (traditional medicine). The underlying belief in dawa was that bullets would be transformed into raindrops. The belief that the overwhelmingly larger governmental forces could be defeated by dawa was enough to mobilize thousands of citizens to fight. The rebels held the best units of the national army at bay, and the army chief of staff, Eugène Ebeya, was even killed by a poisoned arrow in Kwilu (Gérard-Libois and Van Lierde 1965, p. 20). The spectacular success of Mulele partisans in Kwilu, which pitted rebels with spears, machetes, and bows and arrows against the firearms of government forces, was convincing evidence of the effectiveness of dawa. In the east, the Fulero and Bembe warriors rooted out two Congolese army battalions with only their spears, machetes, and a handful of firearms.

The role of magic or war charms is not new in Congo. Going back to colonial times, a miracle worker, Epikilipikili, confronted the CFS in 1904 using a war charm believed to protect against all sorts of evil and capable of rendering its bearers immune to army bullets (*Congo* 1921). The Pende also used a charm in the 1931 revolt against the colonial administration (Gize 1973), and war charms were used in the northern Katanga insurrection, in which rebel leaders used magic as a mechanism to control followers (Chapter 2).

These cases of traditional cosmology were similar, but what made the use of dawa in the two rebellions so different from previous cases was that the power of magic was standardized. When the simba were recruited, they went through an elaborate and mysterious initiation, or "baptism," consisting of three steps (Verhaegen 1969, pp. 554–560). First was the laying on of hands to transmit invulnerability from the supernatural domain to the simba through the agency of a specialist in wizardry. The second part of the ritual was the use of a magic powder prepared by a witch doctor, who made small incisions in the combatant's forehead and inserted the dawa, with ingredients known only to the doctor. Third, the witch doctor sprinkled magic cold water on the back and abdomen of new recruits who kept repeating "Mulele Mai, Mulele Mai" (Bullets! It's water! Mulele protects us) to become invulnerable. This third step was the most important because it involved magic water that was assumed to transform bullets into raindrops. This was not ordinary water but pure water into which were mixed undisclosed plant roots, tree barks, leaves, pieces of animal skins, and other ingredients chosen according to a magic recipe known only to the witch doctors. Belief in the supernatural can be useful when a man with a spear, machete, or bow and arrows must maintain his courage against an army with machine guns. Mulele reportedly demonstrated the power of his magic by firing at himself. Soumialot, the organizer of the eastern rebellion, also conducted such demonstrations. Of course, the two social engineers were firing at themselves with blank cartridges or with rounds that had nearly all the power removed (Anderson, von der Mehden, and Young 1974, p. 154). But the masses believed them. Thus, popular acceptance reinforced the power of dawa. Even in the West, soldiers wear good luck charms to secure divine intervention and protect them from the path of a bullet.

The other aspect of the simba's ceremony was to live according to a strict code of conduct by following a number of specific sets of taboos (Verhaegen

1969, pp. 573–575). The first set of taboos was designed to keep the simba pure—for example, by avoiding sex, which was intended to instill discipline and minimize rapes. The second set of taboos relates to military tactics, including the following: neither move backward during battle nor run away; neither turn the head sideways nor make a half turn; neither pass on the left side of a civilian nor let him follow you; avoid stealing; and remain in the road by avoiding the bush when attacking the enemy. The final two prohibitions were associated with water and food.[6] All these strict rules of conduct instilled discipline and forced the simba to behave according to social norms by respecting communities, women, and private property.

Diffusion and Duration of Rebellions

The Kwilu and eastern rebellions differed in their geographical diffusion. While the former was confined to Idiofa and Ngungu territories, the latter spread from Fizi and Uvira to all directions like wildfire on a hot, dry summer day—devastating but quickly over. What made such a spread possible, and why did it vanish so quickly? Once the eastern rebellion had broken out in the east, the most interesting aspect was not why it had started but rather the mobilizing effect it had to appeal to so many citizens. Compared with the early cases of secessions, a number of factors made the two rebellions quite short.

From 1960 to 1963, Congo could be said to fall into two zones: a zone of despair and one of prosperity. The former embraced the rebellions, while the latter opposed them. Areas included in the zone of prosperity were mining and manufacturing areas in South Katanga Province, Leopoldville, and Kongo Central. Eastern Congo, except South Katanga and most parts of today's Bandundu and Equateur Provinces, were among the zones of despair. In a broader sense, there were marked disparities in well-being between the two zones. In the zone of despair, rebel leaders were political investors who attempted to redress grievances for a better tomorrow. In this sense, economic literature expects a civil war to be longer. In the zone of prosperity, however, because people viewed the rebellions as mistakes and felt threatened, they were immune to rebel solicitations. The duration of both rebellions thus depended on these two contradictory regional perceptions. The diffusion and duration of the rebellions were the result of political events such as ethnic affinities and symbols, the continuing belief in the power of magic, the use of terror, and foreign intervention.

Ethnic affinities and symbols. The literature on civil wars shows how baffling the role of ethnicity remains. However, the diffusion of the eastern rebellion depended upon local populations finding a basis of identity within the rebellion's message. The two most important factors that interacted with ethnic labels were political parties and heroes. First, the rallying political party was the MNC/L, which provided the Fulero with a voice for their political demands against a chieftaincy considered colonial and anachronistic. The party promised liberation from the yoke of oppression and offered a mechanism by which the rural population related to the rebellion.

The role of heroes, Mulele and Lumumba, is the second factor and provides its own contradiction (Young 1970). Mulele was a luminous living legend and a new entry in the symbolic lexicon. His personality was invested with legendary attributes only after the Mulelist ideology camps exploded into view at the beginning of 1964. In Kwilu, he was a charismatic guerrilla leader, with prophetic and superhuman qualities. However, other groups in Kwilu, especially the Mbala and Ngongo groups, opposed the rebellion because they controlled the provincial government and felt threatened by Mulele.

Although both Lumumba and Mulele were heroes in the eastern rebellion, they operated in somewhat different fashions (Young 1970). Lumumba was the hero and martyr who confronted imperialism head on and died to give the people of Congo a better life. He became the human incarnation of the inchoate hopes and aspirations of the first independence (Young 1970). The MNC/L cards issued in 1964 even contained a red spot, symbolic of the blood of this patron saint (Verhaegen 1969). On the other hand, Mulele was less a person than an omnipotent force. Rebel forces marching into battle chanted "Mulele Mai! Mulele Mai!" The chant reinforced the potency of the ritual immunizations provided for the troops by the unit witch doctor with the terrible powers of the man-spirit, Mulele. For example, when Gbenye reached the eastern Congo in August 1964 and ordered the rebel army to chant "Lumumba Mai!" rather than invoke Mulele, his order was not fully executed, presumably because of the specific symbolic properties that the name of Mulele came to incorporate, even though as a real person, he was wholly unknown in eastern Congo (Verhaegen 1969).

Despite these unifying symbols, an element of continuity, ethnic fractionalization, increased the cost of the rebellion. For the Kusu-Tetela groups, the eastern rebellion began in the name of Lumumba; was led by their army; supported by their party, the MNC/L; and reinforced by "their magic and witch doctors" (Anderson, von der Mehden, and Young 1974, p. 162). However, not all the Tetela in Sankuru (Kasai Province), as a monolithic entity, accepted rebel symbols, although the eastern rebellion was identified with the Kusu-Tetela.

Local politics in Sankuru had catalyzed a division between the Tetela Eswa and the Tetela Ekonda (Turner 1973, pp. 309–354). The Eswa, who lived in savannas, had become somewhat acculturated because of their contact with the Afro-Arabs in the nineteenth century and were thus involved in the trading system of the Zanzibari. The Ekonda were forest dwellers who occupied a more inaccessible area where opportunities for socioeconomic change were fewer than for the other Tetela group. More specifically, the Eswa group occupied most administrative and political positions in Sankuru. By 1963, bitterness between the two clans reached the point where a large part of the principal town of Lodja was burned by the Ekonda. The legacy of this conflict may have precluded a unified response to rebellion, despite identification with all the symbols of Lumumba and MNC/L. Thus, rebel operations in Sankuru were ephemeral and superficial. Here, the modernized subgroup embraced the rebellion, while the less advanced subgroup opposed it, perhaps in part because of its exclusion from modernity. This is a paradox because the rebellion intended to improve the livelihood of the least modernized group in Congo.

At the provincial level, the same groups that started the rebellion in the countryside, the Bembe-Zimba, later opposed the Kusu-Tetela. From the start, the former were involved in the eastern rebellion because they strongly believed that they were the principal victims of previous administrations. They rallied to the rebellion and were the most courageous combatants of the rebel army. However, when the rebellion reached Kindu, the capital of Maniema, the Bembe and Zimba felt that "their rebellion" was hijacked by an urban Kusu-Tetela elite. Out of frustration based on a collective conflict of interest and competition over power, the Bembe and Zimba opposed the Kusu-Tetela elite. Again, ethnic relationships were trumped by exclusion.

The second type of opposition came from groups for whom the rebel symbols were inimical. Most Kongo in western Congo recalled Lumumba as an adversary, not a hero. Many of the same grievances of eastern social groups and the Mbunda-Pende groups also existed among the Kongo. However, the Kwilu rebellion did not draw them because the rebel antigovernment feeling was tempered among the Kongo. Many eminent Kongo occupied positions of authority in the central government, starting with President Kasavubu. The rural Kongo may have been cruelly disappointed by the system, but it was still their system.

When the rebels left the Lumumbist zone, reaching the Ubangi district in Equateur, they encountered sharp resistance (Verhaegen 1969). A rebel push toward central Kasai was also abandoned because passing through the territory of the Luba-Kasai could provoke violence; Lumumba, after all, collaborated with the Lulua in June 1960 to exclude the MNC-Kalonji from provincial power (Chapter 2). Furthermore, the Luba held Lumumba responsible for their expulsion from the areas into which they had expanded during the colonial period. Finally, southern Katanga populations identified more closely with the Tshombe regime in Leopoldville than with the Gbenye government in Stanleyville. The Tshombe regime was their regime, much as Kasavubu's regime belonged to the Kongo.

Three other ethnic groups feared domination and fought the eastern rebellion: the Shi, Rega, and Tutsi of Mulenge (now Banyamulenge). The Shi resisted the rebel forces because they feared a political leadership headed by the Kusu and Tetela. Their fear echoed the 1960–1961 politics after the Stanleyville government removed provincial president Jean Miruho, a Shi, and most Shi (except Chief Albert Kabare) from power and installed a new government dominated by the Kusu under Andrien Omari. The Shi became restive under what they called Kusu domination during the Omari regime in early 1961. For the Shi, the rebel column was an invasion of Kusu-Tetela from Maniema. The result was strong opposition to rebel forces, which appeared to halt the rebels' advance and even to weaken it.

The Rega were also strongly opposed to the rebellion, not because of its symbols, but because of a long history of hostility dating back to the late nineteenth century during the caravan period. The Kusu-Tetela dominated the Zanzibari slave trade as Arab auxiliaries, and one of their targets was the Rega. Thus, a history of hatred shaped by memories of oppression was critical in the Rega's decision to oppose the eastern rebellion. However, the Rwandan Tutsi refugees, who had been in Kivu Central (see Map 1.1) since the fall of the Rwandan monarchy in 1961, rallied to the cause of the rebellion because rebel leaders Gaston Soumialot and Laurent Kabila promised to help them return to Rwanda and reinstate Mwami Kigeri V.

On the other hand, the Tutsi of Mulenge (now Banyamulenge) opposed the rebellion's socialist ideology and wanted to protect their cattle from being taken from them. They were accused of being "traitors to the Congolese cause" by the Fulero, Vira, and Bembe, who supported the rebellion (Verhaegen 1969; Willame 1997). Their support of the government helped defeat the rebellion in Sud-Kivu. After the rebellion, President Mobutu confirmed the traditional power of these Tutsi for the Kamanyola area and hills of Itombwe. Other local populations saw this as government compensation for the allegiance of the Tutsi of Mulenge to the central government during the rebellion. This affiliation made them "enemies" of the eastern rebellion and enemies of natives or autochthons.

Power of dawa. Any analysis of the spread and duration of the eastern rebellion cannot overlook the power of dawa that made the simba invulnerable to bullets. The use of dawa was systematized and sanctioned by a range of taboos, any of which had clear social control functions. By screaming "Mulele Mai," the simba attacked and unleashed the magic, sure of their invulnerability. Even though they were killed, the idea that they would resurrect three days later made them even more courageous (Verhaegen 1969, p. 328). The effectiveness of dawa not only depended on its acceptance by the population and the simba but also to a great extent its acceptance by the rebellion's first enemy, the regular army. The sight of the simba walking straight at regular troops was so terrifying that soldiers usually turned on their heels. Soldiers' accounts are illustrative: "you emptied your machine gun at them, but bullets never touched them," or, in Lingala, "obeta ye masasi, ezua ye te."[7]

Another tactic linked to invulnerability was that rebels always attacked a town after announcing their arrival and time of attack, usually by making noises with their drums and other materials (Verhaegen 1969). This created panic among soldiers who feared for their lives and had only one thought: to escape these "invincible warriors." The account of an engagement along the Kabambare-Kasongo road in July 1964 is a prototype of national-popular army combat:

The horde continued to advance, inexorably, like the tentacle of an octopus sliding toward a man to seize and strangle him. The soldiers fired, without interruption. Defying the bullets, the "mulele" came toward them, chanting at the top of their lungs: Mulele-Mai Mulele-Mai! Mulele. . . . Our gendarmes began to doubt the effectiveness of their weapons. The distance diminished: 200 meters . . . 150 . . . and fear built up in our ranks. . . . At their waist hung all sorts of leaves: banana or palm fronds. These leaves concealed their shorts. Branches placed here and there in their belt gave them an even more savage and ferocious appearance. Their chests were covered with animal skins. . . . As they marched, their headdress, made of feathers and skins, shook like the mane of a lion. At their neck and waist, oscillating at the cadence of their step, were diverse amulets and packets of "dawa.". . . The horde approached, like a sinister monster. They were now only 100 meters, very close. A shiver of fear ran through the ranks of the soldiers. Then suddenly, the firing stopped, with only the chants of the rebels breaking the silence. A moment of hesitation, and the same idea came like a flash to the mind of all our gendarmes: "They are invulnerable . . . invulnerable. . . . Run for your lives!" The order was not given, but it was executed. . . . The simba found it beneath their dignity to pursue. (Verhaegen 1969 cited in Young 1970, p. 987)

This description of magic is a vivid example of the psychological effect of the supernatural. The simba advanced under enemy fire without caring if their comrades were shot dead around them. While facing predictable enemy resistance, they never used any military tactics to avoid being killed. As pointed out earlier, their taboos constrained them to advance in open fields without the possibility of dispersing and remain in the road by avoiding the bush when attacking the enemy. Many simba attacked with just spears, using the force of their belief in magic and the supernatural as a psychological weapon that terrorized governmental forces and enhanced the myth of the simba's invulnerability. One element of the simba's conviction was the widespread use of hemp as part of their diet. This is the foundation of stories about simba invulnerability (Verhaegen 1969, pp. 593–595).

Just as the dawa helped the eastern rebellion spread like wildfire, it was also self-defeating because it contained the seeds of its own failure. The continued potency of dawa protection depended upon observing a number of taboos, which were also related to the control and discipline of the popular army. However, the simba could not always follow them. If they broke these rules, the power of the baptism and dawa was lost and could only be regained by confession, rebaptism, and the purchase of a new dawa. Thus, failure to follow the taboos provides an explanation for a reasonable number of failures in the eastern rebellion.

More important was the fact that other ethnic groups, such as the Rega, also developed their own dawa. The result was to boost the morale of government soldiers, who were then able to stop the rebels' advance. Several counterattacks came from the mining center of Kamitunga where the Rega warriors, along with one unit of the ANC from Bukavu, were able to force thousands of rebels to retreat. When the rebellion was in decline, the national army became more effective because rebels' dawa lost its credibility.

The use of terror and external intervention. The spread of the eastern rebellion was concomitant with massacres that occurred immediately after a town fell into rebels' hands. When rebel forces captured an area, important opponents, such as public officials and leaders of opposition political parties, were handed over to the simba either by the local youths or by militant woman groups. The rebels used two types of violence (Verhaegen 1969, pp. 599–632). The first included public executions of government officials. This form of terror was liberating because the regime was perceived to be either oppressive or against the people. The police, the military, and a judicial system that, since 1960, had protected the interests of a corrupt leadership were all targets of terror. The second type of terror was against people in specific functions. Here secret executions represented specific and opportunistic violence that focused on killing individuals associated with the incumbent government to allow rebel administrators to occupy vacant positions of authority.

Later in the eastern rebellion, rebels took no prisoners, massacring whole villages suspected of collaborating with the government. For example, the rebels viewed the Rega as enemies of the people, so any Rega who had been a member of the previous administration was summarily executed. However, violence toward populations that were favorable to rebels was minimal. In Kindu, many Kusu who had worked for the ancient regime were maintained in their positions because the Kusu favored the eastern rebellion. In sum, increasing terror against people suspected of collaborating with the national army resulted in declining popular support of the rebellion at the local level.

Finally, the West was critical in ending the eastern rebellion. Engineered by Belgium and the United States, President Kasavubu appointed Tshombe as prime minister in mid-1964 to quell the rebellions. The nomination of Tshombe after he had drawn Congo into secession and almost divided Congo was unimaginable for many observers (Gibbs 1991, pp. 152–156). Regardless of his role in the Katanga secession, Tshombe called in his former Katanga Gendarmerie, which had fought during the secession. By July 1964, the former Katanga soldiers numbered some 16,800 (Gérard-Libois and Van Lierde 1965, p. 352). Tshombe also hired mercenaries to strengthen the flagging army. Mike Hoare was in charge of recruiting mercenaries when he met with Tshombe, Minister of Interior Godefroid Munongo, and Major General Joseph Mobutu in August 1964. Hoare was one of the commanding officers of the mercenary unit during the Katanga secession. In 1961, he was commissioned to bring twenty trucks from Lubumbashi to Nyunzu, but en route these trucks disappeared without a trace (Gérard-Libois and Verhaegen 1969, p. 352). Mobutu gave Hoare direct orders (Hoare 1967, p. 29):

• A company of 200 men must arrive immediately at Kamina: MISSION – Retake Manono, Albertville, Fizi, Uvira;
• 300 volunteers should be formed into six platoons for the six mobile groups now in creation;

• 500 volunteers in company with elements of the ANC must retake Stanleyville immediately.

On 27 August 1964, the United States provided Congo four C-130s, three B-26 jet bombers, ten C-47s, ten H-21 heavy-duty helicopters, seven T-28s fighter airplanes, seventy jeeps, and 250 trucks (Weissman 1978, pp. 391–392). In mid-August, some fifty paratroopers and fifty-six members of the US army were in Congo to maintain the C-130s. To fly the T-28s, the Central Intelligence Agency (CIA) hired US pilots (mostly anti-Castro Cubans), who had a one-year contract with the Congolese government (Lefever and Joshua 1966, p. 131). Among other Americans operating in Congo, twenty were advisers training the Congolese to use US military equipment. On the Belgian side, as of December 1964, there were some 232 army officers and noncommissioned officers as well as 158 air force troops (Gérard-Libois and Van Lierde 1965, p. 360). The United States was thus instrumental in defeating the eastern rebellion, especially given its interpretation of the CNL as a Chinese-supported leftist movement trying to spread communism in Central Africa. The widespread belief in extensive Chinese influence in Stanleyville, which was later shown to be exaggerated, was probably sufficient reason for the United States to support a policy of destroying the eastern rebellion at all costs.

The central government was able to counter the eastern rebellion effectively thanks to US logistical support, Belgian military aid, government-hired mercenaries, and the former Katanga gendarmes. As the military strength of the rebellion began to fail, its top leaders sought to use Europeans and Americans as hostages in the rebel-held territory to stop government troops and mercenaries. The hostage policy led to a Belgian-US parachute operation in Stanleyville and Paulis (in northeastern Congo), code named "Dragon Rouge" (Hoare 1967). This operation began at dawn on 24 November 1964 in Stanleyville, and, on the same day, the first national army-mercenary column reached Kisangani. Some 2,000 hostages, mostly Belgians and Americans, were evacuated. Five days later, the Belgian paratroopers were withdrawn from Congo. The loss of Stanleyville as the capital seat of the revolutionary government was a mortal blow to the eastern rebellion because it forced its leaders into exile.

The indignation in many African states at the Belgian-US intervention translated into a flow of military supplies via Sudan, Uganda, and Tanzania to help the rebels regain their position. However, without central direction, the rebellion shriveled into localized pockets of resistance. The profoundly altered perspectives of the insurgents eliminated any prospect of regaining momentum. After taking Stanleyville, mercenary units focused on cutting rebel supply lines from Sudan, Uganda, and Tanzania (Verhaegen 1969). By mid-1966, the eastern rebellion was defeated because its three most important leaders—Gbenye, Soumialot, and Olenga—were in exile. The few remaining rebel pockets provided no major challenge to the central government.

Conflict Resolution and Postconflict Management

The diffusion and duration of the Kwilu and eastern rebellions should not over-shadow the efforts at managing them. In the second half of 1964, the Tshombe administration attempted to end the rebellions through mediations. Before arriving in Congo from Europe, where he was in exile, Tshombe made several contacts with rebel leaders to end the civil war. First, he nominated André Lubaya, a member of the CNL, to his government as minister of health. Second, on 15 July 1964, he freed Gizenga, who had been in prison for less than three years, to satisfy one of the rebels' demands. In an attempt to initiate negotiations and find common ground, Tshombe made several contacts with rebel leaders. However, the leaders of the eastern rebellion were so disorganized that he realized that the best strategy was a military one.

The two rebellions also had a number of consequences. The victory of the central government over the two popularly supported rebellions inevitably involved moving against a population, not just an enemy military force. Because mercenaries and the Congolese army were known for their unscrupulousness, uncounted civilians were killed as the eastern rebellion was pushed back. Moreover, because no side took prisoners, countless executions destroyed the social networks so important to building communities. More specifically, the rebels killed some 30,000 to 40,000 public servants and intellectuals accused of being pro-West, while mercenaries and government forces massacred more than 15,000 suspected rebels and their sympathizers (Verhaegen 1969). Accounts of the eastern rebellion also revealed a large number of rapes in rebel-controlled areas in late 1964 and during 1965.

Unlike previous wars, the two rebellions used more than 25,000 child soldiers (Verhaegen 1969). Many traumatized children never received psychological or material help to cope with their situation. Even children who experienced severe physical and psychological abuse and witnessed acts of violence, particularly against their family members, were never assisted. Even worse, women were victims of rape and other abuses. These victims were basically ignored by the international community, partly because they were not socially or politically visible. Unlike the early secessions, the two rebellions shattered traditional structures. In 1960–1961, chiefs regained some of their status because politicians had almost no authority over rural areas. The need for rural votes made politicians rally the chiefs to the cause of independence. The rebellions, however, destroyed many of the symbols of traditional structures because they were associated with a corrupt government. By late 1966, the rural area was deprived of both administrative and traditional authorities. It was a Hobbesian world in search of a Leviathan to impose order and rule of law.

One pacification technique that Mobutu used astutely after he took power in late 1965 to build his new state was to bring together those who fought in the rebellions and those who opposed them. Although he condemned the rebellions, he hailed Lumumba, who was the symbol of the rebellions, as a national hero.

On 1 July 1966, he changed the names of major cities from French to the local language. For example, Leopoldville and Stanleyville became Kinshasa and Kisangani, respectively. Katanga became Shaba.[8]

A few months earlier, on 6 April 1966, Mobutu reduced the number of provinces from twenty-one to twelve. By December 1967, that number was brought down to eight, not including the town of Kinshasa. The provinces became simple administrative entities under the central government, ending the decentralized system that had prevailed since 1962. Furthermore, the police became centralized and dependent on the central government. This unitarism was based on Mobutu's goal of muzzling any opposition from provincial authorities, who were sometimes difficult to control, given the distance between them and the capital city.

Because politicians used the youths to start civil wars, Mobutu decided to capture and include them in his reconstruction plan. He created the Corps des Volontaires de la République, or CVR. The leaders of this organization set forth three objectives: (1) national consciousness (C), (2) vigilance (V), and (3) the interest of the Congolese population in reconstruction (R) without distinction to ascriptive criteria. However, Mobutu's idea of mobilizing the youth was just a prelude to the institutionalization of one man's rule through a unique party system. In fact, after creating his political party in April 1966, the MPR, President Mobutu decided in mid-1967 to incorporate the CVR into the new party by creating the youth MPR (Jeunesse MPR). To consolidate his power further, Mobutu promulgated on 24 June 1967 a new constitution that installed a presidential unitary regime with a two-party system (Article 4, paragraph 2). However, this constitution was modified several times to personalize Mobutu's power. Because the international community abdicated any responsibility for reconstruction, Mobutu was able to reorganize the administration as he wished.

Another major reform was his organization of the army. The eastern rebellion may have had two sides, but four different armies participated: (1) the national army, (2) rebel troops, (3) mercenary units, and (4) Katangan gendarmes. Because the rebellions ended with government victory, rebel units were never demobilized. Integrating the last two groups, however, posed several problems for Mobutu. Although he could have given them a lump sum of money for their services and discharged them, Mobutu decided to reintegrate mercenary units into the regular army. The integration of former Katanga gendarmes raised the issue of their loyalty to the new regime because they first served under the seceded state of Katanga and later during the rebellions when Tshombe was prime minister. To disarm them could have posed a major security risk. Mobutu decided to let former Katanga gendarmes and mercenaries keep their own hierarchical system and autonomous communications networks. They thus constituted two sub-armies within the overall Congolese army. This lack of demobilization of combatants would pave the way toward a new round of civil wars.

Summary and Brief Discussion

Started in early 1964, the Kwilu and eastern rebellions no longer posed any major threat to the central government by mid-1966. Despite their differences, the two rebellions were similar in many respects. First, both rebellions relied heavily on traditional arms. Second was a similar reliance on terror. Third, the same iron discipline existed early in both rebellions among rebel warriors, imposing on rebel troops strict boundaries between them and noncombatants. Fourth, both rebellions appealed to rural masses because they were syncretic movements that combined traditional elements (the use of dawa) with completely modern ones (the military organization). Fifth, they both used symbols familiar to rural masses, such as Lumumba and MNC/L. The shining moment of the eastern rebellion was the installation of the revolutionary government under Gbenye in September 1964, which saw an effort by an older generation of politicians to assume authority and reassert social control over the forces unleashed by the rebellions.

The causes of the two rebellions appear to lie at two levels: elite and mass. At the elite level, the politics of exclusion was likely a critical juncture to trigger the two rebellions, similar to the early wars of secession carried out by federalists who felt either excluded or less well represented in the central or provincial administrations. Unlike the early cases of internal wars, the leaders of the rebellions were able to mobilize the masses to their cause because the masses perceived the rebellions as legitimate. As a consequence, the speeches of the excluded elites that emphasized such catch expressions as "new independence" and the removal of "a non-patriotic, corrupt and sold out to the West government" were only a platform to build a coalition of convenience that could later help these elites to reinsert in the political system, which they likely had no intention to change.

In fact, both rebellions did not deliver on their promise of achieving a "second independence." A paradoxical aspect of the two rebellions was that their leaders had no remedies for Congolese social reality, although they knew what was wrong. The only innovation was the further diminution of administrative capabilities, produced by the purge of intellectuals from public service and the massacre of others, the rupture of supply routes, and confusion resulting from multiple claimants to the various segments of authority. Thus, important as the issues were in rural areas, they were not solved because the two rebellions ended with government victory.

At the mass level, the two rebellions were wars of legitimacy to replace a corrupt and exploitative regime with a socialist one. From the beginning, the rebel movement had spontaneous and powerful popular support, especially from the regions that voted for the nationalist bloc in the 1960 elections and dreamed of Lumumba's vision of a free Congo that would provide the best life that he promised. Unlike previous wars of secession, the rebel movement in 1964 was a continuation of Lumumba nationalist political action. More specifically, the nationalist message appealed to young men and women who aspired to liberate themselves from anachronistic tribal institutions during a period of economic recession and to destroy a political order that gave them nothing but misery. The idea of a "second independence" was a simple and powerful message—a new social and political order beneficial to the masses.

A few elements of continuity and change similar to the early cases of civil war also help account for the masses' mobilization in 1964. First was territorial division within each province. Most colonial divisions that reflected particular ethnic groups and territories became the first ground for mobilizing the masses. Mulele was able to mobilize the Pende-Mbunda in his native Kwilu Province, and Soumialot did the same in Sud-Kivu. Second was an element of change that also explained early civil wars: state weakness that provided ample opportunity for the two rebellions.

The two rebellions also seemed to have many similarities with the two early insurrections in North Katanga and northwestern South Kasai but not with the Katanga and South Kasai secessions (discussed in Chapter 2). First, in the two rebellions and the two insurrections, the rural youth spontaneously participated in massive numbers, providing the most dynamic radical element of the rebel forces. Once the youth's dynamism was unleashed, the leadership lost control. Second, the two rebellions and the two insurrections intended to destroy traditional authority and its symbols. Although the rebels did not want to destroy the set of social privileges associated with the administrative function of traditional authorities, they targeted the function and its symbols, which in the rebels' eyes represented a repressive, anachronistic, and inefficient apparatus. A common feature with the two early insurrections was also the use of terror to create fear. Finally, dawa was used, much as it was in the North Katanga insurrection.

Unlike previous civil wars, the eastern rebellion, in particular, hinged on four structures that played a number of critical roles to connect the elites and the masses. First was the revolutionary government that proclaimed the Popular Republic of Congo in September 1964. It was shared by the revolutionary government headed by Gbenye and the Council of Elders as a government legislative component. The former represented the urban elite while the latter had rural roots. As expected, a conflict of interests emerged, which meant that the government itself comprised two antagonistic groups. The second component was the MNC/L, the unique nationalist party. Although it was supposed to be a unifying and inspirational component, the party could not serve this function because of political incompatibilities within the leadership of the eastern rebellion. Moreover, the MNC/L became a huge bureaucracy without any specific functions and with plethoric committees and divisions along ethnic lines, although the MNC/L intended to be a nationalist party. The third component was the new bureaucracy. Rather than being an entity of change to improve the masses' social well-being, it became concerned with promoting and filling vacant positions in the conquered territories.

Finally was the popular army. The principal body of the eastern rebellion because of its esprit de corps in early days of the rebellion, its principal instrument of cohesion was the use of dawa. The cohesion was possible because of the distance that was created between the army's members, the simba, and the people it intended to serve. However, this dichotomy was the first step to the army's demise. One major conclusion is that the defeat of the two rebellions by the government never solved the issues of contention—most notably, the political inclusion of the excluded elites.

Notes

1. The analysis of the two rebellions relies on the following, in alphabetical order: Coquery-Vidrovitch, Forest, and Weiss (1987); Fox, de Craemer, and Ribeaucourt (1965), pp. 78–109; Verhaegen (1969); and Young (1970), pp. 968–1011.

2. Dawa is a Swahili word meaning medicine or potion, but in the eastern Congo the term referred to supernatural curative and protective powers. See Verhaegen (1969).

3. Gizenga returned to Stanleyville in October 1961 to reconstitute his former government. However, this new tour de force was unsuccessful because General Victor Lundula left for Leopoldville, where, on 13 November 1961, he swore allegiance to the central government.

4. The two men were respectively secretary general of revolutionary armed forces and secretary-general of social affairs, youth and sports in the CNL/Gbenye. Soumialot was not a new figure, but a member of the provincial government of Kivu Maniema in charge of justice in the Andrien Omari cabinet in February 1961.

5. Africans already occupied 759 of the 4,440 positions in the middle level. See Gérard Dupriez (1968), pp. 340–341.

6. With water, taboos included avoiding cold showers, working under rain, crossing a river on foot, cutting hair or nails, and even not combing hair. There were also taboos related to food and so forth. See Verhaegen (1969).

7. This is my recollection of soldiers' accounts of rebel warriors in 1964.

8. For other changes, refer to Kisangani and Bobb (2010), pp. xxvii–xxviii.

4

From Mutinies to Invasions

As the eastern rebellion was winding down, General Mobutu took power in a bloodless military coup d'état on 24 November 1965. As he began consolidating his power, the Baka Regiment, all former Katangan gendarmes under Colonel Ferdinand Tshipola, mutinied on 24 July 1966 in Kisangani. The first day of the clash between the ANC and the mutineers resulted in the death of the commander of the Fifth Mechanical Brigade, Colonel Ferdinand Tshatshi, and hundreds of soldiers. After the mutineers controlled a large portion of the town, they declared victory and the imminent return to power of former Prime Minister Tshombe from exile in Spain (Garrison 1966, A4). The ANC, which included both regular troops and white mercenaries, counterattacked and defeated the mutineers several weeks later.

Less than a year after the mutiny of the Baka Regiment, a number of mercenaries and former Katangan gendarmes mutinied in Kisangani on 5 July 1967. For five months, the national army could not crush the mutiny. On 5 November 1967, the group crossed the border to Rwanda as the ANC was gaining ground over the mutineers. The mercenaries' mutiny marked the first period in the tumultuous history of Congo in the 1960s. Both mutinies qualify as civil wars because they involve a rebel group against government forces, resulting in at least 1,000 deaths and more than 2,000 internally displaced citizens in the first three months of the conflicts.

Almost ten years after the mercenaries' mutiny, the FLNC, composed of Congolese who had received sanctuary in Angola, invaded South Katanga on 8 March 1977. The Mobutu regime was rescued by Moroccan troops. The French government provided military transport planes so that Morocco could airlift troops and materials to Katanga. After eighty days, the FLNC retreated to Angola but attacked again on 11 May 1978. Twenty-three days later, French paratroopers drove the invaders out, while Belgian troops evacuated some 2,500 Europeans from Kolwezi. The US role was limited to providing air transport and materials during the French paratroopers' drop. These two invasions by the FLNC are known as Shaba I and Shaba II because Shaba was the name of the

Katanga Province under Mobutu. Although shorter, Shaba II resulted in more casualties than Shaba I. Thus, an invasion qualifies as a civil war if it involves an armed violation of territorial integrity by natives having sanctuary in neighboring countries and resulting in 1,000 deaths and 2,000 internally displaced persons.

This chapter analyzes these four cases of internal wars as the sequel to the Katanga secession because the "rebels" were part of the secessionist army of Katanga. Like the ghost of Banquo, the specter of Tshombe hovered over this second wave of civil wars in Congo.

Mutiny of the Baka Regiment

Background of the Mutiny

On 30 June 1960, the DRC became independent, and ten days later, Katanga Province seceded, with Tshombe as its president. As mentioned in Chapter 2, Tshombe organized an army of southern tribes sympathetic to the secession to defend the newly created state. By mid-1962, this army numbered some 19,000 troops. However, in early 1963, the UN defeated the secession. While most of Tshombe's gendarmes fled to Angola, other soldiers disappeared with their arms and munitions, and a small number of battalions were integrated into the provincial police force. When Tshombe became prime minister in July 1964, he called in his former gendarmes and quickly integrated them into the national army and hired mercenaries to quell the rebellions. Although Tshombe's gendarmes and mercenaries were part of the ANC, they remained autonomous, keeping their own military commanders while fighting in Congo. One contingent combating the eastern rebellion was the Baka Regiment under the command of Colonel Tshipola, who came from Angola as major commander with 4,000 men in 1964 (Gérard-Libois, Verhaegen, Vansina, and Weiss 1967, pp. 345–355). In late 1965, when Mobutu took power, Tshombe had no choice but exile. Many of his soldiers fled to Angola, but other units remained in the national army. Unfortunately, these units were not adequately integrated into the ANC and remained homogenous entities, especially in Kisangani, retaining their own ethnic commanding officers and their autonomous network of communications.

After the Baka Regiment in Kisangani, composed of the 11th, 12th, and 14th battalions, mutinied on 24 July 1966, thirty-two Belgian mercenaries and more than 700 Katangan soldiers left their positions in the towns of Aba, Mahagi, and Aru in northeastern Congo to join the mutineers. After some combat, they headed to Watsa in northeastern Congo where they acquired all the gold of Office des Mines de Kilo Moto (OKIMO), estimated at several millions of dollars. On 30 July, they controlled Paulis and seized some 400 million francs ($2.5 million) from the vaults of an affiliate of the central bank (Gérard-Libois, Verhaegen, Vansina, and Weiss 1967, p. 353).

Mobutu then asked Bob Denard and the mercenaries he commanded, who were stationed in Kisangani, to intervene in exchange for an undisclosed cash bonus, and they became the vanguard of the flagging national army. Denard was a retired French sergeant who fought in Indochina and later became a policeman in Morocco. He became part of the mercenary unit during the Katanga secession. After the secession, this mercenary nucleus of Tshombe's army was exiled in Angola.

A stalemate persisted in Kisangani until 23 September, when the ANC occupied the airport after several fierce confrontations and heavy casualties. The mutineers were forced to retreat and leave Kisangani. Although the number of people killed was never reported by the authorities, thousands of civilians probably died in the mutiny. Denard's account of the number of mutineers killed is illustrative: "It is possible to estimate the number of those who were evacuated to 300 mutineers, while before leaving Kisangani they were 3,500 men; many of them were killed in an ambush made by special forces of the ANC around the Lolindi; it was there that they scattered after having sustained heavy losses" (Gérard-Libois, Verhaegen, Vansina, and Weiss 1967, p. 358).

Causes and Duration of the Baka Mutiny

The first account of the mutiny is from the survivors. Their version was that the ANC headquarters planned to disperse the regiment and to disarm them without paying their wages, which were several months in arrears (Gérard-Libois, Verhaegen, Vansina, and Weiss 1967). In fact, the government intended to dismantle all homogeneous ethnic armies such as the Baka Regiment by integrating their troops into multiethnic units within the ANC. General Mobutu feared that these homogenous units from South Katanga might support action against his regime with the help of mercenary units. However, his strategy failed because Colonel Tshipola was warned and was able to control the airport and a large portion of Kisangani with his men. The Baka Regiment also had other issues. Since it began fighting against the rebel forces in 1964, General Mobutu had not promoted any noncommissioned officers from the regiment, while he had promoted to high positions many incompetent officers and soldiers without combat experience from his own province of Equateur. Tshipola requested that some of his men be promoted to the officer corps because of their courage and combat experience. When Mobutu ignored the request, Tshipola saw it as a deliberate act to exclude Katanga gendarmes from the officer corps of the ANC.

This perception of exclusion was likely real. From late 1964 to mid-1966, most former Katangan gendarmes remained stationed in rebel-controlled areas without being rotated out or replaced by fresh troops. The feeling among Katangan gendarmes was that the government wanted all of them dead. Thus, the Baka mutiny was generated by a sense of political exclusion. Colonel Tshipola even complained that no commanding officer of Katanga regiments was consulted on Mobutu's decision to take power in November 1965.

Of course, Mobutu could not include these officers, given their strong ethnic affinities with Tshombe. In any case, Tshipola and his men made several demands during the reconciliation process (Gérard-Libois, Verhaegen, Vansina, and Weiss 1967, pp. 348–349):

- Dissolution of "ethnic" headquarters of the ANC headed by Mobutu
- Promotion of officers and noncommissioned officers of the Baka Regiment according to combat experience
- Application of military rules and justice in general, especially the equality of officers, noncommissioned officers, and soldiers
- Replacement of the Supreme Command of the ANC by an impartial corps capable of implementing equality and justice within the ANC without discrimination.

A final demand was to revoke the decision of the high military command of 24 November 1965, which legitimized Mobutu's coup d'état, because the decision never involved the Baka Regiment. The list of demands illustrates the regiment's frustration with their exclusion from the political process. Mobutu rejected all these demands.

The mutiny lasted only two months for three reasons. First, it ultimately failed because Mike Hoare, one of the chief mercenaries, tipped off President Mobutu about the mutiny. Second, Denard and his French mercenaries, who controlled major areas in Kisangani, sided with the government. The duration of the Baka mutiny seems to have no association with any extant theory. Third, local circumstances and the fact that one of the mercenaries tipped Mobutu gave an edge to the president, who relied on mercenaries and the rest of the army to defeat the mutiny. The mutiny of the Baka regiment ended on 25 September 1966.

Conflict Management and Consequences of the Mutiny

The mutiny of the Baka regiment was a real challenge to President Mobutu. First, he tried to accommodate the rebels. On the first day of the mutiny, General Leonard Mulamba, then prime minister, arrived in Kisangani at the request of the mutineers to attempt a peace deal. President Mobutu even requested Governor Godefroid Munongo of South Katanga to broker a peace settlement. However, all efforts at reconciliation failed because the mutineers insisted on the resignation of President Mobutu.

After the mutiny, Colonel Tshipola was captured and accused of crimes against state sovereignty. He was tried in March 1967 and sentenced to death. A year earlier, Tshombe's parliamentary immunity was revoked while he was in exile in Spain. The Mobutu government accused him of proclaiming the Katanga secession, of printing money in an independent state of Congo, of having massacred 80,000 Luba of North Katanga, and of financing the Kisangani mutiny with the help of his brother, Thomas Tshombe. Moïse Tshombe was also deemed guilty of having undermined the economic independence of Congo by giving preferential treatment to big Belgian private companies while he was prime minister of Congo (Piraux 1969, pp. 315–320). On 13 March 1997, he was sentenced to death in absentia by a three-man special military court. Thomas Tshombe was accused of financing the mutiny with one billion francs to help his brother regain power and was sentenced to fifteen years' imprisonment. (Gérard-Libois, Verhaegen, Vansina, and Weiss 1967, p. 354).

The government also dismantled all the remaining ethnic armies. The main body of the Katangan forces was absorbed into the national army, while other battalions were integrated into the Katangan police force. Finally, southern Katanga came under military occupation. Using people from his own Equateur Province, President Mobutu increased the size of security forces in southern Katanga by almost 150 percent. He appointed Jean-Foster Manzikala, from Kibali- Ituri, as governor of South Katanga, with instructions to implement military rule in the province. Once in Katanga, the governor fired more than 3,000 civil servants, mostly from the Lunda ethnic group, and forced many others on leave without pay. He also purged the administration and instituted a reign of terror in South Katanga. Massive layoffs and terror tactics increased the number of former Katangan policemen crossing the border and taking refuge in Angola. Thousands of youths also left, fearing Manzikala's reign of terror. On 10 April 1967, Mobutu reassigned Manzikala to another gubernatorial position without an investigation of his reign of terror and crimes against the people of South Katanga. The mercenaries and other Katangan soldiers mutinied less than three months later in Kisangani.

Mercenaries' Mutiny

On 5 July 1967, eleven mercenaries, under Commander Jean Schramme, and some 100 Katangan gendarmes drove their jeeps to the military Base Ketele in Kisangani where, at 6:15 am, some 500 soldiers were getting ready for the flag ceremony (Gérard-Libois and Verhaegen 1969, p. 370). The day was a holiday to honor the inauguration of an army frigate in memory of Colonel Ferdinand Tshatshi, who was killed by Katangan mutineers in July 1966. Schramme's jeeps took position in the center of the camp and opened fire on unarmed soldiers. In only twenty minutes, more than 400 people, including women, children, and soldiers, were killed (Gérard-Libois and Verhaegen 1969, pp. 370–371). Schramme was a Belgian colon in Maniema who lost his plantations during the tumultuous years following independence. He was promoted to army major in the seceded Katanga.

Schramme decided on this surprise attack because he wanted to force other mercenary units to join the mutiny. The massacre meant that all mercenaries became "enemies of the Congolese people." In fact, mercenaries who were unaware of the Kisangani event were captured by the ANC in Kinshasa on the same day. The second effect Schramme expected was the psychological collapse of the ANC. The brutality of the massacre was intended to paralyze the ANC through terror similar to that inspired by rebel simba during the eastern rebellion, which Schramme witnessed firsthand in 1964–1965.

Schramme's surprise attack, however, turned out to be a mistake. Despite heavy casualties within the ANC, government troops attacked forty minutes later when mercenaries and Katangan gendarmes relaxed their guard. In the next few hours the ANC killed several mercenaries and a dozen gendarmes. The ANC's attacks continued until 12 July and forced mercenaries to evacuate the town of Kisangani. At this time, the mutineers comprised twenty-five mercenaries and some 100 Katangan soldiers. After a week of fighting, Schramme had on his side some 150 mercenaries, 600 Katangan soldiers, and 400 former simba. Another contingent of mercenaries and Katangan troops stationed in Punia and Obokote, in Maniema Province, also joined the mutineers. Meanwhile, forty mercenaries of the tenth commando occupied Bukavu but abandoned it on 7 July 1967 and joined Schramme at his plantation in Punia. Then, the mercenaries, Katanga gendarmes, and hundreds of former simba started the long march toward Bukavu, which they reoccupied on 9 August 1967. The scattered ANC units in the area avoided face-to-face combat with the mutineers until the rebel columns reached Bukavu where heavy casualties occurred, with thousands dead on the army's side (Gérard-Libois and Verhaegen 1969, pp. 388–392).

The mercenaries' mutiny ended on 5 November 1967 with most of the survivors crossing to Rwanda. They numbered 123, of which fifty-five were Belgians.[1] A special commission of the Organization of African Unity (OAU) mediated an accord between Rwanda and Congo, which repatriated all Congolese soldiers involved in the mutiny, along with their families. Some 850 Katangan gendarmes were repatriated, and Mobutu promised them general amnesty (Gérard-Libois and Verhaegen 1969, p. 408). Those who were not part of the revolt were hired by the Katangan police force.

Mercenaries in Congo: Background to the Mutiny

A few weeks after Moïse Tshombe proclaimed the Katanga secession, the leadership of North Katanga rose against him. As discussed in Chapter 2, Tshombe quickly recruited white mercenaries to quell the insurrection because he had no army of his own. On 25 October 1960, twelve Belgian mercenaries, labeled the "frightful ones" (*Affreux*), were assigned the task of defeating the North Katangan insurrection in Kesele. Non-Belgian mercenaries were later recruited to serve as officers for small units of the Katanga Gendarmerie. In March 1961, a large contingent of 200 mercenaries arrived in southern Katanga to reconquer Manono, which was occupied by Gizenga's soldiers from Stanleyville. For the most part these mercenaries were British, Rhodesians, and South Africans. The

UN estimated in early 1961 that mercenaries in Congo numbered 500, of which about half were Belgians. However, this number decreased to less than 150 when the 1961 UN February Resolution requested all foreigners, military or civilian, not under the UN command to leave Congo. Among the remaining mercenaries were Schramme, Hoare, and Denard.

When Tshombe became prime minister in July 1964, he hired mercenaries to help the sagging national army quell the eastern rebellion. The first contingent of mercenary units became the fifth commando unit under Hoare and arrived in the Kamina military base on 23 August 1964. By September 1964, mercenaries in Congo numbered 600 despite repeated requests from the OAU that the Congo government stop recruiting mercenaries and that mercenaries operating in Congo be sent back to their home countries. By February 1965, mercenaries included 790 men divided into two commando units: the fifth Anglophone contingent under Hoare and the sixth French-speaking commando unit. The first counted 350 men and the second had 440 (Table 4.1).

The Mobutu coup d'état on 24 November 1965 broke with the past and ended the honeymoon that mercenary units had enjoyed under Prime Minister Tshombe. To provide some external legitimacy for himself in Africa, President Mobutu wanted to reduce the number of these units. However, he faced a real dilemma. To retain mercenaries meant losing the legitimacy he so badly needed from African leaders. However, an abrupt Mobutu's decision to disband or dismiss the mercenaries might lead to a major mutiny that the ANC could not yet handle. In fact, Denard suggestively asked a newspaper reporter: "Do you know places where I could get a job after this one?" (Gérard-Libois and Verhaegen 1969, p. 363). President Mobutu decided that it would be militarily unwise, however attractive politically, to disband the mercenary units used by his pred-

Table 4.1 Mercenaries in Congo, 1964–1967

Rank	Fifth Unit	Sixth Unit
Colonel	1	—
Major	1	3
Commander	1	3
Captain	7	16
Lieutenant	4	17
First lieutenant	7	18
Chief adjutant	2	14
Adjutant	20	78
Volunteer	307	287
Other	—	4
Total	350	440

Source: Gérard-Libois and Verhaegen (1969), p. 355.

ecessor. He kept them but ordered that they operate within the national army in destroying rebels' remnants in eastern Congo.

Mercenaries were aware of the fact that Mobutu was under considerable pressure from other African states to disband all mercenary units before the OAU summit scheduled in September 1967 in Kinshasa. For a time, it appeared that dismantling mercenary units might be the quid pro quo for the OAU to accept the Congolese invitation to hold the OAU summit in Kinshasa. In fact, by late 1966, Mobutu had reduced the fifth English commando unit, which included an embarrassing number of South Africans and Rhodesians, and dismantled the unit in April 1967. By early July, only the sixth French-speaking commando unit, which consisted mainly of French and Belgian mercenaries and was part of the regular army, remained under Denard, now Lt. Colonel in the national army. However, in mid-1967, Mobutu decided to dissolve the tenth special mercenary unit under Schramme, which was part of the fourth company of the sixth commando unit.

Causes of the Mercenaries' Mutiny and Its Duration

At first glance, the mutiny seems to have been an irrational act of desperation supplemented by the naive belief that the Congolese army was incapable of fighting back. However, a careful analysis reveals that the mercenaries wanted to weaken the Mobutu regime and make their presence felt, because neither greed nor grievance can explain the mutiny. The mercenaries were the best paid units in the ANC, and the mutiny may have been a way of trying to keep what they had gained. The mercenaries felt that it was just a matter of time before President Mobutu dismissed them or dispersed them among different army units to curb their power as homogenous units and thus prevent a coup. President Mobutu stated that the mutiny was financed by the Belgian private sector to bring Tshombe back to power (Gérard-Libois and Verhaegen 1969, pp. 381–382).

Several events prior to the mutiny seem to support his assertion. In late 1966, there were reports of mercenaries' recruitment in Belgium and France to overthrow Mobutu and to reinstall Tshombe (Gérard-Libois, Verhaegen, Vansina, and Weiss 1967, pp. 356–362). For example, some thirty men were arrested at a secluded farm in Basse-Ardèche near Le Vans in southern France, described as a recruiting camp for white mercenaries bound for Congo (Gérard-Libois, Verhaegen, Vansina, and Weiss 1967, pp. 357–359). These men, all young Europeans, were asleep when the French police picked them up. Under heavy interrogation, they confessed to receiving 2,000 French francs ($2,530 in 2010 prices) per month during training and expected 4,000 francs per month during the operation. They were also promised a bonus of 50,000 francs ($63,200 in 2010 prices) once they had completed their mission, which was to participate in a coup d'état in Congo financed by Tshombe. The arrest of these mercenaries gave Mobutu sufficient proof that the training camp in Basse-

Ardèche was part of a network of European mercenaries intending to overthrow him because of his "economic nationalism." As a point of interest, mercenaries' recruitment coincided with Mobutu's decision to nationalize the affiliate of Société Générale, the UMHK, in late 1966. According to Mobutu, the ultimate objective of the mutiny was to occupy Lubumbashi, the headquarters of the mining company the UMHK. He also pointed out that at the UMHK's behest, Colonel Felix van de Waelle, a former Belgian military counselor to Tshombe, conceived a strategic plan to attack the ANC by dividing Congo. The plan, called Kerillis, intended to separate mercenary thrusts. One group of mercenaries under Schramme's command would entice Congolese army detachments to the eastern region around Bukavu, and other groups would invade the west from Angola. There were some discussions about terms, the date for the operation, and the deposit of cash in advance (Kyle 1967). Tshombe had promised to complete these transactions the evening of his return to Spain from Italy. Thus, mercenary units waited for the signal from Tshombe to carry out their mission to overthrow Mobutu.

Five days before the mutiny, Tshombe declared on the morning of 30 June 1967 his desire to return to Congo as president (Kyle 1967, pp. 13–14). However, after bragging that morning of his plan to take power in Kinshasa, Tshombe was kidnapped in the afternoon. As he returned to Spain from Italy, his airplane was hijacked, and Tshombe arrived in Algiers as a prisoner (Kyle 1967). Even though the coup to bring Tshombe back to power died when he was kidnapped, mercenaries mutinied on 5 July 1967. The group behind Tshombe's kidnapping remains obscure. Some observers attribute the kidnapping to the CIA, while others credit it to either the Soviets or French secret services.[2] As Gérard-Libois and Verhaegen (1969, p. 346) succinctly put it, Tshombe was neutralized just when he was planning to retake power in Kinshasa with the help of mercenaries; thus, the kidnapping must have been facilitated by services with access to networks of information within Tshombe's financial circles and with the necessary means and adequate capacity to organize the kidnapping.

Tshombe's kidnapping left the mercenaries without a sponsor and at the mercy of Mobutu, their patron. The mercenaries' intention was to remain part of the institutionalized spoils system. Because the mercenaries feared political exclusion, they preemptively struck first, hoping to create panic among the regular troops and thus to strike a compromise with Mobutu and earn a form of a golden parachute. Unfortunately, President Mobutu refused to compromise and ordered the regular army to regroup and attack the mutineers.

One reason for the short duration of the mutiny was the lack of coordination among mercenary units. Although Schramme warned Denard that the attack was planned for the morning of 5 July 1967, Denard failed to inform his mercenary units by radio contact and concentrate his forces in Kisangani. Moreover, he neglected to recall troops dispersed in the Orientale Province to form a common front in the mutiny.

There is another reason for the mutiny's short duration. According to Kyle (1967), it was at the Rhodesian end that the conspiracy to take Kinshasa began to fall apart. Two of the top English-speaking mercenaries began feuding as they contemplated an attack on Lubumbashi to bring Tshombe back to power. One officer considered the scheme for seizing the Lubumbashi airport as inviting disaster, because it involved landing seventy unarmed men, out of uniform, from a civilian plane and subsequently supplying them with weapons then to seize the airport. Another Englishman had a crisis of conscience about turning against Mobutu while the mercenaries were still on Mobutu's payroll. The conspiracy was later disclosed to the Congolese government.

In the end, institutional failure explains the duration of the mercenaries' mutiny. The column of mercenaries moved freely over hundreds of kilometers from Kisangani to Punia and then to Bukavu despite the presence of Congolese soldiers in these zones. Once the mercenaries' column was sealed off in Bukavu, it took 15,000 troops seven weeks to root it out, although the mutineers had been cut off from all external aid and resupply (Young and Turner 1985, pp. 255–256). Mobutu's army was simply too fragile to confront mercenary units. The Congolese army lacked both logistical support and the skill to crush a handful of mercenaries, backed by a few hundred Congolese auxiliaries of Katanga origin. More than 3,000 Congolese soldiers were killed by the mutineers (Gérard-Libois and Verhaegen 1969).

After the Mutiny

Once the mutiny was put down, President Mobutu took several steps to further consolidate his power and to tighten security in South Katanga. First, he reorganized the provincial structure, reducing the number of provinces from twelve to nine (eight provinces and the capital city) in December 1967. All members of the provincial government were nominated by the central government. Mobutu posted them outside their region of origin, which automatically removed regional sources of patronage that had previously created administrative ineffectiveness and kept provincial politics imperfectly lubricated. He further centralized all provincial police forces and increased security personnel in Katanga Province. Southern Katanga, specifically, was occupied by soldiers from other regions, who behaved like conquerors. A police state was imposed on South Katanga, forcing many youths to flee to Angola and Zambia. Those Katangan gendarmes who did not participate in the mutiny were either absorbed into the national army or integrated into the police force.

However, some 800 Katangan soldiers who participated in the mercenaries' mutiny remained refugees in Rwanda. The diplomatic solution between Rwanda and Congo was the general amnesty Mobutu promised to the Katangan mutineers. On 3 December 1967, these mutineers returned to Congo under the amnesty but subsequently disappeared, apparently killed by government security forces (Young and Turner 1985, p. 255). The methods used to kill these gendarmes were ominous: many were forced to drink gasoline, while others were dropped from helicopters (Braeckman 1979, p. 142). Of some 800 gendarmes, only a few dozen escaped, fleeing to Angola where they told the story of the massacre of their comrades. After 1967, the flow of refugees from South Katanga to Angola continued unabated.

Katanga Invasions: Shaba I and Shaba II

After the mercenaries' mutiny, the main opposition to President Mobutu was from Angola in the form of the FLNC's Shaba invasions in 1977 and 1978. The first invasion, or Shaba I, occurred on 8 March 1977 when a small contingent of 2,500 so-called former Katangan gendarmes under Nathanaël Mbumba crossed the northeastern Angolan border at several points and quickly occupied a number of key towns in the Lunda, Tshokwe, and Ndembu regions of western Katanga (Yakemtchouk 1988, p. 427). Their offensive developed along two axes: first, the railroad Lobito-Lubumbashi and the second attack from Kapanga. The first town to fall was Kisenge on 8 March 1977. Five days later, the main column reached Kasaji after a day of combat in which a battalion of government forces was reported killed, while the remaining troops took to their heels (Yakemtchouk 1988). The rebels advanced within 25 kilometers of Kolwezi, the center of mining production, when 1,500 Moroccan troops in a French-led operation arrived. Code-named Verveine, the operation started on 6 April (Charpentier 1977, p. 1013). The French government indirectly joined Morocco's military contingent by sending ten transport aircraft to help ferry Moroccan troops and arms into southern Katanga. France also sent to Katanga 125 vehicles and some 50 tons of foodstuffs and munitions for the troops. An Egyptian mission of army pilots and technicians also arrived. On 25 May, the rebel troops abandoned the town of Mutshatsha to advancing government and Moroccan troops (*Africa Research Bulletin* 1977, pp. 4399–4402). Several thousand civilian casualties occurred but were never reported by the government to minimize the magnitude of the conflict. Many accounts told of bombs dropping on towns, especially in Mutshatsha and Kapanga (Willame 1980). Most bombs hit civilian targets, both along roads and in the fields, killing women and children as well as hundreds of rebels. The number of internally displaced persons ranged from 5,000 to 9,000 people during the invasion, which lasted eighty days.

The first Shaba war was clouded from the outset by confusion about the identity of the invaders. On the eve of the invasion, the FLNC was the least known movement opposed to Mobutu's autocratic rule, which led the international press to publish rumors identifying the FLNC as "former-Katangan gendarmes" or "a bunch of mercenaries from Angola trained by the Soviet Union" (Willame 1980). What was the FLNC? Who were its members?

Background to Shaba Invasions

From July 1960, when Tshombe declared the Katanga secession, to the defeat of the secession in early 1963, the Katangan gendarmes were the pillar of Tshombe's defense system. After the UN ended the Katanga secession in early 1963, a few thousands gendarmes accepted their integration in the ANC according to arrangements made between Tshombe and Prime Minister Adoula. Still other gendarmes were hired by private companies as security guards, and some 1,500 disappeared into the forest with their arms and munitions. However, a large portion of this force left Congo for Angola (Willame 1980). In early 1964, the number of those living in Angola increased to 6,000–8,000 while Tshombe was in exile in Europe. After being nominated prime minister of Congo in July 1964, he called in these gendarmes. The Katanga units kept their own officers and communication systems, but they remained in a delicate position after the Mobutu coup d'état in November 1965.

A few thousand gendarmes were integrated into the national army after the Baka mutiny in 1966, while some 6,000 became part of the police force in southern Katanga. In late 1966, a parliamentary investigation commission recommended disarming the police force because it constituted a major national security threat (Gérard-Libois, Verhaegen, Vansina, and Weiss 1967, pp. 364–370). Mobutu appointed the former governor of Kibali Ituri, Jean-Foster Manzikala, to the newly created South Katanga Province to implement the commission's recommendations. Instead, Manzikala instituted a reign of terror that impelled many Lunda as well as others to migrate to Angola, among them former Katangan gendarmes. One of Manzikala's victims was Mbumba, a former truck driver in the UMHK before independence who became a police officer in Kolwezi after independence. Under Manzikala's reign of terror in 1967, Mbumba lost his job and was jailed, but he escaped in January 1968 and fled to Angola where he formed a movement of political refugees in June 1968.

After the mercenaries' mutiny of July 1967, more than 800 Katangan gendarmes who had participated in the uprising were killed by Mobutu. Only a few dozen escaped to Angola. Mobutu's repression against the people of South Katanga increased the movement of a large number of Lunda to Angola after 1967–1968. In October 1968, the number of Katanga rebels in Angola was estimated at 3,000 men, while Katangan refugees in Angola numbered some 98,000 people, including Lunda, Tshokwe, Luba, and other ethnic groups (Willame 1980, p. 8). Up to the mid-1970s, the refugees from Katanga in Angola were still labeled "former Katangan gendarmes," which was appropriate for the early refugees who crossed in 1966 and 1967 during Manzikala's reign of terror. In the early 1970s, however, many thousands of refugees were unemployed young men from South Katanga who had no military background.

In Angola, the Portuguese government recruited most former Katangan soldiers and a large number of young refugees to complement its own colonial army. The Portuguese called these recruits *flechas,* or "black arrows," and the task of training them was given to the Portuguese political police force (Willame 1980). Thus, many refugees who became part of the flechas were young people who had never served in the Katanga Gendarmerie, although most were from regions where Tshombe had recruited his gendarmerie in late 1960. The flechas' mission in eastern Angola was primarily to counter one of the Angolan guerrilla forces, the National Union for the Total Independence of Angola (União Nacional para a Independência Total de Angola, or UNITA), which operated in eastern and southern Angola under the leadership of Jonas Savimbi. The Portuguese army's mission was to counter the other two liberation movements in Angola: Holden Roberto's National Front for the Liberation of Angola (Frente Nacional de Libertação de Angola, or FNLA) and Agostino Neto's Popular Movement for the Liberation of Angola (Movimento Popular de Libertação de Angola, or MPLA). The former established a government in exile in Congo in 1963 and controlled much of northern Angola, while the latter controlled much of the central region and the enclave of Cabinda. The MPLA later became divided into MPLA/Neto and MPLA/Daniel Chipenda.

On 24 April 1974, a group of military officers, called the Armed Forces Movement, seized power in Lisbon in a bloodless coup d'état that ended forty years of civilian dictatorship. The new leadership promised to end colonial rule and to move toward self-determination of Portuguese colonies. In mid-May, the leader of the military junta, General António Sebastião Ribeiro de Spinola, assumed the presidency. President Mobutu quickly started negotiations with the new Portuguese government to avert the danger to his regime posed by the flechas residing in Angola. In September 1974, Mobutu and de Spinola met secretly and agreed to form a coalition government for Angola, to be headed by Roberto, Savimbi, and MPLA dissident Daniel Chipenda but excluding the Marxist Neto of the MPLA (Young and Turner 1985, p. 253). Another important agreement was to grant all Congolese refugees living in Angola a general amnesty.

In late September 1974, however, de Spinola resigned as president and was replaced by General Francisco Costa Gomes, who appointed Vasco dos Santos Gonçalves as his prime minister. The agreement signed by Mobutu and de Spinola was no longer valid. The new Portuguese administration quickly recognized the right of overseas territories to self-determination, including independence. As a result, negotiations began with Angolan rebel leaders. Despite their ideological and personality differences, the leaders of the FNLA, MPLA, and UNITA signed an agreement with the Portuguese government in early 1975 calling for the independence of Angola on 11 November 1975. The accord was, however, short-lived because, during subsequent months, the FNLA, the MPLA/Chipenda, and the UNITA formed a tacit alliance against the MPLA/Neto. Then in January 1975, Admiral Rosa Countinho, governor of Angola, decided to deal with the situation of the flechas as Portugal moved to grant independence to Angola. The admiral disliked Mobutu, who had taken him prisoner and inflicted on him a humiliating detention in Kinshasa some years back

(Braeckman 1979). In addition to his personal dislike of Mobutu, the admiral supported the leftist MPLA, which he thought was the most "coherent, the most efficient, and certainly the most progressive of Angolan liberation movements" (Braeckman 1979, p. 144). Admiral Countinho then convinced Mbumba and his men to join the MPLA/Neto against the Mobutu-backed FNLA. This was a major addition to MPLA/Neto for two reasons. First, Neto had fewer trained troops than the other liberation movements. Second, the elite force of the MPLA had joined Chipenda's MPLA in Congo-Kinshasa, leaving Neto with a weak and dwindling military force.

As early as February 1975, a flow of covert foreign support to all parties began. Already by late 1974, President Mobutu and the CIA were considering military intervention in Angola. Some 1,200 of Mobutu's soldiers entered Angola between March and June 1975 when the MPLA/Neto appeared in ascendancy (LeoGrande 1982, p. 23). In subsequent months, more Congolese troops financed by the United States crossed the Angolan border. On 10 November 1975, the Portuguese high commissioner departed after a brief ceremony, and at midnight Neto proclaimed the People's Republic of Angola. On 23 November, the FNLA-UNITA alliance announced the rival Democratic People's Republic of Angola, with the central highland city of Humbo as its capital. Soon after the two republics were proclaimed, the fight for control of the capital city of Luanda began.

The alliance of flechas and MPLA/Neto stopped the advancing Congolese troops and the FNLA. The defeat of Mobutu's troops and his coalition (the FNLA and MPLA/Chipenda) helped President Neto control the capital city before the arrival of Cuban troops in Angola. Mbumba's troops were thus instrumental in the victory of the MPLA. Without the flechas, the MPLA may not have gained power in Angola. Within a month of Angolan independence, Cuba had dispatched nearly 18,000 troops in support of the pro-Soviet MPLA (Yakemtchouk 1988). The former flechas remained a force that preceded the Cubans during the second phase of the MPLA's control of Angola. By early 1976, Cuban troops equipped with Soviet armored vehicles and rocket launchers helped turn the tide in favor of the MPLA/Neto. After his victory, President Neto acknowledged Mbumba's invaluable contributions. He authorized Mbumba and his men to retake the concessions that the Portuguese had given them in the region of Texeira de Souza and promised to support them in their quest to return to Congo (Afri-Ku-Nyeng 1977, p. 15). Mbumba became a warlord with an autonomous fiefdom in the region of de Texeira de Souza where his troops were stationed.

By late 1976, Mbumba had consolidated his reputation as an anti-Mobutu military leader. To achieve his goal, Mbumba visited Cuba and East Germany in July and September 1976 to negotiate for weapons and for training of his men (Willame 1980). East Germany sent hundreds of military experts to train Mbumba's men, with the operations directed by Lieutenant General Helmut Poppe, East German vice-minister of defense; the Chinese government even accused the Soviet Union of financing the operation for aggressive expansionism (Yakemtchouk 1988). However, the supply of weapons from East Germany was delayed for several weeks and thus compromised the FLNC's attack against Mobutu scheduled on 24 November 1976 during the rainy season (Yakemtchouk 1988, pp. 426–427).

Although General Mbumba was an outstanding military commander, as indicated earlier, his major weakness was unwillingness to collaborate with the other opponents of the Mobutu regime who visited him in Angola. On a number of occasions, Mbumba even jailed them without explanation. As a result, President Neto ordered Mbumba to close his prisons and to liberate all political prisoners. Mbumba refused and, in January 1977, Neto confined him to his residence for having violated the territorial integrity of Angola (Yakemtchouk 1988). On 6 March 1977, Mbumba escaped with some of his men already mobilized to attack South Katanga. The decision to attack South Katanga seemed to have been decided without President Neto's collaboration or support.

The First Shaba War

Causes of the war. The first objective of the FLNC was to overthrow Mobutu. In the words of General Mbumba, "Congo, our country, must be an independent, socialist, and progressive country" (Willame 1980, p. 25). Attacking southern Katanga and controlling several mining sites was intended to suffocate the economy. The rebels attacked exactly when the IMF was putting together a financial rescue plan for the country. Their goal was to wreck the crucial copper and cobalt installations and thus strike a blow at the tottering Mobutu regime. In a statement released in Brussels, the FLNC said that its aim was "to liberate the whole Congolese people from the Mobutu's autocratic rule and from exploitation" (Braeckman 1979, p. 142).

Shaba I involved only 1,500 to 2,000 men, who seized several towns in southern Katanga (Mangold 1979, p. 109). Although the local population welcomed them as liberators, the rebels had no coordinated operational plans and stopped short of taking Kolwezi, the second major mining city in southern Katanga after Lubumbashi. The fall of Kisenge and Dilolo gave the rebels the chance to loot Gécamines' depots of minerals. They captured a stock of manganese valued at 120 million French francs ($88 million in 2010 prices), a significant war booty (Willame 1980).

Recruitment, an element of civil war, was facilitated by the socioeconomic situation in Congo. Mass poverty in rural southern Katanga was a source of frustration and grievance. This rural population was sensitive to Mobutu's neglect and the contrast between the potential richness of Katanga and the effective deterioration of its living standard. Southern Katanga may have provided the Mobutu state with most of its revenue, but little was reinvested in Katanga. Mobutu's neglect of Katanga deepened frustration and popular hatred of his regime. Thus, the FLNC invaded the region when the masses perceived the widening gap between the administrative and political elite and themselves. The FLNC understood people's frustrations and used persuasion to show the growing disparity between the politico-administrative class and the masses.

Most people from southern Katanga bitterly hated the Mobutu regime for a number of reasons. For example, the urban population of Kolwezi lived in deplorable conditions that could be described as quasi-famine, although Gécamines' workers were somewhat better off. Some economic indicators in southern Katanga showed that inflation was at its highest since the late 1960s. Unemployment was also high among young men. Gross domestic product had plummeted to its lowest level and was lower than the national average, although the government received most of its ordinary revenue from the mining province (Kisangani 1997).

From 1967 to 1976, Katanga was literally under siege. Mobutu's troops behaved in southern Katanga like conquerors, raping women and girls, arresting people at will, and committing all types of human rights abuses. Moreover, in the wake of the mercenaries' mutiny in 1967, Mobutu requested all state enterprises, such as Gécamines, not to hire people from South Katanga, yet another source of frustration. At the time, most chief executive officers of Gécamines were nonnatives. All these factors contributed to the sharp, passionate hatred among the Lunda, who became increasingly hostile to a political regime that exploited and excluded them from power. It is not surprising that the people of southern Katanga gave a warm welcome to the FLNC because they viewed it as a legitimate group capable of ending Mobutu's regime.

The final cause of Shaba I was regional security. The FLNC kept its commanding staff and its military training camps in eastern Angola. Although never officially expressed, the bond between the FLNC and the Angola regime was strong. This relationship was based on the historical link, with the FLNC and Angola allied against the two other Angolan liberation movements, and the tense situation between Congo and Angola. The relationship between Mbumba and Neto was further reinforced in 1976 when Mobutu, as a US proxy, began supporting Angolan insurgent groups against the pro-Soviet MPLA. Mbumba then became a bargaining chip for Mobutu's support of anti-Neto forces with sanctuary in Congo.

Duration and consequences. Cold War rivalry was enough to stop the rebels as Mobutu was rescued by the West. The Moroccan troops ferried to Katanga by the French Air Force propped up Mobutu's army. Foreign intervention was a major factor in shortening the invasion. Shaba I also had a number of consequences in southern Katanga. The first impact was economic. Export revenues increased from 438.3 million zaires in 1975 to 774.4 million in 1976, but only to 857.2 million in 1977. However, the percentage of Gécamines' exports as a share of total exports declined from 62.3 percent in 1976 to 55.6 percent in 1977 (Kisangani 1997).

On the political front, the FLNC had an impact for a brief time. The first few towns under its control were quick to democratically elect a new administration separate from the previous one. The FLNC even paid seven-month salary arrears to 130 roadmen. It also responded to a local request to install a popular tribunal to judge previous administrators who were abusing their public offices (Willame 1980). The relationships between the FLNC and the population were friendly because the rebels displayed courtesy and discipline. This contrasted to the government troops that had abused the civilian population after Mobutu had removed most Katangan administrators from the province.

Although Mobutu declared publicly that the Lunda people need not fear any retaliation for their support of the FLNC and that he "would never authorize it," the reality was totally different (Kisangani 1997, p. 28). The aftermath included a crackdown on "dissidents," which turned into a nightmare for the local population. The national army, which was incapable of stopping the rebels' advance, turned against the local population and killed thousands of innocent civilians, especially in the region of Dilolo-Mutshasha. Soldiers raped hundreds of girls and women without mercy and looted towns in their path. The repression that followed soldiers' actions increased the number of Katangan refugees in Angola from 45,000 in 1976 to some 200,000 by the end of 1977 (Kisangani 1997).

To deter trouble in the area, Mobutu stationed 9,000 troops of the Kamanyola army division in Kolwezi permanently. This unit was part of the 25,000 troops trained mainly by North Korea and was considered the army's best unit. Mobutu also made sweeping reforms of the army, accusing it of "moral defeat." On 1 July 1977, he reorganized it completely, and, in the process, purged most Lunda officers from the army by accusing them of a plot to overthrow him. After a show trial, Mobutu ordered several army officers from Katanga shot.[3] By May 1978, no Lunda officer was in any position of authority in either the government or the military. More specifically, the former minister of foreign affairs, Nguza Karl-i-Bond from the Lunda ethnic group, was arrested and accused of high treason for having collaborated with the FLNC. Nearly all Lunda elites were purged from state institutions.

Second Shaba War

On 11 May 1978, some 4,000 rebels of the FLNC from Angola attacked the mining town of Kolwezi in the southeastern region of Katanga (Willame 1978). The industrial installation of Gécamines in Kolwezi supplied some 70 percent of copper and cobalt in the region. Kolwezi also housed a plant that treated zinc, with an annual production averaging at that time 67,000 tons, the highest in Africa (Willame 1978). Kolwezi was thus the heart of the national economy. According to General Mbumba, "We wanted to hit the heart of interests that keep the corrupt dictator Mobutu in power" (Willame 1978, p. 167). The attack on Kolwezi appeared well prepared and conceived. Several months earlier, the rebels had infiltrated the local population, which offered them shelter and support. Besides being the second-largest mining center of Katanga, Kolwezi was also the military headquarters of the Kamanyola army division (Kisangani 2000b). However, as in the 1977 invasion, the Kamanyola division evaporated when faced with the FLNC. As with the rest of the army, the troops' morale was low because of salary arrears and food shortages. General Tshikeva, commander of the Kamonyola battalion in Kolwezi, turned tail in the first hour of the attack and was spotted later some 50 kilometers from Kolwezi at the mining headquarters of Société Minière de Tenke-Fungurume (Willame 1978). Along with civilians, other army units left town. When army units were spotted by government French-made Mirages, the pilots took them for rebels and attacked them, killing hundreds.

Just as in the 1977 invasion, Mobutu had to be rescued by foreign troops. On 19 May 1978, 400 paratroopers of the second airborne regiment of the French Foreign Legion were dropped into the center of Kolwezi. Government Mirage fighters provided an escort for the French Legion troops as they parachuted over Kolwezi. A contingent of Belgian paratroopers was also involved in evacuating foreigners, mostly Europeans. Neither France nor Belgium was well-enough equipped to mount this kind of long-range operation on short notice and had to rely on US C-141 heavy transports (*Africa Research Bulletin* 1978, pp. 4854–4862). After heavy fighting, French paratroopers recaptured Kolwezi. The rebels withdrew from Kolwezi to regroup in Lubumbashi and left Congo on 28 May 1978. The French commander, Colonel Yves Gras, described the rebels as well commanded, well organized, and well trained; the rebels' invasion of Kolwezi was one of "the best planned and executed operations seen anywhere in Africa for years" (*Africa Research Bulletin* 1978, p. 4854).

The number of people killed was between 1,600 and 3,500, while 8,000 to 12,000 persons were internally displaced by the invasion. Fearing more invasions, a peacekeeping force returned to the region to protect it. The bulk of this force comprised some 1,500 Moroccans, but several battalions from Senegal, Ivory Coast, Togo, Gabon, and Central African Republic also joined the Moroccan forces to give the impression of an inter-African force.

Causes of Shaba II. The main goal of Shaba II, as articulated by the rebel forces, was to overthrow Mobutu's autocratic regime and set up a government of national unity. Perhaps the rebels thought they had more chance of shaking up the Mobutu regime in 1978 than in 1977 (Shaba I). Before Shaba II, the Congolese military's fighting effectiveness was completely eroded. Mobutu's policies of purges, assassinations, and ethnic armies had produced a disorganized and ineffective army without discipline, leaving the way open for the rebels (Kisangani 2000b). The rebels took Kolwezi and got as far as they did because the national army was weakened by maladministration, corruption, and discontent.

In brief, the invaders were not secessionists. They were calling on Congolese to rise up against a discredited autocrat. After Shaba I, both economic and political conditions in Congo, and in Katanga particularly, deteriorated badly.

The population of Kolwezi was totally destitute, another factor contributing to the invasion. The rebels planned their attack for late 1977. Hundreds of rebels were already inside Kolwezi waiting to join those coming from Angola. Many young men living in Kolwezi were also recruited in late December 1977 and received some rudimentary training (Willame 1978). The rebels infiltrated and started teaching their Lunda recruits to use weapons (Willame 1978, p. 25). General Mbumba even declared that a number of his soldiers never left southern Katanga and remained there like "fish in the water" (Willame 1978, p. 35). The attack on Kolwezi happened with local support; people knew the rebels were present and supported them. Without that support, the invasion could not have occurred. During this period, arms and munitions were brought into Kolwezi hidden in trucks carrying wood charcoal and even transported by some chauffeurs of Gécamines. Most of these arms and munitions were stored in the African quarters of Kolwezi. With rebels divided into small platoons, the infiltration took several weeks. A large number of Mbumba's troops crossed from Zambia dressed like civilian refugees. Within hours of the first shots, the city of Kolwezi fell to the rebels, most of whom wore uniforms of one kind or another with the word "tigers" (*tigres*) printed on their arm bands. They later became known as tigers.

The broad public support that the invading troops enjoyed in mid-May 1978, during their brief occupation of Kolwezi, reflected not so much their own popularity as it did the Mobutu regime's total unpopularity. This support of the rebels stemmed from the frustration and grievances accumulated since the first Baka mutiny in 1966 and the exclusion of most Lunda elites from the political process, although Katanga Province provided more than 60 percent of government revenue in the 1970s.

The third cause of Shaba II involved regional politics. Talks were under way to enhance collaboration between President Mobutu and President Neto. After Shaba I, Mobutu and Neto were converging on many issues and were in the process of ending their differences as the result of diplomatic efforts by President Marien Nguabi of Congo-Brazzaville. Neto, however, faced a dilemma: a military force, the FLNC, remained in his territory, and he had no control over it. In early 1978, Neto decided to move Mbumba and his men away from the Angola-Congo border as part of his move toward reconciliation with Mobutu.

Moreover, Neto wanted to consolidate his own power over Angola. To do this, he moved most refugee camps 300 kilometers away from the border in April 1978. Because he could not impose himself militarily on the FLNC, he publicly announced in February 1978 his intention to move the refugee camps and hence the FLNC away from the border with Congo. This forced Mbumba to begin his second invasion, taking Neto and others off guard. Mbumba's efforts were perhaps aimed at subverting any reconciliation between Mobutu and Neto. With the second attack, General Mbumba demonstrated that he was still a major force in Angola along the border of the two countries.

Duration and consequences. Shaba II was much shorter than Shaba I because the West intervened quickly as the result of media attention on the rebels' brutality against Europeans. One illustration is the capture in Katanga of six French soldiers who were killed by the rebels after intense torture (Yakemtchouk 1988, p. 507). However, Willame (1980, p. 30) pointed out that most acts of brutality against Europeans were committed by Congolese troops. Regardless of this controversy, the rebels discovered that the tide had turned against them when the national army's 311th Battalion under Major Bokoungo Mahele took control of the airport from the rebels. French paratroopers inflicted heavy losses on the rebels, killing more than 300, while Belgian forces' intervention allowed some 2,260 Europeans and Americans to be evacuated (Yakemtchouk 1988). Again, foreign intervention was critical to ending the rebels' invasion.

As with Shaba I, government troops suffered the consequences of their failures against the invaders. Following what Mobutu called "an abortive coup attempt" against him, the government arrested 250 army officers in 1978, and he dismissed more than 200 officers from the service. Military strength was also reduced by 25 percent to eliminate "disloyal and ineffective elements" (Kisangani 1997). Then, Mobutu ordered an increase in the recruitment of soldiers from his own ethnic group and native province. By 1980, 90 percent of the defense ministry personnel were from Mobutu's province of Equateur (Kisangani 2000b). The enlargement of his "ethnic army" stabilized his regime through an ethnic matching of regime and army. However, this policy degraded the military's fighting power still further because it removed the most qualified officers from positions of leadership and replaced them with unqualified personnel.

Meanwhile, foreign commitments to rescue Mobutu created urgent pressure from the West to liberalize the regime, resulting in a constitutional reform in 1978. A key amendment to the constitution was that the Legislative Council became the organ vested with power over the executive branch. For almost two years, members of the government were called before the Legislative Council to justify their spending and the running of their departments. In 1979, a parliamentary commission of inquiry found that the president had illegally withdrawn $150 million ($451 million in 2010 prices) in foreign exchange from the central bank for personal use in defiance of austerity measures imposed by the IMF in its stabilization program (Kisangani 1997, p. 33).

One year later, Mobutu amended the constitution again. Article 80, which had given the Legislative Council the power to control the executive branch and state enterprises, was abolished. With the new amendment, Mobutu regained control over state marketing boards and the state budget. This amendment was followed by a law, no. 80/007 of 15 November 1980, which created a new party institution called the Central Committee, whose 120 members were all appointed by the president. The committee took over most of the roles vested in the Legislative Council. To ensure their loyalty, Mobutu granted its members a salary ranging from $5,000 ($13,528 in 2010 prices) to $9,200 ($24,892) a month, at a time when physicians and university professors were getting less than $350 ($947) a month (Kisangani 1997). Thus, foreign intervention not only failed to liberalize Mobutu's repressive regime but reinforced governmental irresponsibility and venality.

Conflict management. One major consequence of Shaba II was a rapprochement between Angola and Congo, then called Zaire. On 29 June 1978, President Neto announced that he had disarmed Mbumba's men and moved them to refugee camps in the Bie region around the town of Silva Porto. Neto expected Mobutu to reciprocate by removing the threat of the Angolan rebel groups, mainly sponsored by the United States, from Congo's borders with Angola, which Mobutu did in August 1978 as the two leaders attempted to reduce the flow of arms into their respective countries and to curtail rebels' sanctuaries. On 19 August 1978, Neto arrived in Kinshasa for a three-day official visit to seal the reconciliation. The main issue was to make the border between the two countries a "ribbon of entente, fraternity, and peace" (Yakemtchouk 1988, p. 568). This visit was made possible by the mediating diplomacy of President Nguabi of Congo-Brazzaville, in two meetings in Brazzaville on 15 July 1978. Less than a year after Shaba II, Mobutu and Neto had sealed their reconciliation. A joint communiqué said that the two countries would increase security along their common border and would make a joint approach to the OAU about border security. The two leaders also agreed to create a commission to control their borders under the auspices of the OAU, to harmonize their security policies, to obtain aid from international organizations for Congolese refugees in Angola if they wished to return, and to open up the Benguala railways to Congolese merchandise once Congo stopped providing sanctuary to the Angolan rebel groups.[4]

On the rebel side, Mbumba's soldiers became disillusioned with their leader. Their hopes were dashed by his self-serving attitude and his aggrandizement. His refusal to ally with other opposition groups was a clear indication of his attempt to build a cult of personality. Even so, most of his troops refused to return to Congo in spite of Mobutu's message of amnesty because they remembered earlier empty promises and what had happened to their comrades when they returned home. With the signing of a peace accord between Mobutu and Neto, the specter of Tshombe finally vanished along with the remnants of his secession.

Brief Summary and Discussion

Chapter 4 provides a different view of civil wars, showing the importance of regional analysis similar to "regional conflict complex" (Wallensteen and Sollenberg 1998). This complex combines both population movements and hostile neighbors. It was political because refugees from Congo settled in Angola after the defeat of the Katanga secession. When Tshombe became prime minister, he recalled his gendarmes and mercenaries to quell the eastern rebellion. However, Mobutu's coup d'état in late 1965 changed the fortunes of both Katanga gendarmes and mercenaries, completely isolating them from state spoils. President Mobutu made sure that these soldiers remained in combat zones away from the capital city, resulting in their exclusion from military decisionmaking. Two mutinies occurred as these two groups attempted to reassert themselves against the new regime whose main goal was to exclude them from the political process. After their defeat, many Katangan gendarmes crossed back into Angola. Once in Angola, refugees were transformed into a military complex, with the Portuguese training them to fight local rebels. After Angolan political independence, the flechas became Mobutu's opponents and decided to destabilize his regime. Hosted by President Neto, the complex also became social and political. The political link with Neto was the foundation of Shaba I and Shaba II, but social networks also developed in refugee camps and during the two invasions. Thus, from the Baka mutiny to Shaba II a common thread emerges: the need to recapture a previous political position that was lost as the result of the exclusion of Katanga elites from power. The two mutinies and the two Shaba wars were thus the sequel of the Katanga secession.

Just like the Baka mutiny, the mercenaries' mutiny was a war of convenience caused by fear of being dismantled and excluded from a lucrative service after their sponsor, Tshombe, was kidnapped, thus dashing their hopes to remain an important group in the Congolese polity. The mercenaries had to make themselves indispensable or face losing a lucrative job. Thus, the mercenaries' mutiny was a preemptive endeavor to weaken the Mobutu regime in order to extract compromise that could have allowed them to exit with some kind of payoff. Both the Baka and the mercenaries' mutinies were military operations without any political element.

The same can also be said of the FLNC gaining sanctuary in Angola. It remained a military organization rather than a liberation movement. The FLNC espoused military conquest, not arduous long-term guerrilla warfare and the organization of peasants, although the peasants were truly deprived and the first to support the FLNC. However, Mbumba's goal of destabilizing the Mobutu regime by choking off access to the mining province overlooked the dynamics of the Cold War, which brought international intervention to support Mobutu.

Of the four cases of internal wars analyzed here, two mutinies and two invasions, only the latter can be classified as legitimate wars because they received strong popular support from the people of southern Katanga. Thus, a sense of injustice and deprivation developed among Katangans when they compared their situation under Mobutu to the previous period under a more favorable regime. Here a few elements of continuity emerge. First is the role of Katanga in the postcolonial economy. The goal of the rebels was the same: to choke the Congolese economy and thus weaken the Mobutu regime. Second was the role of ethnicity epitomized by both the Baka mutiny and the two Shaba wars. Though Mobutu derived most of his budget from southern Katanga, none of the Katanga subregions benefited from Katangan wealth. Most people in Katanga remained in total destitution. Like the early secessions and insurrections, and perhaps like the Kwilu rebellion, the causes of the specter of Tshombe remain local. In a sense, the people of Katanga felt some level of unfairness from the political system that discriminated against them. This sense of grievance was reflected by the support they gave to the FLNC in both invasions. Here, Mobutu was the cause and was seen by the people of Katanga as a "bad leader" in Brown's (1996) sense. Mobutu's policy toward Katanga aimed to control the region because it provided him more than half of his budget to sustain his patronage system and to avoid the unpleasant consequences of being forcibly removed from power.

In the final analysis, the two Shaba wars never intended to carve up Congo with secession for a number of reasons. First, General Mbumba learned from the early Katanga secession that Katanga was not ethnically homogenous and any call for secession might revive the northern Katanga insurrection. In other words, collective action for separatism did not justify any action that could have created animosity from other groups. Second, the Cold War itself did not allow such a movement, and a "benevolent international society" (Englebert and Hummel 2005, p. 411) opposed secessionist movements. In a sense, in a world where the supply of sovereignty was in short supply, the FLNC wanted only to be inserted into the political process. Thus, the two invasions, like the early civil wars, originated from local conditions. The support that the FLNC received depended on these conditions.

A major lesson from the specter of Tshombe is that the Congolese state was maintained by the international community as a juridical state without an empirical foundation to defend itself. Western diplomats argued in favor of support for Mobutu, believing there was no viable alternative and that Congo needed a strong man to hold together its 336 tribes. This Western fear was enough for Mobutu to consolidate power. Moreover, a major element of continuity remains in the huge disparity in income between the ruler and the ruled. During the colonial period, this inequality in income existed between Europeans and Africans. Although the color of the players had changed, the same vertical inequality persisted. Shaba I and Shaba II illustrated the perception of this growing inequality.

Change was also a dynamic part of the two mutinies and the two invasions. The changing structure of group relations reflected a new definition of ethnicity. The elimination of overt electoral competition under Mobutu never eliminated ethnicity. On the contrary, ethnicity remained part of the political lexicon as Mobutu himself relied on a core group from his own Equateur Province to survive in office. The juggling of appointments in the regular army was primarily concerned with ensuring the regime's safety and minimizing the chances of a coup. Appointing unqualified kin to commanding positions allowed Mobutu to keep his "fingers on the pulse of the armed forces as well as his hands on their operational control" (David 1997, p. 564), but the strategy destroyed the morale of the ablest officers. High-ranking officers were part of a career system that was manifestly corrupt, and troops lost respect for their officers. By creating an atmosphere of intrigue and suspicion among his clients, Mobutu diminished his own effectiveness and destroyed the foundation of state building.

Notes

1. Other mercenaries included twenty-nine French, sixteen Italians, six Portuguese, four South Africans, three British, three Greeks, two Spanish, two Germans, and three other nationals. See Gérard-Libois and Verhaegen (1969), p. 366.

2. According to this view, Francis Bodeman and Lawrence Devlin, two prominent figures in the early history of Congo, were spotted in Rome on 10 June 1967.

3. For example, Colonel Mampa Salamy, former commander of military operations in Katanga Province, was sentenced to death by the war council. He was convicted of high treason, endangering state security, demoralizing troops on the battlefield and the foreign community working in the mining center of Kolwezi, and of misappropriating 40,000 zaires intended for the Kolwezi front. The following officers were also condemned to death on 17 March 1978: Majors Kalume and Panube as principal investigators; Colonels Blamwenze and Mbiye, Mwepu wa Ngongo; Lt. Colonels Tshiunza Mukishi, Muheu Baruani, and Kalonda Katalayi; and Captain Fundi Setu. See Kisangani (2000b).

4. The railway was the shortest and the least expensive route to export Congolese minerals from Katanga to the nearest seaport in Angola. It was closed as the result of civil war in Angola (see Kisangani 1987).

5

Warring Against the President

General Joseph Mobutu, later Mobutu Sese Seko, became president on 24 November 1965 and remained in power for almost thirty-two years despite two mutinies and two invasions. He built his political longevity by cracking down on dissidents, concentrating power, developing a cult of personality, and sustaining a patronage system. Although Mobutu was able to build a strong state in the early years of his tenure, the state never possessed a monopoly on coercion, nor has it ever enjoyed the rule of law or an effective bureaucracy since the mid-1970s (Callaghy 1984; Nzongola-Ntalaja 2002; Young and Turner 1985). To stay in power, he had to rely on the United States. Thus, Mobutu, one of the all-time major scoundrels even in the exclusive league of African strongmen, received sufficient US support over the years to earn him the label of "America's Tyrant" (Kelly 1993). The collapse of the Soviet Union, however, weakened his power as the United States eventually abandoned him. The revolt against him started on 17 October 1996 when violent fighting broke out between the Banyamulenge-RPA coalition and his army in Uvira, Sud-Kivu. A day later, a rebel group emerged, calling itself the AFDL.

The AFDL was a heteroclite group of four political parties with divergent political interests when its members signed an alliance with Rwanda on 18 October 1996.[1] It was not until 7 November 1996 that Laurent Kabila emerged as the spokesperson of the AFDL and announced the group's intention to remove Mobutu from power.

The alliance between the AFDL and Rwanda was not an accidental one. It occurred more than two years after the Tutsi-led RPF from Uganda took power in Rwanda in June 1994 and ended the genocide. The result was a massive wave of Hutu refugees into the DRC. The failure of the UN Assistance Mission to Rwanda to intervene and stop the genocide created a security vacuum in the Great Lakes region. As a result, the UN Security Council passed Resolution 929 on 22 June 1994 to authorize a temporary French-led humanitarian mission to the region, called Operation Turquoise, until the UN could mobilize support for a new operation. This mission was mandated to use "all necessary means" to protect civilians and vulnerable persons by establishing secure humanitarian areas as well as to provide security and support for the distribution of relief supplies and humanitarian operations. The resolution also stressed "the strictly humanitarian character of the mission that shall be conducted in an impartial and neutral fashion." However, the French-led operation was far from neutral, given France's three decades of diplomatic relations with the former Rwandan-Hutu government. As a consequence, French troops allowed the former Rwandan Hutu soldiers and their political leaders to escape across the border with their weapons, money, and munitions along with masses of Rwandan-Hutu civilians. These armed groups received Mobutu's support as well (Kisangani 1997). Once in Nord-Kivu, they began launching military attacks on the Rwandan Tutsi government.

In mid-November 1996, the RPA and the AFDL launched a massive attack on Hutu refugee camps around Goma in eastern DRC. A few days later, the AFDL seized the town, where its leaders established their headquarters. In late 1996, two key US officials, diplomat Denis Hankins and ambassador to Rwanda Peter Whaley, visited the AFDL's headquarters in an important diplomatic gesture, providing an implicit signal to the rising revolt that the United States was behind it (International Crisis Group 2000). This visit implied that Washington was committed to removing President Mobutu from power. After the fall of Goma, the AFDL was reinforced by troops from Burundi and Uganda. In late December, the movement incorporated Mai Mai groups and some 12,000 to 16,000 child soldiers known as *kadogo*, or little boys. Angola joined the rebel movement in late January 1997. The Katanga tigers, discussed in Chapter 4, became part of the AFDL in mid-February 1997.

After the capture of Lubumbashi in April 1997, the headquarters of the state mining company Gécamines, the international community recognized Kabila's movement as a "belligerent community."[2] This recognition gave Kabila rights over the state mining company and allowed him to conclude several deals with potential foreign investors. As the AFDL advanced toward Kinshasa, 2,000 soldiers of the presidential guard supported by UNITA rebel troops set up the fiercest resistance against the AFDL in Kenge, Bandundu Province.

On 17 May 1997, the AFDL forces, spearheaded by troops from Rwanda, Uganda, and Angola, entered the capital city. On 29 May 1997, Kabila proclaimed himself president in a surprise move against the kingmakers—Rwanda and Uganda (Willame 1999). People killed from direct fighting numbered some 3,000 to 5,000. In addition, as the RPA and AFDL crossed the DRC, they tracked down former Rwandan soldiers and *Interahamwe* (group working together) militias who had committed the genocide in Rwanda. In the process, the RPA killed some 233,000 Hutu refugees (Kisangani 2000a, p. 179). Thus, the civil war against Mobutu resulted in the death of at least 236,000 people, with more than 100,000 people internally displaced.

The "internationalization" of civil war against Mobutu was intrinsically linked to regional politics in Central Africa. A number of Mobutu's neighbors helped the AFDL conquer Congo (Kisangani 1997; McNulty 1999; Reyntjens 1997). The fall of Mobutu seemed to pave the way toward reshaping and even resizing the DRC (Kisangani 2003, p. 56). Each of the leaders of the DRC's neighboring states had reasons to support Kabila and to reshape the DRC. It was pay back and get even time.

After a brief honeymoon period, the Mai Mai groups, former allies of Kabila, began an insurrection against him on 7 September 1997 because they were opposed to the presence of foreign troops, especially Rwandan soldiers, in eastern Congo. Within five months, some 6,500 to 10,000 people were killed, and an estimated 13,000 people were internally displaced (U.S. Committee for Refugees 1999). This uprising ended on 28 July 1998 when Kabila ordered all foreign troops to leave. This decision also ended the military cooperation that overthrew Mobutu.

On 2 August 1998, the second civil war against Kabila began and was backed by Rwanda and Uganda. In early January Kabila was assassinated, leaving the DRC occupied by rebel groups, foreign armies, and militias. The war ended in December 2002 after more than four million people had been killed and more than 100,000 had been internally displaced each year.

The purpose of this chapter is threefold. First is to analyze the three internal wars in the context of regional politics in the Great Lakes region because the first and third civil wars were "internationalized," similar to the 1917 Russian Civil War and the Yugoslav War (Levy and Thompson 2010, p. 22). The second objective is to discuss the civil war against Mobutu in terms of a rentier state. Third is to explain the absence of civil wars from 1979 to 1992. For almost fourteen years Congo was peaceful. Because Congo had so many wars in the 1960s—two in the 1970s and many others in the 1990s—should not overshadow the fragile peace of the 1980s. The first three sections analyze these civil wars, while the fourth section summarizes and discusses the findings.

Anti-Mobutu Civil War: Liberation or Path to Autocracy

The civil war against President Mobutu has been a topic of considerable debate and disagreement. According to one view, Angola, Rwanda, and Uganda wanted a friendly government in Kinshasa capable of securing their borders with the DRC (McNulty 1999). For other observers, the US refusal to help Mobutu was critical in the success of the civil war and could be viewed as a victory of the United States over France (P. Leymarie, cited in Ngolet 2000). Some French politicians even saw this refusal as evidence of an "Anglo-Saxon conspiracy" (Huliaras 1998; Ngolet 2000). These arguments provide only half of the story. The author contends that the main critical antecedent of Mobutu's political demise was the declining patronage system he created to keep himself in office. In addition, one critical juncture that precipitated the war against Mobutu was the political exclusion of the Banyamulenge as the result of restrictive and discriminatory nationality laws.

Brief Background: Banyamulenge Nationality Issue

The Banyamulenge are descendants of Tutsi cattle herders from Rwanda, found mostly in the Uvira territory where they live with the Fulero and Vira, as well as in Fizi and Mwenga territories. Map 5.1 highlights the location of the Banyamulenge and major groups in Sud-Kivu. The word "Banyamulenge" emerged only in 1973 and in Kifulero means "people of Mulenge" or "inhabitants of hills of Mulenge." Mulenge is a small Fulero village several kilometers from Lemera, in Sud-Kivu Province. The question among observers is over the number of Banyamulenge in Congo. Before 1933, their number was so small that no mention of the tribe occurred in any ethno-cartography of the Belgian Congo. The ethnic groups of Sud-Kivu Province mentioned in colonial maps were the

Map 5.1 Sud-Kivu and Its People

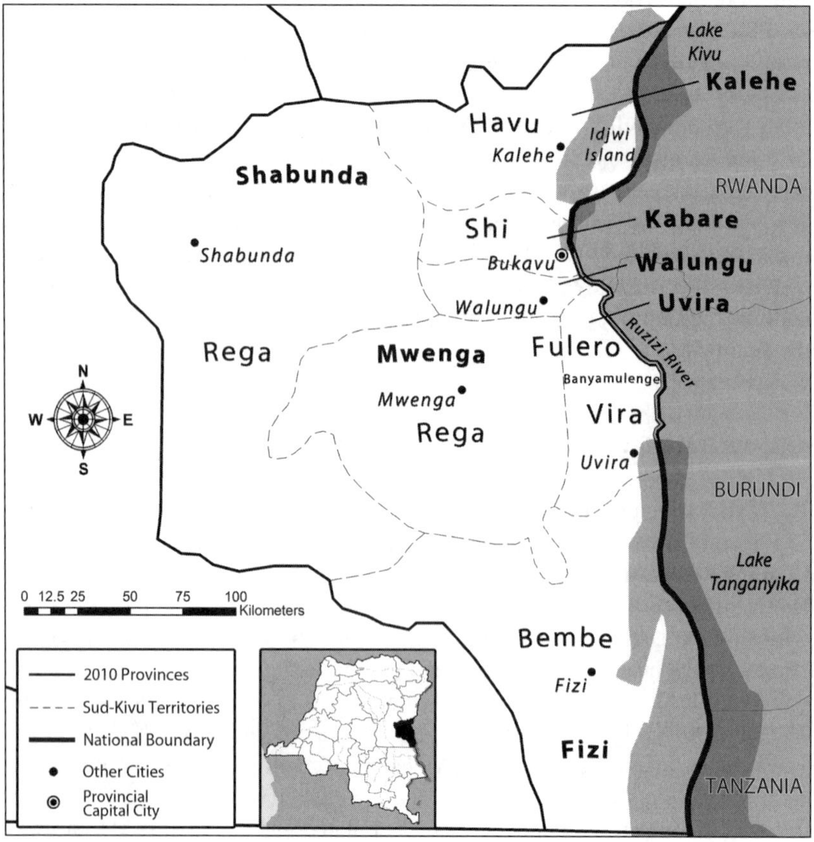

Bembe, Fulero, Havu, Rega, Shi, and Vira. In the 1950s, Van Bulck (1954) indicated no Kinyarwanda speakers in Sud-Kivu. However, Weiss (1954) counted in the same year some 20,000 Kinyarwanda speakers in the chieftaincy of Bavira in Uvira. Assuming that the rate of population growth is 3.1 percent per year in Sud-Kivu, and using a compound formula from 1954 to 1996, or forty-two years, the number of Banyamulenge should have been 72,093 in 1996, not counting deaths. However, most observers have suggested that the Banyamulenge were perhaps 40,000 people in 1996, or some 10 percent of the population of Uvira, thus representing the third-largest population in the territory (Kabamba and Lanotte 1999, p. 127).

Sources also diverge on the date the first group of Rwandan pastoralists came into the region. According to Newbury (1988, pp. 48–49), the Banyamulenge migrated to the Uvira territory in the late eighteenth century as refugees from the southern Kinyaga region of Rwanda to escape the growing power of Mwami (King) Rwabugiri. Other groups escaped the repression unleashed after the Rucunshu coup d'état of 1896 (Prunier 2009, p. 51; Kabamba and Lanotte 1999, p. 126). These pastoralists first settled in the Ruzizi plains around Lemera, in the chieftaincy of the Fulero, and created the Mulenge village named after the neighboring mountain (Kajiga 1956). Before they settled in the area, however, the Banyamulenge concluded a communal contract with their Fulero chiefs consisting of an annual tribute, *ubugabire*, for the right to use the land. They later developed trade, exchanging beef for food crops with their neighbors. These two arrangements helped the Banyamulenge control one portion of the Ruzizi plains around Kamanyola and the high plateau of Itombwe for the grazing needs of their cattle (Ruhimbika 2001).

During colonization, the Belgian government encouraged further migrations from Burundi and Rwanda, relocating people to the so-called less populated areas in the plains of Ruzizi to work on cotton plantations, to build the railway between the port of Kalunda (Uvira) and Kamanyola, and to work in the agro-pastoral industry. The administration granted them control over several small chieftaincies (*chefferies*), which were later grouped into larger units for administrative convenience. In 1933, however, Banyamulenge's autonomous chieftaincies were abolished, and the Banyamulenge became again subjects of the local chiefs. Their claim in 1944 for a chieftaincy that would include all Tutsi immigrants was rejected.

The independence of Congo, Burundi, and Rwanda in the early 1960s brought a new political configuration in the Great Lakes region because it transformed the relationships between the Banyamulenge and their neighbors—the Fulero and Vira. First, the Rwandan revolution in 1959 and subsequent migrations of Tutsi into Sud-Kivu gave the Banyamulenge a Tutsi characterization. This "Tutsization" of Banyamulenge is the "first export of the Rwandan political and ethnic conflict" into Sud-Kivu (Kisangani 1997; Kabamba and Lanotte 1999). The second wave of Tutsi from Rwanda into Sud-Kivu occurred in 1962 when Grégoire Kayibanda became president, ending the Rwandan monarchy.

This inflow consisted mostly of Tutsi royalists from the Rwandan Unitarist Party who supported Mwami Kigeri V. However, the Banyamulenge opposed the unitarists because they were afraid of losing their Congolese status and wanted to distinguish themselves from these Rwandan Tutsi refugees.

In addition to official refugees, undocumented migrations from Burundi and Rwanda have continued unabated since the early 1960s. Given porous borders, these illegal migrants have usually disappeared into Congolese society without a trace, taking either the Banyamulenge or Rundi label in Sud-Kivu and Banyarwanda label in Nord-Kivu. When the 1964 eastern rebellion hit Uvira and Fizi, the Banyamulenge fled. As pointed out in Chapter 3, the Tutsi refugees from Rwanda joined the eastern rebellion with other groups in the area because Gaston Soumialot, the leader of the rebellion, promised to help the Tutsi reconquer Rwanda. When mercenaries, Katanga gendarmes, and government forces penetrated into Sud-Kivu, rebel groups fled to the high mountains of Itombwe, where they killed the Banyamulenge's livestock to feed themselves. In retaliation, the Banyamulenge joined government forces and the mercenaries to protect their families and cattle. The offensive of the national army and the Banyamulenge defeated the eastern rebellion in its fiefdom of Sud-Kivu and Maniema (Verhaegen 1969). Autochthons, such as the Fulero and Bembe, saw this alliance as an act of treason and an "unforgivable expression of collaboration with the enemy" (Vlassenroot 2002, p. 504).

After the eastern rebellion, the central government confirmed the traditional authority of Banyamulenge in Kamanyola despite vehement opposition from local chiefs.[3] A few years later, President Mobutu signed the decree-law no. 72-002 in 1972 that conferred Congolese nationality on all immigrants from Rwanda and Burundi who had been in Congo before January 1950 and had continued to reside in Congo since. According to Article 15, "The people from Ruanda-Urundi who were established in the Kivu province before 1 January 1950 and who had continued to reside since then in the Republic of Zaire until the promulgation of the present law had acquired Zairian nationality on 30 June 1960" (Zaïre 1972, p. 6). The nationality law was followed a year later by the November 1973 "zairianization" that nationalized all small and medium-size foreign businesses and plantations, which Mobutu distributed to his cronies.

Unlike Nord-Kivu (as developed later in Chapter 6), the promulgation of the 1972 nationality law created no major societal issue of coexistence between the Banyamulenge and other ethnic groups in Sud-Kivu for three reasons. First, the Banyamulenge continued to honor their communal contract with their patrons in order to use land. Second, the 1973 nationalization never benefited the Banyamulenge the way it benefited the Tutsi in Nord-Kivu. Third, land was still plentiful for pasture in Sud-Kivu because the province remained less populated than Nord-Kivu. In fact, while there were 102 people per square kilometer in Uvira, the southern Fizi-Baraka area had only 13 people per square kilometer in the 1990s (Willame 1997, p. 76) compared with more than 250 inhabitants per square kilometer in Masisi (Nord-Kivu). Thus, the Banyamulenge's cattle never put pressure on cultivable land in Sud-Kivu as the Tutsi's cattle did in Masisi.

Nonetheless, the central government's recognition of the Banyamulenge increased their self-awareness as a distinct group in the multiethnic environment of Sud-Kivu. With this increasing awareness of their sociopolitical emancipation, the Tutsi immigrants decided to change their identity and differentiate themselves from the massive waves of refugees from Burundi and Rwanda. Thus, the name "Banyamulenge" emerged in 1973 to distinguish this group from Tutsi refugees (Willame 1997, p. 83). This construction of identity was the work of Muhoza Gisaro, who regrouped all the Tutsi living in Sud-Kivu territories of Fizi, Mwenga, and Uvira and even those living in Moba in North Katanga under the same appellation. In other words, all Tutsi became "from Mulenge," although only a portion of this group lived there.

As elsewhere in Congo, the electoral process under Mobutu followed ethnic arithmetic. Gisaro was elected to parliament thanks to his Banyamulenge constituency. While in the parliament, he tried to use the institution to pass legislation that would provide the Banyamulenge with their own territory. His efforts were strongly criticized and failed to gain support. Gisaro's move was later interpreted by traditional authorities in the Uvira territory as an attempt to usurp their land and authority. In sum, the electoral process of 1977 started a new round of political competition between autochthons and the Banyamulenge.

While the situation in Sud-Kivu remained calm, Nord-Kivu was boiling after a number of Tutsi became owners of plantations as the result of the 1973 nationalization law. Most legislators of non-Rwandan origin lobbied in the parliament to change the 1972 nationality law. The result was the promulgation of a new law, no. 81-002 of 29 June 1981, which explicitly canceled the rights of the Tutsi and Hutu in Kivu. According to Article 4 of the law, "Zairian in terms of article 11 of the Constitution, on 30 June 1960, [is] any person whose one of the ancestors is or has been member of one of the tribes established on the territory of the Republic of Zaire within the limits set on 1 August 1885, and as modified by subsequent conventions" (Zaïre 1981, p. 27). The new nationality law intended to exclude most Congolese of Rwandan descent, such as the Banyamulenge, from the political process. This outcome became obvious a year later when the legislative electoral process was under way, and Banyamulenge put their candidate, Joseph Mutambo, on the ballot. However, his nomination was rejected by the electoral commission on the grounds that he was a foreigner, according to the 1981 nationality law, even though the Banyamulenge were allowed to vote. The Banyamulenge refused to vote and burned voting booths in Uvira. In 1987, the nominations of two other Banyamulenge candidates, Dugu wa Mulenge and Musafiri Mushambaro, were again rejected because they were considered of "questionable nationality" (Mugisho 1998). In 1989, the government sent a mission, called Identification Mission of Zaireans in Kivu (Mission d'Identification des Zaïrois au Kivu), to the Kivus and northeast Katanga to identify nationals and to settle the citizenship status of people of Rwandan origin. However, technical and political difficulties hampered the process.

Meanwhile, when the Tutsi-led RPA started its war against the Hutu government of Rwanda in early 1990, a large number of young Banyamulenge, Tutsi of Nord-Kivu, and Tutsi refugees joined the RPA to unseat the Hutu government (Willame 1997, pp. 87–99). The Fulero and Vira populations saw this as yet another indication of Banyamulenge's lack of any nationalist link with Congo and considered such behavior an act of high treason reminiscent of the 1964 rebellion (discussed in Chapter 3). When Mobutu liberalized his political regime in April 1990, political competition ensued, and representatives of Sud-Kivu to the national conference, later sovereign national conference, were able to exclude the Banyamulenge from the political process.

It was not until April 1995 that the situation deteriorated as the result of a parliamentary resolution denying the Banyamulenge their citizenship. Adopted on 28 April, the resolution classified the Banyamulenge as immigrants and refugees from Rwanda. In addition, Articles 3 and 4 required the application of the 1981 nationality law, the cancellation of selling or purchasing land by immigrants from Rwanda or Burundi who had acquired the Congolese nationality "through fraudulent means," and the annulment of their nomination to any public office. Thus, threatened with eviction by the application of the 1995 Resolution, the Banyamulenge declared publicly that they would resist any attack against them (Mugisho 1998, p. 327). While these events were unfolding, the region of Uvira became tense in August–September 1996 as some 1,200 to 3,000 Banyamulenge who had fought alongside the RPA and helped it take power in Rwanda returned to the plateaus of Itombwe (Willame 1997, p. 93).

Causes of Civil War Against Mobutu

This subsection divides the causes of the anti-Mobutu civil war into critical juncture and critical antecedents. A major critical juncture is the politics of exclusion of the Banyamulenge as the result of the nationality issue and the democratization process. This argument goes against a number of scholars and observers who saw the war against Mobutu as an invasion from Rwanda. Critical antecedents include both elements of continuity (colonial borders) and elements of change such as the decline of rentier state and regional politics.

Nationality issue and politics of exclusion. The nationality issue remained dormant for almost nine years, from 1982 to 1990, until April 1990 when Mobutu announced the liberalization of his political regime and the holding of elections. More specifically, Mobutu was strategically planning his 1997 elections to satisfy Congo's major donors and still maintain power. He knew that the Kivus were critical to his reelection because the main tribes in the areas, such as the Bembe, Fulero, Nande, and Shi, not only disliked him but were also hostile to the Banyarwanda in Nord-Kivu and to the Banyamulenge in Sud-Kivu, believed to support Mobutu. He decided to use these hatreds to get reelected. As developed later (in Chapter 6), Mobutu was in the process of creating a Hutuland in Nord-Kivu with the collaboration of former Rwandan army officers and Hutu refugees to tip the balance of numbers in favor of the Hutu at the expense of the Nande. In Sud-Kivu, he sacrificed the minority group, the Banyamulenge, for his electoral strategy to rally the electorate majority.

Mobutu used Anzuluni Bembe, deputy president of the transitional parliament, to bring the nationality issue to the parliament. The irony was that Bembe was stoned by his own Bembe constituency in Uvira because of his support of Mobutu (Lanotte 2003).[4] On 28 April 1995, the parliament passed a "Resolution on Nationality." To follow up, Bembe created a commission presided over by Manbeweni Vangu, the Vangu Commission, to investigate the nationality issue in the Kivus. In its report, the Vangu Commission concluded that all citizens of Rwandan origin should return to Rwanda. The transitional parliament followed with the promulgation of the "Resolution on Refugees and Displaced Populations in the Regions of Nord-Kivu and Sud-Kivu" in late 1995, which required repatriation of all peoples of Rwandan origin and all Hutu refugees who had entered the DRC through the French humanitarian Turquoise mission (Kisangani 2003). The word from politicians and people of Kivus was simple: "Before the end of 1995, all people of Rwandan origin naked and out" (Chamowicz 1996, p. 117).

This message was a threat to the Banyamulenge and their cattle. As a result, the Banyamulenge began buying weapons and arming themselves as early as mid-1995 to defend their villages and cattle against eventual attacks. They used their relations with officers in the Congolese army to stock up weapons and munitions (Prunier 2009, p. 69). According to Mugisho (1998), a large quantity of weapons that Congolese authorities seized from the former Rwandan soldiers in 1994 were sold to the Banyamulenge; Mobutu's son Kongolo Mobutu even sold weapons and munitions to the Banyamulenge (Prunier 2009, p. 69). Finally, the Banyamulenge were counting on a large number of their young men who helped the RPA take power in Rwanda in June 1994 to return home and help defend their cattle.

In sum, the argument advanced by a number of scholars that the war against President Mobutu was an invasion from Rwanda is misleading because it overlooks the fact that the Banyamulenge were contemplating a rebellion since the adoption of the April 1995 parliamentary resolution. For example, Müller Ruhimbikathe, one of the Banyamulenge's leaders, declared in May 1995 that "those who covet our cattle will take them only after they have killed the last Munyamulenge" (Mugisho 1998, p. 327). Until then, it seemed that the Banyamulege were ready for a military option to protect their cattle and defend themselves against what they called "ethnic cleansing" or their deportation to Rwanda.

In 1995, the Banyamulenge could rely neither on Burundi nor on Rwanda. Both countries confronted their own internal security issues as the result of rebel armed interventions from sanctuaries based in Tanzania and Congo, respectively (Kisangani 1997, 2003). Nonetheless, Rwanda responded a year later because its government wanted to end the military incursions of Rwandan rebels from Congo by dismantling the refugee camps where the Hutu rebels were operating freely. In early July 1996, General Paul Kagame started to infiltrate Rwandan soldiers dressed in civilian clothes into Sud-Kivu. In a sense, the civil war against Mobutu started with the issue of Banyamulenge's nationality.

In fact, on 8 October 1996, the deputy governor of Sud-Kivu, Lwabanji Lwasi, gave the Banyamulenge eight days to vacate Mulenge in what he called a "cleansing of the plateau" (Reyntjens 1999, p. 55). With nowhere to go, the Banyamulenge began launching a number of attacks against government forces. Violent combat was reported in Bukavu and Uvira on 18–30 October 1996 when troops from Rwanda and the Banyamulenge attacked the Bukavu and Uvira refugee camps, forcing refugees to flee in several directions.

In retrospect, the critical juncture of the revolt against Mobutu was provincial politics to exclude the Banyamulenge from the political process, similar to Congo's previous civil wars that were precipitated with the implementation of exclusionary policies at the provincial level. The Rwandan Tutsi-dominated government responded to the Banyamulenge's distress call a year after the adoption of the April 1995 resolution. In this situation, the call for help can be considered part of "kin country syndrome" (Huntington 1996, p. 272); that is, ethnic affiliations across international borders can make ethnic groups in one country become alarmed by the grievances of their brethren across borders. This syndrome, which is an element of continuity related to colonial African borders, increased between neighbors and ultimately resulted in the "internationalization of Congo civil war" (Levy and Thompson 2010, p. 22).

At the regional level, the Banyamulenge's call for help well suited the Rwandan government in its struggle to reconcile warring factions within the government and to halt the repeated incursions of former Rwandan troops into northwestern Rwanda (Kisangani 2000a). The only way to solve this dual security problem was for the Rwandan government to attack the refugee camps in Kivu where these troops had sought shelter. This strategy also included a move to prevent the West from intervening in the Great Lakes region with humanitarian assistance, because the Rwandan government feared that any intervention would give the former Rwandan soldiers enough time to regroup and launch an attack on Rwanda (Kisangani 2000a).

Critical antecedents of anti-Mobutu war. De Villers and Omasombo (2002) have argued that Laurent Kabila's success in ousting Mobutu was more an accident of history than the result of a sociopolitical process of change. This view is partly incorrect because it overlooks the historical process of Mobutu's system, which started decaying in the second half of the 1970s (as developed in Chapter 1). First, Mobutu was able to create a strong state and a sense of nation from 1967 to 1975. For almost nine years, the state penetrated the countryside, except in a few mountainous places of Fizi and Uvira, provided security and order, and implemented a number of socioeconomic policies that sustained economic growth for a decade—1966–1975. However, the Mobutu state began showing signs of weakness in 1977–1978 when the army was unable to drive back Congolese insurgents who had sanctuary in Angola (Chapter 4). President Mobutu was rescued by the West, which forced him to liberalize his political regime. The result was an increase in the power of the legislative branch and the defection of some of his clients. A small group of defectors even created a new political party, the UDPS, in 1982. This was treason under the one-party system.

Nonetheless, Mobutu's rescue by the West in 1978 set an unprecedented period of peace that lasted for almost fourteen years—from mid-1978 to 1992. Two levels of analysis—elite and mass—help account for this period of apparent political stability devoid of any internal war, although the state was weak enough to provide ample opportunity for a civil war. At the elite level, Mobutu's patronage helped him muzzle his opponents by co-opting them. The concept of the shadow state (see Reno 2000) is relevant in describing Mobutu's patronage or kleptocracy that resulted in economic decline and state failure. This element of change was the result of institutional failure created by a rentier economy. The term "rentier economy" is often used to describe any resource that is external and plays a dominant role in domestic politics (Mahdavi 1970). Rent-seeking is thus a behavior in institutional settings where individual efforts to maximize value generate social waste rather than social surplus (Yates 1996).

President Mobutu began his rentier state in June 1966 with the promulgation of the Bakajika Law that made all lands state domain. The law cleared the way for new mineral concessions by abolishing colonial arrangements and undeveloped colonial claims and paved the way for the nationalization of the UMHK, later Gécamines, on 1 January 1967. The control of mining resources allowed Mobutu to sustain his rentier state without resorting to direct taxation, which could have spurred unrest among urban forces, whose index of real wages declined from 100 in 1960 to virtually zero in the late 1970s (Kisangani 1997, p. 10).

On 30 November 1973, Mobutu bolstered his rentier state with the nationalization policy. All small and medium-sized nationalized businesses were handed over to fewer than 325 families. Meanwhile, Mobutu created more than twenty state marketing boards to capture any economic surplus generated by the peasants and staffed them with his cronies from different ethno-political constituencies. The nationalization policy allowed Mobutu to control the elites by integrating them into his circle and thus narrowing access to state spoils. Because his policy rewarded clients rather than social groups or regions, it prevented mobilization of broad-based political demands and collective action. Mobutu's clients became dependent on his willingness to keep them on the payroll as ministers or directors of state parastatals. The result was that his clients embezzled billions of dollars and transferred their theft abroad. By 1976, Mobutu institutionalized corruption, and kleptocracy was evident to all. In fron of a crowd of some 50,000 people, he gave public voice to this knowledge when he urged his citizens to steal wisely: "If you want to steal, steal a little in a nice way, but if you steal too much to become rich overnight you will be caught. And if you have succeeded in stealing, please reinvest in our country the product of your theft. You become the republic's enemy if you transfer this product overseas" (cited in Kabwit 1979, p. 397).

However, the number of his clients kept increasing, as new university graduates were co-opted into the patronage system. President Mobutu could not keep up with his patronage as the result of this inflation of clients and declining sources of rents from the mineral sector and foreign aid. The mineral sector, which contributed some 50 percent of total revenue per year in the 1970s, began to decline in the early 1980s, despite an increase in copper production in the late 1980s (Kisangani 1987). For example, the contribution of Gécamines to state revenue averaged only 19 percent a year from 1983 to 1987 (Kisangani 1997). In subsequent years, this portion of revenue increased, averaging some 34 percent a year from 1988 to 1991, but was not enough to satisfy a hyperinflation of potential clients. Things got worse later as mineral production plummeted in the early 1990s. Although the Gécamines' contribution still represented some $121.4 million of revenue for Mobutu (14.8 percent of total), this contribution was almost zero after 1993. The only source of dwindling state revenue was the diamond sector from Kasai, where the state was competing with smugglers and artisanal miners.

Another source of patronage was foreign aid. Prior to 1979, it was quite modest but increased in 1980 and remained above 50 percent of total revenue per year thereafter (Kisangani 1997). The end of the Cold War saw a substantial decline in foreign aid from major patrons. Concomitant with foreign aid was foreign debt, which represented 32 percent of GDP in 1980 and was close to 110 percent of GDP in 1990. By the time Kabila became president in May 1997, foreign debt was 230 percent of GDP (World Bank 2010). The growth in foreign debt did not correspond to foreign direct investments, which declined throughout the 1980s to almost zero by 1992 as the result of a weak exchange rate. Therefore, the decline of rents and the increasing number of college graduates, or potential clients, strained the Mobutu patronage system.

The final critical antecedent of Mobutu's downfall as related to his rentier state was seigniorage: revenue the government earns by printing money and is thus a tax on citizens. From the late 1970s to the mid-1980s, seigniorage revenue varied around $200 million a year, while direct taxes represented less than 5 percent of total revenue, mostly from payrolls of public servants (Kisangani 1997). From the mid-1980s onward, the power to print money increased and then exploded in the 1990s as the result of a decline in mineral revenue and foreign aid. What De Herdt (2002, p. 448) calls a puzzle in 1974–1978 can now be explained; he describes "as puzzling to note that the instrument of seigniorage was not activated to neutralize a much more important fall in ordinary revenue between 1974 and 1978." In fact, the real prices of copper declined by more than 50 percent in 1975, while exports fell by almost one-third of their previous levels. However, foreign aid was forthcoming to compensate for this shortfall in 1974–1978. Thus, Mobutu hardly needed to use his power to print money. Only later, when the West deserted him as the result of his unwillingness to let the democratization process proceed, did seigniorage increase. Although Mobutu caught a break in 1994 after the massive influx of refugees from Rwanda, foreign aid declined in subsequent years.

Seigniorage rose in the early 1990s and remained more than 300 percent of government revenue until Kabila overthrew Mobutu in May 1997. This financing of the deficit made zaire banknotes so useless that they were called "prostates" after Mobutu was diagnosed with prostate cancer. The consequence of this financing was hyperinflation and the breakdown of the formal economy. Consumer prices increased by 81 percent from 1989 to 1990, jumped by 2,154 percent from 1990 to 1991, and then by 4,129 percent a year later (World Bank 2010). Although the increase in consumer prices from 1992 to 1993 was lower than the preceding year—that is, 1,986 percent—the price level jumped by almost 23,773 percent from 1993 to 1994. In 1995, it increased by only 542 percent. The hyperinflation that followed money printing further weakened the Mobutu regime as citizens moved away from the local currency by using dollars for their daily transactions to avoid the seigniorage tax. The "dollarization" of the economy was massive in the first half of the 1990s. Some estimates put the number of dollars in circulation in the early 1990s at $350 million, with a peak of $400 million in 1992 (De Herdt 2002, p. 449). Dollarization meant loss of revenue. If the public tolerated some 50 to 70 percent of yearly inflation in the second half of the 1970s without seeking alternative currencies, the Mobutu regime lost more than $175 million as the result of dollarization (De Herdt 2002, p. 449). This is a further indication of a weak state, one that cannot even control its own currency. The Mobutu state thus completely lost all sovereign power to tax citizens, even through money printing.

In sum, co-optation of the elite from different ethno-political constituencies was Mobutu's strategy to gird the regime against centrifugal elite forces. Although economic growth remained positive in the 1980s, most social indicators show signs of strain. First, Mobutu's spending on himself, which averaged 35 percent of total government spending in the 1980s, increased to more than 40 percent in 1990 (Kisangani 1997, p. 41). The result was a concomitant decline of public spending in a number of social areas such as education and health. Spending on education declined drastically from 40 percent of total spending in 1983 to 10 percent by 1989 and was less than 2 percent a year in the early 1990s (Kisangani 1997). As a result, the number of dropouts and unemployed young men also increased drastically.

At the mass level, two factors explain what seems to be a relatively peaceful decade, the 1980s, devoid of any civil war. First was the liberalization of the mining sector. President Mobutu signed Decree no. 81-013 on 2 April 1981 and ordinance Law no. 82-039 on 5 November 1982 that deregulated the mining industry. Not only did these laws attract an influx of small foreign companies but they also increased artisanal mining activities. In the words of De Failly (2000, p. 184), the deregulation of the mining sector was another "zairianization" or "nationalization that intended to give the poor access to Congo's mineral wealth, seven years after the 1973 zairianization that gave wealth to the politico-administrative elite."

The deregulation policy attracted a large number of young men in the rural mining enclaves. The boom in artisanal mining resulted in a decline of the urban population from an average of 31 percent of the country's total population in the 1970s to 28 percent in the first half of the 1980s (World Bank 2010). Artisanal mining increased in the 1980s, with income being no less than $100 ($198 in 2010 prices) a month in the mining enclaves, compared to an average monthly income of $5 in large metropolitan areas (Kisangani 1998). The flow of minerals followed specific routes to reach centers that included Kinshasa, Mbuji Mai, Tshikapa, Kasubalesa, and Butembo, where artisanal miners traded their minerals for consumer goods. Minerals were flown from some of these centers to other African countries, Europe, or the Middle East through smuggling networks dominated by specific ethnic groups, such as the Nande in eastern Congo (MacGaffey 1987; Kisangani 1998).

If artisanal mining provided a large number of destitute youths a means of survival, the informal economy was also a booming sector in most major cities. A number of activities were carried out in this economy ranging from transportation of goods to that of people, from repair services to health care, and from construction works to local petty trade (Kisangani 1998). As Kisangani (1998) has pointed out, these informal economic activities not only provided most citizens the means to make ends meet but were also widespread to the extent that they challenged the mere existence of state institutions in their ability to collect taxes. Thus, the informal economy was the only sector that perhaps provided urban dwellers means of survival in the 1980s. For example, in 1984 in Kinshasa alone, employment in the informal sector gave 140,000 people some income compared with 120,000 in the formal sector (Peemans 1997b). Overall, the informal sector provided 1.9 million jobs out of 2.8 million jobs—a full 60 percent. From 1980 to 1990, the number of jobs in the informal sector increased by more than 46 percent, while the formal sector increased by less than 20 percent (Kisangani 1998). More specifically, the income earned from the informal economy represented more than threefold what many citizens were earning in the formal sector.

However, two events would have negative effects on artisanal mining and the informal economy, which set the stage for the armed conflicts of the 1990s. First was a decline in revenue in the artisanal mining as the result of increasing number of intermediaries and diggers. The average monthly income derived from artisanal mining dropped from $198 (2010 = 100) a month in the early 1980s to less than $70 by the early 1990s. As artisanal mining became less lucrative, most youths began their march back to urban areas (Kisangani 1998).

The most important factor that had a negative impact on the informal economy in urban areas was the collapse of the formal economy because the informal economy is highly dependent on the formal domestic and importing sectors (Kisangani 1998). A decline in the formal sector can have major negative repercussions on the informal sector as well. The decline of the formal sector started in the capital city after the first massive looting of the official economy by soldiers and civilians on 23–24 September 1991 in Kinshasa (Kisangani 1998). The saddest part of the September looting was that people burned what they could not bring home because they had limited space in their houses to store their loot. After all shops and warehouses were looted, all "formal economic activities" moved to the informal economy. Looting soon spread throughout the country. The official economy in Kinshasa thus disappeared overnight. Within a few months, the informal economy started showing signs of decay as a result of the absence of the formal economic sector. For example, carpenters working on the side had no suppliers of nails or wood. Cobblers and electricians in the informal sector who, before September 1991, bought supplies from the formal importing sector could not rely on the informal sector because of price hikes or supply shortages. In February 1993, still more looting occurred across the country. As a result, a culture of what Congolese came to label "pillage" was born, which has been sustained since by the regular army, militia groups, and unemployed young men. In sum, the informal sector that had helped millions of people survive also declined in the early 1990s. By the time the AFDL and its African allied forces crossed the DRC from east to west, the youths were ready to follow the movement as an alternative to their destitution under the Mobutu regime.

Without schools to provide them some hope and future opportunity, young men flocked to Kabila's army, which had approximately 25,000 kadogo, averaging 12 to18 years old. This picture of young men as a dynamic group that toppled Mobutu should not cloud the fact that the youths were mobilized only several weeks after the war had already started in Sud-Kivu. Thus, lack of opportunity was more critical in shortening the civil war against Mobutu than in explaining it.

The second critical antecedent to explain the civil war against Mobutu was his interference in his neighbors' politics. This topic has been developed elsewhere (Kisangani 2003; Prunier 2009). Suffice it to say that, for many decades, Mobutu sided with rebel groups against governments in Angola and Uganda or protected his own central African clients, such as the presidents of Central African Republic, Chad, and Rwanda. Thus, a number of neighboring countries wanted him ousted. The impact of Mobutu's policy in the region ended when the Tutsi-led RPF seized power in Rwanda, which resulted in a massive influx of Hutu refugees in Congo. The refugees themselves were not a major problem. The armed groups in their midst, which crossed the borders and began destabilizing the Great Lakes region, were, however, the main cause of regional insecurity.

Duration and Conflict Management

The civil war against Mobutu lasted seven months. As pointed out in Chapter 1, this war was popularly perceived as a legitimate war of liberation from the yoke of Mobutu. First came massive rallying of the people and recruitment. Recruiting children was an integral part of the AFDL's policy to increase the number of rebels. A survey of young men done by the United Nations Children Emergency Fund (UNICEF) in Bukavu in 1997 explains this strategy:

Twenty-five percent of kadogo joined Kabila because he promised them generous compensation for their efforts to topple Mobutu; 28 percent decided to join because the civil war provided the only opportunity to make a living; 15 percent were convinced by other child soldiers to join; 15 percent wanted revenge against abusive soldiers of the Congolese army; and 7 percent were moved by patriotism (cited in Van Acker and Vlassenroot 2001, p. 107). In sum, some 53 percent of child soldiers saw economic opportunity in joining the AFDL.

The advance of rebel troops toward Kisangani opened a door for negotiations. The first meeting between the Mobutu administration and the rebels took place in Cape Town on 20 February 1997 and was brokered by the United States and South Africa. However, the talks collapsed despite the presence of high-level envoys from Pretoria (Deputy Foreign Minister Aziz Pahad) and Washington (Assistant Secretary of State for Africa George Moose and President Bill Clinton's Special Assistant on Africa Susan Rice).

The two parties met again in Togo under OAU auspices on 26 March 1997. However, negotiations faltered because the Kabila delegation refused to compromise as it smelled victory. From 5 to 8 April and on 4 May, South Africa President Nelson Mandela tried to broker a peace agreement, but Kabila was reluctant to negotiate as his troops continued to gain ground. Mandela's diplomatic missions failed in part because a number of major powers recognized the AFDL as a belligerent community by early April 1997. This failure set the stage for the AFDL's military victory and thus weakened Congolese democratic forces that had challenged Mobutu and set the stage for Kabila's autocratic leadership.

Another major factor that helped end the anti-Mobutu war quickly was the role of General Mahele Lieko Bokoungo, chief of staff of the army. In late April 1997, Mahele contacted Kabila and provided him with two key facts. First, Mahele gave the ADFL the defense strategy for the town of Kenge, which was guarded by UNITA troops (Lanotte 2003, p. 62). After the defeat of UNITA forces in Kenge, the battle for Kinshasa was averted because General Mahele gave the US ambassador a plan to let the AFDL enter the capital city without bloodshed (Lanotte 2003, p. 65). Second, Mahele dissuaded Mobutu's son, Kongolo Mobutu, from taking foreigners as hostages. By late afternoon, Mahele paid the price for his treason. He was shot dead by Kongolo (Prunier 2009, p. 137).

Finally, the anti-Mobutu war was short because most leaders in neighboring countries wanted him ousted. The regional consensus in eastern and southern Congo resulted from Mobutu's interference in his neighbors' foreign policies. The Angolan engagement displaced the center of the rebel movement from Kigali to Luanda, especially after Angola learned that Mobutu was using UNITA forces (Reyntjens 1997; Kisangani 1997). The role of Angola was thus decisive because it helped the alliance attack Mobutu forces from both the east and the west, placing Kinshasa in pincers.

Internationally, the United States may have warned France not to save Mobutu and seemed to have dispatched in secret some 350 special troops to Kinshasa earlier in May to avoid any intervention from France (N'Gbanda 1998, pp. 317–319). Without this warning, France might have risked direct military intervention to bail out Mobutu, probably with some African forces, reminiscent of Moroccan troops' intervention in 1977, or Shaba 1 (see Chapter 4). In any case, without direct Western intervention, Mobutu was doomed, and he understood it as he left for Morocco where he died of cancer on 7 September 1997.

Consequences of Anti-Mobutu Internal War

The rise of Kabila marked a period of high hopes for the Congolese and their neighbors. The West also expected a change from decades of kleptocracy to democracy and clean management (Clark 2002), but all hopes were dashed by Kabila's leadership style. First, he marginalized political leaders who had gained popularity and legitimacy for their leadership in the sovereign national conference of 1992–1993 and in the democratization process that weakened the Mobutu regime. Once in power, Kabila reinforced political cleavages by arresting a number of Mobutu's ministers and managers of state enterprises as well as by excluding political parties from his government and disregarding the proceedings of the national conference. He specifically accused these ministers and managers of having destroyed Congo or of having "danced in the glory of the monster" (De Villers and Willame 1998, p. 85; Stearns 2011). However, a few months after being president, Kabila and his collaborators began to cut corners in ways that recalled Mobutu's kleptocratic regime. Foreign businesses were told that to get government approval for their investments, they had to deposit large payments in newly created bank accounts whose shareholders were Kabila's associates (Kisangani 1998). Just like Mobutu, Kabila relied on mineral resources, especially diamonds, to finance his rentier state. Less than a year in power, Kabila was equated with Mobutu by a large proportion of his countrymen and by the international community as "Mobutu's clone" (Boissonnade 1998).

The AFDL's victory also reconfigured ethnic relations in the Kivus. The Banyamulenge, former victims, now became victimizers and began their own process of excluding former victimizers. Many local traditional authorities were killed in the Kivus by the Banyamulenge and Tutsi, and those who escaped the ethnic cleansing fled (Bucyalimwe 1999). These changes in leadership caused deep resentment when the Congolese saw people of Rwandan origin, whom they considered foreigners, claim supremacy in Congolese high offices. Moreover, the Tutsi minority claimed the AFDL's victory as their own. More specifically, the Banyamulenge viewed themselves as liberators because they were the vanguard of the civil war. With other Tutsi, they became "arrogant and behaved toward other ethnic groups" as conquerors (Bucyalimwe 1999, p. 327).

This arrogance for having liberated "other tribes" from the yoke of Mobutu further enlarged the social chasm between Tutsi and autochthons, thus making national reconciliation still more distant. The active participation of the Banyamulenge in dismantling the Mobutu regime must be acknowledged; however, other groups who also participated in weakening the Mobutu regime during the democratization process in the early 1990s objected to the Banyamulenge monopolizing the liberation. The Tutsi espoused short-term management of the state and accumulation of state spoils at the expense of long-term goals of recognition as citizens of Congo and peaceful cohabitation with other groups in the Kivus.

At the military level, Commander in Chief James Kabarebe, a Rwandan Tutsi, used his position to modify the ethnic composition of the army in the east, replacing most officers with those favorable to the Tutsi's cause. Some of the officers were even bought outright with large amounts of cash up to $150,000 (De Villers, Omasombo, and Kennes 2001, p. 18). At the regional level, Rwanda and Uganda left no room for free debate and set up barriers to external monitoring of the Hutu refugees who were killed during the war against Mobutu. At the regional level, control of economic resources was also at stake because it involved both commerce and collection of revenue. A new business elite, speaking English and Kinyarwanda, but not French or any of the Congolese languages, emerged in the Kivus. The goal of Rwanda was to make the Kivus its vassal areas in its quest for a buffer zone or annexation. Although President Yoweri Museveni of Uganda dreamed of economic regional cooperation in the Great Lakes region, with Uganda as its center, most Ugandan military officers and businessmen wanted to exploit Congo's eastern mineral resources. On the Burundi side, the Hutu-dominated rebel troops, Forces pour la Défense de la Démocratie, which was the armed wing of the Conférence Nationale pour la Défense de la Démocratie, lost most of their rear area bases in eastern DRC as the result of the anti-Mobutu war. These forces moved to western Tanzania, where they started operating in and around refugee camps because the Tutsi from Burundi and Rwanda were now in charge of eastern DRC.

Clearly, the issues at stake under Mobutu were not solved during the takeover by Kabila, which presaged another conflict. Thus, the attitudes and actions of members of the Kabila administration set the stage for a new civil war, starting with the Mai Mai insurrection in September 1997. This period was also characterized by abuses of human rights, as the Tutsi minority attempted to assert their authority over the Kivus. Terror and large-scale human rights violations occurred in most areas of Nord-Kivu and Sud-Kivu.

Mai Mai Insurrection and Anti-Foreign Sentiment

The Mai Mai groups were part of the army that toppled Mobutu. While the Banyamulenge and the Banyarwanda were gaining power at the local level in the Kivus, other groups felt they were being marginalized by the Kabila administration. For example, a large number of traditional authorities were replaced by the Tutsi in Nord-Kivu (Willame 1998, p. 239). Moreover, the overwhelming presence of the Tutsi in powerful political positions in the Kivus gave most Congolese the impression that they were under foreign occupation and their country was being run from Rwanda. This sentiment was the first call to rally the Mai Mai against President Kabila. On 7 July 1997, the Mai Mai insurrection started in the Kivus. The Mai Mai troops were joined later by former Rwandan Hutu soldiers and even former Mobutu troops. Within two months, between July and September 1997, some 459 government troops were killed while some 700 Mai Mai perished in the confrontation. The number of civilian deaths was even higher. In July alone, when the war started, more than 2,000 people were killed by Kabila's forces and Rwandan troops to avenge attacks by Mai Mai guerrillas, and more than 12,000 people were internally displaced in the Kivus. The insurrection ended in late July 1998.

Historical Account of the Mai Mai

The Mai Mai groups were mostly composed of young men averaging twelve to twenty years old (Kisangani 2003). The word "Mai Mai," which emerged during the 1964 rebellion in Congo (see Chapter 3), is a corruption of the Swahili word for water, *maji*. The Mai Mai of the 1990s wore war charms reminiscent of the early rebellions and sprinkled their body with water before combat to protect themselves against bullets, which they believed were transformed into raindrops. The image from the early 1960s resonates even today in the collective imagination of the West, which associates the Mai Mai with esoteric practices, strange clothing modes, and savage violence in the heart of darkness of the African continent (Lanotte 2003). As Lanotte (2003) has pointed out, this view is far from the truth. More specifically, the use of war charms in the 1960s and the 1990s represents a strict code of conduct that epitomizes an egalitarian society.

Historically, the Mai Mai movement in the 1960s was an expression of discontent in marginalized communities and a reaction to the corruption of traditional and state institutions of authority. A multiethnic conglomerate of people, this early movement was created in the context of the 1964 rebellions to fight against the symbol of neocolonialism or against an elite "sold out to the West" and a corrupt traditional leadership. In 1964, the Mai Mai thus targeted both administrative and traditional authorities.

Unlike the 1960s, the Mai Mai groups of the 1990s emerged as the result of conflict over land in eastern Congo. They were thus part of the local elites and supportive of both local political and traditional authorities. Before the AFDL was formed, most politicians in the Kivus used the Mai Mai in one way or another and encouraged their movement because they saw Rwandan immigrants as political contenders in the post-Mobutu period. Terror against bureaucrats and politicians was no longer an important instrument of deterrence in the 1990s compared with the terror that people witnessed in 1964–1965.

The early Mai Mai movement was also kept cohesive by Lumumbist ideology. The Mai Mai strongly believed in Lumumba's view of a Congo free from the yoke of "imperialism and neo-colonialism." In the 1990s, however, the Mai Mai movement owed its cohesiveness to ethnic affinities rather than to any political or ideological framework. The Mai Mai also tried to mobilize the population in defense of the rural traditional order against what they perceived as foreign occupation, targeting especially the Tutsi and Rwandan soldiers.

Another difference between the two Mai Mai movements is the availability of conflict capital or guns in eastern Congo. Unlike the early Mai Mai rebels who relied mostly on traditional weapons, such as spears or bows and arrows, the Mai Mai of the 1990s benefited from a market where supply of conflict capital was higher than its demand as the result of civil wars in the Great Lakes region and the concomitant proliferation of small arms in the area. Anyone could exchange a few kilograms of red beans for an AK-47.

Finally, there is some continuity between the Mai Mai movement of the 1960s and that of the 1990s in the Fizi-Baraka area in Sud-Kivu, where the eastern rebellion started in April 1964. The defeat of the eastern rebellion elsewhere in eastern Congo never eradicated the Mai Mai movement in Fizi-Baraka. One of its former leaders, Kabila, was able to mobilize the Mai Mai rebels again by creating the PRP in 1967. From 1967 to 1986, the shadow of the 1964 eastern rebellion under Kabila's PRP attracted a number of young men who underwent political and military education. Their attacks on Moba, North Katanga, in 1984 and 1985 indicated that the movement was still alive, although it never had any major effect on destabilizing the Mobutu regime. Some 60 percent of the Fizi population benefited from this education; most women and men thus knew how to use modern weapons everywhere the PRP had penetrated (Wilungula 1997, p. 188). This meant that the Mai Mai in these areas constituted a reserve army ready for action. When the PRP vanished in 1986, many former rebel leaders became involved in local politics. During local elections in Fizi, rebel survivors ran the propaganda machines of a number of candidates. Long years of revolutionary militancy created an increased capacity for popular mobilization over which any group can organize. A number of former leaders of the 1964 rebellion and later the PRP joined the AFDL thirty-two years later.

The Mai Mai movement thus remained dormant for almost twenty years until late 1986 when groups of young Tembo, Hunde, and Nande in Nord-Kivu, who resented Mobutu's protection of the Banyarwanda, formed a low-intensity antigovernment guerrilla army. They called their movement the Parti de la Libération Congolaise (PLC). According to some observers, the PLC remained underground in the Rwenzori Mountains (Willame 1997; Prunier 2004). Their activities were mostly limited to raiding Ugandan border villages to steal goats and chickens; in 1988–1989, they were severely mauled by the Congolese army and were forced to withdraw either north all the way into the Garamba National Park or deeper into the Beni forest (Prunier 2009, p. 83). In November 1994, President Museveni of Uganda contemplated the possibility of overthrowing Mobutu, using a number of Congolese opponents, including the PLC, because of Mobutu's support for the anti-Ugandan insurgents.

The idea died as the Congolese democratization process got under way in the early 1990s. However, the Ugandan secret services continued to fund the PLC movement in Congo. Colonel Kahinda Otafire, a key Ugandan secret service operative and a personal friend of President Museveni, recruited an idealistic young Mutetela, André Kisase Ngandu, who was a member of the PLC (Prunier 2004). Over the next two years, Kisase became Uganda's man in eastern Congo, retaliating against Mobutu's support of anti-Uganda rebel movements.

In 1993, most youth groups that had formed the Mai Mai militias began to destabilize Nord-Kivu, playing a major role in the first ethnic war in Nord-Kivu (developed later in Chapter 6). It was then that the term "Mai Mai" started circulating in Nord-Kivu to designate vaguely all young men with weapons, a premature suggestion of a unified group. In 1995, young men between twelve and sixteen years of age in Rutshuru territory were also using the rebel magic word, "Mai Mai," and adopting a new label, "the Bangilima," reputed to be invincible to bullets (Prunier 2004). Paid by local populations, they portrayed themselves as freedom fighters making common cause to defend the interests of Congolese and halt Hutu territorial expansion.

One significant element of the Mai Mai groups in the 1990s was their fragmentation along ethnic lines, making them a nonunified movement. Despite their diversity and differences, most Mai Mai groups in Sud-Kivu, Nord-Kivu, and North Katanga exhibited some common characteristics in their fight against Kabila and the Rwandan forces. First was their use of the forests and mountains as a base from which to hit the enemy and disappear. Second, their common enemy was the government in Kinshasa, which backed Rwanda and the Tutsi. Therefore, the Mai Mai viewed the Tutsi's claim to Congolese nationality as camouflage for annexing the Kivus to Rwanda and all Tutsi allied with Rwanda as foreign aggressors (Mugisho 2000).

However, viewed from a broader perspective, the Mai Mai groups reflect the political manifestation of the social exclusion affecting a growing number of marginalized young men in eastern Congo. Mugisho (2000) thus classifies the Mai Mai as both a social movement and a political movement. The former had neither political nor ideological goals and included mostly destitute youths whose only goal was to loot, rape, attack truck convoys, and assassinate people in order to survive. Many Mai Mai groups in this category were simply criminal groups, with no specific ideology. They were also involved in illicit trade networks and were sometimes used by certain traditional chiefs as rack-eteers.

Most Mai Mai, however, were part of what Mugisho (2000) calls a "polit-ical movement." This group had an ideology of self-defense and aimed to pro-tect political space against foreign occupying forces, especially Rwandan forces. These Mai Mai, who bore the label of "popular self-defense forces," had total popular support and usually did not disturb the local population from Beni (Nord-Kivu) to Shabunda (Sud-Kivu) (Mugisho 2000, p. 263). Nonetheless, the Mai Mai as a political movement in Sud-Kivu were only loosely connected with the Mai Mai in Nord-Kivu and generally carried out separate military opera-tions. There were several factions in Nord-Kivu, Sud-Kivu, and Maniema: from "Great North" in the Nande area of Lubero, Butembo, and Beni; of Walikale and Masisi, which included the Hunde, Nyanga, Tembo, and Kano; and of Bun-yakiri, Fizi, Mwenga, and Shabunda in Sud-Kivu (International Crisis Group 2000).

Explaining the Mai Mai Insurrection

As pointed out earlier, the victory of the AFDL was made possible because of popular support in eastern Congo, which provided the advancing rebel forces with a quiet rear base (Prunier 2009). More specifically, the Mai Mai groups were critical to the AFDL victory given their connection with local populations. Between 15,000 and 25,000 Mai Mai young men joined Kabila's forces during the war that toppled Mobutu in May 1997 (International Crisis Group 2000). However, keeping peace in eastern Congo, especially in the Kivus, required a number of conditions that President Kabila completely overlooked because he paid more attention to power at the center than at the periphery that helped him become president. Among these conditions were continued support of the Mai Mai militias, a clear distinction between "foreign Tutsi forces from Rwanda" and the Congolese of Rwandan origin, and the promulgation of a decree to re-instate the nationality of these Congolese (Kisangani 2003).

Unfortunately, Kabila completely neglected the Mai Mai. By late June 1997, the Mai Mai groups had sprung up everywhere in the Kivus. On 5 Sep-tember, the Mai Mai attacked Bukavu, but the fighting was particularly sharp in Nord-Kivu because a large number of Tutsi pastoralists moved from Rwanda and Uganda with their cows and settled in Masisi-Walikale territories (Prunier 2009, p. 173). In September alone, more than 1,000 human casualties occurred. The conflict spread to Butembo in the north, where the Mai Mai confronted the Katanga contingent of the national army.

In carrying out their insurrection against Kabila, the Mai Mai even allied with their former enemies: anti-Rwanda and anti-Uganda rebel groups still roaming in eastern Congo. Perhaps the first critical juncture of the Mai Mai in-surrection against President Kabila was the nomination of Tutsi to local ad-ministrative and political positions in Nord-Kivu and Sud-Kivu at the expense of the Mai Mai and other natives. Most Mai Mai leaders were not co-opted into the Kabila government as he had promised. Once in power, Kabila refused to compensate them for their military participation. Under Rwanda's pressure, he requested that the Mai Mai be disarmed and confined to several camps, among them the Kapalate camp near Kisangani, where hundreds perished of cholera and malnutrition (Van Acker and Vlassenroot 2001, p. 111). The exclusion of the Mai Mai from the political process pushed them to oppose Kabila.

The Mai Mai insurrection was also a reaction against the Rwandan government's attempt to extend its territory to the Kivus. Rwanda has always been overpopulated, and Congo has always provided a means to alleviate this lateral pressure since the colonial period. However, once in power in June 1994, the Tutsi-led RPF began claiming land along its western border based on the Berlin II idea, which intended to revisit colonial borders set at the end of the 1885 Berlin Conference by European powers (Kisangani 1998). Pasteur Bizimungu, president of Rwanda after the RPF took power, declared on 10 October 1996, that "if our combatants are actually in Zaire, they are in fact home" (Willame 1997, p. 76). Already in 1996, the Rwandan government had presented a map of "Greater Rwanda" that included a number of Congolese territories.

The idea that some areas of the Kivus were actually part of Rwanda received international support. As McKinley (1996) has described, the "Tutsi forces in Rwanda, Burundi and Eastern Zaire have struck back at their enemies and are trying to reassert control over an area that was part of their ancestral kingdom." The Rwandan effort to propagate the idea of Berlin II was perhaps an international psychological game allowing Rwanda to annex several regions of eastern Congo without becoming an international outcast because the international community upholds the idea of state sovereignty based on colonial boundaries. Moreover, Rwanda's claims overlooked the fact that many parts of Rutshuru territory in Nord-Kivu and all Sud-Kivu were never under the control of precolonial Rwanda (developed later in Chapter 6).

The Rwandan government's interpretations of history and claims over the Kivus were enough to galvanize the people, and the Mai Mai in particular, not only to fight against the Rwandan occupying force but also against Kabila, who was accused of having sold the Kivus to Rwanda. Rwanda's dream of carving up the Kivus further increased anti-Tutsi sentiment that viewed the RPA as a group of mercenaries without borders. In October 1997, the Mai Mai reiterated their intention to rally, to refuse cohabitation with all Tutsi and any negotiation with the enemy, and to chase the Tutsi from eastern Congo (Lubala 1998). To counter the abuses of the Tutsi military that caused antipathy or even hatred among the ethnic groups in the region against the Tutsi population (Lubala 1998), they created the Mouvement National pour la Sauveguarde de la Démocratie. According to Lubala (1998), by late 1997, when the Mai Mai insurrection started, a strong anti-Rwanda or anti-Tutsi sentiment was already rooted, creating a sort of dualism: Bantu versus Hamits, just as the Hutu were opposed to the Tutsi in Burundi and Rwanda. The Mai Mai thus reacted against what

Congolese perceived as Tutsi domination. By attacking the Banyamulenge and Rwandan forces, the Mai Mai were showing their anger against Kabila himself.

The Mai Mai insurrection and the local popular support in the Kivus were based on two factors that existed nowhere else in Congo. First is a type of collective memory found in Nord-Kivu and Sud-Kivu provinces. Liberating violence remains a major factor in the collective memories of the interlacustrine groups of the Kivus. Oral accounts of the past show the process of particularism and homogenization of these communities, with epic wars and myths of origin providing them with some type of cohesion and continuity.

The second factor is the role of a few traditional chiefs, who have the task of reminding people about the collective memories. The chiefs represent a strong monolithic political power and symbols of continuity that these communities identify with. Members of the community view any attempt to weaken or destroy these symbols as an attempt to destroy the community itself. The occupying forces, such as Rwanda, understood this link, and their first act was to harass traditional authorities and even kill the recalcitrant ones. Thus, the Mai Mai insurrection partly represents a reaction against acts viewed as deliberate attempts to destroy local communities.

Duration and Consequences

On 1 June 1998, President Kabila arrested some 500 Mai Mai fighters in eastern DRC (*Africa Research Bulletin* 1998, p. 13152). Despite this move, the Mai Mai continued to attack the Banyamulenge and Rwandan forces in Kivu. Their insurrection ended when Kabila announced the end of military cooperation with Rwanda in late July 1998. Because Kabila partly solved the issue of contention, the Mai Mai ended their insurrection.

One consequence of the Mai Mai insurrection was the massacre of innocent people accused of being Mai Mai supporters by the Banyamulenge and Tutsi soldiers, which human rights groups called genocide (Human Rights Watch 1999). The use of an ethnic base was part of the Tutsi's strategy of control. The dynamism that emerged from this insurrection manifested at three interconnected levels. At the local level, the Mai Mai insurrection helped a large number of young men liberate themselves from increasing alienation by giving them an opportunity to earn a living. Here, violence gave the youths a means to integrate into the local economy and also to be useful to society by protecting their land. The rise of Mai Mai also signaled a different type of organization in a traditional setting in which the use of violence called for a more egalitarian society than ever before. The Mai Mai insurrection indicated that their members opposed deficient state institutions that could not protect their land and families from foreigners. Moreover, the rise of Mai Mai signaled the fact that the Congolese young men would not hold back and were likely to challenge any existing order incompatible with their material survival and political participation.

Anti-Kabila War

When Kabila became president in May 1997, for many of his countrymen, he was just a puppet of Rwanda. However, on 27 July 1998, Kabila decided to liberate himself from the kingmakers by breaking his military cooperation with Rwanda. In response, a mutiny was announced by Commander Sylvain Mbuki of the Tenth Battalion of Congolese Armed Forces (Forces Armées Congolaises, FAC) in Goma on 2 August. The conflict was not limited to the Kivus; a number of clashes occurred in Kindu (Maniema), Kisangani, and across the country, at Camp Tshatshi and Camp Kokolo in Kinshasa, as well as in Kitona military base in Bas-Congo (Prunier 2009, p. 181). On 3 August, more Rwandan troops crossed the border to support the rebels. The next day Commander James Kabarebe hijacked a Boeing 707 at the Goma airport and flew with some 180 troops to Kitona military base, 1,600 kilometers to the west, to attack Kabila from the lower Congo River. The choice of Kitona was intended to attract former Mobutu soldiers who were unhappy with their treatment by the Kabila regime. As the rebels approached Kinshasa, Kabila seemed doomed. However, the "remake" of another victory similar to that which ousted Mobutu was far from over as the first 400 troops from Zimbabwe landed in Kinshasa on 20 August 1998 to support Kabila, while Namibia supplied arms and munitions to the government. On 22 August 1998, Angola intervened abruptly, attacking rebel forces from a base in Cabinda. Troops from Sudan and Chad later joined the coalition to help Kabila (Kisangani 2003). What started as an internal conflict became internationalized as it involved a number of countries on the Congolese soil (Levy and Thompson 2010, p. 22).

The first rebel group to emerge on 16 August was the RCD under the leadership of Ernest Wamba dia Wamba, a former professor of history at the University of Dar Es Salaam. On 12 November 1998, another center of revolt broke out in Equateur under the MLC, which proclaimed to be an autonomous group, although it was mostly dominated by former Mobutists under the leadership of Jean-Pierre Bemba. In July 1999, a peace agreement was signed in Lusaka, Zambia. However, repeated cease-fire violations delayed its implementation.

On 16 January 2001, Kabila was assassinated by his bodyguard, Rashidi Kasereka, who a few minutes later was killed by Kabila's camp aide, Colonel Eddy Kapend (Braeckman 2001, p. 152). Kabila's death left the DRC divided in what Nzongola-Ntalaja (2002) calls the war of "partition and pillage." After several tentative peace deals, the belligerents finally signed a global and inclusive agreement on 17 December 2002, which resulted in the formation of transitional institutions in mid-2003. By then, more than 3.9 million people had died in the war (Brennan, Despines, and Roberts 2006). On average, 200,000 people were internally displaced each year from August 1998 to mid-2003 (Kisangani 2003).

Causes of the Anti-Kabila War

Described mistakenly by many commentators as "Africa's first world war,"[5] the anti-Kabila revolt was the only civil war in the DRC since 1960 to end through negotiations. Levy and Thompson (2010, p. 22) contend that the anti-Kabila war was an "internationalized civil war" similar to the 1917 Russian Revolution and the Yugoslav civil war. The conflict occurred on Congolese soil rather than on the soil of the states involved. Thus, the involvement to support either the rebel groups or the government is termed an "external military intervention" by a number of states in the DRC rather than viewing the the anti-Kabila civil war as a "world war," or a "great war of Africa" as some observers sensationalized it. Moreover, the involvement of a number of states in the anti-Kabila war was not the kind of external involvement that constitutes a life-or-death threat to the states involved, such as the two world wars. In other words, the civil war against Kabila was an additional element in the struggle for power and material benefit between contending domestic strongmen (Sørensen 2001, p. 347).

The causes of the anti-Kabila revolt have been a source of controversy. One group of scholars sees the civil war as the result of Kabila's lack of political skills, his inexperience, autocratic leadership style, reluctance to act on the nationality issue, failure to construct a broad domestic constituency by opening up the political space, and inability to secure eastern Congolese borders (Afoaku 2002). This argument has several problems (Kisangani 2003). First, President Kabila did not have a political base after the defeat of the eastern rebellion in 1966. When he joined forces with the AFDL rebel movement in 1996, he had virtually no troops of his own and no following, and few Congolese had even heard of him. Second, the minority Banyamulenge and Tutsi in the government never wanted a broader political base because it could have marginalized their authority, given an already acute anti-Tutsi sentiment in the 1990s in the DRC.

However, Clark (2002) provides three different perspectives on the causes of the anti-Kabila revolt. The first views the war as an issue of state collapse, followed by a scramble of unscrupulous neighbors for "the lush spoils left unguarded and unclaimed" by a leaderless country. The failed decolonization, followed by Cold War rivalries and the long and corrupt Mobutu regime that left the country bankrupt, provides the reason for the anti-Kabila war. A second broader perspective argues that the war against Kabila, just like the war against Mobutu, was part of a continental trend: the withdrawal of support from powerful patrons—the United States and France—and from international financial institutions. The third is that African states were emulating their European counterparts in the early modern era. Thus, the involvement of Congo's neighbors in the DRC was motivated by nation building or their desire to protect themselves against their own insurgencies.

Despite these different opinions, a more plausible critical juncture of the anti-Kabila civil war was Kabila's decision to avert a coup by excluding the Banyamulenge and other Tutsi from power. By April 1998, he was convinced that Rwanda and the Banyamulenge were plotting a coup (Braeckman 1999, p. 348). According to Weiss (2000), the intelligence chiefs of Angola, Rwanda, and Uganda held discussions regarding the desirability of finding an alternative leader for the DRC as early as January 1998. In late March 1998, Kabila sacked a number of Tutsi in his government and replaced them with members of his North Katanga clan. Thus, the anti-Kabila revolt was caused by his decision to expel Rwandan troops and to remove both the Banyamulenge and the Tutsi from his government. For most Congolese of Rwandan origin in the government, especially the Banyamulenge and the Tutsi from Nord-Kivu, this measure also aimed specifically to exclude them from state spoils. Moreover, their exclusion from the government motivated them to reassert themselves because exclusion from power also meant the denial of their Congolese nationality. The RCD, which started the rebellion, was in fact a coalition of convenience that contained major excluded players from the AFDL. In a sense, the anti-Kabila war was neither a war of liberation nor a war of legitimacy. The RCD leaders were not social outcasts. They were a manifestation of "elite recycling" that has epitomized the history of Congo since the 1960s (Kisangani 1997).

Most RCD leaders had served in senior positions under either Mobutu or Kabila and were thus members of the political establishment (Tull and Mehler 2005, p. 378). They had the connections and resources to organize a civil war as a means to enforce their re-inclusion into a political system that they had few incentives to transform. The RCD's poor record of governance in territories under its control from 1998 to 2003 underscores the lack of an agenda for developing a political renewal. Emerging in late 1998, the RCD never achieved any of its stated goals of restoring a federal state, establishing a liberal political system, developing an open economy to lay the foundation of sustainable economic development, and pursuing regional security (Kisangani 2003, p. 58). First, political parties were prohibited in the RCD's controlled areas, and several human rights groups documented patterns of rebels' involvement in discriminating and extrajudicial killings, summary executions, torture, rape, and mass murder of innocent civilians accused of collaborating with the enemy (Human Rights Watch 2001). Second, the RCD privatized mining concessions that became the property of Rwandan officials. Therefore, the civil war against Kabila intended to bring the Banyamulenge and the Tutsi back into the political system that they had no incentive to change.

Also, the MLC of Bemba was created by Mobutist clients who became isolated when Kabila took power in May 1997. The war against Kabila was a war of replacement to help the excluded elites reposition themselves while they used nationalistic ideology to justify their objectives. This exclusion of former government members also underscores Clapham's (1998, p. 5) suggestion that "insurgencies derive basically from blocked political aspirations." The state is a prize to be won only to gain access to its spoils. In this case, a civil war is motivated by an undisguised drive to capture the state first in order to legitimize looting.

As in the previous cases of civil wars, a number of elements of change and continuity explain the exclusion of the Tutsi group from power. First, Kabila was not a new figure in the political discourse of Congo. As part of change, he was among the Lumumbist group excluded from power in 1962–1963, and this exclusion triggered the 1964 rebellions. Once in power in May 1997, Kabila followed Mobutu's steps to the extent that he was called Mobutu's clone (Boissonnade 1998). He developed his own patronage system and networks and appropriated a number of mining operations with his foreign backers, such as Zimbabwe.

Duration of Anti-Kabila Civil War

The civil war against Kabila officially lasted less than five years, August 1998–December 2002. It was longer than previous Congo wars for a number of reasons. First was the division within the RCD and the concomitant inflation of belligerents. The real breakup of the RCD occurred on 16 May 1999 when Emile Ilunga from North Katanga replaced Wamba dia Wamba. Wamba was removed after he complained openly that the issues of the Banyamulenge nationality and Rwandan security were dominating what should have been a broader struggle for democratization. Moreover, other motives were in the mix, such as access to Congo's minerals. This was attested by Wamba's move to Kisangani, a diamond center, where he formed his political party, RDC-Kisangani.

The second factor was the dominance of foreign armies and foreign rebel groups on Congolese soil. The multiplication of rebel groups and their control by foreign patrons increased the likelihood of stalemate. Once enmeshed in a stalemate, the belligerents' motives are best explained by greed, which maintains that the duration of civil wars is the outcome of an expected utility calculation from rational individuals seeking material advantages. A number of rebel groups were able to recruit combatants because a large base of destitute young men roamed everywhere, ready to join any armed group to loot and to survive. For example, when Bemba started his MLC movement, his army had more than 5,000 young men who began looting plantations in the Equateur Province to survive (Kisangani 2003).

From 1999 to 2001, control of the illegal trade of Congolese resources allowed all belligerents to finance the war at no cost. Cheap labor was used to mine coltan (columbine tantalite), diamonds, and gold. The first UN (2001, p. 36) report on the exploitation of Congolese natural resources by warring groups referred to this as "convincible labor" comprising child workers and prisoners; some 5,000 Rwandan prisoners mined gold and coltan in the Kivus from 1999 to 2001. President Paul Kagame of Rwanda even described the conflict as a "self-financing war" (International Crisis Group 2000). This finding is consistent with the economic view that favorable access to a lootable mineral tends to lengthen the duration of civil war (Collier, Hoeffler, and Söderbom 2004). However, this argument, which emphasizes greedy behavior by African rival warlords, is only partially true because it overlooks the same greedy behavior by the capitalist Western world. As Hari (2006, p. 1) puts it, the war against Kabila was "the most savage war in the world" and "the story of a trail of blood that leads directly to you: to your remote control, to your mobile phone, to your laptop and your diamond necklace . . . it is a battle for metals that make our technological society vibrate and ring." The war was thus longer than previous ones because of direct and indirect participation of the West included a wide network of companies, money changers, brokers, facilitators, and speculators. To facilitate the inclusion of their companies in the organized disorder created by the anti-Kabila revolt, Western government officials also became involved. For example, the "economic section of the United States embassy in Kigali was extremely active at the beginning of the war in helping establish joint ventures between the American corporation Trienitech and the Dutch firm *Cnemie Pharmacie* to exploit coltan" (Nest, Grignon, and Kisangani 2006, p. 87).

The formation of alliances and counteralliances was another factor prolonging the war against Kabila (Lanotte 2003, pp. 159–196). The adage that the enemy of my enemy is my friend held in the war. As Regan (2002) demonstrates, rival interventions—one supporting and another opposing the government—certainly tend to lengthen civil wars. A number of African countries became involved in the war, including Angola, Chad, Namibia, Sudan, and Zimbabwe, while others (such as Burundi) showed some "tolerant complicity," and still others (such as Central African Republic, Congo, Tanzania, and Zambia) avoided involvement to prevent contagion effects. The civil war against Kabila became internationalized (Levy and Thompson 2010, p. 20). For example, the involvement of Angola to support the Kabila administration seems to reflect a consistent foreign policy in the region—to cut supply lines to UNITA. More specifically, Angola decided to attack the anti-Kabila rebels in Bas-Congo to protect an offshore oil field that had been the source of government resources for Angola in its war against UNITA.

The decision of Zimbabwe to intervene dated back to the war against Mobutu with a contribution of $40 million in arms and uniforms (Lanotte 2003). Confronted with a lack of liquidity, Kabila offered Zimbabwe some economic privileges in the mining sector. The same economic interventionism compelled Namibia to send 2,000 to 3,000 troops, nearly one-fourth of its own army, to Congo to rescue Kabila. President Sam Nujoma of Namibia claimed to have dispatched troops to Congo to help pay a moral debt to Congo. However, the prolongation of war against Kabila helped Nujoma benefit as well through the diamond concession of Maji-Munene, some 45 kilometers from Tshikapa, in exchange for his military support (Kisangani 2003; Lanotte 2003).

Sudan's involvement in the war had to do with President Museveni's applying the "enemy of my friend is my enemy" theory. In fact, Sudan dispatched some 400 troops to Kindu, Maniema Province, in September 1998 to defend the town (Kisangani 2003). These soldiers were former Mobutu soldiers integrated into the Sudanese army in 1997 (Lanotte 2003). Moreover, Sudan provided war aircraft to the Kabila regime to attack a number of towns controlled by the rebels.

Finally, after the assassination of Kabila, the inner circle needed to buy time in the absence of a constitutional successor. Angola and Zimbabwe agreed on a successor, Joseph Kabila, and the West backed Laurent's son. On the day of his inauguration, Joseph Kabila referred to the need to implement the Lusaka Peace Accord. Briefly stated, the accord consists of two security chapters and a political section (Nest, Grignon, and Kisangani 2006, p. 70). The two security chapters address the withdrawal of foreign troops as well as foreign rebel forces still roaming the DRC. The political chapter recommends an ICD organized by a neutral facilitator, followed by the establishment of the new dispensation for Congo that would lead to the organization of national elections. Kabila's trip to France, Belgium, and the United States a week after his inauguration increased his external legitimacy and paved the way to the peace process despite the lack of domestic legitimacy.

Consequences of Civil War Against Kabila

Unlike previous civil wars, the anti-Kabila war involved some eight foreign armies, a number of rebel groups from some of Congo's neighbors, and no less than twenty indigenous militias, including the Mai Mai groups, with shifting alliances that completely militarized the DRC. The first consequence was the country's human and social capital. Human capital consists of labor, and its destruction is associated with death, migrations, and worsened nutrition and health. Social capital is about trust, work ethic, respect for property, and community links. The war against Kabila caused the death directly and indirectly of more than three million people, mostly farmers (Brennan, Despines, and Roberts 2006). More than 700,000 of these deaths were thought to have resulted from direct acts of violence; most of the rest were caused by disease and malnutrition. Also, both primary and secondary school enrollments plummeted from 41 percent to 28.8 percent (Kabanga 2005, p. 237). The difference between the eastern Congo war zone and western Congo was also apparent. In 1996–1997, the human development index declined from 0.482 in eastern Congo, especially Nord-Kivu, to 0.380 in 2001, compared to the national average from 0.449 to 0.424 (Kabanga 2005, p. 238).

Millions of children perished, while some 65,000 joined armed or militia groups. Those who survived without parents became homeless. Thus, the war, intermingled with disease and poverty as well as the prohibitive cost of education, contributed to a large number of children living on the streets almost everywhere in Congo's major cities. Another tragedy was the fact that rape became an instrument of war. Women of all ages were victims (Brittain 2002). The most pervasive consequence of rape was the spread of HIV/AIDS. Most armies involved in the war against Kabila had a high HIV prevalence ranging from 16 percent for Namibia to as high as 60 percent for Zimbabwe (Elbe 2002, p. 163). Because many women were raped repeatedly, the chance of transmitting the virus multiplied accordingly. The result of rape was the destruction of social fabric of rural communities.

The second consequence of the civil war against Kabila was environmental. Natural capital is that part of the environment that remains undisturbed and provides a store for future value. For example, some 4,000 elephants from a population of 12,000 were killed in the Garamba National Park, which was controlled by Ugandan forces and their Congolese rebel allies (UN 2001, 2002). This destruction fed soldiers and rebel groups. Much of the forest in the Kivus was destroyed, and endangered species were decimated by belligerents and poachers. In Nord-Kivu and Sud-Kivu, unregulated mining of coltan deposits beneath arable land destabilized hillsides and caused landslides that destroyed fields.

Another environmental tragedy that later affected the demobilization of combatants was the disappearance of the hippopotamus population. In Nord-Kivu, especially around Lake Edward, extensive poaching by various militias resulted in the elimination of an estimated 93 percent of extant hippos. This catastrophe, in turn, reduced the dung-generated phyloplankton feeding the lake's freshwater tilapia (Philips 2005, pp. 1 and 4). The result was a decline in the catch and income that fishermen once derived from the lake. Efforts by nongovernmental organizations to retool former militias into fishermen were unsuccessful because there were no fish to catch. As one local fisherman lamented, "Fifteen years ago we routinely hauled in 500 good size tilapia in one night. . . . [E]ven catching thirty fish now is a blessing" (Philips 2005, pp. 1 and 4).

Civil war also affects economic capital, which refers to productive resources (subsistence economy, plants, buildings, equipment), economic infrastructure (transport and communication systems, power, irrigation, and so forth), and social infrastructure (schools, hospitals, clinics). Three levels of analysis provide a framework for understanding the impact of the anti-Kabila war on the economy. First is the local or provincial level. Unlike previous wars, the war against Kabila had a substantial effect on subsistence agriculture, which employed some 60 percent of the population. In many areas, rebel groups either prohibited villagers from cultivating fields and gathering food and wood in the forest or limited the times when they could do so in an attempt to impede collaboration between villagers and other rebel groups. Because women made up a disproportionate part of the workforce in the subsistence sector, this also meant that their absence from the fields, as the result of repeated rapes, reduced food production and increased food shortages. The result was a drastic decline in food crops from 1999 to 2001, with the worst decline of almost 52 percent for sweet potatoes, a staple in the Kivus (Nest, Grignon, and Kisangani 2006). Other staples, such as beans, declined from 32,274 tons in 1992 to 15,825 tons in 2002. The production of chickens also plummeted from 211,986 to 12,502 during the same period (Kabanga 2005, p. 245).

Second, at the national level, the war had a negative impact on economic growth, which declined from –1.6 percent in 1998 to –6.9 percent in 2000. The official mining sector totally collapsed, which coincided with an increasing level of artisanal mining. More specifically, cobalt and copper ores were being stripped away by handpicking, thus endangering the future of open pit mining in Katanga. More than 60,000 young men and boys as young as seven were involved in artisanal mining in eastern DRC (Vlassenroot 2000, p. 281).

Third, at the regional level, the most obvious and widely advertised consequences were the criminalization of the economy and the plundering and exploitation of Congolese resources by a number of foreign state actors described in detail by UN reports including Rwanda, Uganda, and Zimbabwe (2001, 2002, 2003). These reports viewed as illegal any act that takes place without the consent of the legitimate government, involves the use or abuse of power by some actors, or violates the existing regulatory framework in the country based on international law. However, the distinction between legality and illegality does not provide adequate understanding of the reality that people experience. When laws are few, shifting, unenforced, and violated even by government officials, limiting the study of war-fueled activities and consequences to those deemed illegal misses the point (Samset 2002, p. 466). According to Stefaan Marysse, looting is any activity that takes place when "a part of the value of export is invested in activities that do not benefit the country"; thus, looting is "stripping people of the fruits of their property or their work without providing a just remuneration" (cited in Samset 2002, p. 467).

This view of property is important in analyzing the regional consequences of the looting of Congo's natural resources by warring parties. The anti-Kabila war changed property rights and gave rebel groups and foreign state players more control over Congo's resources. As pointed out by Kisangani (2003), the war resulted in the reconfiguration of smuggling and other informal economic activities. During the Mobutu era, these activities were tolerated, in large part because they enabled citizens to fend for themselves. From the liberalization of the mineral sector in the early 1980s to the beginning of the anti-Mobutu revolt in late 1996, artisanal mining was linked to major urban smugglers in eastern DRC. Most of these smugglers were private citizens, such as the Nande in Butembo, who exported gems to Asia and the Middle East and imported manufactured goods. The war against Kabila gave state leaders control over illegal trade routes. For example, the main trade routes by the belligerents from 1998 to 2010 transited through Butembo to Kampala (Fahey 2008, p. 368) or Kigali. The war against Kabila also allowed those who controlled instruments of violence to shape the market. By subjecting the Congolese population to trade restrictions, Rwanda and Uganda almost destroyed local traders who had flourished before the outbreak of the civil war. Most Congolese traders in eastern Congo left the region and relocated their activities to Kinshasa or elsewhere (Kisangani 2003).

The informal economy that came to dominate the war economy revolved around the illicit exploitation of natural resources and the exchange of minerals and timber for weapons, which were then used to expand control over natural resources. Thus, the informal economy that had helped people to fend for themselves became a captive of warlords—both foreign and local state managers. The result was a vicious circle, involving profits and violence, in which established civilian livelihoods and entitlements were destroyed as criminal activities increased.

The final consequence of the anti-Kabila war was political. Organizational and institutional capital is the most important factor to be affected by conflict. This includes government institutions at all levels. At the local level, the dependence of armed groups on their war businesses resulted in their dependence on locals to supply natural resources such as gold, diamonds, and coltan. In exchange, local populations in mining enclaves came to depend on the same armed groups to supply physical protection against other armed groups trying to control these enclaves. Such interdependence hardly implies that this cooperation was voluntary. The war created violent entrepreneurs who engaged in rent-enhancing divisions of labor where they both plundered and protected by squeezing their targets, such as local producers and artisanal miners. Some observers call it the "protection screw," which captures several organizational forms ranging from warlord competition, competing patron-client relationships, and clan conflicts to the interaction between commercial protection firms and roving bandits (Mehlum, Moene, and Torvik 2002, p. 448). The link between organized plunder and protection is what Lane (1958, p. 403) calls violence-using and violence-controlling enterprises; just as in Europe between 700 and 1700, "a plunderer could become in effect the chief of police as soon as he regularized his 'take,' adapted it to the capacity to pay, defended his preserve against other plunderers."

Protection militias also had a consequence for traditional authorities, who had to adopt different strategies depending on locality (Tull 2003, p. 439). In the RDC-controlled areas, some chiefs were the target of armed groups. Uncooperative chiefs were killed, and others who resisted had to flee to avoid being killed. Other chiefs abandoned their constituencies and collaborated with the rebel groups. In this context, they took the chance of seeing their administrative authority questioned by their constituencies. Nonetheless, this choice provided them some personal physical security. In many parts of Sud-Kivu, many traditional chiefs either accommodated the RCD or collaborated with the movement, while in Lubero and Beni, Nord-Kivu, all chiefs resisted rebel groups (Van Acker 1999; Kisangani 2003).

Also at the local level, the appointment of the Tutsi, viewed as foreigners, in most powerful administrative and political positions under the control of the RCD in the Kivus increased animosity among the autochthons. Another issue was the creation of a number of new territories, without the tacit approval of traditional authorities, to accommodate a few ethnic groups that controlled instruments of violence. The RCD created the Minembwe territory on 16 September 1998 to satisfy the long-standing demand of the Banyamulenge for a territorial base (Bulambo 2000), although the Banyamulenge had no traditional or customary right to own communal customary land. The territory of Kalehe, where the Havu people live with a Tembo minority, was the most seriously affected by the creation of a new territory called Bunyakiri, with a majority population of Tembo. The creation of Bunyakiri was apparently intended to reduce the level of Mai Mai opposition to the RCD administration. Furthermore, the Havu collectivity in Kalehe lost a portion of its land in the creation of a new collectivity of Buzi, where both Havu and Rwandaphones live (Bucyalimwe 2003, pp. 195–196).

At the international level, many observers contemplated the demise of the Congolese state. However, the anti-Kabila revolt had the opposite effect, galvanizing Congolese against a common enemy. The intervention of Rwanda and Uganda in the DRC alongside Congolese rebels, especially the visibility of the Tutsi, forced some sense of commonality among Congolese that helped fulfill some of their psychological needs, such as social cohesion. Hostility toward the out-group tends to increase in-group cohesion (Coser 1956). The threats posed by foreign troops and the Tutsi made it more likely for Congolese to develop a consciousness that strengthened their bonds as they watched the exploitation of their wealth by the out-group. This in-group paradigm was never well articulated in Congolese political discourse until 1998, except in the terminal years of colonial rule. By pointing his finger at the enemy and giving the enemy a name—Tutsi—President Laurent Kabila was able to build a common sense of identity threatened by the Tutsi, despite the ethnic heterogeneity of Congolese society.

Conflict Management and Path Toward Peace?

The revolt against President Kabila created a number of problems for the international community. According to some observers, it was a difficult environment.[6] Most important was the widening ring of African states sucked into the conflict because of the complex regional alliances and motivations of major players as the "civil war became internationalized" (Levy and Thompson 2010, p. 22). Moreover, the proliferation of rebel groups meant that without dialogue and a group of powerful third party states, peace was unlikely. Thus, from the beginning, some initiatives helped level the playing field. A number of external actors became involved to pave the path toward peace and to hold elections.

The role of external players. The first real step in conflict management occurred with the election of Thabo Mbeki as the new South African president. His inauguration on 14 June 1999 paved the way for an impromptu meeting in Pretoria on 17 June 1999, attended by most presidents involved in the conflict. One result of this meeting was a request to the belligerents to meet in Lusaka, which produced a peace agreement that was signed by the state heads of the DRC, Namibia, Rwanda, Uganda, and Zimbabwe on 10 July 1999 after interminable discussions at the ministerial level. Known as the Lusaka Peace Accord, this was the first document that offered some hope of genuine peace since the outbreak of the anti-Kabila revolt.

The peace accord had been exhaustively assessed and need not be discussed here (Kisangani 2003; Prunier 2009; Willame 2002). Suffice it to say that this accord had a number of weaknesses that explained why many belligerents ignored it and continued to fight. First, the agreement recognized Congolese rebel groups as equal partners to the Kabila government, while former Rwandan soldiers in sanctuaries in Congo were considered "negative forces" and hence to be disarmed by the international community. The expression "negative forces" was used by Rwandan authorities in 1995 to disqualify those groups that did not share the hatred ideology of the RPF toward the Hutu (Ruzibiza 2005) and seemed to have been imposed by Rwanda in Lusaka. Second, the agreement not only legitimized the occupation of eastern Congo by Rwanda and Uganda, but it also froze the status quo and distinct zones of influence controlled by different rebel factions under either Rwanda or Uganda patronage. Third, the agreement never mentioned the Mai Mai groups, though they represented popular forces in eastern Congo. Finally, it was signed without much debate over the causes of the conflict and, in particular, the Kivus' dimension of the conflict.

Despite its weaknesses, the Lusaka Accord recognized the need for an ICD. On 14 November 1999, the OAU appointed Ketule Masire, former president of Botswana, to facilitate the application of the Lusaka Accord, especially the organization of the ICD. However, Masire was confronted with a Congolese government unwilling to cooperate. Meanwhile, the UN Security Council passed Resolution 1279 on 30 November 1999 authorizing the United Nations Observer Mission in the DRC (known later as MONUC, or Mission de l'Organisation des Nations Unies au Congo) as stipulated by the Lusaka agreement. The agreement called for a UN Chapter VII to enforce the cease-fire and disarm the foreign militias operating in the DRC. The MONUC was also mandated with coordinating the disarmament, demobilization, repatriation, resettlement, and reintegration (DDRRR) of all rebel foreign troops but was not mandated to disarm them by force. Repeated cease-fire violations delayed the implementation of the Lusaka Accord. Laurent Kabila's uncooperative behavior was also a detriment, especially his rejection of Masire's collaboration, his opposition to UN deployment, and his precondition for the withdrawal of Rwandan and Ugandan forces from Congo. His stalling tactics continually derailed the peace process. However, his death broke the logjam in the peace process by eliminating his preconditions.

After several delays the ICD finally convened in Sun City, South Africa, from 25 February to 18 April 2002. Although it did not produce the expected comprehensive political agreement to shape the transitional government, for the first time it provided a forum for all belligerents to discuss openly their differences. A number of bilateral agreements were negotiated and even concluded between the government and a number of rebel groups with their state backers, but they proved to be futile until a comprehensive peace agreement was reached in December 2002 (Kisangani 2003; Prunier 2009; Nest, Grignon, and Kisangani 2006). After more than five months of international pressure, the UN special envoy to the ICD, Moustapha Nyasse, and South African President Mbeki were able to pressure the major parties to the ICD to sign a comprehensive and inclusive agreement on 17 December 2002 in Pretoria, called Global Act of the Transition (Acte Global et Inclusif sur la Transition en République Démocratique du Congo, or AGI). The Pretoria agreement settled the issue of the organization of power sharing during the period of political transition (Bouvier and Bomboko 2003).

On 30 June 2003, the peace accord resulted in the formation of a national transitional government that included Joseph Kabila as president, four vice-presidents, and thirty-five ministers with their deputies. This became known as the 1 + 4 formula. The four vice-presidents were Yerodia Ndombasi (from the previous government), Jean-Pierre Bemba (MLC), Azaria Ruberwa (RCD-Goma), and Z'Ahidi Ngoma (unarmed opposition). The civil society obtained two ministerial and three deputy ministerial positions plus the chairmanship of five institutions dedicated to the democratization process: the Independent Electoral Commission, the Higher Authority on the Media, the Truth and Reconciliation Commission, the National Human Rights Commission, and the Commission on Ethics and the Fight against Corruption. A Follow Up Commission was created to assess the interpretation and implementation of the transition. On 8 July 2003, this commission adopted not only the list of 500 deputies and 120 senators as the result of the December agreement that set a bicameral legislature but also appointed people in charge of institutions to sustain democracy. More specifically, Apollinaire Malu Malu Wolongo became the president of the electoral commission.

On 6 March 2003, the parties to the ICD agreed on a constitution of transition and a protocol on the reform of the security services, especially the shape of the future national army, called the Armed Forces of the DRC (Forces Armées de la République Démocratique du Congo, or FARDC). They signed these documents at a special session of the ICD concluded in Sun City on 2 April 2003. The belligerents agreed to restore democracy and stability in Congo. They also created an Implementation and Monitoring Commission to help interpret the agreement, resolve conflict, oversee power sharing at the provincial level, and decide on the nominations of ambassadors and other members of the government.

The monitoring commission was assisted by the Comité International d'Accompagnement de la Transition (CIAT), which comprised ambassadors of the UN Security Council, members of countries with particular interest in the Congolese transition, financiers of the transition, and the European Union. Its primary goal was to sustain the fragile peace process by controlling state sovereignty and the behavior of members of the government. Second, the

CIAT's role was also to pressure the parliament to produce a number of critical pieces of legislation, such as a nationality law for national reconciliation, which dealt with the definition of a Congolese.

After several weeks of hesitation, on 15 August 2003, the RCD-Goma finally presented its list of army officers to be nominated. However, some officers, among them Laurent Nkunda, refused to report to Kinshasa because of security considerations. A number of interviews with some Tutsi defectors from the RCD and the Rwandan government indicated that President Kagame played a key role in Nkunda's desertion; that is, he needed a "Plan B" just in case the transition did not work in Kigali's favor (cited in Stearns 2008, p. 246). This defection caused the first armed conflict for the control of Bukavu in May 2004 between government troops and Tutsi troops under Colonel Jules Mutebutsi (International Crisis Group 2005). The violence sparked an anti-Tutsi crackdown that forced some 3,000 Tutsi to leave Bukavu (International Crisis Group 2005). Nkunda reacted by leading a force of 1,000 soldiers to Bukavu, thanks to financial support from Governor Eugène Serufuli of Nord-Kivu and weapons from Rwanda, to prevent what Nkunda called another "genocide against Tutsi." Pressure from the United States and France on both Rwanda and RCD forced Nkunda to retreat to Masisi in Nord-Kivu, where he began recruiting soldiers to start his war against the central government.

Thus, the role of Belgium, France, and the United States was critical during the transition. They imposed conditions on the belligerents to halt the zero-sum political games each side planned during the conflict (Willame 2007). The DRC was under de facto international trusteeship. The UN Security Council also authorized an increase in MONUC troops to 17,000 at an annual cost of $1 billion under Chapter VII. This force, as a military arm of the CIAT, was later complemented by a 2,500-strong European Force (EUFOR) in Kinshasa during the elections in late 2006 to deter any insurgency.

Conflict management and institutional changes. The international community assigned to transitional institutions a number of tasks to achieve peace, including a new nationality law, a new constitution, and free elections. The transitional parliament passed the nationality law, no. 04/024, on 12 November 2004, which was critical for national reconciliation (DRC 2004).[7] Article 6 of the law stipulates that "any person belonging to an ethnic group or nationality whose people and land were part of the territory that became Congo upon independence is of Congolese origin." With the passing of the law on nationality, Rwandan immigrants in Congo before July 1960 automatically became Congolese. No nationality reinstatement procedure is required. Because the new law remains silent on the refugees who migrated to Congo after 1960, these immigrants and their descendants are not citizens of Congo. However, these descendants can choose Congolese nationality and have to apply voluntarily upon reaching maturity (Article 21). Given porous borders and the continuous movement of people in the area, this issue remains unresolvable.

The second institutional change concerned a new constitution and the electoral process. The Independent Electoral Commission became fully operational in November 2004 when its provincial offices were in place. On 20 June 2005, the registration of voters began in Kinshasa. Some 25.4 million voters registered across the country, out of an estimated population of 59.1 million. On 18–19 December 2005, the constitutional referendum drew a 67 percent turnout. Of the 15 million people who cast ballots, some 84 percent approved the constitution.

Promulgated in February 2006, the constitution has a number of provisions. The first is the division of power between the executive and legislative branches of government. The constitution sets a semipresidential-semiparliamentary system. The idea is to have a figurehead president when the opposition controls the lower house and an executive president when the ruling party controls it. Second is the issue of decentralization as a mechanism of conflict management. According to the constitution, the DRC is comprised of the federal capital city of Kinshasa and twenty-five provinces. By late 2010, the law on decentralization was not yet adopted by the legislature.

Although the referendum was a success, it uncovered a mood of deep popular dissatisfaction and suspicion toward the elites who had been the Kinshasa authorities prior to reunification and their international backing. As Weiss (2007, p. 141) rightly pointed out, the most important objection was the fear that the whole process was for the sake of legitimizing leaders who held power in Kinshasa during the years of war and transition and who enjoyed the backing of Europe, the United States, MONUC, and South Africa.

The second phase of the transition was the electoral law promulgated in March 2006. It includes the rule that any candidate for president must receive at least 51 percent of the votes (absolute majority), or a runoff election, a party list, and a proportional representation system with no runoff provision to fill both the National Assembly or parliament and the provincial assemblies.

Guns, power, and peace. The forty-member government backed by the 620 appointed members of the parliament and five "institutions to support democracy" were charged with laying the foundation for the Third Republic. The cost of the transition was enormous, mostly financed by international institutions and the West. Foreign aid increased from 21.2 percent of GDP in 2002 to a record high of 95.5 percent of GDP a year later and remained on average 25 percent of GDP during the transition (Table 5.1). Most aid in 2003–2004 came from Congo's godfathers—Belgium, France, and the United States. In 2003, they provided some $3.5 billion (or 64 percent of total foreign aid).

The massive amount of aid that poured into the hands of members of the transitional institutions only fueled corruption. In the first year of the transition, former enemies and now collaborators maximized their limited time dur-

Table 5.1 Development Assistance to the DRC, 2000–2006 (millions of current $US)

Source	2000	2001	2002	2003	2004	2005	2006
All donors	177.12	243.11	1,174.95	5,416.03	1,824.06	1,827.25	2,056.71
DAC[a]	102.71	143.36	351.01	5,009.49	1,164.99	1,036.58	1,500.31
Multilateral	74.22	99.58	823.68	406.37	658.90	792.83	557.90
Belgium	26.68	43.23	41.26	789.63	265.27	151.72	221.50
France	8.21	7.94	0.82	1,274.00	134.68	87.96	57.20
Germany	12.76	12.92	21.11	541.56	59.29	51.09	35.00
Italy	0.96	1.59	3.87	428.98	23.80	1.02	1.20
Japan	0.47	0.32	0.85	0.63	48.47	376.26	23.10
Netherlands	4.67	12.00	135.03	220.55	58.75	46.23	29.80
UK	8.03	17.04	14.93	22.66	300.97	77.57	139.90
US	12.75	20.23	79.99	1,415.45	189.63	143.64	838.40
Percentage of GDP	4.1	5.2	21.2	95.5	27.8	25.7	24.11

Source: Data used to compare percentages are from World Bank (2010).
Note: a. DAC = Development Assistance Committee.

ing the transition by plundering state resources rapidly. Payments to civil servants and soldiers regularly evaporated before reaching their intended recipients. The government even inflated the troops in the national army to 350,000 in August 2005, while the MONUC declared that the real number was only 152,000 troops (UN 2005). The fictive list allowed a few in the government to pocket the difference. More than 40 percent of spending took place outside proper budgetary processes, and the presidency exceeded its budget by 89 percent, while Vice President Bemba spent more than seven times his allocation (Willame 2007). Similar figures were reported for all executive and legislative organs of the transition. In sum, the transition was a legal way to buy off former warring parties.

Another issue was the demobilization of combatants. Congolese armed groups underwent the disarmament, demobilization, and reintegration (DDR) process, coordinated by the National Commission for Demobilization and Reinsertion (Commission Nationale de la Démobilisation et de la Réinsertion, or CONADER) and financed by the World Bank. As a political goal, the DDR intends to incorporate different militia factions into a unified national army and thus to restore the state. However, the government inflated the national army with incompetent and undisciplined elements through what it called *mixage* and *brassage*. Mixage provided military integration at the platoon level with a view to form six brigades and allowed troops to remain in their province of origin. Brassage aimed to create a unified national army by merging the individual members of various armed forces operating in the country and involved the transfer of troops to provinces other than their own home province. Foreign troops had to undergo the DDRRR, which was coordinated mainly by the Multi-Country Demobilization and Reintegration Program spearheaded by the UN Development Programme.

The DDR process focused on a number of objectives that were discussed elsewhere (Prunier 2009). Suffice it to say that the CONADER failed to achieve its mission as the result of many factors. First was lack of food and water in brassage centers. Second, a number of militia groups took advantage of the transitional political climate and resisted the demilitarization process. With the exception of the Mai Mai, no armed groups that flourished in eastern Congo were signatories of the AGI signed in December 2002. They all wanted the government to perceive them as threats to security so they could make demands. This open policy resulted in the co-optation of many militia leaders into the national army. The consequence was an inflated (by some 70 to 80 percent) officer corps with barely 25 to 30 percent soldiers. By December 2008, the national army was literally overrun by commanders without any military formation or background. The integrated FARDC soldiers also continued their private activities, including looting, terrorizing, and abducting members of the local population with impunity. By December 2010, political insecurity remained the biggest issue in the DRC as regular troops, militia groups, and armed bands kept terrorizing civilians in the countryside and major cities.

Third and most importantly, the failure of the DDR was also due to its politicization. Some twenty militia groups were given special privileges by the international community, resulting in in the failure of the DDR process (Prunier 2009). For example, the international community and the government allowed the Tutsi armed groups to undergo mixage, which gave these troops the right to remain in the Kivus rather than being dispersed throughout the country, as other troops were required. Furthermore, the Tutsi troops under renegade General Nkunda and his political party, the National Congress for the Defense of the People (Congrès National pour la Défense du Peuple, or CNDP), were treated differently in the DDR process. Although the process called for the eradication of the former Rwandan soldiers still roaming in eastern Congo, it considered Nkunda and his rebels as a legitimate group in eastern Congo.

Finally, the DDRRR faced a number of problems and never completely succeeded in disarming rebel groups from Burundi, Rwanda, and Uganda, which had sanctuaries in the DRC. The hurdle with the DDRRR was that it only targeted the former Rwandan soldiers and the former Rwandan militia groups known as the Democratic Forces for the Liberation of Rwanda (Forces Démocratiques pour la Libération du Rwanda, or FDLR) and labeled by the Rwandan government as "negative forces." By 2002, some 15,000 of these forces were repatriated to Rwanda out of 25,000 (Kisangani 2000a). However, the intensification of attacks against the FDLR, first by joint forces of the UN and Congolese army, the Congolese army, and Rwandan troops and then by the CNDP and Congolese army, further indicated that the DDRRR was dead by 2007. Thus, the Rwandan government was never committed to the DDRRR of former Rwandan soldiers.

The electoral process. The last phase of the transition was the electoral process that started with legislative and presidential elections. The international community donated some $450 million to fund the elections and deployed the world's largest UN peacekeeping operation, MONUC, for their smooth operation. No less than thirty-three candidates ran for president and 9,707 for the 500 seats in the national assembly. Nearly 14,000 more competed for the 690 seats available in the eleven provincial legislatures. Legislative elections, on 30 July 2006, revealed a new geographic distribution of legislators different from the early 1960s when ethnic affinities were critical in the electoral process. The electoral results showed that the presidential party, the Party for Reconstruction and Development (Parti pour la Reconstruction et le Développement or PPRD), carried 111 seats, mostly from the eastern provinces; Bemba's MLC received sixty-four seats; Antoine Gizenga's Unified Lumumbist Party (Parti Lumumbist Unifié, or PALU) won thirty-four seats; and independents received sixty-three votes. The RCD received only fifteen seats. The legislative elections clearly indicated the fragmentation of the political landscape. Of 500 seats, five parties obtained twenty seats or more. However, these represented slightly over half of the total. Sixty-three independent candidates were elected, and thirty-one parties obtained only one seat. Together, these ninety-four single member groups accounted for almost 20 percent of the National Assembly.

In the past, major ethnic groups tended to vote in homogenous blocs, but this pattern never appeared in the 2006 elections. The ethnic breakdown was replaced by a regional and linguistic divide: east versus west, or Swahili versus Ngala. An enduring pattern is the low number of elected women because the electoral law provides no reserved seats or quotas for underprivileged citizens. Thus, women captured only 10 percent of seats in the National Assembly. Voters also threw out "the rascals" who had ruled them from 1998 to 2003 by sending back to Kinshasa only forty-five members from the 500-seat transitional parliament. Preferring new leadership, they rejected more than 90 percent of Kinshasa appointees during the transition.

The first round of presidential elections also occurred on 30 July 2006. On 20 August 2006, the electoral commission released its full provisional presidential election results, indicating that no candidate was able to secure a majority, which led to a runoff election on 29 October 2006. Joseph Kabila and Jean-Pierre Bemba received 44.8 percent and 20 percent, respectively, of the 17.9 million votes. The third highest candidate was Antoine Gizenga, the heir of Lumumba in the 1960s, with 13 percent of the votes, mostly from his province of Bandundu. When the final votes were announced on 20 August 2006, a fight broke out between Kabila's guards, behaving like a militia, and Bemba's men. Kinshasa was the scene of three days of fighting with heavy weapons, leaving a number of people killed, before the MONUC-EUFOR quelled it.

Kabila won the second round of presidential elections with 59.05 percent of the total votes, or 9.4 million. However, in the eastern provinces, he was a net winner, with more than 70 percent of the votes. In November, the Supreme

Court officially declared Kabila winner of presidential elections. Bemba officially conceded defeat and agreed to be nominated as senator and take over the role of leader of parliamentary opposition. In December 2006, the CIAT held its last meeting, marking the formal end of the supervised Congo transition.

In sum, the elections were peaceful, and turnout quite impressive, with 70 percent during the first round of presidential elections and 65 percent in the second round. More specifically, the voters used the ballot box to send two messages to the elites. First, the Congolese rejected those who ruled them from the war to the end of the transition, 1998–2006. Second, voters rejected the belligerents, who they thought committed crimes against them. It was a referendum against the war. Third, the advent of the Kabilas made the east predominant. In a sense, the electoral outcome was to have the east rule the DRC.

On 30 December 2006, Gizenga obtained the job of prime minister as agreed when he backed Kabila during the second round. After a number of post-electoral deals and bribes, a coalition of parties behind the president called the Alliance for the Presidential Majority (Alliance pour la Majorité Présidentielle, or AMP) gained the majority in the lower house, and its secretary-general, Vital Kamerhe, was elected president of the National Assembly in December 2006. In early February 2007, Gizenga announced his colossal government of sixty ministers and vice ministers.

On the same day of the second round of presidential elections, provincial assemblies were elected, mostly by direct suffrage. Of the 690 provincial assembly members, 632 were directly elected, and fifty-eight were co-opted in early January 2007 from among traditional chiefs. The AMP was able to secure 309 out of 632 available seats, obtaining a majority in seven out of eleven provincial assemblies. The Union pour la Nation of Bemba's coalition controlled assemblies in Kinshasa, Equateur, Bas-Congo, and Kasai Occidental.

In addition to their importance at the provincial level, and in line with the federal formula, provincial assemblies were in charge of electing members of the upper house, the Senate, which they did on 19 January 2007. Because the AMP secured 309 seats in the provinces, it also secured 58 senators out of 108 in January 2007. Thus, the patrimonial structure of the political landscape of the DRC seemed to have not changed after the 2006 elections. One consequence of this indirect voting rule for senators was that more than 30 percent of senators were former members of government under Mobutu, who were able to bribe provincial representatives or buy votes in order to represent their provinces in the upper house. Gubernatorial elections were also held on 27 January 2007. The governors and vice governors were chosen through indirect elections by members of the provincial assemblies.

After the elections, a number of old issues emerged that delayed the peace dividend. First, the victory of Joseph Kabila created another round of instability, especially in the Kivus. Three days before the presidential election results were announced in November 2006, dissidents under the command of renegade

Laurent Nkunda renewed attacks on the national army in Nord-Kivu in an attempt to control Goma despite warnings from MONUC forces. The UN forces reacted strongly against Nkunda by using helicopters and infantry, killing some 200 to 400 insurgents (Stearns 2008, p. 252). Despite this show of force, the UN troops and the government were unable to create political stability in the Kivus. Then, under the auspices of Rwanda, Nkunda's backer, President Kabila, brokered a deal with Nkunda to integrate his troops into the national army, but the deal failed to specify the modalities needed for launching operations against the former Rwandan soldiers still roaming in eastern Congo. Each side thought it could exploit the ambiguity of the deal to manipulate the other. As a result, fighting resumed in August 2007 with massacres of some 185 people and some 370,000 people internally displaced.

Political instability created by the CNDP resulted in the Amani (peace in Swahili) Program on 2 February 2008 by presidential Decree no. 08/008 for a six-month period. Amani followed the Goma Engagement Act of January 2008 as conceived by the accords of Nairobi in November 2007 and Addis Ababa in December 2007. The goal of the Amani Program was to create political security and pacification in Nord-Kivu and Sud-Kivu (Bucyalimwe 2010). However, the program collapsed as the result of repeated cease-fire violations, leading to Nairobi II and Nairobi III agreements. By late 2010, political instability remained a major problem in the Kivus and Uele despite the presence of one of the largest UN missions in the world.

Most observers blamed political instability in 2004–2010 on spoilers—leaders and parties who used violence to undermine peace. However, Autesserre (2010) views these outbreaks of conflict as the result of local dynamics. She contends that after the national and regional settlements were reached, some local conflicts over land and power became increasingly self-sustaining and autonomous from the macrolevel development. Thus, the generalized fighting affected three main changes in the grassroots dynamics of violence: (1) it reinforced some preexisting local antagonisms, (2) it led to militarization of others, and (3) it created new decentralized tensions. According to her narratives, decentralized antagonisms over land and political power motivated local violence against the people of Rwandan descent and enticed some Congolese groups to allow a strong Rwandan Hutu presence in the Kivus. In turn, these two issues were the main stated motivations for the continued Rwandan involvement in Congo and the main reasons why Nkunda's troops and RCD-Goma hard-liners continued to fight in the east. Thus, microlevel conflicts eventually jeopardized the national and regional settlements. In sum, many conflicts became autonomous from national and regional developments.

This argument is partly incorrect. First, the round of conflict in eastern Congo by Nkunda signaled Rwanda's effort to keep destabilizing eastern Congo and thus shift the Rwandan conflict entirely into the DRC. What Autesserre (2010) viewed as outbreaks of conflict from local dynamics were only local reactions to national and regional issues. The UN (2008) threw considerable light on the link between Nkunda and Rwanda, especially military, financial, and logistical support that Nkunda's CNDP was getting from Rwanda. The UN report was an embarrassment for President Kagame and resulted in the removal of Nkunda and his arrest in January 2009 near Kigali.

Furthermore, the 2004 nationality law remains discriminatory against the people of Rwandan origin who migrated to the DRC after June 1960. This national issue is still a hindrance to peace in the Kivus. Like previous nationality laws, the 2004 law not only automatically excluded more than 150,000 Rwandan Tutsi refugees who migrated to Congo in the first half of the 1960s, but also required their descendants to follow an arduous application process to gain citizenship. Thus, most conflicts that occurred in 2004–2010 in the Kivus started with the sons of these refugees of the early 1960s from Rwanda, including Nkunda, who was born in 1967. In a sense, Nkunda was not a national of the DRC according to the new law on nationality beause he never voluntarily applied in writing (see Chapter 3, Article 23 of the 2004 nationality law). In other words, what Autesserre (2010) perceives as local may be linked to the colonial legacy and thus remains regional in nature.

Second, she overlooked the role of the 2006 elections that marginalized the Tutsi. The lack of representation of the Tutsi at all levels means they are unlikely to favor any democratic framework in the DRC. This picture resembles the behavior of the Tutsi governing elites in both Burundi and Rwanda against the majority Hutu. After provincial elections, the situation continued to worsen as the political balance shifted away from the Rwandan-backed RCD. More specifically, the elections completely denied the Tutsi any access to political representation, and their exclusion from provincial politics was a clear indication that the Tutsi had no political base in the Kivus. In the Kivus, political representation also means land ownership.

Another issue in the Third Republic is the level of corruption that reached unimaginable proportions. The government of Kabila remained a colossal political machine, averaging forty ministries. In addition, government ministries averaged some twenty advisers, each earning no less than $2,500 per month, while the average worker's pay averaged $10 a month. The most egregious case was the office of the prime minister with some sixty-four advisers in 2009–2010. Meanwhile, public funding for health care, education, and infrastructure had plummeted to less than 2 percent of total government spending.

The third issue after the 2006 elections was a sense of authoritarianism. President Kabila had been quite reluctant to face his critics from the parliamentary opposition and from civil society. A widely publicized assassination of human rights activist Floribert Bahizire Chebeya, who was usually critical of the Kabila administration, in June 2010 prompted a quick international reaction and the suspicion that the government was responsible. A few days after the assassination, the inspector general of the national police, General John Numbi, was suspended from his functions, and a number of other officers were later arrested.

Moreover, Kabila's efforts to consolidate power gave ample evidence to worry about a return to the type of dictatorship that had plagued Congo for decades with devastating economic and social results. The Kabila administration had fallen short on many critical fronts. For example, the quest to amend the new constitution was reflective of the government's misplaced priorities (Dizolele 2010, p. 153). The most important article of the constitution, which was related to the election of the president, was amended in late December 2010 and adopted by both houses of the parliament in a joint session on 15 January 2011 despite efforts by the opposition. The amendment removed the system of runoff elections and adopted the "first past the post" principle. Meanwhile, political instability remained a major threat to people in eastern Congo.

Summary and Brief Discussion

President Mobutu took power in November 1965. He overcame the opposition and remained in power for almost thirty-two years, creating a strong state that provided not only order but economic prosperity for a decade from 1966 to 1975. However, Mobutu's state started showing signs of weakness in the late 1970s. Congo, then Zaire, was so weak by the 1980s and early 1990s that anyone with few dollars could bribe customs officials and smuggle any type of weapons and even missiles into Congo without any problem, given the kleptocratic nature of the polity. The weak Congolese state provided the opportunity for any warlord to march toward Kinshasa and take power. As Prunier (2009, p. xxxi) puts it, "what passed for a government structure was so rotten that the brush of a hand could cause it to collapse."

State weakness that characterized the early 1990s was similar to that of the early 1960s because the government lost control over its central instrument of coercion—the army. Thus, the AFDL's march from east to west should not have been a surprise. For most Congolese, the war against Mobutu was a legitimate one as the AFDL and its alliance received popular support and protection as they advanced toward Kinshasa (Prunier 2009). After a brief honeymoon, Laurent Kabila confronted an insurrection by the Mai Mai movement, which was a war of convenience because it was never intended to remove him from power. The Mai Mai's goal was to choke off the regime and force Kabila to change his policy toward foreigners—in particular, Rwanda and the Tutsi. In fact, Kabila asked Rwanda and all foreign troops to leave Congo in late July 1998, ending the coalition that brought him to power. The result was another round of conflict intended to remove him from power and install someone amenable to Rwanda and the Tutsi's interests.

Like the early civil wars, the analysis of these three internal wars indicates that the politics of exclusion was a critical juncture to explain them. The war against Mobutu showed that the Banyamulenge were contemplating an uprising to protect their families and cattle as early as April 1995, given their political exclusion. The Mai Mai movement was also a manifestation of social exclusion. The second war against Kabila reveals that the politics of exclusion remains a critical juncture. Among the people who felt excluded this time from the political process were the Mobutists and people of Rwandan origin. The former wanted to be reintegrated into the political process, while the latter felt expelled from the process they thought they created. Thus, the anti-Kabila revolt was no more than a war of replacement.

Unlike the early wars of secession (discussed in Chapter 2), which intended to carve Congo into ministates, the wars of the 1990s aimed to keep a unitary state in order to have legitimate access to state spoils. Elites' attachment to postcolonial boundaries is really a consequence of their material rewards, which are acquired only within the state apparatus. As Englebert and Hummel (2005, p. 411) point out, the capacity to appropriate privately the resources of the weak state or to use it as an instrument of predation because of its widespread lack of accountability are crucial elements of the logic of the state's survival and reproduction. Sovereignty provides a legal way to loot state resources. As the Congolese government spokesman, Kikaya bin Karubi, told the British Broadcasting Corporation in reference to accusations in UN reports that the government and its allies siphoned more than $5 billion in one year: "The Congolese government is the legitimate government of this country. . . . Whatever we do is legitimate" (cited in Englebert and Hummel 2005, p. 414). Unlike previous wars where a number of elements of continuity prevailed, the wars of the 1990s were mostly dominated by elements of change. First, the declining supply of rents and the increasing demand from numerous clients were critical antecedents in toppling Mobutu. These elements of change started with the Mobutu rentier state. The argument is that a country is vulnerable to civil wars whenever the source of rents declines. The weakening of the Mobutu rentier state and its institutions opened up his state to centrifugal forces. In particular, disruptions in resource distribution among the ruling elites minimized cohesion within them. Added to this was an increase in the number of clients without enough rents to satisfy competing demands. The democratization process in the first half of the 1990s was not a major force to weaken the Mobutu regime. Although it unleashed centrifugal forces against his regime, Mobutu was able to mitigate its impact because the process failed to remove him from power.

One element of continuity remains the role of colonial boundaries and colonial policy to alleviate lateral or population pressures in Burundi and Rwanda. The wars against presidents were linked to the massive wave of refugees from Rwanda. When the Hutu crossed the borders with their arms and munitions, a number of them disappeared in the local Hutu communities. In launching attacks against the new Tutsi government of Rwanda, the former Rwandan soldiers in refugee camps created insecurity along the borders. As a weak state, the DRC was unable to control these armed refugees. Their attacks against Rwanda prompted the Rwandan government to be involved in the Congolese conflict between the Banyamulenge and the Congolese state. When the Mai Mai turned against Kabila, the former Rwandan soldiers roaming in eastern Congo joined the Mai Mai to fight against both Rwandan troops and Banyamulenge.

On 2 August 1998, a second war against Kabila began, and the president needed capable forces to support him. He turned to former Rwandan soldiers and rebels from Burundi who fought alongside the Congolese army against the AFDL in eastern Congo. By late 2010, a few thousand of these former Rwandan soldiers were still roaming in eastern Congo. The Rwandan government considered these combatants as part of those who committed genocide in Rwanda. Those who returned to Rwanda were forced to undergo *ingando,* or indoctrination, in solidarity camps to eradicate their hatred of the other—the Tutsi. Meanwhile, the Tutsi-led government of Rwanda blocked any entry of the Hutu elites into the political process. In other words, the ingando was to condition Rwandans with the RPF ideology and to contain any type of opposition to the government (Mgbako 2005). In sum, the eastern Congo is likely to remain unstable until the Tutsi-dominated government of Rwanda engages in dialogue with the leaders of the FDLR and other moderate Hutu in exile to start a real process of reconciliation for peaceful coexistence.

The wars against Mobutu and Kabila also seemed to be linked to the 1964 eastern rebellion. The Banyamulenge and the Mai Mai are not newcomers to Congolese politics. After the eastern rebellion, the political context became favorable for the Banyamulenge as they began to expand southward and northward. The defeat of the eastern rebellion by government troops and the Banyamulenge as well as the bloody memories of the war divided the Banyamulenge and the autochthons. Another mistake made by the Banyamulenge that revived the 1964–1965 war memory was the RPF recruitment of Banyamulenge in the early 1990s when it was preparing its attacks against Kigali. In other words, the decision to fight in another country was seen by the autochthons as opportunistic for people who want to call themselves Congolese. Despite a common cause—to remove Mobutu from power—the Banyamulenge and autochthons never had the same vision of the post-Mobutu era.

Thus, the war against Laurent Kabila in August 1998 was a direct consequence of state politics despite the weak capacity of the states involved. As a result, the duration of the second war against Kabila became linked to natural resources—an outcome that appeared nowhere in the previous civil wars. As the war dragged on, the goals of combatants changed, and state preservation was partly replaced by the desire to plunder. With unfettered access to riches, the emergence of these new priorities was not surprising, and war became a business in the hands of those who controlled instruments of violence. As different armed groups dug themselves in along major mineral frontiers, military operations were stuck in a stable, self-serving stalemate. The anti-Kabila revolt was also interconnected with both regulated and unregulated global trade and financial flows. War entrepreneurs often begin with predatory operations—looting and destroying property and goading population movement to accompany or counterbalance military power. The traditional objective of war—to defeat the enemy militarily—was replaced by economically driven interests in continued fighting because the war was more profitable than peace. The duration of civil wars previously considered political uprisings, to which a state responds through counterinsurgency, needs to be understood in terms of the interests of warlords who benefit from violent economic activity and have incentives to prolong conflict and sabotage peacemaking efforts. Thus, the peace process became the hostage of spoilers. The status quo became profitable for state players, although devastating to the population.

This is the dilemma of collective action. Some combatants are better off as long as they keep fighting, because war grants power and wealth that would not be available in peacetime. Prolonging the war provides all sides with a rationale to keep looting. Rebel groups are likely to settle for local pillage because they cannot seize control of state power. A war of attrition tends to create a new system of predation where one loots a neighbor's resources without attempting to conquer the neighbor. In a vicious cycle of conflict-based rapine, the plundering of resources elevated the level of violence. Profits increasingly motivate the need to protect their sources and, in the process, increase the level of violence, which makes those profits possible.

The second war against Kabila was also the only civil war in the Congolese history to end with negotiations as the result of the number of foreign armies involved, rebels from neighboring countries having sanctuaries in the DRC, and the inflation of Congolese rebels. The interaction of these groups created a difficult environment and stalemate that favored neither group. However, in the balance of power, Kinshasa enjoyed one advantage that none of the rebel movements opposed to it could duplicate: the legitimacy of the state. Precarious though that legitimacy might have been, Kinshasa drew an advantage from its relations with the wider community of states. The achievement of a cease-fire was the result of UN intervention and pressure from the West. These participants increased the costs of fighting, making it more attractive for the parties to stick to the peace deal in the short run. Moreover, the international community reduced the level of fear among rebel groups that the government would renege on its commitments. Powersharing was critical to rebel groups that obtained access to state spoils. The massive foreign aid that poured into Congo was an indirect bribe to bring all belligerents to Kinshasa to set the electoral timetable as a force for peace. After the euphoria brought about by the elections, the Kabila government rapidly demonstrated an ambition to control all levels of power and a willingness to repress the opposition.

Just as in the past, the West remains unwilling to tackle the deeply ingrained, heavy-dominance pattern of the executive and the often pervasive blending of state and ruling party. This pattern tends, as in the past, to circumscribe the overall freedom of political choice and to sustain abuses of human rights that are so pervasive in Africa. As a result, once an election is over, the new leadership concentrates power and the opposition is forgotten, leading to another round of clientelism, authoritarianism, and civil unrest (Sisk 1996). As

Chabal and Daloz (1998, pp. 37–38) contend, politics on the African continent are essentially factional because of the particularistic links between big men and their constituent communities. So, they conclude, it is doubtful that a process of democratization will result in a fundamental political transformation because most leaders continue to associate with their supporters through the same old networks of patronage.

Notes

1. These groups included the Alliance Démocratique du Peuple of Deogratias Bugera, the Conseil National de Résistance pour la Démocratie of Kisase Ngandu, the Mouvement Révolutionnaire pour la Libération du Congo-Zaire under Anselme Masasu Nindaga, and the PRP of Laurent Kabila established in 1967. The alliance seemed to have been made in a Kigali hotel, but the Lemera location was announced only to make it sound more "authentically Congolese." See Prunier (2009), note 1, p. 396 and Willame (1999), p. 34.

2. Three conditions must be satisfied to extend recognition to a rebel group or to recognize it as a "belligerent community": (1) a government and military organization must have been established and be operative in the rebel-controlled area; (2) the rebellion must have reached a stage beyond mere local revolt—that is, a condition of warfare equivalent to conflict between states has to have developed; and (3) the rebel group must control a reasonable portion of the territory. See von Glahn and Taulbee (2010), pp. 159–161.

3. See Arreté Départemental No. 0229 of 23 August 1970, cited in Mba (2003), p. 33.

4. Bembe, who was pro-Mobutu, was stoned by his own Bembe people in 1990 for tracking down the democratization process by supporting President Mobutu. He knew that the Banyamulenge issue or their quest for Congolese nationality was a key for his people to forgive him of his mischief. He offered them Banyamulenge's assets or cattle in the hills of Itombwe. The same scenario occurred for most politicians of the Uvira territory. They promised their people the same gift—Itombwe hills and its wealth, gold. This gold was discovered in the early 1970s and was exploited by the Banyamulenge. See Lanotte (2003) and Willame (1997).

5. According to Duke (2003), the expression "first world war" originated with Susan Rice, the US assistant secretary of state for Africa.

6. Downs and Stedman (2002, pp. 55–56) provide the following features of a difficult environment: state collapse, the existence of more than two belligerent groups, the presence of armed combatants that number over 50,000 soldiers, the presence of hostile neighbors or regional networks, and disposable natural resources.

7. The nationality law fixes the fundamental options of Congolese nationality and institutes two distinct legal statutes. It is composed of ten chapters: Chapter I deals with the general provisions; II defines the nationality by birth; III refers to the Congolese nationality by acquisition; IV provides for the loss, deprivation, and regaining of the Congolese nationality; V applies to the procedures of declaration, deprivation, and regaining of the Congolese nationality; VI talks about the proof of nationality; VII designates the competent authority for issuing the nationality certificate; VIII provides the tax provisions; IX contains the particular and transitional provisions; and X covers the rescinding and final provisions.

6

Ethnic Wars in Nord-Kivu and Ituri

The last four chapters recounted the distinctive causes, duration, and management of secessions, rebellions, mutinies, invasions, insurrections, and revolts in Congo. These chapters also showed why, how, and when each group became involved in political conflict with the state in which it lived as well as the ways in which members of each group interacted with other groups. Although these conflicts remained nonethnic, Congo has experienced ethnic wars as well. A number of these wars occurred in the 1990s—three in Nord-Kivu and one in Ituri. Broadly speaking, an "ethnic community" is a named human population having "a myth of common ancestry, shared memories, cultural elements, a link with a given territory or homeland, and a measure of solidarity" (Smith 1986, pp. 28–29). An ethnic conflict qualifies as a civil war if "one or more contenders define themselves using communal criteria and makes claims on behalf of the group's collective interests against the state, or against other communal actors" (Smith 1986, pp. 28–29), with the familiar threshold of at least 1,000 deaths and 2,000 internally displaced persons in the first three months of the conflict. The next two sections analyze ethnic conflicts in Nord-Kivu and Ituri, respectively. The last section summarizes and discusses the findings.

Conflicts in Nord-Kivu

Nord-Kivu was a district of Kivu Maniema before becoming a province on 14 August 1962 as the result of a decentralization law promulgated in April 1962. In December 1966, it was again a district of Kivu until 1988 when Mobutu separated Kivu into three provinces by Decree no. 88-031 of 20 July. Nord-Kivu extends over 59,483 square kilometers. Park reserves represent 26 percent of Nord-Kivu, while inhospitable areas such as lakes, forests, and mountains too steep for human settlement represent 11 percent. Its temperate climate makes Nord-Kivu ideal for livestock and agriculture. The main cash crops include coffee, tea, and pyrethrum, but gold, tin, and coltan are also found in the area. As

Map 6.1 indicates, Nord-Kivu has six territories: Beni, Lubero, Masisi, Nyi-rangongo, Rutshuru, and Walikale. In 1993, its diverse ethnic population was estimated to be close to 3.7 million, with no less than a dozen ethnic groups, including the most politically vocal groups the Hunde, Nande, Nyanga, and Banyarwanda (both Hutu and Tutsi).

The first ethnic conflict in Nord-Kivu broke out on 20 March 1993 in the marketplace of Ntoto in Walikale territory when the Nyanga attacked the Banyarwanda. A week later, the conflict expanded to Masisi territory, and, within a month, some 996 Nyanga and Hunde and as many as 1,238 Banyarwanda were killed (Mathieu and Mafikiri 1999, p. 60). In March–April 1993 alone, ethnic conflict in Masisi and Walikale displaced more than 59,000 Nyanga and Hunde as well as some 72,000 Banyarwanda (Willame 1997, p. 66). When the conflict ended on 31 August 1993, between 7,000 and 16,000 people were dead, and some 250,000 were internally displaced (U.S. Committee for Refugees 1994, p. 73). On 17 July 1995, a new round of deadly confrontations between the Hunde and the Banyarwanda in Masisi began, which ended on 21 December 1995 with 6,000 to 9,000 deaths; in July–August alone, some 450 people were killed in the confrontation (U.S. Committee for Refugees 1996, p. 76). The number of internally displaced people was about 150,000. However, the bloodiest ethnic confrontation in the history of the province happened four months later, beginning on 17 April 1996 and lasting until 12 October 1996. Some 30,000 people were killed in Masisi territory, and more than 220,000 people were internally displaced. In sum, from 20 March 1993 to 12 October 1996, ethnic conflicts in Nord-Kivu, especially in Masisi, claimed 40,000 to 70,000 lives, and an average of 120,000 people were internally displaced per year.[1] A brief precolonial and colonial background of the Nande, Hunde, and Banyarwanda will help explain these ethnic conflicts.

Historical Context

The Nande are agriculturalists of Bantu origin (Bergmans 1979; Cirhagarhula 1981; Mashauri 1981). In the fifteenth century, they migrated to their present area, Beni and Lubero territories, as the result of political changes in the region of Kitara-Bunyoro, Uganda. Although the Nande migrants found their present habitat already occupied by the Mbuti pygmies, other agriculturalists, and Bahera pastoralists, they easily conquered and assimilated these "natives." The Nande ethnic group comprises a dozen Bantu groups or clans, but all these groups speak Kinande. Despite differences among Nande clans, they have similar laws, customs, mores, and traditions that make them almost homogenous or an "ethnic-nation" (Mashauri 1981).

Major Nande groups developed six confederal principalities that were similar to other interlacustrine polities: the Bamate, Banyisanza, Bashu, Basongora, Baswanga, and Batangi (Mashauri 1981). They were part of the *bwami* system, or small principalities with strong ties to the land and sophisticated modes of

Map 6.1 Nord-Kivu Province: Its Territories and People

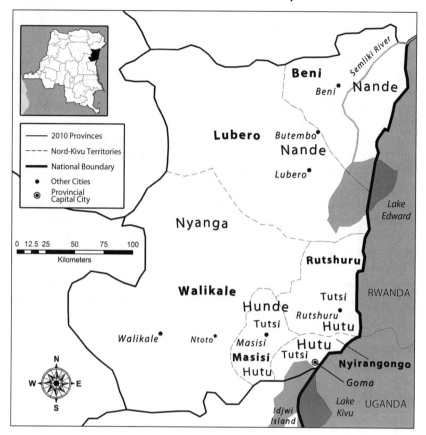

coronation and burial ceremonies of their princes in the Great Lakes region. Another historical bond is their land, which keeps them together and gives them a common memory.[2] Traditionally, the Nande land is communal but the ruler, the *mwami,* provides land to his notables—barons, or *vakama*—as a hereditary right or a contract to use land in exchange for an annual tribute, or *muhako* (Mafikiri 1994, pp. 90–116). This tribute plays a dual role: first, it helps stabilize traditional political relationships over land because it recognizes traditional authority, and second, it upholds the right of the first occupant and thus helps integrate strangers into the community.

The second group of interest resides in Masisi territory and is called the Hunde. Like the Nande, the Hunde are an agro-pastoralist society with predominantly small livestock (Viane 1952). The cattle were introduced in Masisi by Rwandan immigrants in the 1930s. The Hunde originated in Bunyoro, Uganda, in the eleventh century and migrated into their present space, Masisi, through Bwito in northern Rutshuru (Cirhagarhula 1981). They are linguistically similar to the Shi group of Sud-Kivu. Four independent principalities co-existed for centuries in Masisi: Bunyungu, Bafumando, Bugado, and Kishali (Cirhagarhula 1981, p. 235). In their early history, the last three polities paid tribute to the first principality.

The political organization of these Hunde principalities paralleled the Nande system. At the top of each principality was the ruler (*mubake*), followed by governors of provinces (*batware*), and village chiefs (*batambo*). Royal succession was not automatic. Unlike the Nande political system, the Hunde mwami was both a military and spiritual leader. However, his power was limited by the inner council, the *Bakungu*, which could depose the reigning prince and even kill him. Land was also a common good among the Hunde, and the mwami its custodian. He distributed land among his subjects who received rights to use it. Users of land gave the mwami a tribute called *mutulo* in the form of animal skin, goat, tusk, cowa, local wine, and food when the mwami traveled to the area. In return, the notables could provide user rights to others and also received gifts as participants in the mwami's tribute. This was the second-level tribute.

The final group of interest in Nord-Kivu is the Banyarwanda that comprises the Hutu and the Tutsi (Munanira 1981). However, precolonial Rutshuru was mostly occupied by the Hutu before the arrival of the Tutsi in the area. As a result, most of these Hutu prefer the name Banyabwisha (people of Bwisha). Precolonial Bwisha comprised a number of localities that came under the rule of two monarchies. First, a few localities were under the Rwandan monarchy from the mid-nineteenth century to 1910, while a number of other Hutu principalities remained autonomous until 1910. Second, from 1910 to 1960, Bwisha was under Belgian rule. The three groups of people under these monarchies were the Hutu, Tutsi, and Twa. The first occupants of Bwisha, the Twa lived by hunting and gathering and were difficult to integrate into other cultural groups. In the late nineteenth century, they revolted at Bufumbira against the despotic rule of the Rwandan ruler and the dominating tutelage of both Hutu and Tutsi. Among the Twa's demands were broader political participation and management of interethnic relations (Munanira 1981). The repression of the Twa was bloody and most were killed.

The Hutu are agriculturalists and seem to have occupied today's Rutshuru territory in two waves. The first occurred around 1000 AD and consisted of migrations from Uganda (Munanira 1981, pp. 180–181), which established a number of principalities in the area. The second group migrated from Rwanda in the nineteenth century to escape the despotic rule of the Rwandan mwami. The third group is the Tutsi from Rwanda, and their presence in Rutshuru goes back to the nineteenth century. Although they are predominantly shepherds of large livestock, they were also farmers in precolonial Bwisha. Their penetration into Bwisha was mostly pacific because they intermarried with the Hutu, easily adopting Hutu language, the Kinyarwanda, and agricultural activities.

Economically, the land tenure system in Bwisha differed from that of many principalities in today's Nord-Kivu. The first occupants to displace the Twa were the Hutu. As the first group to rule the area, they called themselves the Bakonde (clan or lineage chief) and gave portions of land to latecomers, the Bakeberwa (Munanira 1981). While land tenure in Rwanda was based on the system of clientelism, or *ubuhake*, land tenure in Bwisha was based on lineage. This system created a decentralized sociopolitical organization in which lineage chiefs were political leaders in their own lineages. However, the coronation of Rwandan Mwami Yuhi IV Gahindiro in 1876 changed the Bwisha configuration when he expanded his kingdom to a number of localities in Bwisha where Rwandan rulers installed the patron-client system. Under the new Rwandan ruler, Hutu lineage leaders or chiefs had to provide an annual tribute to the royal court. Despite frequent revolts of Hutu chiefs, the system persisted until 1910 when Belgium and Germany modified their colonial boundaries in eastern Africa.

The terms "Hutu" and "Tutsi" were constructed to characterize two classes of citizens in Rwanda, not two separate groups of migrants. The label "Tutsi," which was in use by a court elite by the early nineteenth century in Rwanda, became by extension a label applying to all warriors serving the king, as militarism developed, and was subsequently attached more generally to cattle owners (Vansina 2000). Cirhagarhula (1981) and Vansina (2000) categorically refute the thesis that the Tutsi originated as an immigrant group of conquerors who subdued and subjugated the existing populace in relatively recent historical times. The term "Hutu," Vansina states, was originally a term of disdain, applied to court servants. During the decades preceding colonial rule, it became generally applied to subject agricultural populations, who continued to have important regional and local identities. Thus, ethnic categories in Rwanda should be understood as political identities that changed with the changing nature of the Rwandan state (Mamdani 2001; Vansina 2000).

In the late nineteenth century, the colonial period transformed the region's communal land tenure into a new system. As pointed out in Chapter 1, King Leopold II introduced a system of private land management by declaring that all unoccupied lands were state property and could not be occupied without state's authorization. However, the decree-law of 1 January 1885 also upheld Africans' rights to land. Thus, land inhabited and in use by the natives under their traditional authorities was administered by customary law and nobody could dispossess them, according to the law. The traditional or communal land tenure regime remained and coexisted with the colonial or written law. When the CFS became a Belgian colony, on 15 November 1908, Article 15 of the Colonial Charter, which was modified on a number of occasions, gave the colonial administrator the power and rights to give or sell land to private companies and Europeans for either fiscal or developmental purposes. Nonetheless, all land transactions took place subject to Africans' land rights and after detailed investigations on land availability.

One important factor after the Belgian annexation of the CFS in 1908 was the protocol that modified colonial boundaries in eastern Africa, signed on 14 May 1910 between Belgium and Germany. The convention also gave Belgium several islands in Lake Kivu, including the largest island, Idjwi, as well as four zones in the Rutshuru territory, some of which were part of precolonial Rwanda. On 8 November 1920, a law created ethnically based sectors and chieftaincies (Magotte 1934). The subsequent reorganization of the rural area transformed precolonial principalities into chieftaincies, and a number of these chieftaincies were staffed by warrant chiefs, mostly colonial puppets. For example, tension began with the imposition of a Hutu warrant chief, Daniel Ndeze, in 1920 as the great chief of the Rutshuru territory. In 1921, the imposition of André Kalinda as the great chief of Masisi territory followed, although the Hunde had histori- cally four autonomous principalities. While Chief Ndeze and his heirs faced strong opposition from the Hutu of Bwito and from his rivals within the Bwisha, Chief Kalinda was also challenged in Masisi.[3]

The existence of many autonomous principalities with strong myths of ori- gin in today's Nord-Kivu (also Sud-Kivu) was a major challenge to the colonial administration as it attempted to impose its authority in the area. By the late 1920s, the Kivu area was still ungovernable, and the colonial administration decided to attract Europeans to help establish its authority. On 13 January 1928, it promulgated a decree creating a charter company called the National Com- mittee of Kivu (Comité National du Kivu, or CNKi), which obtained unlimited forest, mining, and land rights over a vast territory in Kivu. The CNKi's goal was to identify appropriate lands for agriculture and pasture for European colonists. Once it had identified so-called vacant lands, it then divided and fenced them in "blocs of colonization" that were either sold to or rented by colonists coming directly from Europe, especially Belgium. However, this un- limited ownership was later reduced to 800,000 hectares in 1930 and to 300,000 hectares in 1947 as the result of complaints to the colonial administration by local populations, especially in populated areas of Masisi and Rutshuru (Lemarchand 1964; Young 1965).

Migrations from Rwanda-Urundi between 1928 and 1955 would further complicate land relationships in an already overpopulated Masisi territory. Early migrations were organized by the colonial state for two primary reasons. First, famine had frequently struck Rwanda. As early as 1928–1929, Belgium moved a large number of Rwandans into Kivu to alleviate population pressure caused by the famine. Famines occurred again in 1940–1943 and 1950–1952.

The second organized movement of Rwandan migrations was the result of a labor shortage in the Belgian Congo to satisfy the growing demand for work- ers in mines and plantations. The colonial administration of Kivu, Rwandan au- thorities, and the CNKi signed an agreement that created the Immigration Mission of the Banyarwanda (Mission d'Immigration des Banyarwanda, or MIB), known then as Mission Henard. It targeted several territories of Kivu to house Rwandan immigrants and contacted traditional chiefs of Lubero, Walikale, and Masisi. The first two categorically refused to welcome the new migrants, and only the chief of the Hunde gave his approval. Several waves of migrations into Gishari, in Masisi territory, followed.

The first wave began in 1937, following an act of cession signed by Hunde Chief Kalinda and the MIB. The colonial government paid Kalinda 29,600 Belgian francs ($41,836 in 2010 prices) in compensation for 350 square kilometers of land (19.5 x 18 kilometers) in Gishari to host the first group of Rwandan migrants (Kisangani 2002, p. 13). This piece of land was administered by a Tutsi subchief chosen by the first group of immigrants. One year later, local Hunde chiefs in Masisi complained about the high percentage of Tutsi (72 percent) over Hutu (28 percent) within the first group of immigrants. Because the Tutsi are pastoralists and the Hutu are farmers, more Tutsi meant more land under pasture, leaving little land for farming in the agrarian Masisi area. In mid-1939, the governor-general of the Belgian Congo reversed the trend by a decree that allowed more Hutu than Tutsi to migrate to Congo. In 1937–1940, some 25,000 Rwandans, mostly Hutu, moved to Gishari.

In the early 1940s, a major famine swept Rwanda again, resulting in some 60,000 additional Rwandans moving into Masisi. Because the new migrants could not be accommodated in the 350 square kilometers allocated to them in Gishari by the 1937 contract, they were moved deep into the Hunde zone of Washali-Mokoto. In addition to these early organized migrations, the colonial administration recruited some 80,000 Rwandans to work on Congolese plantations and in the mines (Kisangani 1997). As migrants moved into the Nord-Kivu District, they became a distinct group of people. Thus, the issue of "autochthons" versus "allochthons" started in 1940 when the colonial administration created the chieftaincy of Gishari and appointed Bideri, a migrant, as chief of the new entity. For the Hunde chiefs, Bideri was a vassal who would continue to pay an annual tribute to the Hunde mwami in order to use land (Bucyalimwe 1990).

However, things changed in 1944 when Wilfrid Buchanayande replaced Bideri and was invested as chief of the autonomous Gishari chieftaincy by Decision no. 1/1944 of the district commissioner of Nord-Kivu.[4] Social tension developed between the migrant chief and Hunde chiefs. This political decision to build an autonomous chieftaincy of migrants was a political aberration, as stated by the governor-general in his letter dated 1 March 1953: "[I]nhabitants of Ruanda-Urundi who are being installed in the Belgian Congo in the region of MIB and its intervention must be considered at individual title and not at chieftaincy level and must be eventually integrated within their traditional or customary notables in the local native circumscriptions under the high authority of these circumscription chiefs."[5] In other words, Gishari was not a chieftaincy but a sector under Hunde chiefs. In the mid-1950s, the Hunde chiefs vehemently opposed its existence, resulting in its abolition. Their argument was that Rwandans were given land in the chieftaincy as long as they remained under the jurisdiction of a local Hunde mwami. As a consequence of friction between "natives" and the migrants from Rwanda, a new ethnic identity began to emerge in both Masisi and Rutshuru as the number of migrants from Rwanda increased in the 1950s. By 1960, the Hutu and Tutsi in both territories became known as Banyarwanda, or people from Rwanda.

Postcolonial Period

To prepare for independence, the Belgian legislature passed the electoral law of 23 March 1960, which gave migrants from Rwanda the right to vote as residents. Article 1 states that "A voter must be Congolese or born of a Congolese mother, or come from Ruanda-Urundi and having resided in Congo for at least ten years. Second, eligible voters had to be male, twenty-one years and older" (Gérard-Libois and Verhaegen 1961, p. 257). The electoral law thus alluded to people of Ruanda-Urundi as residents and excluded those who migrated to Congo after 1950. The law clearly distinguished refugees from the migrants of the 1930s and 1940s. As stated in Article 10, early immigrants had residency status and were even allowed to run for legislative office if they had been legally in Congo for five years.

The electoral law also assigned seventy seats to Kivu in the national and provincial legislatures. The first provincial government of Kivu included Jean Miruho, a Shi from Sud-Kivu, as governor, and a number of Banyarwanda legislators. As developed in Chapters 1 and 2, this government lasted until late December 1960 when several platoons of soldiers from Kisangani took Bukavu, making Kivu part of the Stanleyville government under Antoine Gizenga. The Miruho government was replaced by the Anicet Kashamura-Andrien Omari government, which was brief but provided several important seats to representatives of Goma and Rutshuru. The reconciliation in 1961 brought an end to the Stanleyville government and the reelection of Miruho as provincial president.

From the beginning of his second mandate, Miruho confronted a high unemployment rate among youths (Verhaegen 1962). Meanwhile, politicians were cashing in on smuggling activities in Kivu, which was known then as a safe haven for illegal trade activities with Uganda. Masson (1970) described Kivu in 1961–1962 as an exceptional province where politicians, businessmen, and foreigners (especially Asians) were involved together in lucrative smuggling activities. Parallel networks among these groups developed and became well integrated. In 1961–1962, illegal trade through Uganda cost the Congolese government some 5 billion francs (Masson 1970, p. 70), or $226.7 million (2010 = 100) alone, while the government received only 10 million francs, or less than $453,206 (2010 = 100) in customs duties.

More specifically, Governor Miruho and a number of prominent Banyarwanda were also involved in illegal trade activities. For example, in May–June 1961, Marcel Bisukiro, a Hutu from Rutshuru and minister of commerce in the central government, issued to Governor Miruho and a group of Banyarwanda politicians, including Cyprien Rwakabuba and Celestin Rwamakuba, a trade license that helped them establish a fictitious enterprise called Socogeki (Gérard-Libois and Verhaegen 1963, pp. 73–75). This company automatically supplanted and almost eliminated the state marketing board, Office des Produits Agricoles du Kivu, which had a monopoly to buy coffee and other agricultural products from local farmers at fixed government prices and to process and export them. Socogeki managed all exports of agricultural products without paying any export tax. From July 1961 to May 1962, Socogeki made a colossal profit equivalent to 800 million francs (Masson 1970, p. 72), or $35 million in 2010 prices.

Most legislators of Nord-Kivu were aware of these operations and decided to create their own province. Their decision was also based on the fact that they were underrepresented in the provincial government while their resources were being plundered by the representatives of other territories. In accordance with the April 1962 law, the majority of legislators from Nord-Kivu introduced a petition to the parliament to have their own province because it met all the criteria set by the April 1962 law.[6] This decision was not well received by the Shi leaders in Bukavu, Sud-Kivu, who never wanted to lose a rich region and a major generator of provincial revenue. Despite their vehement opposition, Nord-Kivu became a province on 14 August 1962. However, the Banyarwanda legislators opposed attaching Goma and Rutshuru territories to Nord-Kivu and requested a referendum in Masisi and Walikale, where other Banyarwanda lived with the Hunde and the Nyanga, respectively.

On 28 November 1962, representatives of Kivu Central (today Sud-Kivu) introduced a petition to the central government to create their own province. The law of 18 May 1963 made Kivu Central a province, which also included Goma and Rutshuru territories. Thus, the parliamentary decision to include Goma and Rutshuru in Kivu Central without a referendum caused partisans of Nord-Kivu, especially the Nande, to harden their position on keeping Goma and Rutshuru in Nord-Kivu Province. In the words of a Nande legislator, "The two territories of Goma and Rutshuru no longer belong to the Congolese people, Mr. Kasavubu has given them to Rwandans" (Beys, Gendebien, and Verhaegen 1964, p. 353). After Nande legislators vehemently opposed the May 1963 law attaching Goma and Rutshuru to Kivu Central, the central government retreated and declared both territories as contested and appointed a special administrator until a referendum could decide their status.

As the referendum approached, the Banyarwanda legislators developed a strategy aimed to increase their numbers in the polls in order to remain in Kivu Central. They distributed Congolese identification cards to Tutsi refugees in Goma and Rutshuru (Beys, Gendebien, and Verhaegen 1964, p. 349). Tensions further mounted between the Nande and the Banyarwanda as new waves of refugees continued to enter Nord-Kivu as the result of ethnic conflict in Rwanda. Violence erupted as legislators became suspicious of the Banyarwanda, accusing them of trying to conquer Rutshuru, Walikale, Kalehe, and Masisi territories by force.

The 1964 constitution dug the hole deeper between the Banyarwanda and other groups in Nord-Kivu by making the Congolese nationality more restrictive. According to Article 6, the Congolese nationality is exclusive to those people whose ancestors were members of any ethnic group that had lived in the DRC before 18 October 1908, unless they made a special request within twelve months to change their nationality. This article automatically excluded most Banyarwanda of Masisi, who migrated to Congo from 1937 to 1950 under the MIB policy, and all refugees from 1959 to 1964, unless they made a special request to change their nationality.

Meanwhile the results of the referendum on Goma and Rutshuru, in April–May 1965, attached the two contested territories to Nord-Kivu, and its results were officially promulgated by the decree of 18 September 1965. Legislative elections, which occurred between 18 March and 20 April 1965, gave a net majority to the Nande in both provincial and national legislatures.[7] However, Banyarwanda contested the electoral results in Masisi, which gave most seats to the minority Hunde group in the provincial assembly. An ethnic clash ensued, with as many as 195 people killed in June 1965 (Gérard-Libois and Van Lierde 1966). As stated in Chapter 3, the authorities of Nord-Kivu attributed the disorder to collusion between the Banyarwanda and the rebels of Gaston Soumialot and called it the Kinyarwanda rebellion. Torture and extrajudicial killings of Banyarwanda by the Hunde and Nande also occurred, and many were thrown into Lake Vert near Kirotse (Gérard-Libois and Van Lierde 1966, pp. 79–80).

From 1961 to 1965, the political environment in Nord-Kivu was tense, with the Banyarwanda facing off with the Nande, Nyanga, and Hunde. This tense political environment never escalated into a civil war, although traditional Hunde authorities complained to the central government about their fear of "the number of Banyarwanda immigrants" that was "likely to lead to a major revolt against us" (Gérard-Libois and Van Lierde 1965, p. 15). However, President Mobutu ignored the complaint and in 1967 closed all Tutsi refugee camps in Nord-Kivu, effectily turning some 55,000 Tutsi refugees into Congolese residents (Kisangani 1997).

Mobutu's decision to close refugee camps came from one of his advisers, Barthélémy Bisengimana, a Tutsi from Rwanda. Less than two years after closing the camps, Mobutu nominated Bisengimana as the chief of staff (or director) of his office. From his nomination in May 1969 until his removal in 1977, Bisengimana was the architect of most of Mobutu's policies. For example, three years after the nomination, Mobutu signed on 5 January 1972 Decree-law no. 72-002 that conferred Congolese nationality on all immigrants from Rwanda and Burundi who had been in Congo before January 1950 and had continued to reside in Congo since. As pointed out in Chapter 5, Article 15 of the law states that "The people from Ruanda-Urundi who were established in the Kivu province before 1 January 1950 and who had continued to reside since then in the Republic of Zaire until the promulgation of the present law had acquired the Zairian nationality on 30 June 1960." The law affected more than 190,000 Tutsi immigrants in Masisi and, to a lesser degree, Rwandan immigrants in Rutshuru,

Goma, and Walikale. The main issue was in Masisi where these immigrants outnumbered the Hunde, as natives, by a ratio of two to one. Table 6.1 gives a picture of the impact of this nationality law in Masisi territory where 70.6 percent of immigrants became citizens by a stroke of a pen. These immigrants also represented 24 percent of the population of Goma and Rutshuru.

However, the 1972 law on nationality would not have generated the animosity that it did if not coupled with the historical land law on 20 July 1973 and the zairianization law on 30 November 1973. The first law, no. 73-021, laid out the principle that "land is the exclusive, inalienable and indefeasible property of the state" (Article 53). The new law disqualified customary law on land tenure and institutionalized private land tenure in Congo. Thus, anyone could buy rural land without the approval of traditional authorities. It also automatically replaced customary rules for accessing land without actually destroying traditional land tenure. As pointed out in Chapter 5, Mobutu then decided to nationalize all small and medium-sized foreign businesses in November 1973, including foreign plantations, and handed them over to fewer than 350 families of the ruling political class. Most Tutsi in Nord-Kivu benefited enormously from the policy, acquiring vast concessions of land and plantations in Nord-Kivu (Kisangani 1997, 1998).

In the early 1980s, the conflict over land and nationality became even more acute as the result of two events. First was a complaint to the parliament by a legislator from Walikale, Mihia Bamwhisho, about the cession of 230,000 hectares of land, or one-tenth of the Walikale territory, to Rwacico enterprise, which belonged to Cyprien Rwakabuba, a Tutsi. The government annulled the concession after the Legislative Council recommended that the land cession be voided. The second event was the nomination of four Tutsi to the newly created supreme institution of the unique party state, the Central Committee, by Law no. 80-221 of 2 September 1980. This nomination sparked vehement protests from the Hutu of Bwisha in the Rutshuru territory. In reaction to the nomination, the Hutu created the Mutuelle Agricole des Virunga (Agricultural Mutuality of the Viruga) to further the interests of the Bwisha Hutu. This was the first subtle division within the Banyarwanda of Rutshuru.

Table 6.1 Distribution of Rwandan Immigrants in Nord-Kivu, 1970

Territory	Total Population (1)	Immigrant Population (2)	Percentage (2)/(1)
Walikale	78,334	1,882	2.40
Goma	74,835	17,713	23.70
Rutshuru	333,916	81,509	24.40
Masisi	273,920	193,428	70.60

Source: Data from De Saint Moulin (1976); also see Willame (1997), p. 54.

The nomination of Tutsi as members of the Central Committee forced legislators from Nord-Kivu to introduce a nationality bill in the parliament. The result was the promulgation of a new law, no. 81-002 of 29 June 1981, which explicitly canceled the nationality of the Banyarwanda, except for the Banyabwisha, as "natives." Article 4 of the law states that a person is "Zairian on 30 June 1960 in terms of article 11 of the constitution, any person whose one of the ancestors is or has been member of one of the tribes established on the territory of the Republic of Zaire within the limits set on 1 August 1885, and as modified by subsequent conventions." Therefore, the people of Rutshuru were Congolese, given the 1910 convention between Germany and Belgium, but migrants from Rwanda since the 1930s and their children were not. In this case, the new law upheld the *jus sanguinis* doctrine (law of the blood).

The Tutsi retaliated immediately by the creation of their own organization, called Umoja (Unity), for what they perceived as a sign of political exclusion. By stripping people of Rwandan descent of Congolese nationality, the government created stateless people without even identifying who they were. Article 15, however, provided the president of the republic discretionary power to grant Congolese nationality to "anyone on the basis of past services to the nation" after consultation with the Central Committee of the party (paragraph 3). Since the 1981 law was never implemented, and given porous borders between Congo and Rwanda, illegal migrations continued unabated.

A final policy under Mobutu setting the course for ethnic wars in Nord-Kivu was his decision in 1987 to divide Kivu Province into three separate entities reminiscent of the early 1960s. His rationale was to bring power closer to the people through decentralization, which intended to improve accountability and administrative efficiency. Ordinance law no. 88-031 of 20 July 1988 established Nord-Kivu as a province. Mobutu's decision was a prelude to organized elections scheduled for March 1989. However, elections were not held in Nord-Kivu because the central government was unable to carry out a census of the population to identify eligible voters.

This confusion over nationality was exacerbated after Mobutu announced the liberalization of his political system in April 1990 and the organization of a national conference to set new institutional arrangements. At this juncture, a native administration was appointed in Nord-Kivu for the first time since 1967. Appointing natives to govern their own province was known in the Congolese political lexicon as "geopolitics." Mobutu nominated Chrysostome Kalumbo, a Nande, and Miha Bamwisho, a Nyanga, as governor and vice governor of Nord-Kivu. The duo purged all Banyarwanda in the government and replaced most administrators with the Nande, Hunde, and Nyanga. Geopolitics also meant representation at the sovereign national conference according to the share of an ethnic group in the province. Since nobody knew this share, the idea was to exclude from the conference whoever the Nande, Hunde, and Nyanga called "foreigners," or the Banyarwanda.

In late 1992, several Banyarwanda leaders were assassinated, and thousands of cattle belonging to the Banyarwanda were slaughtered by the Hunde and Nande in Masisi. The Tutsi responded to this threat by killing a Hunde chief and cutting his body in pieces to undermine the chief's authority, the chieftaincy, and traditional customs (Willame 1997). The Hunde retaliated violently. The attack of Banyarwanda by the Nyanga on 20 March 1993 in the local market of Ntoto in Walikale, which started the first ethnic war in Nord-Kivu, was the natural consequence of these events. In early July 1993, President Mobutu visited Goma and invited all parties to discuss the issues of land and power sharing. To reinforce the peace in the spirit of pacification, he decided to send 140 troops of his Presidential Special Guards to Goma. He also replaced the incumbent native administration of Kalumbo-Bamwisho by another native governor, Christophe Moto Mupenda from a small ethnic group called Kano, for the purpose of ethnic reconciliation.

However, the influx of 1.2 million Hutu refugees from Rwanda in mid-June 1994 wrecked any hope of a lasting peace. Some 860,000 of these refugees, among them former soldiers and militiamen who had committed the genocide, were relocated in Nord-Kivu along Rwandan borders (Kisangani 2000a; U.S. Committee for Refugees 1996). The Hutu refugees changed the ethnic configuration of Nord-Kivu. First, the increase in the Hutu population created a new majority in Nord-Kivu, thus posing a threat to the Nande should elections take place while refugees were still in Congo. Second, the influx of Hutu refugees also created a new identity for the Banyarwanda. Before 1990, they were a single group that included both the Hutu and the Tutsi living in Nord-Kivu. They had a common purpose against the Hunde, Nande, and Nyanga groups, even when the Tutsi and the Hutu fought each other in Rwanda. The massive influx of Hutu refugees openly broke the old Tutsi-Hutu alliance within the Banyarwanda, indicating the malleability of ethnicity. The split widened as Hutu militiamen in refugee camps began attacking the Tutsi-dominated government of Rwanda.

Third, most politicians from the Kivus panicked in the presence of Hutu refugees and lobbied in the transitional parliament for the passage of the resolution of 28 April 1995. The panic was caused by fear to see these Hutu refugees disappear in the local Hutu population before the elections. This resolution not only stripped Banyarwanda of their Congolese nationality but also denied all people of Rwandan descent even simple residency in Congo. Another round of ethnic conflict began on 17 July 1995 in the Masisi area and continued until 21 December 1995. After more than three months of calm, conflict reemerged on 17 April 1996 as Hutu militias and the Congolese army launched a hunt for Tutsi in Nord-Kivu. The crisis continued until 12 October 1996. On 12 November 1996, the AFDL-RPA coalition occupied Goma, ending the Moto Mupenda administration and Mobutu's rule in Nord-Kivu. The AFDL nominated a Tutsi, Léonard Kanyamuhanga, as governor of Nord-Kivu, resulting in the exclusion from major provincial offices of Nande and Hutu, considered the two largest groups in the area.

To sum up, three distinct ethnic conflicts occurred in Nord-Kivu from 1993 to 1996, while none occurred in Sud-Kivu, although the nationality laws affected the Banyamulenge equally. Thus, specific features that differentiate the two provinces should be highlighted to understand why these laws never provoked a high level of hatred and animosity in Sud-Kivu the way they did in Nord-Kivu. First, as pointed out in Chapter 5, the Banyamulenge developed social relations with other groups in Sud-Kivu because they were part of the socioeconomic fabric of Uvira and Fizi territories. Second, their settlement in Itombwe never created an issue of land scarcity for local farmers with whom they shared a larger territory than Rwanda. In other words, the Banyamulenge's cattle never competed with land the way the Tutsi's cattle did in Nord-Kivu. Third, although local authorities and urban populations were hostile to them, the Banyamulenge kept good relations with army officers and secret service agents. Thus, the Banyamulenge avoided taking part in the interethnic conflict in Uvira and Fizi areas.

Fourth, the Banyamulenge never benefited from the 1973 nationalization policy the way the Banyarwanda did in Nord-Kivu. Fifth, the Banyamulenge had acquired some auto-defense potential since 1964 when they helped defeat the eastern rebellion. They used their relations with army officers to accumulate weapons to defend their cattle against marauding bands. This war capital provided them with the means to defend themselves against other groups. It was not until the application of the 1995 resolution threatening the Banyamulenge with eviction that they declared publicly that they would resist any attack against them (Mugisho 1998, p. 327).

Causes of Ethnic Wars in Nord-Kivu

Most analysts who have analyzed conflicts in Nord-Kivu have relied on the idea of grievance and hatred of migrants from Rwanda as the result of pressures they placed on land in a predominantly agrarian region of Nord-Kivu. What most experts have overlooked is that both legal and illegal migrations have not been unique to Nord-Kivu. These migrations also occurred along most Congolese borders, especially in Bas-Congo Province where the influx of refugees from Angola averaged 228,000 migrants a year in the 1960s, with a peak of 500,000 in 1967, and 480,000 refugees a year in the 1970s and the 1980s (Kisangani and Bobb 2010, p. 452). Two major differences between Bas-Congo and Nord-Kivu emerge here, however. First, the Angolan refugees were mostly absorbed into the formal and informal economies of Kinshasa and other major cities in the province. Second, they never sought political or elected offices the way Rwandan immigrants did. This low political visibility of Angolan refugees perhaps explains the absence of any conflict between the refugees and autochthons in Bas-Congo.

Conventional wisdom also tends to relate ethnic wars in Nord-Kivu to the democratization process of the early 1990s and the concomitant anarchy that followed Mobutu's intransigence to the process. As Posen (1993) contends, under conditions of anarchy, groups within states fear for their own security much as states do. Efforts to improve one group's security in anarchy make other groups feel insecure and hence reduce security for all. After the collapse of the Soviet Union, the lid on ancient rivalries was taken off, and long-suppressed grievances kept checked by the Cold War were settled as different groups claimed their spaces. Rather than developing a broad-based political alliance, the argument goes, political elites of all ethnic affinities became divided and polarized to the extent that building a peaceful coexistence was no longer possible as ethnic groups used their own militias to destroy each other. Thus, the local cop became the Muhunde, Munande, Munyarwanda, or Munyanga cop in Nord-Kivu.[8]

However, the security dilemma is not sufficient in and of itself to explain the conditions under which leaders or subgroups succeed in garnering the support of an often reticent public audience that typically prefers peace to violence (DeFigueiredo and Weingast 1999). As DeFigueiredo and Weingast (1999, pp. 262–263) point out, the elites are predatory and use violence either to remain in power or to gain power. When the mass public notices this violence, even if unsure about who provoked it, it can become concerned that the other group might be dangerous. The public may therefore rationally support policies preparing for war, calculating that the costs of violence are lower than the costs of facing threatened violence unprepared.

These rational choice explanations of ethnic wars fail to explain the absence of ethnic wars, defined by the threshold of 1,000 deaths, anywhere else in Congo. Although illegal immigration and the security dilemma provide some explanations of the first ethnic war in Nord-Kivu, they do not fully account for the recurrence of ethnic wars in the province because they fail to separate critical juncture from critical antecedents.

Critical juncture and ethnic wars in Nord-Kivu. Since the 1960s, a political issue in Nord-Kivu has remained the politics of exclusion between majority and minority groups according to ethnic arithmetic. However, both groups perceived the numbers through different lenses. On the one hand, minority groups, such as the Hunde, Nyanga, and Tutsi, viewed the electoral process as the sword of Damocles hanging above their heads because it provided them little access to state spoils. Political salvation thus resides in striking an alliance with one of the two majority groups—either the Nande or the Hutu—and hoping that the majority group would not renege on its commitment in postelectoral institutional arrangements.

On the other hand, the Hutu and the Nande hoped to prevent both the minority groups outside their alliance and the other majority group from gaining access to state spoils. Moreover, the fear of majority groups is a minority group controlling the political process. Politics of exclusion and alliance systems tend to dichotomize politics in Nord-Kivu, with minority Hunde and Nyanga groups allying with the Nande because they saw themselves as autochthons, while the Tutsi had allied with the Hutu as Banyarwanda.

The Nande, as a homogenous group, also control Beni and Lubero territories and have often gained the most from the electoral process. They are well represented in Goma and Rutshuru, the fiefdoms of Hutu and Tutsi, and also live in Masisi and Walikale. The domination of Banyarwanda immigrants in Masisi became apparent in the beginning of the democratization process, launched on 24 April 1990 by President Mobutu, and provided the location of deadly confrontation. The ratio of people of Rwandan extraction to autochthons in Masisi was almost two to one. In 1990, they represented some 65 to 70 percent of the total population of Masisi and almost 17 percent of the population of Nord-Kivu (Pabanel 1991, p. 36). If electoral arithmetic had been applied in 1990, the people of Rwandan extraction would have received at least 65 percent of seats from the Masisi territory, and locals such as the Hunde would have obtained less than 33 percent. In general, the Rwandan population could have controlled almost 17 percent of elected offices in Nord-Kivu.

The critical juncture of the first ethnic war in Nord-Kivu was thus the politics of exclusion. The appointment of two natives as governor, Kalumbo, and vice governor, Bamwisho, was intended to give leaders familiar with their province easy access to local means to solve local problems. Rather than solving socioeconomic issues of the province, the two chief executives embarked on a campaign of exclusion in which the alliance among the Nande, Hunde, and Nyanga gave the Nande the lion's share of administrative and military positions in the province. Even the Rutshuru territory, predominantly inhabited by the Banyarwanda, was under a Nande administrator, Musokoni Matabazi. The notion of geopolitics intensified local ethnic competition because leaders identified with their own ethnic groups. Clearly, this policy was another Mobutu

Table 6.2 Ethnic Composition of Provincial Government, Jan. 1992–Nov. 1996

| | Nande Dominated (Jan. 1992–July 1993) | | | | Tutsi Dominated (July 1993–Nov. 1996) | | | |
	Government	Urban Zones	Rural Zones	Total	Government	Urban Zones	Rural Zones	Total
Hunde	0	1	11	12	1	1	3	5
Hutu	0	1	5	6	0	1	2	3
Nande	2	1	26	29	1	1	21	23
Nyanga/Kano	2	1	7	10	1	0	6	7
Tutsi	0	0	1	1	1	1	18	20
Kumu	0	0	1	1	0	0	1	1
Tembo	0	0	0	0	0	0	1	1

Sources: Data from Bucyalimwe (2000), pp. 252–253.

strategy to stall the democratization process by giving the elites access to provincial spoils, which in turn triggered the politics of exclusion.

The politics of exclusion first targeted the Hutu of Bwisha with whom the Nande compete politically. This exclusion was also critical for the survival of the Hunde minority in the Masisi territory, especially in the Bwito chieftaincy, where all Hutu and Tutsi chiefs as well as notables were removed and replaced by the Hunde. Table 6.2 illustrates this exclusion of the Hutu and Tutsi in January 1992–July 1993 and shows the dominance of minority groups, Hunde and Nyanga, at the expense of the second majority group, Hutu, and minority Tutsi.

On 17 July 1995, the second war broke out. The critical juncture of this outbreak was the appointment of a new native governor, Moto Mupenda, in early July 1993. Mupenda is from the Lenga minority of Walikale, commonly called Kano, which was usually not involved in the conflicts of Nord-Kivu. However, to the Nande, Hunde, and Nyanga, the new governor was a Tutsi puppet. In fact, the new governor reconfigured the politics of Nord-Kivu by replacing appointees from the previous administration with mostly Tutsi administrators or Tutsi sympathizers to end the Nande hegemony. The purge also involved the control of the gendarmerie. Even his chief adviser was a Tutsi, Léonard Gafundi Kanyamuhanga, who later became governor after the AFDL took Goma in November 1996. The new administration also targeted the Hutu of Rutshuru because this group had controlled the territory with the family of Chief Ndeze.

The goal of the new administration was to break this Hutu political monopoly by appointing mostly Tutsi in the territorial administration of Rutshuru. Once in power, the Tutsi minority also built its own coalition with Nyanga and Hunde minorities by excluding the Hutu, the other majority group.

According to Table 6.2, the number of Hutu administrators in the rural areas declined from five in the previous administration to two in the Tutsi-dominated provincial government. The number of minority Tutsi appointed to rural areas suddenly jumped from one in the Nande-dominated administration (1992–1993) to a record high of eighteen in the Tutsi-dominated administration. The number of Hunde also declined from eleven to three, signaling that most Tutsi were appointed in Masisi, the Hunde's land. The overwhelming number of Nande in rural territories is the result of their homogeneity in the two most populous territories of Nord-Kivu—Beni and Lubero. The Tutsi could not exclude the Nande from their territories without bloody consequences. In this game of exclusion, the Hutu group suffered the most discrimination.

The final Tutsi strategy was to help the rebel-dominated Tutsi RPF, which had sanctuary in Uganda, to take power in Rwanda. As the Tutsi armed groups were consolidating their positions along the borders, troop movements began in Uganda as the RPF planned a massive attack against the Hutu Rwandan government in late 1993. The RPF's attack occurred in December 1993 when the assassination of President Juvenal Habiarimana of Rwanda in a plane shot down by the RPF set the course for genocide (Kisangani 2000a). The RPF's offensive helped stop the genocide but created a massive wave of refugees into Nord-

Kivu. All Hutu refugees in Nord-Kivu were relocated to predominantly Hutu chieftaincies of Bwisha (Rutshuru), Bukumu (Nyiragongo), and Kamuronza (Masisi). The arrival of Hutu refugees in Nord-Kivu also reinforced fears among non-Hutu groups as the population balance tipped in favor of Hutu at the expense of other groups. Most non-Hutu elites feared that these refugees would disappear into the local Hutu population and participate in the electoral process and thus exclude them from state power.

Although the politics of exclusion explains how ethnic wars started in Nord-Kivu, it provides little insight into the structural causes of the three ethnic wars and the rationale behind masses' involvement. The historical background highlights several economic and political antecedents in Nord-Kivu, which warrant careful examination because they help explain why ethnic conflicts emerged in Nord-Kivu in the early 1990s and nowhere else in Congo.

Critical antecedents. The first critical antecedent is an element of continuity and consists of colonial boundaries set in 1910. A portion of Hutu and Tutsi who were subjects of the Rwandan ruler became subjects of the Belgian king. This element of continuity created two antagonistic alliances in Nord-Kivu and also epitomized the regional politics of the 1990s that set the stage for ethnic wars in Nord-Kivu. In fact, regional politics became critical in explaining the last two ethnic wars when the RPF took power in Rwanda and created a massive wave of Hutu refugees in Congo. As long as the refugees were confined to their camps, the electoral issue did not cause much alarm. Once they began to integrate into the local Hutu community, ethnic arithmetic became a major political issue and an object of contention.

The second critical antecedent is the combination of land scarcity and land tenure laws. The interaction of demographic, ecological, and legal factors is critical to understanding the three ethnic wars in Nord-Kivu. A number of scholars in the Malthusian tradition argue that wars are often over renewable resources such as fresh water, cropland, forests, and fisheries (Galtung 1982; Homer-Dixon 1998). As pointed out in Chapter 1, scarcity of such resources can cause violent conflict, under certain conditions, because the availability of these resources determines people's day-to-day well-being.

The first time land scarcity became an issue in Nord-Kivu was when the colonial administration created the charter company CNKi, whose goal was to allocate land to European colonists, and began expanding the National Reserve Park of Virunga (former National Park Albert) from 70,000 hectares in 1925 to 220,000 in 1929 and then from 380,000 in 1934 to 809,000 hectares in 1935. Related to this expansion is the ecology of Nord-Kivu with its active volcanoes that erupt at fairly regular intervals (Meyer 1955). During eruptions, volcanic ash covers large areas, destroying vegetation and pasture. Caught between volcanoes and the national park, people usually have no exit or no place to move to.

For example, the Jomba area, in the vicinity of Lake Edward, was officially described as "over-saturated in 1957 as each family household had less than

1.9 hectares of land to raise crops and cattle" (Bucyalimwe 2005, p. 229), although the colonial administration estimated that a rural family of four required at least 1.2 hectares of land to survive in Kivu (Belgium 1956). The colonial administration also reported that the Masisi territory had 37.9 inhabitants per square kilometer in 1955, which represented the highest population density in the Belgian Congo, with Leopoldville (now Kinshasa) a distant second with 8.14 inhabitants per square kilometer (Belgium 1956, pp. 59–64). In 1970, the average density in Masisi was 62, with 103 in Rutshuru (Mathieu and Mafikiri 1999, p. 27). After inhospitable areas, such as volcanoes, parks, inaccessible mountains, and grazing land, have been taken into account, the population density was even higher, averaging 200 inhabitants per square kilometer in the province and 330 per square kilometer in Masisi alone in 1990 (Mathieu and Mafikiri 1999, pp. 26–29). By 1987, 47 percent of rural families in Nord-Kivu had access to only 0.3 to 0.5 hectares of land (Fairhead 1991), which was far below the 1.2 hectares necessary to sustain a decent rural livelihood of a family of four.

The increasing population density in Nord-Kivu and the pressure on land can also be explained in terms of demographics. First is rapid growth of the population, which averaged 3.1 percent a year since the 1940s as the result of the temperate mountainous climate and improved sanitation during the colonial period. Nord-Kivu has thus been overpopulated since the late 1950s, and immigrations from Rwanda have increased lateral pressure on an already saturated area. Thus, the second cause of demographic pressure in Nord-Kivu lies with both organized and unorganized migrations from Rwanda. As discussed earlier, the first wave of migrations was organized by the colonial administration as the result of famines in Rwanda in 1928–1929, 1940–1943, and 1950–1952. The second organized wave was in response to labor needs in 1937–1945 and 1949–1955. By 1954, more than 175,000 Rwandan migrants had registered in Congo (Belgium 1955, p. 67). The first unorganized migrations occurred as the result of Hutu resistance to the Tutsi monarchy, which culminated in the November 1959 revolt overthrowing Mwami Kigeri V. Of the more than 150,000 Tutsi who fled Rwanda, some 60,000 relocated in Nord-Kivu and the rest in Uganda. In late 1963, Tutsi migrants in Uganda invaded Rwanda at Bugesera in an attempt to overthrow the Hutu government. This brought another wave of more than 60,000 Tutsi refugees into Nord-Kivu. In 1967, the Mobutu administration closed refugee camps, and some 55,000 Tutsi refugees disappeared into the Banyarwandan community of Nord-Kivu.

Another migration came from Burundi in 1972. An attempted coup against the Tutsi regime of Captain Michel Micombero resulted in the genocide of some 200,000 Hutu, with thousands fleeing to Congo and Tanzania (Lemarchand 1994). One year later, the revolt of Tutsi students in Rwanda resulted in the exile of elite Tutsi from Rwanda to Congo, where many graduates later sought employment in education and administration. In mid-1994, the massive wave of Hutu refugees followed.

Finally, because Hutu and Tutsi live on both sides of common porous borders between Congo and Rwanda, illegal migrations from overpopulated Rwanda to Congo have continued since the early 1960s. In brief, the Banyarwanda population varied between 15 percent and 20 percent of the local population in the early 1990s (Kisangani 1997). More specifically, the Banyarwanda represented at least 60 percent and maybe 70 percent of the local population in Masisi (Pabanel 1991, p. 36). The result was further pressure on already limited land in Masisi. Therefore, a basic causal relation is that the likelihood of ethnic war increases as population increases and cultivable land becomes scarce in an agrarian economy. Though this view provides a cause of conflict, it underspecifies a number of factors that have exacerbated tensions in Nord-Kivu but did not lead to conflicts elsewhere in Congo.

Scarcity of land cannot be attributed to population pressure alone. Institutional arrangements are also crucial and can contribute to this scarcity. One of these arrangements and an element of change was the Bakajika Law, promulgated on 7 June 1966, by which the Congolese state took possession of all lands. It was followed by the General Property Law No. 73-021 of 20 July 1973, which remained the cornerstone of land tenure in the postcolonial period. Because the state owns all lands, five public institutions in descending order are allowed to allocate land: the parliament, the presidency, the ministry of land titles, provincial governor, and curator of real estate titles. Second, the state can give land in the form of concessions, which represent the right to use land. The law removed traditional authorities from being managers of state land. In sum, the law nationalized the Congolese land and, by ricochet, not only abolished private land tenure but also ended the colonial distinction between modern land tenure based on written laws and unwritten traditional land tenure.

The main objective of the 1973 land law was thus to weaken the power of traditional authorities to grant land. In the process, however, it created an ambiguous land tenure system that upheld the territorial base of ethnicity. Articles 385 and 386 of the law indicate that land occupied by local communities and exploited individually or collectively according to customs become state domain; however, the right to use land regularly acquired would be regulated by presidential decrees (Article 389). Because these presidential decrees were never promulgated, the Mobutu state considered the occupation of land by Congolese in rural areas neither as a right nor as a state obligation but rather as a privilege.

The saddest part of this ambiguous land law was that the Congolese jurisprudence was also unable to settle the issue of rural land. The Supreme Court of Justice gave two contradictory rulings in less than three months in 1988. On 20 January 1988, the high court ruled that the rights to use land were still under customary legal system until a presidential decree ordained otherwise (cited in Matabaro 2008, p. 390). However, on 9 April 1988, it stated that the 1973 law was the sole text on land tenure. The ambiguity of the 1973 law has perpetuated a vague system of land tenure that has left plenty of room for abuse of power, corruption, and massive land spoliation. Before this law, every rural dweller had access to land as long as he remained under a given chief and respected the traditional hierarchy. There was no need to register land or fence it. With the new law, registration and fencing became part of the rules of the game. Meanwhile, most peasants have continued to rely on traditional authorities to deal with land issues, although traditional customs are no longer the source of land rights.

At the district or territorial level, most administrative officials had no authority to allocate or cede land but were in charge of implementing the law. However, district and territorial commissioners whose role was to implement land law or to validate the accuracy of information or investigation related to "unoccupied lands" became grantors of land rights, selling land to the highest bidder, most likely to the urban elites. Corruption abounded, and the subsistence farmer remained the victim who has no legal recourse. By 1991, less than 30 percent of wealthy urban elites, mostly Tutsi immigrants, owned 71.2 percent of land in Masisi, leaving most peasants without enough land to earn a living.

The 1973 land law would not have created animosity and friction in Nord-Kivu without the zairianization policy of 30 November 1973. Crafted by Bisengimana (a Tutsi), the director of President Mobutu's office, the nationalization of small and medium-size businesses made it easier for the Banyarwanda to acquire vast plantations in Nord-Kivu. More specifically, the Banyarwanda acquired 45 percent of the arable land in Masisi, which they used as pasture in a region where agriculture provided a livelihood for more than 70 percent of the population (Kisangani 1997; Gnamo 1999). They also obtained 93 percent of all nationalized businesses and plantations in Nord-Kivu, especially in the Masisi and Rutshuru territories. Bisengimana emerged as a big winner, acquiring plantations on the island of Idjwi in Lake Kivu and becoming a quasi-sovereign there.

The land and nationalization laws added a third critical antecedent to the conflict equation: the development of the cattle sector. Cattle were introduced in Masisi by the first Tutsi migrants in 1937. The Masisi high-altitude climate was ideal for livestock and had been used for cattle by Rwandan immigrants when they first arrived in the area. However, the colonial administrator carefully regulated the cattle sector in the area to the extent that, by 1958, only some 45,000 head were allowed, leaving enough room for croplands in Masisi (Bucyalimwe 2001). From 1960 to 1973, Nord-Kivu had no major development project for cattle ranching. As a result, there was no intense conflict over land. From 1973 to 1980, however, the development of cattle ranching by the Banyarwanda caused resentment among other ethnic groups, who viewed this development as domination by foreigners. The government, more specifically Bisengimana, revitalized livestock production by rationalizing that the policy would assure food security and improve peasants' livelihoods (Bucyalimwe 2001). The Mobutu government even provided funding for the cattle project to members of the political elite and their associates, mostly Tutsi. The development of the cattle business was based on intensive ranching that required at least 4 hectares of pasture per head.

Table 6.3 gives the number of cattle in Masisi and its relationship with available land to assess land vulnerability in the area. Masisi covers 4,374 square kilometers. Because the area of nonhuman settlement, such as lakes and volcanoes, represents 25 percent of total land, available land is thus only 3,280 square kilometers (see column d). Given one animal for 4 hectares of land, this was a highly productive investment for the Tutsi elites. By 1992, more than 374 inhabitants could be assumed to live in one square kilometer of land compared to 100 cattle per square kilometer (one additional cow per one hectare). According to column d in Table 6.3, land necessary for subsistence farming was, over the years, eaten up by the cattle, declining from 3,100 square kilometers in 1958 to 1,433 square kilometers in 1992. In a systematic analysis of land disputes, Bucyalimwe (1990, pp. 237–240) showed an increase in land disputes as the number of cattle increased in Gishari, Masisi: twelve land disputes in the 1960s, forty in the 1970s, and 106 from 1980 to 1988.

By the late 1980s, potential for open armed conflict was already present in Nord-Kivu as the cattle took cultivable land away from subsistence farmers. More specifically, a few Tutsi ranchers controlled more than 300,000 head of cattle by the late 1980s. As the market for land expanded after the promulgation of the 1973 land law, most lands that peasants had cultivated for generations under communal ownership increased in value, and pressures arose to enclose pastures. Another critical antecedent that explains ethnic conflicts in Nord-Kivu seems to have originated from an interaction between a perception of inequal-

Table 6.3 Cattle Production and Land Availability in Masisi

	Cattle (a)	Additional pasture (b)	Population projection (c)	Available land [(3,280)–(b)] (d)	Density (c)/(d)
1958	45,000	180	219,314	3,100	71
1982	253,800	1,015	395,123	2,265	174
1983	263,400	1,054	407,372	2,226	183
1984	273,800	1,095	420,001	2,185	192
1985	285,300	1,141	433,021	2,139	202
1986	297,800	1,191	446,445	2,089	214
1987	310,800	1,243	460,285	2,037	226
1988[a]	324,400	1,298	474,554	1,982	239
1989[a]	338,300	1,352	489,265	1,928	254
1990[a]	353,726	1,506	504,432	1,774	284
1991[a]	369,997	1,669	520,069	1,611	323
1992[a]	387,757	1,847	536,191	1,433	374

Source: Number of cattle from 1958 to 1987 is from Bucyalimwe (1990).
Note: a. Projected values, which are conservative.

ity (class system) and the mode of production. Pastures and markets increased the perception of inequality in two ways. First, cattle production requires far more land than food cultivation. Second, control over land means political power and the exclusion of political rivals. Pressure on the elites to respond to citizens' demands for land meant the exclusion of other groups in order to replace cattle by plowshare.

Institutionally, the ambiguity of the 1973 land law seemed to have been deliberately motivated by urban elites to own rural land. Beause the law was followed by the nationalization of foreign businesses and plantations, this indicated that the president and his urban clients intended to destroy traditional authorities and start the process of primitive accumulation of wealth. More specifically, the legislative body under the Mobutu regime was comprised of the same group that acquired vast plantations in rural areas and even expanded pastures by encroaching on peasants' land for subsistence production.

In addition to conflict between cattle and plowshare is a set of critical sociopolitical antecedents that explain ethnic conflicts in Nord-Kivu but are not present anywhere else in Congo. First is leadership style. According to Brown (1996), internal wars occur not because one group hates another but rather because of the rational and deliberate decisions of "bad leaders." Characteristics such as "bad leadership" or "charismatic leadership" describe the ways in which leaders matter. These terms are hard to quantify, so it is not surprising that quantitative studies have not been able to test the effects of leadership style on the onset of civil wars. Current operational definitions of this variable, such as autocracy, hardly capture the individual psychological characteristics of leaders. For example, during his tenure as president, Mobutu used a "divide and rule" policy in the Kivu area, playing one group against another and creating antagonistic relationships, which increased polarization and mistrust among groups. In the 1970s, Mobutu sided with the Banyarwanda against local groups that contested his authority. The result was the 1972 nationality law that granted Congolese nationality to all Rwandan immigrants who arrived in Congo before the early 1950s. However, in the 1980s, he encouraged an anti-Banyarwanda sentiment among local ethnic groups. The centerpiece of this game was the promulgation of the 1981 nationality law that canceled the Congolese nationality of people of Rwandan descent. In mid-1994, Mobutu used the Hutu refugees to plan the creation of a Hutuland in order to increase the number of voters, which would counterbalance unfavorable votes from non-Hutu groups that contested his authority and leadership.

Another sociopolitical antecedent relates to the notion of an "effective link." In international law, an effective link emerges as another way of acquiring nationality in addition to naturalization and the two traditional modes—jus sanguinis and jus soli. An effective link describes a legal, political, and social tie between a citizen and the state. The issue of an effective link emerged in 1955, when the International Court of Justice ascertained whether the nationality conferred on Friedric Nottebóhm by the principality of Liechtenstein was sufficient enough to protect Notteböhm from arrest and seizure of his assets by the government of Guatemala in the famous case known as *Liechtenstein v. Guatemala* (Lissitzyn 1955). Although international law leaves the issue of conferring nationality to each state, which lays down the rules, the court pointed out in its decision that there must be a "real and effective" relationship between an individual and his state of citizenship—a "genuine link." This link must neither be tenuous nor ephemeral. From this view, the court defines nationality as

> a legal bond having its basis a social fact of attachment, a genuine connection of existence, interests and sentiments, together with the existence of reciprocal rights and duties. It may be said to constitute the juridical connection of the fact that the individual upon whom it is conferred either directly by the law or as the result of an act of the authorities, is in fact more closely connected with the population of the State conferring nationality than with that of any other state. (Lissitzyn 1955, p. 395)

The Hunde, Nande, and Nyanga thus argued that the Banyarwanda should not be considered Congolese citizens because they have no effective link with Congo. First, they accused the Banyarwanda of relentless attempts to divide Nord-Kivu and being politically "secessionist." The year 1962 remained fresh in the mind of most autochthons, when the Banyarwanda refused to join other groups to create Nord-Kivu and instead joined Kivu Central Province. Second, they also accused the Tutsi living in Congo of massive participation in the Rwandan war of liberation in 1993–1994, which ultimately installed a Tutsi-dominated government in Rwanda. This accusation was substantiated by interviews of Tutsi by the government-led Vangu Commission (Willame 1997, p. 48). Huntington (1996) refers to such behavior as "kin country syndrome," where communities sharing similar cultural ties are mobilized across national boundaries in supporting or opposing a government. This syndrome is an element of continuity related to colonial borders and started in the Great Lakes region in the 1960s by the diffusion of conflict from Rwanda to Burundi when the Hutu took power and drove the Tutsi to Burundi and Uganda. In 1973, it moved back to Rwanda after the genocide that killed some 200,000 Hutu in Burundi, driving Hutu to Rwanda and Tanzania. In the 1990s, the syndrome moved to Congo when Tutsi refugees in Uganda took power in Rwanda, driving some 1.2 million Hutu refugees into Congo. The Tutsi's participation in the Rwandan civil war illustrated to autochthons a recurring behavior of social distancing from Nord-Kivu.

Critics may accuse the autochthons of "cognitive dissonance." The argument is that autochthons tend to discount any new information that portrays the Banyarwanda as truly Congolese because this information contradicts preexisting beliefs dating back to the early 1960s about the Banyarwanda. Moreover, autochthons seem to have built "schemas," or "mental constructs," that portray the Banyarwanda as "evil" or "unpatriotic" in order to make sense of their behavior. As a result, the depiction of Banyarwanda as secessionists and "people without borders," trying to conquer Congo by force, is so deep in the subconsciousness of autochthons of Nord-Kivu that their minds tend to close and reject any new information that depicts the Banyarwanda in favorable and positive ways.

However, the autochthons in Nord-Kivu are likely to disagree. In fact, they usually accused migrants from Rwanda of double standards in their quest for citizenship (Kisangani 2002). According to autochthons, Rwandan immigrants wanted to be "politically and economically integrated" without being socially integrated. For example, the Banyarwanda, especially the Tutsi, practiced endogamy—having little or no intermarriage with other people in the area. Other groups viewed the high rate of endogamy among the Tutsi as "social exclusion" and potential for ethnic conflict.

Duration, Consequences, and Conflict Management

The three ethnic wars in Nord-Kivu averaged 159 days each, with the first lasting 162 days. They were longer than the early mutinies of the 1960s and the two Shaba wars of the 1970s but were shorter than the two secessions, the two rebellions, and the three wars against the presidents. They remained shorter than the average Congolese conflict of 538 days. The duration of ethnic wars in Nord-Kivu seems to defy any explanation in extant literature. For example, Fearon's (2004) explanation of "rebel motivation" does not account for the short duration of ethnic wars in Nord-Kivu. His view is that wars emerging from coups, revolutions, and anticolonial struggles are relatively brief, while "sons of the soil" civil wars tend to be long. Although this view suggests that ethnic wars in Nord-Kivu should have been long, the first ethnic war in Nord-Kivu ended after less than six months after the cattle were destroyed. In July–August 1994 alone, more than 300,000 cattle were slaughtered by the Hunde in Masisi and Walikale (Willame 1997, p. 74). Here the cattle represented not a symbol of wealth and class but strangers taking the land of the "sons of the soil" to feed cows and then dominating autochthons. Thus, ethnic wars in Nord-Kivu were viewed as legitimate struggles between two modes of production and were short (as hypothesized in Chapter 1).

Like the second war against Kabila, the three ethnic wars in Nord-Kivu had a devastating effect not only on people and their property but also on subsistence agriculture because they occurred in the countryside. Another major consequence of these wars, especially after the inflow of Hutu refugees from Rwanda, was the deconstruction of the Banyarwanda label. Although some distancing between the Hutu and Tutsi started in the 1980s, this early division was more subtle than open. In the 1990s, however, it became visible as the result of the massive flow of Hutu refugees into eastern Congo in mid-1994. The Hutu-Tutsi coalition that had prevailed against the coalition of the Nande, Hunde, and Nyanga broke down under the pressure of refugee numbers. The Tutsi emerged as a separate group, distinct from the Hutu.

Despite the degree of antagonism in Nord-Kivu after the first ethnic war, all the groups were willing to talk and end the violence. The first round of conflict management occurred between 13 and 16 October 1993 in what the parties called "journeys of reflection" that involved all members of civil society, professional organizations, and traditional authorities. The goal was to create an inclusive mediator corps comprised of members from nongovernmental organizations and churches. The approach was inclusive and encouraged respect for ethnic diversity in finding common solutions. At the second meeting, on 13–16 February 1994, former belligerents agreed to resolve some issues of their disagreement peacefully. For the first time since the end of hostilities in August 1993, many internally displaced persons returned home. However, the arrival of Rwandan Hutu refugees in Nord-Kivu in mid-1994 created a setback. The result was the second ethnic war in Nord-Kivu in April 1995.

Mobutu took the first step toward conflict management of ethnic wars in Nord-Kivu by spending a month in Goma, capital city of the province. He brought groups together but also imposed his troops in the region to keep order. Rather than negotiating a solution, Mobutu used force and appointed a different governor in the name of pacification after the first ethnic war. The new incumbent administration purged previous administrators and appointed new ones by favoring Tutsi and Tutsi sympathizers. No mechanism of conflict management was possible in this round of conflict. In April 1996, President Mobutu dispatched his special guards in Nord-Kivu to carry out Operation Kimya (Operation Silence) to control ethnic militias. He began a second operation, Operation Mbata (blow with the fist), in late May to pacify the area, but his troops ended up only providing services to the highest bidders, mostly former Rwandan troops and militia leaders who committed the genocide in Rwanda. Thus, joint operations between Mobutu's soldiers and armed Hutu elements targeted mostly the Tutsi of Masisi. Human Rights Watch (1996) estimated that some 8,000 Tutsi refugees from Masisi were regrouped in two camps in Gisenyi, Rwanda; by late May 1996, an estimated 18,000 refugees were in Rwanda as the result of this operation.

The diffusion of the Rwandan conflict, in the absence of working institutions, shattered any hope of peaceful coexistence in Nord-Kivu. It started with the fall of Bukavu on 30 October 1996. The next day Goma was in the hands of the AFDL, which appointed mostly Tutsi administrators, including the governor, to administer Nord-Kivu. The two other minority groups in Nord-Kivu, Hunde and Nyanga, were co-opted and received important positions in the provincial government. The victory of the AFDL (developed in Chapter 5) added another layer of conflict in Nord-Kivu. The Mai Mai war against Kabila was partly caused by this dominance of Tutsi in most politico-administrative positions in eastern Congo. The second war against Kabila and its aftermaths remained key issues in eastern Congo, especially in Nord-Kivu, as the politics of exclusion continued to affect elites' strategy to access power.

For example, the transitional period in 2003–2006 was dominated by the Tutsi in Nord-Kivu. Of some seventy-four positions occupied by people of Nord-Kivu in the central government, the Tutsi minority had twenty-two in transnational institutions, including five in the army, nine in the lower house, three in the upper house, and two in the government, including one vice presidency. On the other hand, the majority Nande had twenty-three positions, including thirteen in the lower house, three in the upper house, and two in the government. Meanwhile, as the other majority group in the Nord-Kivu, the Hutu were a distant third, with only nine positions, followed by the Hunde (eight), and the Nyanga (six).

However, the 2006 elections ratified the demise of Banyarwanda, the Tutsi in particular, and reinforced the reality of demographic and ethnic polarization. Kabila's parliamentary coalition, the AMP, won thirty of forty-eight seats in the national legislature. Most Hutu in Masisi and Rutshuru voted for Kabila's PPRD and a pro-Kabila Hutu-led party in Nord-Kivu, the Party of Nationalists for Integrated Development. As expected, the RCD received only seven seats. The Nande secured twenty-six deputies, while other groups had eleven (Hutu), six (Hunde), two (Nyanga), and one (Tutsi). The AMP also overwhelmingly won the provincial elections, taking twenty-five of the forty-two seats as follows: Nande (twenty-five), Hutu (ten), Hunde (seven), and Nyanga (seven). No Tutsi received any seat in the provincial assembly after the only elected Tutsi in the institution, Edouard Mwangachuchu, was elected senator. The Nande and the Hutu managed to find agreement and shared the top positions in the provincial government. The consequence of the electoral process in Nord-Kivu turned the tide against the Tutsi. As discussed in the previous chapter, the round of conflict initiated by Laurent Nkunda and his Tutsi followers was also a reaction against this electoral outcome.

Revisiting an Old Wound: The Ituri Conflict

Ituri was a district of Orientale Province until 1962 when the law of 27 April enlarged the number of provinces and Ituri became Kibali-Ituri in August 1962. Five years later, it was again a district of the Orientale Province, but the 2006 constitution made Ituri a province once again. However, by December 2010, Ituri was still a district awaiting the promulgation of a decentralization law to implement the 2006 constitution on the new administrative division. As Map 6.2 indicates, Ituri has five territories: Aru, Djugu, Irumu, Mahagi, and Mambasa. Its capital city is Bunia.

The center of the Ituri conflict between the Hema and the Lendu is the Djugu territory, the most populated area of Ituri and with many coffee plantations. Other sources of livelihood include herding livestock and fishing in Lake Albert. To this wealth should be added gold. The principal center of gold exploitation is Mongbwalu and Kilomoto controlled by the OKIMO with its social headquarters at Bambumines/Camp Yalala in the Djugu territory. Because it borders Uganda, Ituri has always been a center of transborder trade, which offers lucrative opportunities for transporting and taxing goods. Moreover, the discovery of coltan, rare timber, and oil reserves means that the Hema and the Lendu occupy the most fertile and resource-rich area in the Great Lakes region. This section starts with a brief historical background to assess critical antecedents of the conflict between the Hema and the Lendu.

Brief Political Background

The Hema and Lendu communities reside mainly in Djugu and Irumu territories. Map 6.2 shows the other major ethnic groups in Ituri: Alur, Bira, Lese, Logo, Kakwa, Lugbara, and Nyari. Besides these natives, other groups had migrated into the area, among them the Nande of Nord-Kivu, who live mostly in Bunia and Mongbwalu. In 2002, the Ituri population was close to 4.5 million (International Regional Information Networks 2002). The Lendu comprise al-

Map 6.2 Ituri District and Its People

most 17 percent, while the Hema represent 3.5 percent. The second-largest group in Ituri is the Alur with 11 percent. The two antagonistic communities, Lendu and Hema, can be subdivided into two groups each. The Lendu include a southern group, called Lendu-Bindi or Ngiti, and a northern group, comprised of Pitsi, Djatsi, and Tatsi clans. The Lendu are mostly agriculturalists and claim first occupancy of land in the Djugu territory. The Hema also have a southern group, Nyoro, and a northern one, Gegere. The Gegere intermarried with the Lendu and speak Kilendu. In this sense, they show similarity to Tutsi living in Rutshuru and Masisi who speak Hutu or Kinyarwanda. The southern Hema are mostly pastoralists, while northern Hema are a mix of traders and pastoralists.

Neither Hema nor Lendu are natives to Ituri. According to historical accounts of migrations in Ituri, the Mbuti pygmies were the first occupants of an area extending from Ituri to Nord-Kivu (Ndaywel 1997). The first wave of migrations into Ituri started perhaps between the sixteenth and seventeenth centuries with the Lese and Nyari groups who drove away the Mbuti pygmies. In the eighteenth century, the Lendu migrations pushed out the Lese and the Nyari. The last movement of people in the area consisted of small waves of Hema in the late eighteenth and early nineteenth centuries, with their cattle, in search of pasture land (Thiry 2004). They relocated along the western bank of Lake Albert and became associated with the Lendu. This mix between the Hema and Lendu created no problem because the Hema came to adopt the Lendu language. Another group of Hema, the Nyoro, pushed the Lendu farther north, thus delimiting their own land without mixing with the Lendu. Even in the late nineteenth century, other small migrations continued.

King Leopold's agents penetrated the area during the Revolt of Expedition Dhanis, or the Batetela Mutiny, in the 1890s (Flamant et al. 1952; Moulaert 1950). The people of Ituri were thus among the first in eastern Congo to come under the rule of the CFS. In 1895, the Ituri area was part of the Stanley Falls District, which also included today's Maniema, Nord-Kivu, Sud-Kivu, and Tanganyika. It was not until the administrative reform of the Belgian Congo in 1912 that Ituri became a district, and, in 1926, part of Orientale Province. Although the situation was politically satisfactory in Ituri in the early years of Belgian rule, the Lendu remained difficult to subdue. For example, in 1911, the Lendu-Bindi of Irumu revolted and killed a Hema chief, Bomera, over a land issue (Johnson 2003). And, in 1919, according to colonial archives, the "natives of Kilo area refused to be involved in any type of employment; seditious movements erupted among the Lendu and the Lese" in 1919 (Belgium 1920, p. 12). To reestablish order, the colonial authority had to carry out police operations in the area.

On 8 November 1920, the colonial administration introduced ethnically based sectors, and the decree of 5 December 1933 created new chieftaincies (Magotte 1934). The two laws institutionalized indirect rule and were extensively implemented in the Kivus and Ituri (Bucyalimwe 2005). The 1920 decree imposed a Hema chief on the Lendu, reminiscent of Masisi and Rutshuru in

Nord-Kivu. However, the Lendu revolted and again killed the Hema chief. Because the Djugu territory remained unruly, the district commissioner of Ituri suggested having the area under military occupation to suppress the Lendu revolt. His rationale was based on the fact that the occupation would not only help the gold mine company of Kilo Moto recruit labor among the Lendu but it could also help the colonial administration control the Lendu (Moulaert 1950, p. 96 and pp. 225–257). Thus, Djugu and Irumu territories became heavily exploited by the colonial administration, especially after the discovery of gold deposits in Kilo Moto.

The Belgians also sponsored a plantation-based economy run by European settlers. This exploitation led to the displacement of populations as well as alienation of land and grazing rights, as in the Kivus. In 1923, the colonial administration decided to separate the Hema and the Lendu by limiting the collectivities of Djugu to the north and Irumu to the south to avoid future ethnic confrontation. However, the policy to subdue the Lendu was unsuccessful. In fact, six years later, the colonial administration sent another military occupation to control the Lendu in the Geti area because they refused to pay taxes (Belgium 1930, p. 104). The administration also introduced private titles to land and a system of registration, declaring them vacant lands and hence state property, which resulted in state alienation of thousands of hectares of land from the local Lendu communities.

Furthermore, the colonial state implemented social policies at the expense of the Lendu. Because the Hema cooperated with the colonial rule in Ituri, the state opened schools to Hema children. This policy was based on a colonial myth of superiority that "the Hema supposedly had more leadership qualities and were more intelligent than the Lendu" (Moulaert 1950, pp. 255–256). The education of Hema later allowed them to dominate most clerical jobs in the colonial administration, the Kilo Moto mining company, and plantations. The only alternative left to the Lendu was to remain in the village farming or to become manual laborers in the mining industry or in the plantations. The result was a new social stratification that associated ethnicity with class; the Hema became the upper class in the African community. Although this perception of inequality increased the chance of conflict between the Hema and Lendu, the colonial administration was able to subdue the Lendu with military or police operations in the Ituri District, thus avoiding any kind of revolt.

In 1960, when Congo became independent, the Ituri District overwhelmingly voted MNC/L. Of the twenty seats allocated to Ituri, nineteen went to Lumumba's MNC (Gérard-Libois and Verhaegen 1961, p. 183). The nationalist and unitarist ideology of the MNC/L gave the people of Ituri District a forum to voice ethnic demands within the national agenda. On 14 August 1962, Kibali-Ituri became a province, with Jean-Foster Manzikala as its president. The centrifugal forces that split many provinces along ethnic lines did not disturb the ethnic relationship between the Hema and the Lendu. Because the province was also predominantly under the MNC/L, ethnic politics did not become an issue despite the fact that most administrative positions in Ituri were in the hands of Hema, a consequence of the colonial system. It was not until 1966 that the Lendu revolted and refused to pay taxes to what they considered a Hema administration. The provincial authority repressed the movement with heavy losses in life (International Crisis Group 2003).

In 1973, Mobutu promulgated the land law, which gave the Hema easy access to land at the expense of the Lendu. This law was followed by the nationalization policy in November 1973. The two laws benefited the Hema more than any other ethnic group in Ituri because they dominated the political state apparatus. A year later, a Lendu leader, Soma Mastaki, created a pseudo-party called the Party for the Liberation of Walendu (Parti de Libération des Walendu, or PLW), whose goal was to serve as a forum to voice Lendu political demands for representation in state institutions where they had been marginalized and excluded by the Hema, although the Lendu represented some 17 percent of the Ituri population (International Crisis Group 2003). However, the movement soon turned to terrorism, ambushing and killing Hema civilians. Reports from district administrative officials indicated that the movement used poison to kill Hema school-age children, which was so widespread that the PLW became synonymous for poison in Ituri. The consequence of these acts was so devastating to the Hema that they requested a truce between the two communities. In 1975, community leaders of both groups signed a reconciliation pact under Governor Assumani Busanya Lukili. The pact reestablished peace between the two groups for ten years, from 1975 to 1984. Although some tensions reemerged in 1985, the situation returned to calm without any major incident.

The relationship between the two groups changed after President Mobutu announced the liberalization of his political regime in April 1990. Similar to Nord-Kivu, the Ituri elites also created organizations to further the interests of their groups. The Hema were the first, establishing ETE, which in the Hema language means "cattle." It represented a symbol of nobility to distinguish themselves from others, especially the Lendu, although the Hema were never part of any type of nobility in precolonial Ituri. The ETE's goal was to reinforce ethnic solidarity and to establish a common goal by strengthening the group against the Lendu's threat.

The Lendu followed suit and created LORI, which means "under the palaver tree." However, LORI really stood for the Liberation of Oppressed Race in Ituri (Libération de la Race Opprimée en Ituri). The purpose of the group was to increase political self-awareness and to fight against the dominating power of the Hema, who were perceived as an occupying force that had taken the Lendu's land. As everywhere else in eastern Congo, self-help groups, such as the LORI and the ETE, tried to mobilize ethnic constituencies in case elections took place. They also provided an intellectual vehicle for mobilizing the youths and justifying violence.

It was not until 1993 that the Lendu-Ngiti and Hema clashed in Irumu, with more than 270 people dead (International Crisis Group 2003). Mobutu sent the

412th Battalion to Ituri, but the battalion became uncontrollable and even used heavy artillery against the Lendu warriors, deliberately killing more than 300 civilians. The war against Mobutu in late 1996, which ended in May 1997 with Laurent Kabila as president, did not change ethnic relations in Ituri. In August 1997, however, the Lendu-Pitsi in the locality of Tsunde, Djugu, began protesting against the activities of a Hema rancher, Magbo Mugenyi, who was extending his pasture into Lendu farmers' fields. A Lendu leader, Ngbadhengo Gobba, was able to intercede before the protest escalated to armed conflict. Gobba organized a meeting with the Hema rancher. Not only did the meeting diffuse tension, as the Hema rancher backed down, but it also brought most traditional chiefs together to discuss land issues. The result was some type of reconciliation in mid-1998 among traditional chiefs. The meeting ended with the creation of the Consultative Council of Customary Chiefs of Ituri (Conseil Consultatif des Chefs Coutumiers de l'Ituri). Its goal was to avert armed conflict and to solve land issues without resorting to violence. The Consultative Council brought some semblance of peace until the anti-Kabila civil war erupted on 2 August 1998 and the Ugandan army occupied the Ituri District.

In early 1999, some skirmishes occurred in the Djungu territory as Ugandan forces began evacuating Lendu farmers from their land adjacent to the ranch of a Hema businessman, Singa Kodjo, in exchange for cash payments. Most Lendu officials and local councilors who intervened to stop the move were arrested and sent to prison for having disturbed public order. These arrests fueled an already tense environment in Ituri. In late May 1999, written threats from Lendu chiefs in Pitsi collectivity demanded that the Hema, considered "visitors who are living here in these hills," vacate the Blukua areas, in the Djugu territory (International Crisis Group 2003, p. 4). The Hema perceived this as a preliminary to premeditated "ethnic cleansing." The administrator of Djugu had to intervene to diffuse the situation and to convene an urgent meeting of all community leaders on 19 June 1999 in the Djugu territory. However, the meeting fizzled. Meanwhile, self-help groups dominated by unemployed young men began stirring animosity and circulating tracts of hatred. On the same day in Djugu, a clash between the Hema and the Lendu flared up and quickly spread. Some 700 people were killed on 19 June 1999 alone, the first day of the conflict.

On 18 October, only four months after the conflict began, some 5,000 to 7,000 people had been killed and more than 100,000 people were internally displaced (U.S. Committee for Refugees 2000). By mid-2000, the conflict had spread to other territories, embroiling other ethnic groups. For example, it reached Mongbwalu, the center of the OKIMO, in 2002 and within a year battles for control of the town resulted in more than 2,000 ethnically related deaths (Human Rights Watch 2005, p. 23). Despite peace attempts, the conflict between the Hema and the Lendu continued, and, by July 2005, when the conflict officially ended, 80,000 to 100,000 people had been killed, and an average of 46,000 people had been displaced every year from 1999 to 2005. During the conflict, Ituri had at least eleven armed groups with an estimated average of

12,000 men each (International Crisis Group 2008). The most important were the Hema Union of Congolese Patriots (Union des Patriotes Congolais, or UPC), created in 2000 by Thomas Lubanga, and the Lendu Forces de Résistance Patriotique en Ituri, established in 2002 by Lendu Bindi as the armed group of the Nationalist Integrationist Front (Front National Intégrationiste, or FNI).

Although the Hema and the Lendu had clashed in the past, local authorities had intervened promptly and cut short the violence by calling upon customary mechanisms of arbitration and mediation. The powerlessness of traditional authorities in June 1999 provides a different perspective of the violence, which occurred in the midst of the war against Kabila and also involved Ugandan People's Defense Forces (UPDF). Ugandan generals in Ituri supported and replaced Congolese rebel leaders in the area as they pleased. Wamba dia Wamba, Mbusa Nyamwisi, John Tibassima, Jean-Pierre Bemba, Thomas Lubanga, Chief Kahwa, and many others ruled Ituri as protégés of Ugandan generals.

Causes of Hema-Lendu Conflict

In early 1998, when traditional authorities created the Consultative Council, most observers hoped that Ituri was on the right path and its natural wealth would help rebuild the area. However, the presence of the Ugandan army changed the situation in Ituri. One important critical juncture to the Hema-Lendu conflict was thus the role of the Ugandan army operating in Ituri to preserve President Museveni's sphere of influence in the anti-Kabila war. Before June 1999, Ugandan officers gave military training to both the Hema and the Lendu, which was intended to increase the size of the armed wing of the RCD–Movement of Liberation (Mouvement de Libération, or ML), the rebel group backed by Uganda that nominally controlled the Ituri District. However, a large portion of Ugandan officers favored the Hema by giving them preferential treatment and promoting them to lead militia groups, thus excluding the Lendu.

The Ituri conflict, which started in Djugu on 19 June 1999, was not the spontaneous act of a mob of unemployed young men. One month before the incident, a number of Lendu chiefs were warning Hema ranchers to take their belongings and get out of Lendu lands or face disastrous consequences. Fearing such an attack, most Hema ranchers hired Ugandan soldiers to protect their ranches in late May 1999. In the eyes of the Lendu, Ugandan troops were accomplices in taking Lendu land. Although the role of Ugandan troops was critical, the Lendu's sense of exclusion was not new but became acute in the late 1960s. Since then, Lendu elites have been trying to position themselves in the political process of Ituri, only to find that the main hurdle to their political aspirations was the Hema's domination at all levels of the politico-administrative apparatus.

In addition to this politics of exclusion, a number of critical antecedents also help explain the Ituri conflict. First is an element of continuity. Conflict in

Ituri began when the colonial system upset the traditional institutional arrangements by nominating Hema to head Lendu chieftaincies. In fact, precolonial hatreds between the Lendu and Hema are not found in any historical records (Ndaywel 1997). Before the arrival of Europeans, the two groups had peacefully coexisted. Thus, the tension between the largely pastoralist Hema and largely agriculturalist Lendu began in the early 1910s, occasionally flaring into violence as the result of colonial policy. The Belgian government accentuated divisions and social inequalities between the two communities and other ethnic groups in the region. The Hema had access to education and clerical jobs in the colonial administration because they cooperated with the colonial system. Similar situations occurred all over Congo, much like the situation in Kasai between the Lulua and the Luba (see Chapter 2). This colonial policy of "divide and rule" allowed a climate of animosity and hatred to develop, and the postcolonial period reinforced the growing inequality between the Hema and the Lendu. A Hema elite took over and became a major landowning group, a business class, and an administrative core, with greater access to wealth, education, and political power. This was reflected in the greater prominence of Hema in positions of influence in the provincial and central governments. Despite these differences, both the Hema and Lendu communities generally coexisted peacefully, especially in rural areas. Intermarriage was common, especially between northern Lendu and northern Hema.

The second critical antecedent or an element of change was the promulgation of the 1973 land law. As pointed out earlier, the law modified property rights of land and made all lands state property, removing the constraints of customary law in granting user land rights. As in Nord-Kivu, bureaucrats in charge of implementing land law in Ituri became grantors of land. In allocating land, they completely disregarded both the 1973 land law and customary law and gave themselves implicit authority to grant land. Hema ranchers could buy land in many parts of Ituri easier than the Lendu could because Hema's transactions were facilitated by other Hema who dominated the politico-administrative apparatus of Ituri. Furthermore, the 1973 nationalization law gave further advantage to the Hema, who became owners of most nationalized businesses and plantations.

The Ituri conflict thus revolved around the unscrupulous use of the 1973 land law, which forced many Lendu families to leave their homes because they were unaware that their land could be, and indeed had been, bought by someone else, likely by a Hema rancher. In essence, most land dealings that Ituri administrators authorized were illegal. Nonetheless, the Hema kept increasing their holdings and displacing the Lendu from their villages. Much of this paralleled the conflict in Nord-Kivu between the Tutsi and the subsistence farmers in Masisi and Walikale territories, where customary land law was pushed aside by those in power. As pointed out by Vlassenroot and Raeymaekers (2003, p. 210), the eruption of the Ituri conflict must be understood as the result of the use of local and regional actors in a local political conflict profoundly rooted around land access, available economic resources, and political power.

The third critical antecedent of the Ituri conflict, paralleling what happened in Nord-Kivu, involved the mode of agricultural production: crops versus livestock or plowshares against cattle. The sole difference between Nord-Kivu and Ituri was that pastoralists migrated to Ituri in the precolonial period, while the Tutsi introduced cattle to Masisi in the 1930s. The expansion of pasture land as the result of the 1973 land law also undermined Lendu traditional authority. The immediate reaction of the Lendu was to fight back.

The last factor is the interaction between ethnicity and the democratization process. The process began in April 1990 and unleashed ethnicity as one major avenue to mobilize electoral bases. However, ethnicity by itself does not cause violence, but "when ethnicity is linked with acute social uncertainty, a history of conflict and, indeed, fear of what the future might bring, it emerges as one of the major fault lines along which societies fracture" (Newland 1993, p. 16). The Hema and Lendu elites sought out their own ethnic groups for support because there was no political party with nationalist and unitarist ideology such as the MNC/L of the early 1960s. Ethnic lexicon rather than a national ideological language became the political call of the elites. Creating self-help organizations was the first step toward conflict, as unemployed youths were mobilized by inflammatory political speeches and became instruments of terror and death.

Although ethnicity was critical in mobilizing the young men, primordial sentiments hardly explained ethnic conflict in Ituri. A perception of exclusion to modernity, created in the colonial period, has been perpetuated in the postcolonial era. This perception was the first factor to increase animosity. Ethnic symbols became immensely powerful in the Ituri conflict because they usually enabled politicians to reinterpret a conflict of interest and the politics of exclusion as a struggle for security, survival, status, and the future of the group. Using these symbols to evoke emotions such as resentment, fear, and hatred is how politicians motivate supporters to act. A precondition for ethnic war is political opportunity, which consists of two elements. First, there should be enough political space as the result of state weakness to mobilize without facing possible repression; access to state institutions obviously increases that opportunity. Second is a territorial base because ethnic rebels cannot mobilize unless they are territorially concentrated in specific regions (Toft 2003).

Duration and Conflict Management

The Ituri conflict lasted seventy months. In a sense, the Hema-Lendu conflict was the longest internal war in Congolese history. Unlike Nord-Kivu, acts of terrorism and extreme violence were key features of the Hema-Lendu conflict. Locally, the violence took the form of terrorism and became a ritual as both the Hema and Lendu groups publicly paraded in the streets displaying the heads of their victims. Body mutilation, cannibalism, and exhibition of body parts as trophies were regularly practiced by the Lendu warriors as part of a protection ritual (Amnesty International 2003). As the conflict deepened, the consumption of human body parts used to reputedly increase invulnerability to bullets became common (International Crisis Group 2003). Even the Hema came to practice the same ritual. Instead of creating fear, these acts of violence only exacerbated retaliation that further perpetuated the conflict. Yet extant research hardly considers such horrific acts and the way that they can perpetuate revenge and a vicious cycle of killing.

The second factor to have prolonged the Ituri conflict was the divisive role of the Ugandan army. Its presence favored the Hema at the expense of the Lendu (Human Rights Watch 2001). For example, on 22 June 1999, or a few days after the Ituri conflict had started, General of Brigade James Kazini of the Ugandan army fused the district of Haut-Uélé with Ituri to create the Kibali-Ituri Province. He then appointed Adele Lotsove Mugisa, a Hema businesswoman and member of the RCD-ML, as governor of the newly created province, despite strong opposition from rebel leaders in Bunia. This nomination further inflamed the Lendu, who saw this nomination as another act intended to exclude the Lendu from state spoils. In subsequent years, the Ugandan army commanders used this tactic quite often.

The third factor was competition for power among leaders of the RCD-ML and the resulting inflation of militia groups with shifting alliances. The fluid landscape emerged when Rwanda evicted the chairman of the RCD, Wamba dia Wamba, from his position. He moved to Kisangani with several founding members of the RCD and created the RCD-Kisangani in contrast to RCD-Goma. The choice of Kisangani was intended to benefit from the diamond trade to finance the new party. Kisangani was then controlled by both Rwandan and Ugandan forces, which confronted each other in August 1999 and twice in 2000 for the control of the diamond trade in town. Rwanda won all these military confrontations and forced Uganda to relocate to Ituri. In late August 1999, Wamba also left Kisangani and relocated his office to Kampala, Uganda. A month later he established the RCD-ML, which replaced RCD-Kisangani, and announced that Bunia would be the headquarters of the movement. He nominated two deputies: Mbusa Nyamwisi, a Nande businessman turned politician, as his prime minister and John Tibasima Ateenyi, a Hema and former chief executive of OKIMO, as minister of mining, finance, and budget. Soon after, Wamba's two deputies began a move to unseat him. To avoid having the conflict spiral out of control, President Museveni summoned them to Uganda. On 12 October 2000, Wamba, Nyamwisi, and Tibasima Ateenyi signed a declaration in Kampala that confirmed Wamba as president of the RCD-ML; the other two were first and second vice presidents.

In 2000, when Nyamwisi and Tibasima Ateenyi dominated the political scene of Bunia by seeking control of the RCD-ML, each appealed to specific ethnic groups for support, with the former relying on the Lendu and the latter drawing on the Hema. As a result, the RCD-ML became enmeshed in the Hema-Lendu conflict. Throughout this period, the RCD-ML suffered an internal power struggle that sharply divided the group into Wamba's supporters and

Nyamwisi's supporters. When Wamba left the area, Nyamwisi became the leading figure in Bunia. However, the alliance of convenience between him and Tibasima broke off, and Nyamwisi began fostering ties with the Lendu. In early 2002, the government of Joseph Kabila sought greater rapprochement with the RCD-ML. To shore up this relationship, Congolese government officials visited Ituri and even sent troops to Beni to support the RCD-ML. As a result, Nyamwisi left Bunia in April 2002 to participate in the Sun City talks. To strengthen his base in Nord-Kivu (Beni and Lubero) and in Ituri, he established ties with the Kabila administration.

Rwanda also became involved in the Ituri crisis, supplying arms to the Hema militia UPC. Nonetheless, Ugandan troops remained the main foreign force in Ituri. Thus, Ugandan military officers created the conditions that required the presence of their troops to cover their continued involvement in commercial operations. Ironically, the UN Secretary-General requested in September 2002 that security responsibilities should continue to be discharged by the Ugandan army in an impartial manner until such time as it could be replaced by a capable police force representing a legitimate authority acceptable to the communities in Ituri (UN 2002). The continued conflict was blamed on the lack of any effective authority and the competition among the various armed groups for control of natural resources in the area, both a result, at least in part, of Ugandan policy to obstruct the peace process in Ituri.

In a bold move in early September 2002, Angola affirmed its political role in Ituri by brokering a deal between Museveni and Kabila, which became known as the Luanda Accord. The two leaders agreed to withdraw the UPDF from northeastern Congo within three months and to establish, with MONUC assistance, a joint Ituri Pacification Committee (IPC) within twenty days. The IPC intended to bring together leaders of the armed groups and representatives of civil society in Ituri as well as the two governments in an effort to resolve differences and to create an administrative authority for the region acceptable to all parties. While the two leaders were seeking means to implement the Luanda Accord, a number of militia groups emerged with different agendas in February 2003.

In short, Uganda played an ambiguous role in Ituri that lengthened the conflict. On many occasions, the UPDF units took part in attacks on civilian communities, mainly against the Lendu. Meanwhile, Ugandan officers sold small weapons to both warring factions in Ituri and trained militias, including child combatants. They also accepted bribes, mainly but not exclusively, from Hema businessmen in return for protection. The quasi-alliance of Ugandan officers with Hema politicians may have created suspicion among the Lendu, but the Lendu also occasionally found allies within the Ugandan army, which supplied them with weapons and munitions. Uganda thus used the colonial technique of "divide and rule," setting the fire and fighting it at the same time (International Crisis Group 2003). This confused situation was a smoke screen, allowing Ugandan officers to continue looting Congolese resources, as UN reports documented (UN 2001, 2002, 2003). In a sense, Ituri was the scene of multiple alliances and counteralliances, making the Ituri conflict quite intractable.

Just like the second war against Kabila, the multiplication of ethnic militia groups under different patrons prolonged the Ituri conflict, as groups tried to control mining enclaves in the region. On 11 February 2003, however, representatives of Rwanda and Uganda met in Dar es Salaam, Tanzania, to revisit the calendar for implementing the Luanda Accord. To launch the IPC, they set the date of 25 February 2003. The Ugandan government promised to withdraw the rest of its troops from Ituri on 20 March 2003, by which time the IPC should have completed its work. A cease-fire agreement scheduled for February, which had to precede the establishment of the IPC, was postponed after the UPC issued a communiqué questioning the good faith of Uganda, DRC, and MONUC.

In March 2003, relative calm returned to Bunia, which allowed the 177-member IPC under MONUC auspices to meet and establish an interim administration in Ituri. However, its deliberations failed as the result of deteriorating security from the sudden withdrawal of a large contingent of the Ugandan army in April 2003. As Ugandan troops withdrew, the UN deployed 800 soldiers in Bunia. On 3 May 2003, the Lendu militias launched a massive campaign of violence against the Hema in Bunia. Rather than protecting civilians under imminent threat of physical violence, the MONUC concentrated its efforts to protect its own installations and members. Nine days later, the UPC regained control of Bunia. The failure of the UN to protect civilians, exacerbated by its inability and unwillingness to act decisively even within these apparent constraints, had severe consequences for stability in Ituri.

In late May 2003, UN Secretary-General Kofi Annan called for establishing and deploying a temporary multinational force to the area until the weakened MONUC mission could be reinforced. On 30 May 2003, the UN Security Council adopted Resolution 1484 that authorized the deployment of an Interim Multinational Emergency Force to Bunia with the task of securing the airport and protecting internally displaced persons in the town. This force, called Operation Artemis, consisted of 1,800 French troops and a small 80-man Swedish Special Forces group. The operation was launched on 12 June as the Ugandan troops completed their final withdrawal from Congo.

The French mission, under General Jean-Paul Thonier, remained in Bunia until 1 September 2003 and was able to act decisively and with force against local militias that refused to comply with the Luanda Accord. It also extended its influence beyond Bunia by disrupting the flow of arms to militia groups. On 28 July 2003, the UN Security Council passed Resolution 1493 that defined the tasks of the reconstituted MONUC's 10,800 troops (UN 2003). Called MONUC II under Chapter VII, its mission was to protect UN personnel, facilities, installations, and equipment as well to ensure the security and freedom of movement of all its personnel involved in different missions in Congo. Moreover, it was mandated to protect civilians and humanitarian workers under imminent threat of physical violence and to contribute to improving security for human-itarian assistance.

Although the UN brigade in Ituri had enough military personnel to estab-lish security, it was not proactive in dealing with the inflation of militia groups in Ituri and remained weaker than anticipated by many observers in Bunia (Nest, Grignon, and Kisangani 2006; International Crisis Group 2005). The UN brigade also had many deficiencies that undermined its role and delayed the peace process in Bunia. The UN troops were unable to emulate the success of Operation Artemis because they did not have the ability to monitor either the militias' movements or their communications. For example, on 25 February 2005, a number of militias murdered nine UN Bangladeshi peacekeepers near the town of Kafe. In response, UN forces assaulted a stronghold of one of them, killing fifty people. As a result, a new round of conflict escalated, leading to the kidnapping of a number of UN soldiers by militia groups.

Three events changed the management of the Ituri conflict and paved the way toward some semblance of peace. First, the CIAT gave an ultimatum to all militia groups in Ituri to voluntarily disarm by the end of March 2005 or face major consequences. In early April, the CIAT requested that the government launch both national and international arrest orders against leaders of militia groups in Ituri accused of crimes against humanity. Between March and April 2005, most militia chiefs were thus neutralized. Even before the ultimatum, a number of militia groups began the disarmament process. Although the disar-mament was unsuccessful because militia leaders feared losing lucrative sources from mining enclaves, it helped diffuse a tense situation that was developing.

The second event was the arrest by Congolese authorities of Lubanga, the leader of the UPC, and other militia leaders and their imprisonment in Makala. Lubanga was accused of having ordered the killing of the peacekeepers in Feb-ruary 2005 and of fomenting continuous insecurity in Ituri. On 10 February 2006, the International Criminal Court issued an arrest warrant for Lubanga for the war crime of conscripting and enlisting children under the age of fifteen years and using them to participate actively in the Ituri conflict. On 17 March 2006, Kinshasa authorities transferred Lubanga to the custody of the interna-tional court.

Another critical event was the upcoming elections. President Kabila had much to lose if Ituri voters stayed home in the 2006 elections. On 10 July 2006, Peter Karim, the leader of the Lendu FNI, and the Congolese government signed a memorandum of understanding on the conditions to integrate his FNI militias into the national army. The government also gave him an undisclosed amount of money to make sure that Ituri remained calm during the elections and no major incident occcurred. Most people of Ituri voted for the presidential party, the PPRD.

The electoral victory of Kabila provided another chance for peace in Ituri. A number of government delegations were dispatched to Bunia to negotiate the disarmament of militias and their integration into the national army. In late

2006, several agreements were signed with the leaders of Ituri militias, but only a handful of combatants were disarmed and integrated into the national army by March 2007. The last phase of the DDR process, which took place on 4 August 2007, disarmed only 1,840 combatants out of 15,000 (International Crisis Group 2008, p. 36). However, the victory of Kabila seemed to have stabilized Ituri. By December 2010, Ituri was apparently more politically stable than Nord-Kivu.

Consequences of the Ituri Conflict

The usual consequence of any conflict is the loss of human lives. Added to this was the creation of a cycle of hatred and violence. One constant in the Ituri conflict was the role of the Ugandan army, which controlled profitable exports of natural resources that its officers enjoyed with impunity because President Museveni and his inner circle benefited from these exports as well (Human Rights Watch 2005; Perrot 1999). This exploitation of Congolese resources was facilitated by the cooperation of Congolese rebel leaders and businessmen with the occupying Ugandan army. In 1997, when the Ugandan military force entered Ituri after the fall of Mobutu, it discovered the mineral wealth of Ituri, an area that Perrot (1999) called a "mini Eldorado." When Kabila ended his military cooperation with Uganda a year later, Ugandan forces were quick to rush into Ituri to make sure that the area remained within Uganda's sphere of influence.

At the local level, different rebel leaders struggling for political power in Ituri continued to profit from the ethnic resentment originally created by land disputes. From 1999 to mid-2003, a series of splits resulted in Bunia being the stage for repeated power struggles and skirmishes. At each stage in the fragmentation of rebel groups, new militias recruited members loyal to one or another commander or faction leader. Often half of the militias were children aged eight to fifteen, deployed not only to fight each other but also to whip up insecurity in the countryside and seize strategic localities and commercial opportunities.

The increased intensity of the violence was also the result of the ethnic ideology in the Hutu-Tutsi standoff. The Lendu thought of themselves as kin to the Hutu, while the Hema identified with the Tutsi. Although no historical basis existed for this new construction of identity, it increased the imagined stakes of the conflict.

Summary and Discussion

In their economic models of civil war, Collier and Hoeffler (2002) predicted an 8 percent probability of civil wars in Congo from 1975 to 1979 and 70 percent between 1995 and 1996. Their model failed to predict the first ethnic war in Nord-Kivu, which began in March 1993 and ended in August 1993. Unlike civil wars of the 1960s and 1970s, Nord-Kivu emerged as a unique case because it was the setting of the first ethnic war in the political history of the DRC. The fourth ethnic war—the Hema-Lendu, Ituri, conflict—ran concomitantly with the anti-Kabila civil war but continued after the peace accord signed in Pretoria in December 2002. Though this conflict took place within the context of a much larger conflict, its antecedents were quite different.

Lake and Rothchild (1998, p. 4) argue that "ethnic conflict is most commonly caused by collective fears of the future. . . . As information failures, problems of credible commitment, and the security dilemma take hold, the state is weakened, groups become fearful, and conflict becomes likely." This contention seems partly to hold in Nord-Kivu. The natives or autochthons accused the Banyarwanda of being secretive and of not sharing information on land laws and nationalization policies in the 1970s and could not commit themselves to uphold mutually beneficial agreements regarding Nord-Kivu Province. In other words, they accused the Banyarwanda of not being trustworthy.

Although fear and a weak state apparatus reinforced each other to provide a setting for a civil war in Congo, such a context does not explain the fact that ethnic wars, as defined by the 1,000-death threshold, happened in Nord-Kivu but nowhere else. Like previous civil wars, the politics of exclusion was a critical juncture to explain ethnic wars in Nord-Kivu. The Ituri situation was similar, as the Lendu felt excluded from leadership positions in a district where they felt they represented some 17 percent of the population, the highest percentage in the Ituri District. Though the politics of exclusion triggered ethnic wars in both settings, a major factor of continuity was institutional and related to traditional land tenure. This factor had an impact at both the elite and the mass level.

At the elite level, clientelist and urban politics manipulated land law to make land accessible to corrupt urban elites. At the mass level, most subsistence farmers were plunged into a modern land tenure they little understood; they only saw the cattle taking their best land, leaving them without means to survive. While the urban elite relied on modern land tenure, the masses followed communal land tenure because it minimized their transaction costs. In a sense, ethnic wars were wars of legitimacy to transform the relationship between farmers and the state represented by urban elites and their cattle. In Ituri and Nord-Kivu, ethnic wars had deep roots in the land issue. Both colonial and postcolonial rulers tried to change traditional land tenure, although without success. Uncertainty about land tenure and opportunistic elite behavior reinforced each other to create a feeling of insecurity among the masses. As ethnicity interacted with scarcity of arable land, it became an important element of continuity.

Although institutional change tends to stress collective benefit, most institutional arrangements established during Mobutu's autocratic rule deviated from their functions of resolving recurring problems in society. Mobutu's institutions weakened the link between the elites and the masses that could force them to work together in order to produce beneficial social goals because these institutions never constrained society to help individuals avoid the negative emerging effects of collective actions, such as free riding. However, the masses never revolted against the 1973 land law until they were mobilized by the urban elites in the early 1990s. An element of change that interacted with ethnicity and polarized Ituri and Nord-Kivu was institutional weakness, or a political vacuum created by the democratization process. This process set the stage for conflict as political entrepreneurs in search of an electoral constituency mobilized the only group they knew—their ethnic group—to exclude potential political rivals. For many groups, the process meant a preemptive strategy to avoid being excluded from state spoils. To deter conflict, the process also occurred in the absence of local institutions. Traditional authorities were weakened, and civil society was nonexistent. The state was thus unable to provide order, while its instrument of violence, the army, was captured by private groups. This is similar to the security vacuum that set the stage for the early cases of secessions. Privatization of security interacted with ethnicity to increase the likelihood of conflict. Ethnic militias replaced state instruments of coercion to defend claims of groups' rights.

A number of differences also exist between Nord-Kivu and Ituri. Just like in early civil wars in the DRC, the youth in Ituri became uncontrollable and took over, resulting in a spiral of violence at the local level. Unlike Nord-Kivu, traditional authorities in Ituri lost their power at the profit of youth now roaming the countryside in quest of looting. One major consequence that differentiated Nord-Kivu from Ituri was a total disintegration of the social fabric as the result of the brutality of violence in the latter. The dehumanization of the other that led to the consumption of human body parts was a symbol of social disintegration. This dehumanization of the enemy also became a justification for extermination (International Crisis Group 2003, p. 6).

In Ituri, the Lendu never questioned the identity of the Hema. However, in Nord-Kivu, the nationality issue was an important and crucial element of change that interacted with ethnicity to create a highly volatile environment. In less than ten years, from 1972 to 1981, the government promulgated two contradictory laws on nationality as the result of pressures from Nord-Kivu groups. The discrepancy between the laws and their implementation shaped the images of social groups competing over power at the local and national levels.

In addition to the nationality issue was the unending movement of people from Rwanda to the DRC. Migrations of people into Ituri ceased in the nineteenth century, but migrations from Rwanda to Nord-Kivu have continued unabated. For example, in November 2009 alone, Nord-Kivu Province was the scene of a massive return of some 12,000 Tutsi refugees from Rwanda who entered Masisi and Rutshuru through Kibumba, which was the same route that Rwandan troops crossed in January–February 2009 (Bucyalimwe 2010, p. 208).

This massive return of Tutsi refugees was perceived as the ultimate betrayal because their resettlement signified the entrenchment of a Tutsi population in Masisi and Walikale, where land claimed by Hunde and Nyanga groups was dispossessed by successive waves of migrants during colonization and after independence. Such massive movements of Tutsi should have been organized with the accord of the communities involved, the Office of the UN High Commissioner for Refugees, the Congolese government, and Rwandan authorities through an adequate commission that could have verified the nationality of each Tutsi under the 2004 law on nationality.

Moreover, the nationality issue in Nord-Kivu is a local issue linked to land—the most important element of group survival and representation. Commitment to peaceful coexistence is likely to remain uncertain in Nord-Kivu, and the chance of conflict high, because the ethnic balance of power is constantly in flux, and some uncertainty over the intentions of others is always present. Ethnicity is perhaps more accentuated in Nord-Kivu (also Sud-Kivu) than anywhere else in Congo. Since the early 1960s, political language had always been formulated in terms of ethnic arithmetic at every electoral cycle. For example, political elites from the Hunde, Nande, Tembo, and Nyanga groups view all Hutu and Tutsi as allochthons without exception and believed that the Banyarwanda should not be part of the political process. On the other hand, the Hutu of Bwisha kept distancing themselves from other Hutu in Nord-Kivu. Political entrepreneurs in Nord-Kivu probably triggered ethnic conflicts, but they did not create ethnic identities by linking them to social distinction, as constructivists contend.

In fact, Nord-Kivu, as well as Sud-Kivu, had settings of micro or ethnic nations dating back centuries ago. Myths of origin in the areas and sophisticated rituals of coronation and burial of their chiefs or princes result in perpetual representation in state institutions either through appointments or elections to exclude "strangers." Representation remains a symbol of hegemony in an area where land represents wealth and political power. Including the ethnic-nation in state institutions is critical because it means participation in land management, in particular, and state management, in general. Of course, this representation is false or "false consciousness," because in reality, ethnic representatives do not care about bringing the pork back home. However, in the eyes of the masses and their chiefs, this elites' connection is real because state management means protection of political and temporal space. Being part of the system means the system becomes part of the ethnic nation.

Unlike Ituri, Nord-Kivu also shows that historical memories actively select and frame aspects of existing cultural repertoires to differentiate one ethnic group from another. These memories of nation-tribes within their own time-space continuum build the internal cohesion of the group. Historical memories also build political identities to assert and acquire political power, economic benefits, and social status for members of the group or the group as a whole (Perrot 1999). More specifically, representation in state management is not only part of symbolic prestige for nonelite members of the community and spoils for the elite itself, but this representation is, above all, about temporal and geographic space and the right of autochthons to manage the state. Political competition is no longer limited to land but extends to representation in state organs. To exclude the other is the political norm, limiting the other side's access to political institutions and hence their access to land. In sum, access to land and interaction with political exclusion tend to increase the chance of ethnic wars.

Despite holding elections in 2006–2007, Nord-Kivu remained politically unstable as the result of Rwanda's unwillingness to be politically inclusive. As a consequence, Rwandan conflict between the Tutsi and the Hutu is likely to be fought in Congo for many years to come unless the Rwandan Tutsi-dominated leadership decides to open its political system to the majority Hutu. The most critical menace to peace in Nord-Kivu will thus remain the destabilizing role of the Tutsi. In other words, fragile political institutions imposed on the DRC by Western peacekeepers never envisioned developments beyond elections because they prioritized the holding of elections before disarming rebel groups. Elections also marginalized the Tutsi, and without a voice in the political process, they are likely to destabilize eastern Congo with help from Rwanda.

The Hema and Lendu in Ituri as well as all ethnic groups in Nord-Kivu cannot survive without strong cooperation from each other. Making political space an ethnic space is a self-defeating mechanism in the long run. Only an ideology of development that cuts across ethnic groups can provide a lasting peace in ethnically divided societies. The path to lasting peace in both Ituri and Nord-Kivu should aim to lessen deep resentment and rivalry among communities and address the issue of equitable access to land and economic resources as well as economic opportunities for all.

Notes

1. A conservative assessment by the U.S. World Refugee Survey (U. S. Committee for Refugees 1997, p. 105) provides a number between 10,000 and 40,000 of people who were killed.

2. The Bashu still pay an annual tribute today to the chief of Basongora, while the Baswaga pay tribute to the Bashu chief. There was a time when the Bamate paid their birthright to their elders, the Batangi (Mashauri 1981).

3. In 1971, Bwito became a chieftaincy as the result of this challenge. In the 1980s, Ndeze lost power. People in Bashali fought for autonomy and achieved it only after the death of André Kalinda in 1974 when the chieftaincy of the Hunde was divided into four small autonomous chieftaincies reminiscent of the precolonial period: Bahunde in 1974, Bashali in 1974, Osso in 1976, and Katoryi in 1977.

4. This autonomy gave migrant Hutu chiefs the advantage of receiving 35,000 francs from the colonial administrator, which allowed them to buy land in the area.

5. Letter no. 21/7329/780/v-c/3.a (cited in Bucyalimwe 1990).

6. The law of 27 April 1962 set the following prerequisites: a population of 700,000; economic viability, and a petition submitted by two-thirds of the provincial and national deputies from the region included in the putative province (see Young 1965, p. 549).

7. In Nord-Kivu, of thirty-five seats, Awabelo (Association Wanande Beni Lubero) received twenty-one seats. In the two contested territories of Goma and Rutshuru, eight seats were split between Panaco (five seats), Alliance des Socialistes Chrétiens du Congo, or Asco (two), and Awabelo (one). Electoral results in Masisi gave an overwhelming representation to the Hunde. See Gérard-Libois and Van Lierde (1966).

8. This is borrowed from Doyle and Sambanis (2000) in their example of former Yugoslavia.

7

Conclusion

After seventy-five years under Belgian rule, the DRC became independent on 30 June 1960. Four days later, the army mutinied and, as a result, it was no longer an instrument to help the state keep law and order. Without its instrument of coercion, the new state was no more than a political vacuum that separatist forces filled by declaring the Katanga secession on 11 July 1960. On 2 August 1960, South Kasai also seceded. From 1960 to 2010, the DRC had some seventeen internal wars. More specifically, political instability has remained the rule rather than the exception. The result was five decades of socioeconomic decay and poor governance.

In fact, Congo's GDP in 1967 ($4.4 billion), which was above that of South Korea ($3.8 billion) at the time, barely experienced perceptible growth in the four decades that followed (World Bank 2010). When factored against population growth of 3 percent per year, per capita GDP that stood at $430 (2010 = 100) in 1960 had plummeted to less than $90 in 2010. In 1959–1960, Congo had 145,213 kilometers of road, far ahead of the second African country, Nigeria, which had 67,000 kilometers (Huybrechts 1970, p. 67). By 2010, Congo had some 57,000 kilometers of road, mostly located in the capital city, Lower Congo, and southern Katanga.

In 1959–1960, local industries produced 44 percent of total consumer (local and imported) goods (Lacroix 1967). The result was an increase in the number of wage earners. In 1959–1960, employment in the public sector represented 20 percent of total employment in the private sector; thus, there was one public job for twelve jobs in the private sector (Lacroix 1967). In 2010, the industrial sector had almost disappeared, except for the beer industry, which continues to thrive. As a consequence, the state has become the largest employer, with salaries that hardly help people make ends meets. For example, a private in the national army earned an annual salary of 58,030 Congolese francs ($1,161) in 1960, or $97 a month—equivalent to $685 per month in 2010 prices (Dupriez 1968, p. 380). His highest-ranked officer at the time, Colonel Joseph Mobutu, received 240,000 francs ($4,800) a year, or $400 a month in 1960—equivalent to $2,826 in 2010 prices. In contrast, in 2010, the real monthly salary of a private was a mere $5, while that of a colonel was only $50 a month. Meanwhile, salaries in the political market ranged from at least $2,500 per month for ministerial advisers to large paychecks for the president and his cabinet ranging from $15,000 a month to as high as $75,000 a month.

Chapter 1 highlighted the fact that the medical infrastructure in the Belgian Congo was "the best in Tropical Africa" in 1959–1960 (Brausch 1961). Fifty years later, in 2010, this infrastructure was no more than a carcass, except for a few operational hospitals mostly located in Kinshasa, Lubumbashi, and a few other cities. Socially, the embryonic welfare system of the later years of the colonial rule has atrophied to the point that death from the common cold no longer surprises anyone. Diseases that disappeared in the 1950s have reappeared with a vengeance. In brief, the hope and the euphoria of independence have made room for despair. What went wrong?

The goal of this book was to look at fifty years of independence in the DRC to understand the causes of internal wars that have wracked it since July 1960 with devastating consequences. Of seventeen of Congo's internal wars, ten occurred in the Cold War period. Kaldor (2001) has drawn a sharp distinction between "old wars" of the Cold War era and the "new wars" of the 1990s. Such "new wars," she argues, can be understood only in the context of political, economic, military, and cultural globalization. They have blurred the distinction between war and organized crime; are at once local and depend on transnational connections; have fostered a war economy that is built on plunder, black market transactions, and external assistance; and are usually sustained through continued violence. The analysis of Congo's civil wars requires a careful examination of this assertion. The book has thus disaggregated Congo's civil wars in terms of legitimacy, replacement, and convenience to explain not only elites' strategies in mobilizing the masses but also masses' willingness to follow the elites.

Preventing deadly conflict remains a key priority for scholars, policymakers, and the international community because conflict not only widens political divisions and disrupts socioeconomic activity, but it also corrupts the very fabric of society, resulting in chronic societal and state weakness. Civil wars can also spill across borders, creating complex humanitarian emergencies and undermining regional stability. Moreover, internal conflicts tend to engage major powers and the international community as well. These consequences make any civil war an important problem for both social sciences and policy. Thus, Congo's internal wars offer several lessons to those concerned with research and policies related to conflict and conflict resolution. The next section summarizes the findings in light of the case studies. The second section of this conclusion provides policy options. A few final thoughts follow.

Summary Assessment of Congo's Internal Wars

The analysis developed in this book used a process-tracing strategy to understand the causes of Congo's internal wars. This book argued that the politics of exclusion was a critical juncture in explaining Congo's wars, as excluded elites tried to (re)insert themselves in the political system. With two exceptions—the Katanga and South Kasai secessions of the early 1960s—the excluded elites never desired to secede from the state. Constrained by international norms of inviolability of colonial borders, the excluded elites preferred to capture the weak state as a whole in order to access political power and its spoils. The masses were likely to follow these elites if they believed the conflict was legitimate, only to find later that these elites were trying to re(insert) themselves within a political system that they had no intention of transforming socially or economically.

Although the book emphasized the politics of exclusion as a critical juncture that explained Congo's internal wars, it also contended that the interaction between elements of continuity and change, labeled as critical antecedents, help to explain elites' strategy of exclusion. The elements of continuity include the state itself with its artificial and juridical boundaries, the integration of Congo's provinces into the world economy as providers of a few primary commodities, urbanization as an enforcer of ethnic affinities rather than an agent of modernization, and the coexistence of traditional and modern land tenures. Elements of change represent the deinstitutionalization of the military and the institutionalization of corruption. Figure 1.1 highlighted this process-tracing approach.

The first four cases of civil wars occurred in Katanga and South Kasai. Although critical antecedents were similar all over the DRC, the two areas seceded earlier because they espoused federalism or provincial exclusion. They thus favored separatism over a unitarist state. However, the nationalist-unitary ideology of the MNC/L and its coalitions triumphed in mid-1960 and provided a multiethnic forum to voice ethnic-based grievances within the broader national agenda. The role played by the federalists was also apparent in 1964. By 1963, they had completely excluded the nationalists from power. The result was the two rebellions that broke out in Kwilu and eastern Congo. At the mass level, however, a sense of deprivation in 1963 was not only widespread but was also perceived by the masses in terms of temporal space, vertical social space between strata, and horizontal communal space among groups. Thus, the two rebellions were politically legitimate at the mass level.

When Mobutu took power in late 1965, he promised to curb separatist and exclusionary tendencies of the past. However, he began the same politics of exclusion, starting with people from southern Katanga. The mutinies of the Baka Regiment and mercenaries, as well as the two Shaba wars, were motivated by this politics of exclusion. More interesting was the fact that, prior to the 1990s, Congo had no ethnic wars despite the existence of some 336 ethnic groups. However, four ethnic wars occurred in the 1990s—three in Nord-Kivu in the first half of the 1990s and one in Ituri in the late 1990s. The 1990s also witnessed three internal wars against the president. One critical antecedent of Congo's ethnic wars was institutional: the liberalization or marketization of land that weakened the communal contract without destroying it. As political barons appropriated land, subsistence farmers became deprived and isolated. The perception of vertical inequality reinforced this deprivation as pasture expanded at the expense of cultivable land. The scarcity of arable land and population pressure made ethnic conflict inevitable, especially when two modes of production—pasture and plowshare—collided. Thus, ethnic wars tend to be associated with wars of legitimacy.

In May 1997, Laurent Kabila became the third president of the DRC after a seven-month civil war that toppled Mobutu. Although the exclusion of the Banyamulenge provided a critical juncture in this war, the evidence also suggested that the anti-Mobutu war was rooted in three decades of Mobutu's mismanagement and in a kleptocratic system that never responded to citizens' needs. This revolt was thus viewed by the masses as a war of legitimacy.

Less than a year into his presidency, Kabila's former allies, the Mai Mai, revolted against him by accusing him of having sold eastern Congo to Rwanda. In reality, Kabila marginalized the Mai Mai and excluded them from his government, setting the war against him. In late 1998, he ordered all foreign troops to leave, thus ending the cooperation with Rwanda. Kabila's decision started another war as former collaborators, especially the Tutsi, felt excluded from state spoils. However, the revolt against Kabila was a war of replacement because the excluded elites wanted to regain their previous political positions in the government.

The most interesting finding from the process-tracing approach is that the politics of exclusion remains the main critical juncture to explain civil war or peaceful coexistence, while critical antecedents shape how the elites tend to be exclusive or inclusive. This approach probably explains why eastern Congo has been endemic to civil war. The same approach may also help explain why civil wars are common in countries around Congo, except in Tanzania and Zambia.

On the duration of civil wars, the book's framework argued that a war of legitimacy is likely to be shorter than those of replacement and convenience. However, empirical analysis of Congo's civil wars provides mixed results. Although mineral resources have been advanced in the literature as critical to the duration of civil wars, only the war against Kabila can be viewed as a paradigmatic case of resource-driven or loot-seeking civil war because it was sustained by a high level of primary commodity dependence.

The duration of civil wars also depends on the role of external players or third-party military interventions. Usually, the impact of third-party interventions on the evolution of intrastate conflicts is a function of the interveners' motives (Balch-Lindsay and Enterline 2000). Three sets of external players intervened in a number of Congo's internal wars: the UN, the West, and other African countries.

The UN intervened twice—in the early 1960s and late 1990s. The first was to prevent Congo's crisis from escalating into a global security crisis during the era of Cold War rivalry. The UN served as a surrogate for the national army and was able to defeat the Katanga and South Kasai secessions because the United States wanted to keep the Soviet Union out of Congo. However, the UN left Congo without rebuilding its army, and, as a consequence, the eastern rebellion almost toppled the government. In the 1990s, the role of the UN was to stop the Congolese crisis from expanding. Here, the UN became a peacekeeper in the traditional sense and within the framework of new interventionism based upon humanitarian premises. In essence, the UN accepted rebels as legitimate contenders to the government and, by ricochet, forced all belligerents to negotiate and share power. Although the international community was able to bring belligerents to share power and run for elections, all efforts to restore peace failed because a large number of peace spoilers were still roaming in eastern Congo by late 2010.

The involvement of the West occurred mostly in the Cold War period. The first intervention was carried out by Belgium to restore order after the army's mutiny in early July 1960. This intervention seemed to have given Moïse Tshombe enough time to consolidate his position. Other Western interventions countered the influence of either China or the Soviet Union during the two rebellions and the two Shaba wars. Most Western military interventions in the post–Cold War aimed to reinforce the military authority of the UN as part of the new humanitarian agenda, while the intervention of African countries in the DRC was mostly motivated by states' diverse interests—security or plunder.

A final issue discussed in the book relates to consequences of civil wars because these wars shaped postconflict coexistence. The literature on the consequences of civil wars is immense. These consequences are analyzed at economic, social, and political levels in terms of disruption, diversion, and destruction. First, civil wars disrupt the flow of goods and services as well as social interactions so critical for peaceful coexistence in multiethnic societies. For example, the degree of violence encountered in ethnic wars tends to break societies apart and create a cycle of revenge. Of all the Congo civil wars, ethnic conflicts and the anti-Kabila revolt had the most devastating impact on the people: ethnic conflicts aimed at eliminating the other group before being eliminated, while the anti-Kabila revolt involved a large number of rebel groups and foreign countries all attempting to access economic resources. The consequence related to diversion was an increase in the market for small arms and the control of the informal economy by warring parties, thus depriving the Congolese of what helped them survive economically in the 1980s.

In terms of destruction, three groups of activities provide a way of assessing the effects of civil wars on the economy: war-invulnerable, war-vulnerable, and unclassified activities (Collier 1999). Usually, one war-invulnerable is subsistence agriculture. However, ethnic wars and the war against Kabila destroyed this sector, which employed more than 60 percent of the population. Of all seventeen civil wars, the second anti-Kabila war was the one that destroyed most war-vulnerable sectors, such as mining, construction, transport, distribution, finance, and manufacturing, because it involved not only foreign countries but a mushrooming of rebel groups and regular troops in plundering Congolese resources. Politically, civil wars tend to break institutionalization of the polity, resulting in an unending cycle of institutional rebuilding. In sum, of seventeen Congolese civil wars, only the anti-Mobutu and the second war against Kabila were internationalized.

Policy Implications and Rebuilding Society

Peace-building success refers to an end to conflict, uncontested sovereignty, a modest measure of political openness, and sustained economic growth (Doyle and Sambanis 2000; Kisangani 2003). Doyle and Sambanis argue that the space for postwar peace is determined by the interaction of the root causes of the civil war, the local capacity for change, and the magnitude and type of international assistance. In fact, this book shows that the nature of conflict tends to shape policies to prevent it because this nature helps capture the root causes of the conflict and the local capacity to enhance peaceful coexistence.

Congo's internal wars were diverse and had particular characteristics. However, the politics of exclusion is a critical juncture to explain them, thus making generalizations feasible. All Congo's internal wars started with the same process: the exclusion of one segment of the elite rather than the creation of an all-encompassing elite community. Unfortunately, the counterelites also saw the state as a prize that would allow them to exclude others. Congo's civil wars indicated that both the incumbent and the challenger looked at the weak state as a prize to keep or to be won to access spoils by excluding others. Given that most elements of continuity are structural and may not be amenable to short-term solution, the first policy lesson comes from two elements of change: the deinstitutionalization of the military and the institutionalization of corruption.

The two factors stand out in the analysis of Congo's wars as they relate to the politics of exclusion and concomitant culture of impunity that has perpetuated violence, crimes against humanity, and economic crimes on a large scale. In most cases, committing these crimes was a passport to socioeconomic upward mobility and access to political offices. The atrocities committed by the government's security forces and other armed groups for fifty years, 1960 to 2010, should not absolve the elites from arrest and prosecution. More specifically, because the DRC has been under the tutelage of the international community since its creation in 1885, the West should no longer allow Congolese elites to perpetuate these crimes. An approach that integrates international law, especially the International Criminal Court, should be included in the state-building process because Congolese courts lack the required capacity, credibility, and political neutrality to judge crimes against humanity.

Looking back at the five institutions of democracy created during the transition, 2003 to 2006, only the Independent Electoral Commission, which aimed to organize elections, received adequate financial resources from the international community. The other critical institutions of civil society for long-term human development were neglected by this community and operationally disappeared. They included the Truth and Reconciliation Commission, the National Human Rights Commission, the Commission on Ethics and the Fight against Corruption, and the Higher Authority on the Media.

The Truth and Reconciliation Commission was supposed to be the foundation of a process of national healing after more than three million people had been killed, thousands of women were raped savagely by the warring parties, and thousands of children were forced to bear arms. However, reconciliation never occurred, and abuses of human rights on an unimaginable scale continued unabated by late 2010. More disturbing is the fact that one key element of the Western blueprint to end civil wars is to bribe belligerents with massive foreign aid after bringing them to the negotiating table to share power. For example, members of the transnational government set up in mid-2003 in Kinshasa received an unprecedented level of foreign aid equivalent to 93 percent of GDP, which they were quick to share and spend without investing a dime in any major social infrastructure. In other words, the message from the international community was loud and clear: "take it and forget about the Commission on Ethics and the Fight against Corruption." Corruption has remained endemic, and a few politicians, less than 2,500 citizens out of 59.6 million Congolese, still retain the lion's share of Congo's resources, leaving the rest in total destitution. It is probable that neither the electoral system nor massive foreign aid will be able to rescue the poor soon because the international community attempted to build Congo's new institutions on the run by neglecting the two critical foundations of democracy and development: respect for human rights and rule of law. Therefore, political renewal and economic recovery appear bleak, and human security is likely to remain a distant dream for many years to come.

The first policy choice should be similar to the colonial policy that separated political power from economic power by ending the Leopoldian state monopoly over the economy in the 1910s. In other words, the Congolese political market, which currently offers the highest salaries in the country, should become less attractive. This would require a paradigm shift. The political market has become subject to imperfect competition, which exists not only because barriers to entry are significant but also because elements of natural monopoly are related to ethnic affinities. The attributes of the market for political offices create conditions conducive to opportunism so pervasive to long-term economic development, while the range of contractual agreements that might minimize such opportunism is nonexistent. Because international financial institutions have strong leverage over Congo, it is up to them to transform a wasteful rent-seeking system to a more economically wealth-creating apparatus. One example might be to have the Congolese private sector invest in services, such as electricity production and water delivery.

Another possibility is to require international financial institutions to invest in research and development rather than wasting money on government projects that sustain rent-seeking activities. This should make the academic market more attractive than the political market, which tends to deplete universities of their teachers who cannot make ends meet or survive on their academic salaries. Corruption can also be mitigated if these financial institutions invest in Congolese bureaucracy by making promotions and salary adjustments based on a competitive merit system a part of their program on institution building. Any opposition from the government should result in a suspension of financial aid. Although the military forms part of the bureaucracy, its reform would require more than increasing salaries. A cultural and psychological change is required to make it more functional and more effective.

Related to political inclusion is freeing minority groups from fear of majority rule, especially in provincial governments. This fear can be overcome by including minority groups in the decisionmaking process even if they lose in the electoral process. Safeguards must assure minority groups that they have an important place in the political process. To create mutual trust, power sharing can be both formal and informal. A number of policies exist, including multiple vetoes, reserved seats in the legislature and executive branches of government, corrective equity in appointments, revenue allocations, and quotas (Lijphart 1977).

Another policy of inclusion is to empower women, who have been the most vulnerable group in Congo's civil wars. Research on gender and development has shown that providing basic rights and entitlements to less represented groups, such as women, can have large positive effects on economic development (Wilson 2007). More specifically, empowering women by facilitating their access to positions of authority is likely to lead to lasting peace and development. An institutional arrangement that can enhance this process of gender empowerment is to reserve a large number of legislative seats for women and let women compete among themselves to fill them.

The advantage of democracy with safeguards to both majority and minority groups is that it provides a way of sharing the pie without reneging on promises to increase its size. A policy to increase the pie must be built into an institutional arrangement that makes it difficult to renege on commitment. Such an institutional mechanism is the granting of autonomy to subnational administrative and political entities. Decentralization usually refers to fiscal and political federalism, which includes a number of policies, among them deconcentration, or the transfer of power to local units; devolution, or the transfer of power to subnational political institutions above the local level; and delegation. Unfortunately, the decentralization law, as enshrined in the 2006 constitution, has yet to be passed by the legislature as of December 2010.

Decentralization has its advantages and drawbacks. However, after more than forty-five years of failed centralization in the DRC, an experiment with decentralization is overdue, and a different politico-administrative reform is badly needed. For example, a free electoral process and decentralization at the local level can empower local communities and let them decide on the best way to rule themselves. Decentralized units are usually more flexible, more efficient, and more innovative than centralized systems. For example, one area of reform would be to decentralize the police force to make it a local entity. This reform will not only help create jobs but will also sustain stability because it would be staffed by people who know their communities.

One issue with decentralization in the Congolese context is the fear that it is likely to break Congo into pieces because subnational entities can attempt to secede from the union. With its 336 ethnic groups and no dominant ethnic group, the likelihood of the DRC to explode into ministates appears quite remote. Marivoet's (2009) measure of ethno-linguistic homogeneity supports this contention. Of the twenty-six provinces (including Kinshasa) under the new constitution, only three are more than 50 percent homogenous: Haut-Lomami (72 percent), Mongala (67 percent), and Lualaba (51 percent). Most rich provinces, such as Nord-Kivu and Ituri, are extremely heterogenous.

Another area of contention concerns land as a divisible resource. As an issue, land defies peaceful settlement in eastern Congo. Accommodating territorial demands may be necessary after a careful analysis of customary law and with the consent of the governed and those who are assumed to represent tradition. Traditional authorities remain major key players in the process of building the state and should be given due authority related to land issues.

Final Thoughts

There are three ways of solving collective action problems, which helps explain why civil wars occur. First is to change the situation until the problem disappears. This is an institutional solution, and most economic approaches rely on this outcome. Second is to rely on individual capacity for nonegoistic cooperation—a motivational and mostly political solution. Motives other than self-interest must be invoked to explain collective action, cooperation, and social order. Third is a community-based solution that implicitly combines the first two.

Social structures that facilitate interactions and social control can produce cooperation. People are different and can be grouped into four categories: altruistic (maximization of others' benefit), cooperative (maximization of joint benefit), individualistic (maximization of own benefit), and competitive (maximization of relative advantage) (Liebrand 1986). In many studies, cooperation tends to be dominant if people communicate by minimizing individualistic behavior, but group solidarity tends to increase cooperation.

How then can cooperation be enhanced and self-interested behavior be minimized in the sociopolitical realms? One approach to understanding civil wars is rooted in the tradition of state building in Western Europe (Tilly 1985). The argument centers on the revenue imperative that all rulers face to acquire the income with which to govern. Revenue is seen to form the "sinews" of the state-building process, while a lack of revenue increases the risk of state collapse, which, in turn, increases the risk of civil wars. Thus, spending on administrative and coercive infrastructure can lengthen the reach of the state, thereby making it harder for rebels to organize. Moreover, spending on social welfare may help mitigate social grievances, whereas wasteful consumption by rulers may foment grievances.

State building thus implies the creation of a political entity that accommodates centrifugal and contradictory interests, and economic development means mobilizing resources to improve societal goals. The attempt to create a strong state on a weak economic basis requires incorporating a small group of loyal followers into the ruling group to legitimize the regime. By creating an atmosphere of intrigue and suspicion among their followers, rulers diminish their own effectiveness and hence sacrifice economic development, which in the long run destroys the foundations of the state-building process. The result is a cycle of unending political instability, or civil wars, and institutional rebuilding, which epitomizes many of Congo's civil wars.

A democratic system that frees citizens from anxiety can set the course of development because it will free the mind (Sen 1999) and make innovation possible, a critical element for the advancement of society. Since institutions are complex forms of norms and behaviors, which persist over time and serve socially valued purposes, they must be carefully crafted to avoid political instability. An understanding of institutions is important in preventing civil wars because institutions affect people's opportunities by establishing and maintaining their access to social, material, and natural resources. Institutions can also reinforce collective action and self-help. Understanding the relationship between institutions and those they serve is critical to understanding how different social groups and actors secure rights, opportunities, and power.

Economically, free enterprise creates wealth. Although economic diversification remains the best policy possible to create jobs capable of sustaining economic growth and minimizing the probability of conflict, the state remains the critical factor to revitalize the private sector. This revitalization should allow citizens to accumulate wealth outside the state apparatus and serve as a counterweight to state managers' rent-seeking behavior.

If citizens are prone to being manipulated by the elites, it is because they fear losing their livelihood. This fear is at the root of mass mobilization and manipulation. If civil war is easy to motivate, then the distinction between the leader's influence and the masses' proclivity to follow the elites becomes smaller and is, at best, a distinction between proximate and permissive causes of violence. It thus becomes harder to see "greed" and "grievance" as competitive explanations of internal wars. Political institutions can reduce grievances by implementing laws. Efficient economic institutions can influence the stability of political institutions and minimize greedy or corrupt behavior. Structural factors can be shaped by good governance.

Good governance and economic growth can create a virtuous circle that sustains the positive development and the peacefulness of a polity. In the Congolese case, such attributes can only be accomplished through institutional and normative change. Institutional change can be wrought with problems, but the benefits outweigh such initial concerns. Adam Smith (1969 [1763]) made this clear when he argued that institutional rules have the initial effect of stabilizing expectations, which in themselves create an atmosphere conducive to wealth generation. The critical formula remains the same: to build a strong state that is not predatory.

Acronyms

ABAKO	Alliance des Bakongo
AFDL	Alliance des Forces Démocratiques pour la Libération du Congo (Aliance of Democratic Forces for the Liberation of Congo)
AGI	Acte Global et Inclusif sur la Transition en République Démocratique du Congo (Global Act of the Transition)
AMP	Alliance de la Majorité Presidentielle (Alliance for the Presidential Majority)
ANC	Armée Nationale Congolaise (Congolese National Army)
BALUBAKAT	Baluba of Katanga
CEPSI	Centre d'Etudes des Problèmes Sociaux Indegènes
CFS	Congo Free State
CIA	Central Intelligence Agency
CIAT	Comité International d'Accompagnement de la Transition
CNDP	Congrés National pour la Défense du Peuple (National Congress for the Defense of the People)
CNKi	Comité National du Kivu (National Committee of Kivu)
CNL	Conseil National de Libération (National Council of Liberation)
CONACO	Convention Nationale Congolaise (Congolese National Convention)
CONADER	Commission Nationale de la Démobilisation et de la Réinsertion (National Commission for Demobilization and Reinsertion)
CONAKAT	Confédération des Associations Tribales du Katanga (Confederation of Tribal Associations of Katanga)
CRISP	Centre de Recherche et d'Information Socio-Politiques
CSK	Comité Special du Katanga
CVR	Corps des Volontaires de la République
DDR	disarmament, demobilization, and reintegration

DDRRR	disarmament, demobilization, repatriation, resettlement, and reintegration
DRC	Democratic Republic of Congo
EUFOR	European Force
FAC	Forces Armées Congolaises (Congolese Armed Forces)
FAO	Food and Agriculture Organization
FARDC	Forces Armées de la République Démocratique du Congo (Armed Forces of the DRC)
FDLR	Forces Démocratiques pour la Libération du Rwanda (Democratic Forces for the Liberation of Rwanda)
FLNC	Front pour la Libération Nationale du Congo (Front for the National Liberation of Congo)
FNI	Front National Intégrationiste (National Integrationist Front)
FNLA	Frente Nacional de Libertação de Angola (National Front for the Liberation of Angola)
Forminière	Société Internationale Forestière et Minière
GDP	gross domestic product
Gécamines	Générale des Carrières et des Mines
HCR	Haut Conseil de la République (High Council of the Republic)
HCR/PT	Haut Conseil de la République/Parlement de Transition (HCR/Parliament of Transition)
IAC	International Association of Congo
ICD	Inter-Congolese Dialogue
IDPs	internally displaced persons
IMF	International Monetary Fund
IPC	Ituri Pacification Committee
IRSA	Immigration and Refugee Services of America
JMPR	Jeunesse du Mouvement Populaire de la Révolution
LORI	Libération de la Race Opprimée en Ituri (Liberation of Oppressed Race in Ituri)
MIB	Mission d'Immigration des Banyarwanda (Immigration Mission of the Banyarwanda)
MLC	Mouvement pour la Libération du Congo (Movement for the Liberation of Congo)
MNC	Mouvement National Congolais (Congolese National Movement)
MNC/K	Mouvement National Congolais/Albert Kalonji
MNC/L	Mouvement National Congolais/Patrice Lumumba
MONUC	Mission de l'Organisation des Nations Unies au Congo
MONUSCO	Mission de l'Organisation des Nations Unies pour la Stabilisation du Congo (UN Stabilizaiton Mission in the DRC)
MPLA	Movimento Popular de Libertação de Angola (Popular Movement for the Liberation of Angola)

MPR	Mouvement Populaire de la Révolution (Popular Movement of the Revolution)
OAU	Organization of African Unity
OKIMO	Office des Mines de Kilo Moto
PALU	Parti Lumumbiste Unifié
PLC	Parti de la Libération Congolaise
PLW	Parti de Libération des Walendu (Party for the Liberation of Walendu)
PNP	Parti National du Progrès (National Party of Progress)
PPRD	Parti pour la Reconstruction et le Développement (Party for Reconstruction and Development)
PRP	Parti de la Révolution Populaire
PSA	Parti Solidaire Africain (African Solidarity Party)
RCD	Rassemblement Congolais pour la Démocratie (Congolese Rally for Democracy)
RCD-ML	Rassemblement Congolais pour la Démocratie–Mouvement de Libération (Congolese Rally for Democracy–Movement of Liberation)
RPA	Rwandan Patriotic Army
RPF	Rwandan Patriotic Front
UCOL	Union pour la Colonisation (Union for Colonization)
UDPS	Union pour la Démocratie et le Progrès Social (Union for Democracy and Social Progress)
UMHK	Union Minière du Haut Katanga
UN	United Nations
UNHCR	United Nations High Commissioner for Refugees
UNICEF	United Nations Children Emergency Fund
UNITA	União Nacional para a Independência Total de Angola (National Union for the Total Independence of Angola)
UPC	Union des Patriotes Congolais (Union of Congolese Patriots)
UPDF	Ugandan People's Defense Forces

References

Afoaku, Osita. 2002. "Congo's Rebels: Their Origins, Motivations, and Strategies." In *The African Stakes of the Congo War*, ed. John F. Clark. New York: Palgrave Macmillan.

Afri-Ku-Nyeng, N'Zimba K. 1977. "Zaïre-Angola: Les Origines Secrètes de la Guerre," *Jeune Afrique* no. 857 (10 June): 14–15.

Africa Diary. 1963. "Bloody Fighting in Kasai," 2, no. 2 (26 January–1 February): 973–974.

Africa Research Bulletin. 1977. "Zaire: Response to Invasion," 14, no. 4 (April): 4399–4402.

———. 1978. "Zaire," 15, no. 5 (May): 4854–4862.

———. 1998. "Democratic Republic of Congo: Explosive Kivu Region," 35, no. 6 (June): 13152–13153.

Amnesty International. 2003. *On the Precipice: The Deepening Human Rights and Humanitarian Crisis in Ituri*. New York: Amnesty International.

Anderson, Benedict. 1983. *Imagined Communities: Reflections on the Origins and Spread of Nationalism*. London: Verso.

Anderson, Charles W., Fred R. von der Mehden, and Crawford Young. 1974. *Issues of Political Protest*. Englewood Cliffs, NJ: Prentice-Hall.

Anstey, Roger. 1966. *King Leopold's Legacy: The Congo under Belgian Rule, 1908–1960*. London: Oxford University Press.

Autesserre, Séverine. 2010. *The Trouble with the Congo: Local Violence and the Failure of International Peacebuilding*. New York: Cambridge University Press.

Balch-Lindsay, Dylan, and Andrew Enterline. 2000. "Killing Time: The World Politics of Civil War Duration, 1820–1992," *International Studies Quarterly* 44, no. 4: 615–642.

Banks, Arthur. 2010. *Cross-National Time-Series Data Archive*. CD-ROM. Binghamton, NY: Center for Social Analysis.

Belgium, Chambre des Réprésentants. 1920. *Rapport Sur l'Administration de la Colonie du Congo Belge pendant l'Année 1919 Présenté aux Chambres Législatives*. Brussels: M Hayez, Imprimeur.

———. 1930. *Rapport Sur l'Administration de la Colonie du Congo Belge pendant l'Année 1929 Présenté aux Chambres Législatives*. Brussels: F. Van Gompel, Imprimeur Editeur.

———. 1955. *Rapport Sur l'Administration de la Colonie du Congo Belge pendant l'Année1954 Présenté aux Chambres Législatives*. Brussels: Etablissements Généraux d'Imprimerie, S.A.

———. 1956. *Rapport Sur l'Administration de la Colonie du Congo Belge pendant l'An-née 1955 Présenté aux Chambres Législatives.* Brussels: Etablissements Généraux d'Imprimerie, S.A.

Belgium, Ministère du Congo Belge et du Ruanda-Urundi. 1958. *Statistiques des Mou-vements des Capitaux au Congo Belge et au Ruanda-Urundi de 1887 à 1956.* Brussels: Direction des Statisitques.

Bergmans, Lieven. 1979. *L'Histoire des Baswagha.* Butembo, DRC: Procures.

Beys, Jorge, Paul-Henry Gendebien, and Benoît Verhaegen. 1964. *Congo 1963.* Brussels: CRISP.

Bézy, Fernand. 1957. *Problèmes Structurels de l'Economie Congolaise.* Louvain, Belgium: Institut des Recherches Economques et Sociales.

Bézy, Fernand, Jean-Philippe Peemans, and Jean-Marie Wautelet. 1981. *Accumulation et Sous-Développement au Zaïre 1960–1980.* Louvain-la-Neuve, Belgium: Presses Universitaires de Louvain.

Boissonnade, Euloge. 1998. *Kabila, Clone de Mobutu?* Paris: Moreux.

Bouvier, Paule, and Francesca Bomboko. 2003. *Le Dialogue Inter Congolais: Anatomie d'une Négociation à la Lisière du Chaos; Contribution à la Théorie de la Négoci-ation.* Tervuren, Belgium: Institut Africain-CEDAF.

Braeckman, Colette. 1979. "La Saga du Shaba," *La Révue Nouvelle* no. 2 (February): 135–149.

———. 1992. *Le Dinosaure: Le Zaïre de Mobutu.* Paris: Fayard.

———. 1997. "Zaire at the End of a Reign," *New Left Review* no. 222 (March–April): 129–138.

———. 1999. *L'Enjeu Congolais. L'Afrique Centrale après Mobutu.* Paris: Fayard.

———. 2001. "La Mort de Kabila: Nouvelle Donné dans la Guerre en RDC," *Politique Africaine* no. 82 (June): 151–159.

Brass, Paul R. ed. 1985. *Ethnic Groups and the State.* London: Croom-Helm.

Brausch, Georges. 1961. *Belgian Administration in the Congo.* New York: Oxford University Press.

Brennan, Richard J., Michael Despines, and Leslie F. Roberts. 2006. "Mortality Surveys in the Democratic Republic of Congo: Humanitarian Impact and Lessons Learned," *Humanitarian Practice Network* no. 35 (November). www.odihpn.org/report.asp?id=2838. Accessed 9 August 2009.

Brittain, Victoria. 2002. "Calvary of the Women of Eastern Democratic Republic of Congo (DRC)," *Review of African Political Economy* 29, no. 93/94 (September–December): 595–601.

Brown, Michael. 1996. "Introduction." In *The International Dimensions of Internal Conflict*, ed. Michael Brown. Cambridge, MA: Center for Science and International Affairs.

Bucyalimwe, Stanislas M. 1990. "Land Conflicts in Masisi (Eastern Zaire): The Impact Aftermath of Belgian Colonial Policy (1920–1989)." PhD dissertation, University of Indiana, Bloomington.

———. 1999. "La Société Civile au Kivu: Une Dynamique en Panne?" In *L'Afrique des Grands Lacs: Annuaire 1998–1999*, eds. Stefaan Marysse and Filip Reyntjens. Paris: L'Harmattan.

———. 2000. "La Guerre des Chiffres: Une Constante dans la Politique Au Nord-Kivu." In *L'Afrique des Grands Lacs: Annuaire 1999–2000*, eds. Stefaan Marysse and Filip Reyntjens. Paris: L'Harmattan.

———. 2001. "Pouvoirs, Elevage Bovin et la Question Fonçiere au Nord-Kivu." In *L'Afrique des Grands Lacs: Annuaire 2000–2001*, eds. Stefaan Marysse and Filip Reyntjens. Paris: L'Harmattan.

———. 2003. "L'Administration AFDL/RCD au Kivu (Novembre 1996–Mars 2003). Strategie et Bilan." In *L'Afrique des Grands Lacs: Annuaire 2002–2003*, eds. Stefaan Marysse and Filip Reyntjens. Paris: L'Harmattan.

——. 2005. "Kivu et Ituri in the Congo War: The Roots and Nature of a Linkage." In *The Political Economy of the Great Lakes Region in Africa. The Pitfalls of Enforced Democracy and Globalization*, eds. Stefaan Marysse and Filip Reyntjens. New York: Palgrave Macmillan.

——. 2010. "La Question de la Réintégration des Déplacés et des Réfugiés dans le 'Programme de Stabilisation et de Reconstruction en Zones Post-Conflict' au Kivu." In *L'Afrique des Grands Lacs: Annuaire 2009–2010*, eds. Stefaan Marysse, Filip Reyntjens, and Stef Vandeginste. Paris: L'Harmattan.

Buhaug, Halvard, Lars-Erik Cederman, and Jan Ketil Rød. 2008. "Disaggregating Ethno-Nationalist Civil Wars: A Dyadic Test of Exclusion Theory," *International Organization* 62, no. 3 (July): 531–551.

Buhaug, Halvard, Scott Gates, and Päivi Lujala. 2009. "Geography, Rebel Capability, and the Duration of Civil Conflict," *Journal of Conflict Resolution* 53, no. 4 (August): 544–569.

Bulambo, K. A. 2000. *Mourir au Kivu*. Paris: L'Harmattan.

Callaghy, Thomas. 1984. *The State-Society Struggle: Zaire in Comparative Perspective*. New York: Columbia University Press.

Chabal, P., and J.-P. Daloz. 1998. *Africa Works*. London: James Currey.

Chamowicz, Monique. 1996. "Kivu: Les Banyamulenge enfin à l'Honneur!," *Politique Africaine* no. 64 (December): 115–120.

Charpentier, J. 1977. "Pratique Française du Droit International," *Annuaire Française du Droit International* 23, no. 1: 1012–1085.

Chomé, Jules. 1959. *Le Drama de Luluabourg*. Brussels: Remarques Congolaises.

Cirhagarhula, Bashizi. 1981. "Mythe Hamite, Formation Etatiques et Acculturation Interlacustres." In *La Civilisation Ancienne des Peuples des Grands Lacs. Colloque de Bujumbura, 4–10 Septembre 1979*, ed. Jean-Baptiste Ntahokaja. Paris: Editions Karthala.

Clapham, Christopher. 1998. *African Guerillas*. Bloomington: Indiana University Press.

Clark, John. 2001. "Explaining Ugandan Intervention in Congo: Evidence and Interpretations," *Journal of Modern African Studies* 39, no. 2: 261–287.

——. 2002. "Introduction." In *African Stakes of the Congo War*, ed. John Clark. New York: Palgrave.

Collier, Paul. 1999. "On the Economic Consequences of Civil War," *Oxford Economic Papers* 51, no. 1 (January): 168–183.

Collier, Paul, and Anke Hoeffler. 1998. "On the Economic Causes of Civil War," *Oxford Economic Papers* 50, no. 4 (October): 563–573.

——. 2002. "On the Incidence of Civil War in Africa," *Journal of Conflict Resolution* 46, no. 1 (February): 13–28.

Collier, Paul, Anke Hoeffler, and Nicholas Sambanis. 2005. "The Collier-Hoeffler Model of Civil War Onset and the Case Study Project Research Design." In *Understanding Civil War: Evidence and Analysis. Vol. 1, Africa*, eds. Paul Collier and Nicholas Sambanis. Washington, DC: World Bank.

Collier, Paul, Anke Hoeffler, and Måns Söderbom. 2004. "On the Duration of Civil War," *Journal of Peace Research* 41, no. 3 (May): 253–273.

Congo. 1921. "Fétiche Indigène de Guerre Tonga Tonga," no. 2: 423–428.

Coquery-Vidrovitch, Catherine, Alain Forest, and Herbert Weiss. 1987. *Rébellions-Révolution au Zaïre, 1963–1965*. Paris: L'Harmattan.

Coser, Lewis A. 1956. *The Functions of Social Conflict: Political Opportunism and Ethnic Conflict*. New York: Free Press.

David, Steven R. 1997. "Internal War, Causes and Cures," *World Politics* 49, no. 4 (July): 552–576.

De Failly, Didier. 2000. "L'Economie du Sud-Kivu 1990–2000: Mutations Profondes Cashées Par Une Panne." In *L'Afrique des Grands Lacs: Annuaire 1999–2000*, eds. Filip Reyntjens and Stefaan Marysse. Paris: L'Harmattan.

DeFigueiredo, Rui, and Barry R. Weingast. 1999. "The Rationality of Fear: Political Opportunism and Ethnic Conflict." In *Civil Wars, Insecurity and Intervention*, eds. Barbara Walter and Jack Snider. New York: Columbia University Press.

De Herdt, Tom. 2002. "Democracy & the Money Machine in Zaire," *Review of African Political Economy* 29, no. 93/94 (September–December): 445–462.

DeRouen, Karl, and David Sobeck. 2004. "The Dynamics of Civil War Duration and Outcome," *Journal of Peace Research* 41, no. 3 (May): 303–320.

Deschamps, Hubert J. 1965. *Les Religions d'Afrique*. Paris: Presses Universitaires de France.

De St. Moulin, Léon. 1976. *Atlas des Collectivités du Zaire*. Kinshasa: Presses Universitaires du Zaïre.

De Villers, Gauthier, and Jean Tshonda Omasombo. 2002. "An Intransitive Transition," *Review of African Political Economy* 29, no. 93/94 (September–December): 399–410.

De Villers, Gauthier, Jean Tshonda Omasombo, and Erik Kennes. 2001. *Guerre et Politique: Les Trente Derniers Mois de L. D. Kabila (Août 1998–Janvier 2001)*. Tervuren, Belgium: Cahiers d'Etudes Africaines.

De Villers, Gauthiers, and Jean-Claude Willame, eds. 1998. *République Démocratique du Congo: Chronique d'un Entre-Deux-Guerres, Octobre 1996–Juillet 1998*. Paris: L'Harmattan.

De Witte, Ludo. 2001. *Assassination of Lumumba*. New York: Verso.

Dizolele, Mvemba P. 2010. "The Mirage of Democracy in the DRC," *Journal of Democracy* 21, no. 3 (July): 143–157.

Downs, Georges, and Stephen Stedman. 2002. "Evaluation Issues in Peace Implementation." In *Ending Civil Wars: The Implementation of Peace Agreements*, eds. Stephen J. Stedman, Donald Rothchild, and Elizabeth M. Cousens. Boulder, CO: Lynne Rienner Publishers.

Doyle, Michael W., and Nicholas Sambanis. 2000. "International Peacekeeping: A Theoretical and Quantitative Analysis," *American Political Science Review* 94, no. 4: 779–801.

DRC, Ministère de l'Education Nationale et des Affaires Culturelles. 1964. *Statistiques Scholaires 1963–1964*. Kinshasa.

DRC, Présidence de la République. 2004. "Loi No. 04/024 du 12 Novembre 2004 Relative à La Nationalité Congolaise," *Journal Officiel de la DRC* 45 (17 November): 1–16.

Duke, Lynne. 2003. *Mandela, Mobutu, and Me*. New York: Doubleday.

Dunn, Kevin C. 2003. *Imagining the Congo: The International Relations of Identity*. New York: Palgrave Macmillan.

Dupriez, Gérard. 1968. "Legislation et Marché du Travail." In *Indépendance, Inflation, Développement: L'Economie Congolaise de 1960 à 1965*, ed. Institut des Recherches Economiques et Sociales. Paris: Mouton.

Dupriez, Pierre. 1968. "La Politique du Commerce Extérieur." In *Indépendance, Inflation, Développement: L'Economie Congolaise de 1960 à 1965*, ed. Institut des Recherches Economiques et Sociales. Paris: Mouton.

Duverger, Maurice. 1955. *Political Parties: Their Organization and Activity in the Modern State*. Translated by Barbara and Robert North. New York: Wiley.

Easman, Milton J. 1994. *Ethnic Politics*. Ithaca, NY: Cornell University Press.

Elbe, Stefan. 2002. "HIV/AIDS and the Changing Landscape of War in Africa," *International Security* 27, no. 2 (Fall): 159–177.

Emizet, Kisangani, and Vicki Hesli. 1995. "The Disposition to Secede: An Analysis of the Soviet Case," *Comparative Political Studies* 27, no. 4 (January): 493–536.

Englebert, Pierre, and Rebecca Hummel. 2005. "Let's Stick Together: Understanding Africa's Secessionist Deficit," *African Affairs* 104, no. 416 (July): 399–427.

Epstein, Howard M. 1965. *Revolt in the Congo 1960–1964*. New York: Facts on File.

Fahey, Dan. 2008. "Le Fleuve d'Or: The Production and Trade of Gold from Mongbwalu, DRC." In *L'Afrique des Grands Lacs: Annuaire 2007–2008*, eds. Stefaan Marysse, Filip Reyntjens, and Stef Vandeginste. Paris: L'Harmattan.

Fairhead, J. 1991. *Securité Alimentaire au Kivu du Nord et du Sud*. London: Oxfam.

Fearon, James D. 2004. "Why Do Some Civil Wars Last So Much Longer Than Others," *Journal of Peace Research* 41, no. 3 (May): 275–301.

———. 2005. "Primary Commodities Exports and Civil War," *Journal of Conflict Resolution* 49, no 4 (August): 483–507.

Fearon, James D., and David D. Laitin. 2000. "Violence and the Social Construction of Ethnic Identity," *International Organization* 54, no. 4 (Autumn): 845–877.

Flamant, F., F. Vandewalle, J. Dargent, J. Van Moll, and H. Franckx. 1952. *La Force Publique: De Sa Naissance à 1914*. Brussels: Institut Royal Colonial Belge, Section des Sciences Morales et Politiques.

Food and Agriculture Organization. 1965–2009, annual. *Production Yearbook*. Rome: FAO.

Fox, Renée, Willy de Craemer, and Jean-Marie Ribeaucourt. 1965. "The Second Independence: A Case Study of the Kwilu Rebellion in the Congo," *Comparative Studies in Society and History* 8, no. 1 (October): 78–109.

Galtung, Johan. 1982. *Environment, Development and Military Activity. Towards Alternative Security Decline*. Oslo: Norwegian University Press.

Gann, Lewis H., and Peter Duignan. 1984. *The Rulers of Belgian Africa*. Princeton, NJ: Princeton University Press.

Garrison, Lloyd. 1966. "Congo Accuses Tshombe of Plotting a Rebellion," *New York Times*, July 29, A4.

Geertz, Clifford. 1980. *Negara: The Theatre State in Nineteenth-Century Bali*. Princeton, NJ: Princeton University Press.

Gérard-Libois, Jules. 1963. *Secession au Katanga*. Brussels: CRISP.

———. 1967. *Congo 1966*. Brussels: CRISP.

Gérard-Libois, Jules, and Jean Van Lierde. 1963. *Congo 1962*. Brussels: CRISP.

———. 1965. *Congo 1964*. Brussels: CRISP.

———. 1966. *Congo 1965*. Brussels: CRISP.

Gérard-Libois, Jules, and Benoît Verhaegen. 1961. *Congo 1960*. Vols. 1 & 2. Brussels: CRISP.

———. 1963. *Congo 1962*. Brussels: CRISP.

———. 1969. "La Révolte des Mercenaires." In *Congo 1967*, eds. Jules Gérard-Libois, Benoît Verhaegen, Jan Vansina, and Herbert Weiss. Brussels: CRISP.

Gérard-Libois, Jules, Benoît Verhaegen, Jan Vansina, and Herbert Weiss. 1967. *Congo 1966*. Brussels: CRISP.

Gibbs, David N. 1991. *The Political Economy of Third World Intervention: Mines, Money, and U.S. Policy in the Congo Crisis*. Chicago: University of Chicago Press.

Gize, Sikitele. 1973. "Les Racines de la Révolte Pende de 1931," *Etudes d'Histoire Africaine* 5: 99–153.

Gnamo, Abbas H. 1999. "The Rwandan Genocide and the Collapse of Mobutu's Kleptocracy." In *The Path of a Genocide: The Rwanda Crisis from Uganda to Zaire*, eds. H. Adelman and A. Suhrke. New Brunswick, NJ: Transaction Publishers.

Goldstone, Jack. 1991. *Revolution and Rebellion in the Early Modern World*. Berkeley: University of California Press.

Gould, David. 1980. *Bureaucratic Corruption and Underdevelopment in the Third World: The Case of Zaire*. New York: Pergamon Press.

Habermas, Jurgen. 1979. *Communications and the Evolution of Society*. Boston: Beacon Press.

Hardin, Russell. 1995. *One for All: The Logic of Group Conflict.* Princeton, NJ: Princeton University Press.

Hari, J. 2006. "A Journey into the Most Savage War in the World," *The Independent* 6 May.

Herbst, Jeffrey. 2000. "Economic Incentives, Natural Resources, and Conflict in Africa," *Journal of African Economies* 9, no. 3 (October): 270–294.

Hoare, Mike. 1967. *Congo Mercenary.* London: Robert Hale.

Hochschild, Adam. 1998. *King Leopold's Ghost: A Story of Greed, Terror, and Heroism in Colonial Africa.* Boston: Houghton Mifflin.

Homer-Dixon, Thomas F. 1999. *Environment, Scarcity and Violence.* Princeton, NJ: Princeton University Press.

Horowitz, Donald. 1985. *Ethnic Group in Conflict.* Berkeley: University of California Press.

Hoskyns, Catherine. 1962. *The Congo: A Chronology of Events, January 1960–December 1961.* London: Royal Institute of International Affairs.

Howard, Lise Morjé. 2008. *UN Peacekeeping in Civil Wars.* Cambridge: Cambridge University Press.

Huliaras, Asteris C. 1998. "The 'Anglosaxon Conspiracy': French Perceptions of the Great Lakes Crisis," *Journal of Modern African Studies* 36, no. 4: 593–609.

Human Rights Watch. 1996. "Zaire. Forced to Flee. Violence Against the Tutsis in Zaire," *Human Rights Watch* 8, no. 2A (July).

———. 1999. "The Democratic Republic of Congo (formerly Zaire)." In *Human Rights Watch World Report 1998.* New York: Human Rights Watch.

———. 2001. "Uganda in Eastern DRC: Fueling Political and Ethnic Strife," *Human Rights Watch* 13, no. 2(A) March: 1–37.

———. 2005. *The Curse of Gold.* Washington, DC: Human Rights Watch.

Huntington, Samuel. 1996. *The Clash of Civilizations and the Remaking of World Order.* New York: Simon & Schuster.

Huybrechts, André. 1970. *Transports et Structures de Développement au Congo: Etude du Progrès Economique de 1900 à 1970.* Paris: Mouton.

Ilunga, Kabongo Mbiye. 1973. "Ethnicity, Social Classes, and the State in the Congo, 1960–1965: The Case of the Baluba." PhD dissertation, University of California, Berkeley.

International Crisis Group. 1999. "The Agreement on a Cease-Fire in the DRC: An Analysis of the Agreement and Prospects for Peace." Report No. 5, August 20. Nairobi, Kenya: International Crisis Group.

———. 2000. "Scramble for the Congo: Anatomy of an Ugly War." Africa Report No 26, Brussels: International Crisis Group.

———. 2003. "Congo Crisis: Military Intervention in Ituri." Africa Report No. 64 (June). Brussels: International Crisis Group.

———. 2005. "A Congo Action Plan." Africa Briefing No. 34, 19 October. Brussels: International Crisis Group.

———. 2008. "Congo: Quatre Priorités pour une Paix Durable en Ituri." Rapport Afrique No. 140 (13 May). Brussels: International Crisis Group.

International Regional Information Networks. 2002. "In-Depth: Ituri in Eastern DRC." www.irinnews.org/InDepthMain.aspx?InDepth=33&ReportId=70762. Accessed 9 March 2008.

James, Selwyn J. 1943. *South of the Congo.* New York: Random House.

Johnson, D. 2003. "Shifting Sands: Oil Exploration in the Rift Valley and the Congo Conflict." Unpublished manuscript. Goma, DRC: Pole Institute.

Kabamba, Bob, and Olivier Lanotte. 1999. "Guerres au Congo-Zaïre (1996–1999): Acteurs et Scénarios." In *Conflicts et Guerres au Kivu et dans la Région des Grands*

Lacs. Entre Tensions Locales et Escalade Régionale, eds. Paul Mathieu and Jean-Claude Willame. Paris: L'Harmattan.

Kabanga, Musau D. 2003. "Le Remodelage du Paysage Socio-Economique dans les Zones de Conflict du Nord-Kivu et du Maniema (R. D. Congo)." In *L'Afrique des Grands Lacs: Annuaire 2002–2003*, eds. Stefaan Marysse and Filip Reyntjens. Paris: L'Harmattan.

Kabwit, Ghislain C. 1979. "Zaire: The Roots of the Continuing Crisis," *Journal of Modern African Studies* 17, no. 3: 381–407.

Kajiga, Gaspar. 1956. "Cette Immigration Séculaire des Rwandais au Congo," *Bulletin Trimestriel du Centre d'Etudes des Problèmes Sociaux Indigènes* no. 32 (March): 10–11.

Kalb, Madeleine. 1982. *The Congo Cables*. New York: Macmillan.

Kaldor, Mary. 2001 *New and Old Wars: Organized Violence in a Global Era*. Palo Alto, CA: Stanford University Press.

Kalivas, Stathis. 2008. "Promises and Pitfalls of an Emerging Research Program: The Microdynamics of Civil War." In *Order, Conflict, Violence*, eds. Stathis Kalivas, Ian Shapiro, and Tarek Masoud. Cambridge: Cambridge University Press.

Kamitatu, Masamba. 1977. *Le Pouvoir à la Portée du Peuple*. Paris: Maspero.

Kanyinda-Lusanga, Théodore. 1970. *Institutions Traditionnelles et Forces Politiques au Congo. Le Cas de la Societé Luba du Kasai*. Brussels: CRISP.

Kelly, Sean. 1993. *America's Tyrant: The CIA and the Mobutu of Zaire*. Washington, DC: American University Press.

King, Gary, Robert Keohane, and Sidney Verba. 1994. *Designing Social Inquiry: Scientific Inference in Qualitative Research*. Princeton, NJ: Princeton University Press.

Kisangani, Emizet F. 1987. "Implementation of Stabilization Policies in an Authoritarian Setting: Zaire, 1970–1980," *Canadian Journal of African Studies* 21, no. 2: 175–200.

———. 1997. *Zaire After Mobutu: A Case of Humanitarian Emergency*. Helsinki: World Institute for Development Economics.

———. 1998. "Confronting Leaders at the Apex of the State: The Growth of the Unofficial Economy in Congo," *African Studies Review* 41, no. 1 (April): 99–137.

———. 1999. "Political Cleavages in a Democratizing Society: The Case of the Congo (formerly Zaire)," *Comparative Political Studies* 32, no. 2 (April): 158–228.

———. 2000a. "The Massacre of Refugees in Congo: A Case of UN Peacekeeping Failure and International Law," *Journal of Modern African Studies* 38, no. 2: 163–202.

———. 2000b. "Explaining the Rise and Fall of Military Regimes: Civil-Military Relations in the Congo," *Armed Forces & Society* 26, no. 2 (Winter): 203–227.

———. 2000c. "Congo (Zaire): Corruption, Disintegration, and State Failure." In *War, Hunger, and Displacement: The Origins of Humanitarian Emergencies, Volume 2: Case Studies,* eds. E. Wayne Nafziger, Frances Stewart, and Raimo Väyrynen. Oxford: Oxford University Press.

———. 2002. "The DROC: Non-State Actors on Center Stage." In *Proceedings Central African Security: Conflict in the Congo*, eds. Kent Hughes Butts and Arthur L. Bradshaw, Jr. Carlisle, PA: Center for Strategic Leadership.

———. 2003. "Conflict in the Democratic Republic of Congo: A Mosaic of Insurgent Groups," *International Journal on World Peace* 20, no. 3 (September): 51–80.

Kisangani, Emizet F., and F. Scott Bobb. 2010. *Historical Dictionary of the Democratic Republic of the Congo*. Lanham, MD: Scarecrow Press.

Kisangani, Emizet F., and Jeffrey Pickering. 2008. "International Military Intervention, 1989–2005." Inter-University Consortium for Political and Social Research, Data Collection No. 21282, University of Michigan, Ann Arbor.

Kyle, Keite. 1967. "Plot and Counter-Plot, What Happened in the Congo," *New Republic* 157, no. 12 (16 September): 10–16.

Lacroix, Jean-Louis. 1967. *Industrialisation au Congo. La Transformation des Structures Economiques*. Paris: Mouton.

Laitin, David D. 2001. "Secessionist Rebellion in the Former Soviet Union," *Comparative Political Studies* 34, no. 8 (October): 839–861.

Lake, David A., and Donald Rothchild. 1998. "Spreading Fear: The Genesis of Transnational Ethnic Conflict." In *The International Spread of Ethnic Conflict: Fear, Diffusion, and Escalation*, eds. David A. Lake and Donald Rothchild. Princeton, NJ: Princeton University Press.

Lane, Frederic C. 1958. "Economic Consequences of Organized Violence," *Journal of Economic History* 18, no. 4 (December): 401–417.

Lanotte, Olivier. 2003. *Guerres sans Frontières en République Démocratique du Congo*. Brussels: Editions GRIP.

Lefever, Ernest W., and Wynfred Joshua. 1966. *United Nations Peacekeeping in the Congo: 1960–1964; An Analysis of Political, Executive, and Military Control*. Washington, DC: Brookings Institution.

Lemarchand, René. 1964. *Political Awakening in the Belgian Congo*. Berkeley: University of California Press.

———. 1994. *Burundi: Etnocide as Discourse and Practice*. New York: Cambridge University Press.

———. 2006. "The Geopolitics of the Great Lakes Crisis." In *L'Afrique des Grands Lacs: Annuaire 2005–2006*, eds. Filip Reyntjens and Stefaan Marysse. Paris: L'Harmattan.

———. 2009. "Reflections on the Crisis in Eastern Congo." In *L'Afrique des Grands Lacs: Annuaire 2008–2009*, eds. Stefaan Marysse, Filip Reyntjens, and Stef Vandeginste. Paris: L'Harmattan.

LeoGrande, William M. 1982. "Cuban-Soviet Relations and Cuban Policy in Africa." In *Cuba in Africa*, eds. Carmelo Mesa-Lago and June S. Belheim. Pittsburgh, PA: Center for Latin American Studies, University of Pittsburgh Press.

Levy, Jack S., and William R. Thompson. 2010. *Causes of War*. Oxford, UK: Wiley-Blackwell.

Licklinder, Roy, ed. 1993. *Stopping the Killing: How Civil Wars End*. New York: New York University Press.

Liebrand, W. B. G. 1986. "The Ubiquity of Social Values in Social Dilemmas." In *Experimental Social Dilemmas*, eds. H. A. M. Wilke, D. M. Messick, and C. G. Rutte. Frankfurt: Verlag Peter Long.

Lijphart, Arend. 1977. *Democracy in Plural Societies*. New Haven, CN: Yale University Press.

Lissitzyn, Oliver J. 1955. "Notteböhm (Liechtenstein v. Guatemala)," *American Journal of International Law* 49, no. 3 (July): 396–403.

Lubala, Emmanuel. 1998. "La Situation Politique au Kivu: Vers une Dualisation de la Société." In *L'Afrique des Grands Lacs: Annuaire 1997–1998*, eds. Stefaan Marysse and Filip Reyntjens. Paris: L'Harmattan.

Lujala, Päivi, Nils P. Gleditsch, and Elisabeth Gilmore. 2005. "A Diamond Curse: Civil War and a Lootable Resource," *Journal of Conflict Resolution* 49, no 4 (August): 538–562.

Mabika, Kalanda A. 1959. *Baluba et Lulua: Une Ethnie à la Recherche d'Un Nouvel Equilibre*. Brussels: Editions de Remarques Congolaises.

Mabusa, Basile. 1966. "Post-Independence Education in the Congo," *Africa Report* 11, no. 6: 24–28.

MacGaffey, Janet. 1987. *Entrepreneurs and Parasites: The Struggle for Indigenous Capitalism in Zaire*. Cambridge: Cambridge University Press.

————. 1991. "Historical, Cultural and Structural Dimensions of Zaire's Unrecorded Trade." In *The Real Economy of Zaire*, ed. Janet MacGaffey. London: James Curey.

Mack, Andrew. 2002. "Civil War: Academic Research and the Policy Community," *Journal of Peace Research* 39, no. 5 (September): 515–525.

Mafikiri, Tshongo. 1994. "Problématique d'Accès à la Terre dans les Systèmes d'Exploitation Agricole des Régions Montagneuses du Kivu." PhD thesis, Université Catholique de Louvain (Belgium).

Magotte, J. 1934. *Les Circonscriptions Indigènes. Commentaires du Dècret du 5 Décembre 1933*. Dison, Belgium: Winandy.

Mahdavi, Hossein. 1970. "Patterns and Problems of Economic Development in Rentier States: The Case of Iran." In *Studies in the Economic History of the Middle East*, ed. M. A. Cook. Oxford: Oxford University Press.

Mamdani, Mahmood. 2001. *When Victims Become Killers: Colonialism, Nativism, and the Genocide in Rwanda*. Princeton, NJ: Princeton University Press.

Mangold, Peter. 1979. "Shaba I and Shaba II," *Survival* 21, no. 3 (May–June): 107–115.

Marivoet, Wim. 2009. "Decentralizing the Challenges of Poverty Reduction in the DRC." In *L'Afrique des Grands Lacs: Annuaire 2008–2009*, eds. Stephan Marysse, Filip Reyntjens, and Stef Vandeginste. Paris: L'Harmattan.

Marshall, Monty, and Keith Jaggers. 2010. Polity IV Project. http://www.cidcm.umd.edu/inscr/polity. Accessed 1 September 2010.

Mashauri, Kule T. 1981. "Organisation Etatique des Yira et son Origine." In *La Civilisation Ancienne des Peuples des Grands Lacs: Colloque de Bujumbura, 4–10 Septembre 1979*, ed. Jean-Baptiste Ntahokaja. Paris: Editions Karthala.

Masson, Paul. 1970. *Dix Ans de Malheurs: Kivu 1957–1967*. Brussels: Arnold.

Matabaro, Séverin M. 2008. "La Crise Foncière à l'Est de la RDC." In *L'Afrique des Grands Lacs: Annuaire 2007–2008*, eds. Stefaan Marysse, Filip Reyntjens, and Stef Vandeginste. Paris: L'Harmattan.

Mathieu, Paul, and Tsongo Mafikiri. 1999. "Enjeux Fonciers, Déplacements de Population et Escalades Conflictuelles (1930–1995)." In *Conflicts et Guerres au Kivu et dans la Région des Grands Lacs*, eds. Paul Mathieu and Jean-Claude Willame. Paris: L'Harmattan.

Mba, Bigiramana C. 2003. "L'Evolution des Violences à Caracter Ethnique Chez les Banyamulenge du Sud-Kivu (1990–1998)." BA thesis, political science, National University of Rwanda, Butare.

McKinley, J. C. 1996. "Rwanda Claims Eastern Congo," *New York Times*, 28 October.

McNulty, Mel. 1999. "The Collapse of Zaire: Implosion, Revolution or External Aggression," *Journal of Modern African Studies* 37, no. 1: 53–82.

Mehlum, Halvor, Karl O. Moene, and Ragnar Torvik. 2002. "Plunder & Protection Inc.," *Journal of Peace Research* 39, no. 4 (July): 447–459.

Merlier, Michel. 1962. *Le Congo de la Colonisation Belge à l'Indépendance*. Paris: Maspero.

Meyer, A. 1955. *Aperçu Historique de L'Exploitation et de l'Etude des Regions Volcaniques du Kivu*. Brussels: Institut des Parcs Nationaux.

Mgbako, Chi. 2005. "Ingando Solidarity Camps: Reconciliation and Political Indoctrination in Post-Genocide Rwanda," *Harvard Human Rights Journal* 18, no. 2 (Spring): 201–224.

Miller, Joseph C. 1970. "Cokwe Trade and Conquest." In *Pre-Colonial African Trade*, eds. Richard Gray and David Birmingham. London: Oxford University Press.

Morel, Edmund D. 1906. *Red Rubber*. London: R. Fisher Unwin.

Moulaert, George. 1950. *Vingt Années à Kilo Moto, 1920–1940*. Brussels: Dessart.

Moutoulle, L. 1946. *Politque Sociale de l'Union Minière du Haut Katanga*. Brussels: Académie Royale des Sciences d'Outre Mer, Sciences Morales et Politiques, Tome XIV, fasc. 3.

Mugisho, Emmanuel L. 1998. "La Situation Politique au Kivu: Vers Une Dualisation de la Société." In *L'Afrique des Grands Lacs: Annuaire 1997–1998*, eds. Stefaan Marysse and Filip Reyntjens. Paris: L'Harmattan.

———. 2000. "La Contre-Résistance dans la Zone d'Occupation Rwandaise au Kivu (1996–2000)." In *L'Afrique des Grands Lacs: Annuaire 1999–2000*, eds. Stefaan Marysse and Filip Reyntjens. Paris: L'Harmattan.

Munanira, Ruriho. 1981. "Pour Une Révision Profonde de l'Histoire de la Région des Grands Lacs: Le Cas du Bwisha Precolonial." In *La Civilisation Ancienne des Peuples des Grands Lacs: Colloque de Bujumbura, 4–10 Septembre 1979*, ed. Jean-Baptiste Ntahokaja. Paris: Karthala.

Namegabe, Paul-Robain. 2005. "Le Pouvoir Traditionel au Sud-Kivu de 1998–2003: Rôle et Perspectives." In *L'Afrique des Grands Lacs: Annuaire 2004–2005*, eds. Stefaan Marysse and Filip Reyntjens. Paris: L'Harmattan.

Ndaywel è Nziem, Isidore. 1997. *Histoire Générale du Congo. De l'Héritage Ancien à La République Démocratique*. Paris: Duculot.

Nest, Michael, François Grignon, and Emizet F. Kisangani. 2006. *The Democratic Republic of Congo: Economic Dimensions of War and Peace*. Boulder, CO: Lynne Rienner Publishers.

Newbury, Catherine. 1988. *The Cohesion of Oppression*. New York: Columbia University Press.

Newland, Kathleen. 1993. "Ethnic Conflict and Refugees." In *Ethnic Conflict and International Security*, ed. Michael E. Brown. Princeton, NJ: Princeton University Press.

Ndikumana, Léonce, and Emizet F. Kisangani. 2005. "The Economics of Civil War: The Case of the Democratic Republic of Congo." In *Understanding Civil War: Evidence and Analysis, Volume 1: Africa,* Paul Collier and Nicholas Saurbanis, eds. Washington, DC: World Bank.

N'Gbanda, Honoré Nzambo Ko Atumba. 1998. *Ainsi Sonne Le Glas! Les Derniers Jours du Maréchal Mobutu*. Paris: Editions Gideppe.

Ngolet, François. 2000. "African and American Connivance in Congo-Zaire," *Africa Today* 47, no. 1 (Winter): 65–85.

Ntahokaja, Jean-Baptiste, ed. 1981. *La Civilisation Ancienne des Peuples des Grands Lacs: Colloque de Bujumbura, 4–10 Septembre 1979*. Paris: Karthala.

Nzongola-Ntalaja, Georges. 2002. *The Congo from Leopold to Kabila: A People's History*. London: Zed Books.

O'Brien, Conor Cruise. 1962. *To Katanga and Back: A UN Case History*. London: Hutchinson.

Pabanel, Jean-Pierre. 1991. "La Question de la Nationalité au Kivu," *Politique Africaine* no. 41 (March): 32–40.

Page, Melvin E. 1976. "The Manyema Hordes of Tippu Tip: A Case Study in Social Stratification and the Slave Trade in Eastern Africa," *International Journal of African Historical Studies* 7, no. 1: 69–84.

Peemans, Jean-Philippe. 1968. *Diffusion du Progrès Economique et Convergence des Prix: Le Cas Congo-Belgique, 1900–1960*. Louvain, Belgium: Editions Nauwelaerts.

———. 1975. "Capital Accumulation in the Congo under Colonialism: The Role of the State." In *Colonialism in Africa 1870–1960*, ed. L. H. Gann. Cambridge: Cambridge University Press.

———. 1997a. *Le Congo-Zaïre au Gré du XXe Siècle: Etat, Economie, Société 1990–1990*. Paris: L'Harmattan.

———. 1997b. *Crise de la Modernisation et Pratiques Populaires au Zaïre et en Afrique*. Paris: L'Harmattan.

Pelissier, R. "La Guerre en Angola Oriental," *Revue Française d'Etudes Politiques Africaines* no. 103: 87–109.

Perrot, Sandrine. 1999. "Entrepreneurs de l'Insécurité: La Face Cachée de l'Armée Ougandaise," *Politique Africaine* 75 (October): 60–71.

Philips, M. 2005. "More Dung, Please: Vanishing Hippos Break a Food Chain," *Wall Street Journal,* 19–20 November, pp. 1. and 4.

Piraux, Maurice. 1969. "La Condamnation et l'Enlèvement de Moïse Tshombe." In *Congo 1967*, eds. Jules Gérard-Libois, Benoît Verhaegen, Jan Vansina, and Herbert Weiss. Brussels: CRISP.

Posen, Barry R. 1993. "The Security Dilemma and Ethnic Conflict," *Survival* 35, no. 1: 27–47.

Prunier, Gérard. 2004. "Rebel Movements and Proxy Warfare: Uganda, Sudan, and the Congo," *African Affairs* 103, no. 412: 359–383.

———. 2009. *Africa's World War: Congo, the Rwandan Genocide, and the Making of a Continental Catastrophe.* Oxford: Oxford University Press.

Raymaekers, Paul. 1964. *L'Organisation des Zones de Squatting.* Paris: Mouton.

Regan, Patrick. 1996. "Conditions of Successful Third-Party Intervention in Intra-State Conflicts," *Journal of Conflict Resolution* 40, no. 2 (April): 336–359.

———. 2002. *Civil Wars and Foreign Powers.* Ann Arbor: University of Michigan Press.

Reno, William. 2000. "Shadow States and the Political Economy of Civil Wars." In *Greed and Grievance: Economic Agendas in Civil Wars*, eds. Mats Berdal and David M. Malone. Boulder, CO: Lynne Rienner Publishers.

Reyntjens, Filip. 1997. "La Rébellion au Congo-Zaïre; Une Affaire des Voisins," *Hérodote* no. 86–87: 57–77.

———. 1999. *La Guerre des Grands Lacs: Alliances Mouvantes et Conflicts Extraterritoriaux en Afrique Centrale.* Paris: L'Harmattan.

Rigby, S. H. 1995. "Historical Causation: Is One Thing More Important than Another?" *History* 80, no. 259: 227–242.

Roberts, Leslie F. 2000. *Mortality in Eastern Democratic Republic of Congo: Results from Five Mortality Surveys by the International Rescue Committee.* New York: International Rescue Committee.

Rubbens, Antoine. 1958. "La Consultation Populaire au 22 Décembre à Elisabethville," *Bulletin CEPSI* no. 42 (September): 70–90.

Ruhimbika, M. 2001. *The Banyamulenge (Congo-Zaire) entre Deux Guerres.* Paris: L'Harmattan.

Ruzibiza, A. J. 2005. *Rwanda. Histoire Secrète.* Paris: Editions Panama.

Sahr, Robert C. 2008. "Consumer Price Index (CPI) Conversion Factors to Convert to 2007 Dollars Using the CPI-U-X1 Series, which Applies the Post-1982 CPI to 1950–1982." http://oregonstate.edu/cla/polisci/facultyresearch/sahr/infcf17742007.pdf. Accessed 1 February 2011.

Sambanis, Nicholas. 2004. "What Is Civil War? Conceptual and Empirical Complexities of an Operational Definition," *Journal of Conflict Resolution* 48, no. 6 (December): 814–858.

Samset, Ingrid. 2002. "Conflict of Interests or Interests in Conflict? Diamonds & War in the DRC," *Review of African Political Economy* 29, no. 93/94 (September–December): 463–480.

Sen, Amartya. 1999. *Development as Freedom.* Oxford: Oxford University Press.

Sisk, T. D. 1996. *Power Sharing and International Mediation in Ethnic Conflicts.* Washington, DC: United States Institute of Peace Press.

Sklar, Richard L. 1967. "Political Science and National Integration," *Journal of Modern African Studies* 5, no. 1: 1–11.

Slater, Dan, and Erica Simmons. 2010. "Information Regress: Critical Antecedent in Comparative Politics," *Comparative Political Studies* 43, no. 7 (July): 886–917.

Small, Melvin, and J. David Singer. 1982. *Resort to Arms: International and Civil Wars, 1886–1980*, 2nd ed. Beverly Hills, CA: Sage.

Smith, Adam. 1969 [1763]. *Lectures on Justice, Police, Revenue and Arms.* Edited by Edwin Cannan. Oxford: Clarendon Press, 1896 [Louisville, KY: Lost Cause Press].

Smith, Anthony D. 1986. *The Ethnic Origins of Nations.* Oxford, UK: Basil Blackwell.

———. 1993. "The Ethnic Sources of Nationalism." In *Ethnic Conflict and International Security*, ed. Michael E. Brown. Princeton, NJ: Princeton University Press.

Sobek, David, and Caroline L. Payne. 2010. "A Tale of Two Types: Rebel Goals and the Onset of Civil Wars." *International Studies Quarterly* 54, no. 1 (March): 213–240.

Sørensen, Georg. 2001. "War and State-Making: Why Doesn't It Work in the Third World?" *Security Dialogue* 32, no. 3: 341–354.

Stearns, Jason K. 2008. "Laurent Nkunda and the National Congress for the Defence of the People (CNDP)." In *L'Afrique des Grands Lacs: Annuaire 2007–2008*, eds. Stefaan Marysse, Filip Reyntjens, and Stef Vandeginste. Paris: L'Harmattan.

———. 2011. *Dancing in the Glory of Monsters: The Collapse of the Congo and the Great War of Africa.* New York: Public Affairs.

Stedman, Stephen J. 1997. "Spoilers Problems in Peace Processes," *International Security* 22, no. 2 (Autumn): 5–53.

Stedman, Stephen J., D. Rothchild, and Elizabeth M. Cousens, eds. 2002. *Ending Civil Wars: The Implementation of Peace Agreements.* Boulder, CO: Lynne Rienner Publishers.

Stewart, Francis. 2010. "Horizontal Inequalities as a Cause of Conflict: A Review of CRISE Findings." Background Paper for *World Development Report 2011.* wdr2011.worldbank.org/sites/default/files/pdfs/WDR%20Background%20Paper_Stewart.pdf. Accessed 6 June 2011.

Thiry, Edmond. 2004. *Une Introduction à l'Ethnohistoire des Hema du Nord (Congo du Nord-Est).* Tervuren, Belgium: Musée Royale de l'Afrique Centrale.

Tilly, Charles. 1985. "War Making and State Making as Organized Crime." In *Bring the State Back In*, eds. Peter Evans, Dietrich Ruescemeyer, and Theda Skocpol. Cambridge: Cambridge University Press.

Toft, M. D. 2003. *The Geography of Ethnic Violence: Identity, Interests, and the Indivisibility of Territory.* Princeton, NJ: Princeton University Press.

Tshilombo, Augustin. 1964. "Le Développement Economique du Sud-Kasaï avant et après l'Indépendance du Congo." Mémoire de Licence, Université de Liège, Wallonia, Belgium.

Tull, Denis. M. 2003. "A Reconfiguration of Political Order? The State of the State in Nord-Kivu (RD Congo)," *African Affairs* 102, no. 408 (July): 429–446.

Tull, Denis M., and Andreas Mehler. 2005. "The Hidden Costs of Power-Sharing: Reproducing Insurgent Violence in Africa," *African Affairs* 104, no. 416 (July): 375–398.

Turner, Thomas E. 1973. "A Century of Political Conflict in Sankuru: Congo-Zaire." PhD. dissertation, University of Wisconsin, Madison.

———. 2006. *The Congo Wars: Conflict, Myth and Reality.* London: Zed Books.

United Nations. Security Council. 2001. *Report of the Panel of Experts on the Illegal Exploitation of Natural Resources and Other Forms of Wealth of the Democratic Republic of the Congo.* S/2001/357. New York: United Nations.

———. 2002. *Report of the Panel of Experts on the Illegal Exploitation of Natural Resources and Other Forms of Wealth of the Democratic Republic of the Congo.* S/2002/565. New York: United Nations.

————. 2003. *Report of the Panel of Experts on the Illegal Exploitation of Natural Resources and Other Forms of Wealth of the Democratic Republic of the Congo.* S/2003/1027. New York: United Nations.

————. 2005. *Twentieth Report of the Secretary-General on the United Nations Organization Mission in the Democratic Republic of the Congo.* S/2005/832. New York: United Nations.

————. 2008. *Final Report of the Group of Experts on the Democratic Republic of the Congo.* S/2008/773. New York: United Nations.

Urdal, Henrik. 2005. "People vs. Malthus: Population Pressure, Environmental Degradation, and Armed Conflict Revisited," *Journal of Peace Research* 42, no. 4 (July): 417–434.

U. S. Committee for Refugees. 1994. *World Refugee Report 1993.* Washington, DC: Immigration and Refugee Services of America (IRSA).

————. 1996. *World Refugee Report 1995.* Washington, DC: IRSA.

————. 1997. *World Refugee Report 1996.* Washington, DC: IRSA.

————. 1999. *World Refugee Report 1998.* Washington, DC: IRSA.

————. 2000. *World Refugee Report 1999.* Washington, DC: IRSA.

Van Acker, F. 1999. "La 'Pémbénisation' du Haut Kivu: Opportunisme et Droits Fonciers Révisés." In *L'Afrique des Grands Lacs: Annuaire 1998–1999*, eds. Stefaan Marysse and Filip Reyntjens. Paris: L'Harmattan.

Van Acker, Franck, and Koen Vlassenroot. 2001. "Les 'Maï Maï' et les Fonctions de la Violence Milicienne dans l'Est du Congo," *Politique Africaine* no. 84 (December): 103–116.

Van Bulck, G. 1954. *Carte Linguistique du Congo Belge.* Brussels: Institut Royal Colonial Belge, Commission Central de l'Atlas du Congo.

Vansina, Jan. 1962. "Long-Distance Trade Routes in Central Africa," *Journal of African History* 3, no. 3: 375–390.

————. 1966. *Kingdoms of the Savanna.* Madison: University of Wisconsin Press.

————. 2000. *L'Evolution du Royaume de Rwanda des Origines à 1900.* Brussels: Académie Royale des Sciences d'Outre-Mer.

Verhaegen, Benoît. 1962. *Congo 1961.* Brussels: CRISP.

————. 1969. *Rébellions au Congo. Vols. 1 and 2.* Brussels: CRISP

Viane, L. 1952. "L'Organisation Politique des Bahunde, "*Kongo Oversee* 18: 8–34.

Vlassenroot, Koen. 2000. "Identity and Insecurity: The Building of Ethnic Agendas in Southern Kivu." In *Politics of Identity and Economics of Conflict in the Great Lakes Region*, eds. Ruddy Doon and Jan Gorus. Brussels: VUB Press.

————. 2002. "Citizenship, Identity Formation and Conflict in Sud-Kivu: The Case of the Banyamulenge," *Review of African Political Economy* 29, no. 93–94 (September–December): 499–515.

Vlassenroot, Koen, and Timothy Raeymaekers. 2003. "Le Conflit en Ituri." In *L'Afrique des Grands Lacs: Annuaire 2002–2003*, eds. Stefaan Marysse and Filip Reyntjens. Paris: L'Harmattan.

von Clausewitz, Carl. 1976. *On War.* Michael Howard and Peter Paret, eds. and trans. Princeton, NJ: Princeton University Press.

von Glahn, Gerhard, and James L. Taulbee. 2010. *Law among Nations: An Introduction to Public International Law*, 9th ed. New York: Pearson/Longman.

Wallenstein, Peter, and Margareta Sollenberg. 1998. "Armed Conflict and Regional Conflict Complexes, 1989–97," *Journal of Peace Research* 35, no. 5 (September): 621–634.

Weiner, Myron. 1978. *Sons of the Soil: Migration and Ethnic Conflict in India.* Princeton, NJ: Princeton University Press.

————. 1996. "Bad Neighbors, Bad Neighborhoods: An Inquiry into the Cause of Refugee Flows," *International Security* 21, no. 1 (Summer): 5–42.

Weiss, George. 1954. *Le Pays d'Uvira, Etude Géographique Régionale sur la Bordure Occidentale du Lac Tanganyika*. Brussels: Académie Royale des Sciences Coloniales.

Weiss, Herbert F. 1967. *Political Protest in the Congo*. Princeton, NJ: Princeton University Press.

———. 2000. *War and Peace in the Democratic Republic of the Congo*. Uppsala, Sweden: Nordiska Afrikainstitutet.

———. 2007. "Voting for Change in the DRC," *Journal of Democracy* 18, no. 2 (April): 138–151.

Weissman, Stephen R. 1978. "The CIA and U.S. Policy in Zaire and Angola." In *American Policy in Southern Africa: The States and the Stance*, ed. René Lemarchand. Washington, DC: University Press of America.

Willame, Jean-Claude. 1964. "Les Provinces du Congo: Kwilu-Luluabourg-Nord Katanga-Ubangi," *Cahiers Economiques et Sociaux* 1, no.1 (May): 17–50.

———. 1978. "La Seconde Guerre du Shaba," *Enquêtes et Documents d'Histoire Africaine* 3: 165–206.

———. 1980. "Contributions à l'Etude des Mouvements d'Opposition au Zaïre: Le F.L.N.C.," *Les Cahiers du CEDAF* 6, no. 2: 1–41.

———. 1997. "Banyamulenge and Banyarwanda," *Cahiers Africains* no. 25 (March): 1–156.

———. 1998. "Les Relations du Régime Kabila avec la Région du Kivu." In *République Démocratique du Congo. Chronique Politique d'un Entre-Deux-Guerres, Octobre 1996–Juillet 1998*, eds. Gauthier De Villers and Jean-Claude Willame. Paris: L'Harmattan.

———. 1999. *L'Odyssée Kabila*. Paris: Karthala.

———. 2002. *L'Accord de Lusaka: Chronique d'une Négociation Internationale*. Paris: L'Harmattan.

———. 2007. *Les "Faiseurs de Paix" au Congo. Gestion d'une Crise Internationale dans un Etat sous Tutelle*. Paris: GRIP-Editions Complexe.

Wilson, Marie C. 2007. *Closing the Leadership Gap: Add Women, Change Everything*. New York: Penguin.

Wilungula, B. C. 1997. "Fizi 1967–1986: Le Maquis de Kabila," *Cahiers Africains* 26 (May): 1–136.

World Bank. 2010. *World Development Indicators*. CD-ROM. Washington, DC: World Bank.

Yakemtchouk, Romain. 1988. "Les Deux Guerres du Shaba. Les Relations entre la Belgique, la France et le Zaïre," *Studia Diplomatica* 41, no. 4–5–6: 375–742.

Yates, Douglas A. 1996. *The Rentier State in Africa: Oil Rent Dependency & Neocolonialism in the Republic of Gabon*. Trenton, NJ: Africa World Press.

Young, Crawford. 1965. *Politics in the Congo*. Princeton, NJ: Princeton University Press.

———. 1970. "Rebellion and the Congo." In *Protest and Power in Black Africa*, eds. Robert I. Rotberg and Ali I. Mazrui. New York: Oxford University Press.

———. 1993. *The Rising Tide of Cultural Pluralism: The Nation-State at Bay?* Madison: University of Wisconsin Press.

Young, Crawford, and Thomas Turner. 1985. *The Rise & Decline of the Zairian State*. Madison: University of Wisconsin Press.

Zacher, Mark W. 2002. "The Territorial Integrity Norm: International Boundaries and the Use of Force," *International Organization* 55, no. 2 (Spring): 215–250.

Zaïre. 1972. Présidence de la République. "Loi No. 72-002 du 5 Janvier 1972 Relative à la Nationalité Zaïroise," *Journal Officiel*, pp. 4–11.

———. 1981. "Loi No. 81-002 du 29 Juin 1981 sur la Nationalité Zaïroise," *Journal Officiel*, pp. 27–36.

Zaïre, Haut Conseil de la République. 1995. "Résolution sur La Nationalité." Kinshasa: Palais du Peuple. 28 April.

Zartman, William I. 1995. *Elusive Peace: Negotiating an End to Civil War*. Washington, DC: Brookings Institution.

_____. 2005. "Need, Creed, and Greed in Interstate Conflict." In *Rethinking the Economics of War: The Intersection of Need, Creed, and Greed*, eds. Cynthia J. Arnson and William I. Zartman. Baltimore, MD: Johns Hopkins University Press.

Zeilig, Leo. 2008. *Lumumba. Africa's Lost Leader*. London: Haus Publishing.

Index

About the Book

Wars of secession, ethnic wars, rebellions, mutinies, and Congolese-led invasions have been part of the political landscape of the Democratic Republic of Congo since the country became independent in 1960. Why? And what can we learn from this seemingly unending series of internal conflicts? Emizet François Kisangani explores these fundamental questions within a rigorously systematic and uniquely comprehensive framework.

Looking closely at five decades of civil wars in the DRC, Kisangani finds ample evidence to challenge popular paradigms. His focus on the politics of exclusion and his attention to both the micro- and macroprocesses of the wars provides an analytical lens through which not only the nature of civil wars, but also Congo's politics more broadly, are brought into clearer focus.

Emizet François Kisangani is professor of political science at Kansas State University. He is coauthor of *The Democratic Republic of Congo: Economic Dimensions of War and Peace* (a *Choice* Outstanding Academic Book in 2006) and of the *Historical Dictionary of the Democratic Republic of Congo*.